Microsoft® SQL Server™

Planning and Building a High Performance Database

Robert D. Schneider

To join a Prentice Hall PTR internet mailing list, point to:
http://www.prenhall.com/register

Prentice Hall PTR
Upper Saddle River, New Jersey 07458
http://www.prenhall.com

Editorial/production supervision: *Camille Trentacoste*
Manufacturing manager: *Alexis R. Heydt*
Composition: *Mary R. Strunk*
Acquisitions editor: *Mark L. Taub*
Editorial assistant: *Kate Hargett*
Cover design: *Anthony Gemmellaro*
Cover design director: *Jerry Votta*
Marketing Manager: *Dan Rush*

The publisher offers discounts on this book when ordered in bulk quantities.
For more information, contact:

    Corporate Sales Department
    Prentice Hall PTR
    One Lake Street
    Upper Saddle River, New Jersey 07458

    Phone: 800-382-3419, Fax: 201-236-7141
    E-mail: corpsales@prenhall.com

Printed in the United States of America
10 9 8 7 6 5 4 3 2

ISBN 266222-1

Prentice-Hall International (UK) Limited, *London*
Prentice-Hall of Australia Pty. Limited, *Sydney*
Prentice-Hall Canada Inc., *Toronto*
Prentice-Hall Hispanoamericana, S.A., *Mexico*
Prentice-Hall of India Private Limited, *New Delhi*
Prentice-Hall of Japan, Inc., *Tokyo*
Simon & Schuster Asia Pte. Ltd., *Singapore*
Editora Prentice-Hall do Brasil, Ltda., *Rio de Janeiro*

For Melanie

Contents

Preface

Microsoft® SQL Server™ lets you quickly build powerful and reliable database applications. This alone is often not enough; users also demand high performance. It takes skill and experience to produce such high-quality systems, but many Information Systems (IS) professionals don't have the time to learn the intricacies of the SQL Server engine. This book gives you the insight you need to produce the fast database applications your users want.

Intended audience

Microsoft SQL Server: Designing and Building a High Performance Database is a tool for application developers, database administrators, systems analysts, and system administrators who are interested in designing, developing, maintaining, and administering efficient applications that use the SQL Server engine, version 6.0 and newer.

To get the most out of this book, programmers and analysts should be comfortable with:

- Basic Structured Query Language (SQL)

Database administrators should understand:

- Relational database design concepts
- Intermediate or advanced SQL
- Microsoft SQL Server engine architecture

System administrators should understand:

- Microsoft SQL Server engine architecture
- The Windows NT™ operating system at an intermediate level

Benefits of using the book

Microsoft SQL Server: Designing and Building a High Performance Database provides you with these benefits:

- **Enhanced productivity.**   It's hard for a user to be productive if a typical query takes three minutes to return data. End-of-week reports that take 36 hours to run generally don't lead to a more robust bottom line, either. In this book, we cite dozens of specific changes you can make to your applications and systems to upgrade your organization's productivity.

- **Increased application reliability.**   Generally, an inefficient application is an unreliable application. At the very least, slow systems are perceived as being less reliable than fast systems. When you increase a system's speed, you will improve its reliability.

- **Reduced hardware expenditures.**   Few organizations can afford to continually upgrade their hardware environments to get better performance. Therefore, they expect their IS staff to do more with less. You can use the suggestions in this book to squeeze extra speed out of your existing hardware.

- **Simpler applications.**   In many cases, the simplest solution is the fastest solution. You will find many tips in this book to help you increase a system's speed while reducing its complexity.

- **More satisfied users.**   In the past, most users were mainly concerned with whether a system worked; performance wasn't a major consideration. Today's users are more sophisticated than ever and view system speed as the crucial element. Many organizations have learned this painful lesson the hard way, when users don't approve a slow system, no matter how well-designed.

How to use this book

This book is divided into these major sections:

1. **Chapter 1.**   In this chapter, we discuss how to set up the most effective optimization test environment.

2. **Part 1—Creating a Well-Designed Database.**   Your entire application relies on an efficient database design. In this part, we review some of the most important facets of a good database design.

3. **Part 2—Improving Database Access.**   Whether via direct SQL, or stored procedures, it's important that your database access be as effective as possible. In Part 2, we describe how to write efficient SQL, stored procedures, and triggers. In addition, we cover several other important topics, such as transactions, concurrency, and cursors.

4. **Part 3—Tuning the Database Engine.**   Even the most efficient application can be sluggish if the underlying database engine is tuned incorrectly. In Part 3, we review many techniques you can use to make your database engine run as rapidly as possible.

    A. **Case Studies.**   This appendix contains several case studies. Each case study features several interrelated problems.

    B. **Software.**   We've also included a powerful utility, SQL Replay, to help you gather and analyze SQL Server performance statistics. SQL Replay collects data about SQL Server activity by making periodic snapshots of system information. Information derived from system tables, sysprocesses, syslocks, and some of the SQL Server global variables allows you to review past SQL Server activity, and find performance problems or bottlenecks, research locks contention, or heavy usage time intervals.

You don't need to read this book from cover to cover. To get the most benefit from our suggestions, review only those sections that apply to your particular situation. However, there are several sections that deserve your attention, regardless of your situation. These include:

- **Setting Up an Optimization Test Environment.**   It is a big mistake to rush in and start making performance enhancement changes to your system without first observing a few very important details. This chapter covers these details.

- **Relational Database Design Concepts.**   A good database design is the foundation of a system that performs well. This section teaches you how to implement the relational model when you design a database. It also covers specific situations where the relational model is not appropriate.

- **Indexing Strategies.**   The wrong indexing strategy can wreck an otherwise perfect database design. We list some straightforward indexing techniques you can use to dramatically raise your system's throughput.

- **SQL Tips.**   Without SQL, you can't access data. In this chapter, we cite several ideas you can incorporate to improve your SQL statements.

- **General Tips.**   This chapter contains numerous suggestions that can help you develop better, faster applications, no matter what engine or tools you use.

- **Case Studies.**   This appendix contains a number of multifaceted case studies. Spend some time reviewing them: chances are you may already have experienced some of the problems we illustrate.

How to use the examples

You'll find numerous examples in each chapter, which we have made as clear and concise as possible. This will help you implement our suggestions quickly. Because this book is intended as a reference, the examples in one chapter do not necessarily rely on one another. This will help you concentrate on specific problems and solutions. Keep in mind that while the examples in this book may not exactly match your database design, application software, and/or engine configuration, you can still apply them to your specific problems.

Acknowledgments

The author wishes to acknowledge the following people for their invaluable assistance in creating and publishing this work. Andrew Zanevsky and Bill Vaughn for their detailed technical and content reviews, Mary Strunk for composition, Richard Shrout for indexing, Mary Lou Nohr for copy editing, and Maureen Diana and Marjorie Shustak for proofreading. Camille Trentacoste for production, and Mark Taub for project management. Lynn Z. Schneider and Nicole Sierra Schneider for their patience and support. Danielle Jolie Schneider for motivation, as well as setting a realistic schedule.

Chapter 1

Setting Up an Optimization Test Environment

When faced with a sluggishly performing application or an engine that appears out of tune, most administrators and programmers are eager to roll up their sleeves and begin the optimizing process. Unfortunately, there are a number of potentially tiresome, yet very important steps that you must first take before you begin the "real work" of tuning. If you don't set up a stable, accurate test environment, you face the very real risk of making inaccurate judgments about the root cause(s) of your system's current woeful performance. You might then use these incorrect assumptions as the base of an entire action plan, only to later learn that your original hypotheses were wrong.

In this chapter, we address these important issues. We've divided the chapter into three major sections. The first section deals with the agenda you should cover before you even begin your testing efforts. This agenda includes ensuring that the right hardware, operating system, database, and application software are in place. In addition, we discuss some organizational issues that you should address immediately at the start of the optimization.

Next, we spell out some methods that you can use to help point the way while your testing is going on. While the most successful system testers and tuners rely heavily on their test plan to guide them during this process, they also choose the right blend of discipline and creativity when following up on new, promising performance leads.

Finally, we illustrate how you can translate the knowledge that you gained during testing process into real performance improvements.

While this chapter is primarily designed for people tuning existing systems and applications, you can still apply these suggestions if you're doing new development. In fact, one way to help guarantee a production system that meets your standards is to treat good performance as one of the most important development deliverables.

Steps to follow before testing

Hardware considerations

Your hardware environment really consists of a number of different components, each of which plays a meaningful role in your overall performance picture. Let's illustrate each of these components in more detail.

- **CPU.** Ideally, both your production and test environment have similar CPU speeds and capacities. If not, you'll always have to wonder which numbers you should believe: those from the production system or those from the test system. The same problem often arises at multiprocessor sites, where the production machine may have four CPUs, while the test machine has one. This difference really becomes a problem if you're trying to tune the engine.

- **Memory.** It's crucial that your test platform have the same amount of memory as your production system. Slow-running applications can experience a "miracle cure" when you add a few megabytes of memory to the hardware. If your test and production systems have vastly different memory configurations, be careful before you draw conclusions from your research.

- **Disk drives.** If your production system uses older, slower disk drives, and your test system has the speed benefits of the newest generation data storage devices, you're bound to come to some erroneous conclusions about each machine's capacity and response. If you're attempting to test your SQL Server engine's response, try to match the production machine's disk configuration when you set up your test machine. Disk sizing and layout can have a big impact on engine throughput; you'll get more realistic results if you're working with a real-life disk profile.

- **Connections (local and network).** If your production application uses a distributed database or works in a client/server environment, it's important that you configure your testing platform to accurately reflect these connections. Network and client/server overhead can be substantial; if you omit these factors from your testing, you might not get completely accurate performance information.

Ideally, your test system and production system are carbon copies of each other. In reality, however, most administrators and developers are lucky even to have a test machine; few organizations can afford to have a production-caliber machine sitting idle. If this is the case in your organization, try to use the production machine for your tests whenever possible. This may mean that you only have access to the equipment after hours or on weekends. See the "Operational considerations" section of this chapter for more information about gaining access to the production system for testing.

Software considerations

Once you've set up a testing system, your next challenge is to obtain the right software and correctly configure it. In this section, we divide the software into the following elements:

- **Operating system.** It's important that your optimizing platform have the same operating system configuration as your production system. Slight differences in Windows NT operating system parameters can cause wide disparities in performance; these differences might skew your findings. If you don't know how to check your operating system parameters, ask your system administrator to check them for you. If possible, try to work with identical operating system parameters.

- **Database and tools.** Try to ensure that you've installed the same versions of your production system's database server and tools in your test environment. This is especially important if you're examining a client/server system. Even if you don't use any client/server features, remember that Microsoft continually enhances the query optimizer. You can expect your performance statistics to vary, depending on which version of the database engine you're using.

- **Application.** One way to guarantee an unpleasant optimizing experience is to work with different versions of your application on the development, production, and test machines. Sometimes, a one-line difference in a program can have a tremendous influence on performance. Insist on testing the same version of application software that the users are complaining about. Otherwise, you may (rightly) come to the conclusion that there is no performance problem: When you ran your version of the application, it performed perfectly.

Data considerations

After you have set up your hardware and software environment, the next topic to consider is the data that you plan to use during your testing. Ideally, your test database should exactly match the database that's currently in development or production. This means having the same number of tables, indexes, views, stored procedures, and triggers under the testing environment as you do on the production environment.

One common mistake that administrators and developers make when setting up a test database is using an undersized data set. If you don't make your test database big enough, it's possible that you might get an incorrect picture of true system performance. Even the most poorly written query may perform well on a tiny database, whether or not the underlying database design is good.

If possible, use an exact copy of your production database on your test platform by using the Database/Object Transfer menu option from the SQL Enterprise Manager. If your production database is too large or if your test system doesn't have enough storage space, it's still important that you create a test database with the same number of tables, indexes, views, triggers, and stored procedures. You can use the schema creation utility on the production database to obtain the SQL necessary to create a duplicate test database. If you're testing a query that works only with two moderate-sized tables from your production database, you only need to copy the contents of those two tables from the production system to the test system.

Once you've set up your testing database and filled it with the correct amount of data, don't forget to run UPDATE STATISTICS with the same options that you chose for your production database.

Setting up a test plan

It's not absolutely essential that you write a test plan prior to beginning your experiments. However, a well-designed test plan can make your tasks much easier by providing a clear sense of direction. This is especially important if you have a multi-person test team. Without a plan, team members might duplicate each other's work and potentially damage the integrity of your test results. You can also use your test plan to form the basis of your summary report once you finish your examinations.

You don't need to spend an inordinate amount of time on your plan; it should simply define, at a high level, which procedures you expect to follow when conducting your evaluations, along with any assistance you might need from other users or developers.

For example, look at the following set of entries from a sample test plan:

Example 1.1   Test Plan:

```
    ...
    ...
    ...
    Test #:              17
    Date:                03/09/97
    Start time:          08:00
    Finish time:         11:00
    Platform:            Production
    Action:              Experiment with adding/changing indexes on the
                         call_tracking table.
```

Special needs:	May need to briefly lock tables when adding/changing indexes.
Team members:	Nicole - Primary Jed - Assist Li - Assist
Test status:	<unfinished>
Test results:	<unfinished>

Test #:	18
Date:	03/09/97
Start time:	12:15
Finish time:	16:30
Platform:	Production
Action:	Raise number of shared memory buffers to test SQL Server engine performance. Monitor engine statistics for balance of day.
Special needs:	Need to restart engine - will result in approx. 2 minutes database downtime.
Team members:	Lynn - Primary Karl - Assist
Test status:	<unfinished>
Test results:	<unfinished>

Test #:	19
Date:	03/10/97
Start time:	08:00
Finish time:	17:30
Platform:	Development
Action	Alter cc01288, cc03432 programs to use read uncommitted isolation levels instead of current repeatable read isolation. Monitor application response times before & after modification.
Special needs:	None
Team members:	Miguel - Primary Lynn - Assist
Test status:	<unfinished>
Test results:	<unfinished>

Test #:	20
Date:	03/11/97
Start time:	08:00
Finish time:	17:30
Platform:	Production
Action:	If test #19 improves performance, move the cc01288 and cc03432 programs into production.
Special needs:	Need user input regarding response times.
Team members:	Miguel - Primary Meyer - Assist Sandra - Assist

```
Test status:          <unfinished>
Test results:         <unfinished>
...
...
...
```

You could even store your test plan in the database and then use SQL to create helpful queries.

Operational considerations

After you've finished setting up your hardware, software, and database and have designed a good test plan, you face perhaps your biggest challenge: obtaining operational support for your tuning efforts.

Operational issues are often the most frustrating part of optimizing an application. Management may be unwilling to allow you full or partial access to the resources that you need. Users are often reluctant to help isolate a performance problem, even though they have the most to gain from any discoveries that you make. The designers and/or developers of the application may be nervous about what your investigation might uncover.

Unfortunately, you can only get a true picture of what is really happening on the system by requesting cooperation from management, users, and developers. Before you begin your experiments, you have every right to ask for each of the following:

- **System availability.**   If you don't have a dedicated test platform, you'll have to run your experiments on the production system. This probably means you'll be working some late nights or weekends, but it's better than having no system at all. If management is reluctant to grant access to you, point out that you'll be able to solve their performance problems much faster if you can work on the platform where the response delays are occurring. Unfortunately, if your production system is continuously active 24 hours a day, 7 days a week, you may not be able to isolate a "safe" time to work.

- **Realistic system load.**   As we've just seen, it's best to run your tests in a production environment. However, it's often not enough to have access to the production system during off-hours, because no matter how hard you try, you may never be able to replicate a performance problem if you're using a relatively idle platform. Some bottlenecks simply can't be reproduced on a placid system. For example, your network load can widely fluctuate, depending on the time of day. If you're running your tests at 2 a.m., the network may appear fine; 12 hours later it may be sluggish. This highlights the importance of running your tests under the most realistic conditions possible.

- **User input and support.** You should try to make your tuning experiments as scientific as possible. If users are complaining about response time, it's reasonable for you to ask them to cite specific examples. It's even better if you can sit by their side as they work. You will have a much better chance to diagnose a problem if you observe it while it happens, instead of hearing about it three days later. Once you've investigated and (hopefully) corrected the problem, you still need feedback and assistance from your user community. Otherwise, you may never truly know if your enhancements helped.

- **IS staff support.** Unless you're the only person in the IS department, chances are you'll need to work with your peers when optimizing new or existing applications. If you're an administrator, you need good rapport with the programmers and analysts who designed the system. If you're a programmer or an analyst, you need the cooperation of the database administrator. Unfortunately, a large proportion of tuning exercises become mired in politics and finger-pointing. Therefore, whatever your job responsibility, it's important that you conduct your investigation and present your suggestions with sensitivity and tact. (Almost) no one sets out to design a deliberately slow application or database. In addition, a well-designed application can slow down over time under the weight of increased volume and altered requirements. Remember that there are many ways to solve design challenges; the decisions that your peers made during the design process may have been, at that time, the right ones to meet the requirements. Few people find nonconstructive criticism enjoyable; keep this in mind as you proceed with your work.

Steps to follow during testing

Discipline vs. creativity

What should you do if, during testing, you discover a completely new and potentially exciting path that you feel bears further investigation? Do you abandon your carefully thought-out tuning strategies? Do you merely write down your idea and get back to the original plan? What if you realize that your plan doesn't really meet your needs?

The most practical answer to all of the above questions is to remain flexible while you conduct your tuning exercises. Don't be afraid to yield to your creative impulses; sometimes the most promising optimizing leads appear out of nowhere. You should never allow an idea to escape because you were too busy to write it down.

On the other hand, don't discard your testing plan just because it's now partially obsolete. Instead, why not incorporate your new ideas into the existing plan? For example, using the example from earlier in this chapter, suppose that you've just run test 19:

Example 1.2

Test #:	19
Date:	03/10/97
Start time:	08:00
Finish time:	17:30
Platform:	Development
Action:	Alter cc01288, cc03432 programs to use read uncommitted isolation levels instead of current repeatable read isolation. Monitor application response times before & after modification.
Special needs	None
Team members:	Miguel - Primary
	Lynn - Assist
Test status:	COMPLETED
Test results:	Yielded no performance gain, but we discovered an indexing problem. See test 19.1.

You learned that the problem with the two programs wasn't the transaction isolation levels, as you had originally thought. Instead, you realized that each program used an ORDER BY clause in several SELECT statements. By reviewing the output from SHOWPLAN, you discovered that there was no index on the columns listed in the ORDER BY clause. Once you added an index, each program ran in one-fifth of its original time. How can you record this information? One way is to add a new test that reflects the results of your additional test:

Example 1.3

Test #:	19.1
Date:	03/10/97
Start time:	08:00
Finish time:	17:30
Platform:	Development
Action:	Place a composite index on the territory_number and zip_code fields in the 'leads' table. Test impact on cc01288 and cc03432 programs. See test 19 for original plan.
Special needs:	None
Team members:	Miguel - Primary
	Lynn - Assist
Test status:	COMPLETED
Test results:	cc01288 and cc03432 both ran much faster.

This approach lets you follow your creative ideas without straying from a disciplined methodology.

Steps to follow after testing

Formal assessment

Once you've finished your testing and (hopefully) confirmed your hypotheses, it's time to formally document your findings. Unfortunately, this is true even if you learn that every one of your hypotheses was completely wrong. It's important that you commit your conclusions to paper for several reasons:

- **Better communication.**   If you enlisted the support of other people during the optimization process, it's only fair that you provide them with the results of your examination. You could do this verbally, but you'll reduce the potential for confusion and misunderstanding by writing the results. If your recommendations include database, engine configuration, or application modifications, you definitely need to put them in writing if you expect anyone to take them seriously and implement the changes. Even if you didn't need the help of any users or developers or don't recommend any alterations, chances are that your management will want to know what you learned.

- **Future testing.**   Unless this round of testing solved every performance issue that you faced, chances are that you'll need to retest and retune your applications and environment at some point in the future. In fact, even if you eliminated every problem, it's still a good idea to periodically monitor your system's response. You'll find written documentation of earlier test plans and results to be a very useful tool when faced with subsequent assessments.

- **Assisting new personnel.**   Current turnover rates virtually guarantee that you'll need to explain your testing methodologies and procedures to a new hire at some point in the future. By documenting your findings now, you can help reduce the amount of time that you'll be obligated to spend during future orientations, as well as increasing the accuracy of your presentations.

Determining the next step

Even if you feel that you've located every performance bottleneck, it's important not to rush in and immediately make widespread changes after you finish your tuning experiments. Instead, consider applying one change at a time. After you apply each modification, run some simple performance tests to see what effect your change had on throughput.

For example, suppose that you learn, through your experiments, that your system is hampered by three major performance impediments:

- Not enough memory buffers
- Unnecessarily high levels of isolation
- Insufficient indexing

How should you proceed in this case? Generally, it's a good idea to implement the simplest alterations first. It's also wise to make one change at a time. By modifying only one variable each time, you stand a better chance of learning which variations had the most impact.

Regardless of which alteration you implement, always remember to keep a copy of the original code, database structure, or engine configuration. It's a chilling thought to have made a change that ends up hurting, rather than helping, performance and then realizing that you have no way to get back to the original configuration. In the above example, the shared memory buffers problem is easiest to address: It requires no code or database modifications, and you need only briefly bring SQL Server down for the new buffers parameter to take effect. Once you raise the number of memory buffers, your next step should be to monitor performance to see what effect your change had. Try to make your evaluations as scientifically as possible, but don't be afraid to go back to your users and get their opinions as well.

Once you've obtained some updated throughput statistics, your next step is to evaluate whether or not your enhancement was helpful. If it wasn't or if the improvements weren't substantial enough, return the system to its original state. If it was, leave it in place and move on to the next modification. However, don't forget that certain changes may have far-reaching effects on other users, applications, or the engine itself. For example, you might find that a new index speeds up queries on a table but might degrade the response of another program that inserts rows into the same table. You can help reduce the chances of these unwanted side effects by taking some time to observe what happens after each performance enhancement. If a change helps one area but hurts another, you may have no choice but to reverse the alteration.

Continue following this cycle until you've investigated each performance enhancement. When you have finished, you should have a better performing system.

Creating a Well-Designed Database

Whether you are designing a new system from scratch, or maintaining one that has been in production for years, your database design is one area that should receive special attention. In Part 1, we cover several topics that fall under the heading of database design. Our focus will be on the logical aspects of database design. For more details about the physical implications of database design, see Part 3 on efficient engine management. For more information about SQL, stored procedures, and triggers, see Part 2 on improving database access.

In Chapter 2, we examine a number of items that interest database designers and systems analysts during the design process. These include:

- Data normalization, along with the three normal forms
- Situations where full normalization may not be appropriate
- Special data types
- Constraints and referential integrity
- Views

A good indexing strategy can help even the most badly designed database perform acceptably; a bad indexing strategy can ruin the response of even the most efficient database design. With that in mind, Chapter 3 reviews all facets of indexing, from determining if your existing indexes are sufficient through specific situations that require index modification.

Finally, we'll look at the Microsoft SQL Server optimizer in Chapter 4. This includes the mechanisms the optimizer uses to process queries, as well as a detailed description of the SHOWPLAN command, which is a valuable report provided by the optimizer. We'll also learn how to tell what the optimizer is doing and how we can "help" it reach the right conclusions.

Relational Database Design Concepts

Your database design is the most important factor in determining the kind of performance you can expect from your application. Many applications that benefit from well-written programs and well-thought-out procedures still collapse under the weight of a bad relational database design. On the other hand, a good database design doesn't always guarantee good system performance, and a bad database design doesn't always ensure poor performance. Even with those caveats in mind, you should still strive to design your databases as efficiently as possible.

A full exploration of relational database design would take up an entire book. In fact, there are many excellent books on this topic. In Part 1, we take a more streamlined approach to this subject, focusing on normalization and the three normal forms. We'll also discuss situations where you should back away from full normalization. We then focus on how to make the best use of SQL Server's special data types, including text and images. Finally, we'll explore constraints, and how they can help simplify and speed up your applications.

If you want more information on normalization in particular, consult any of the numerous books on relational database design. As part of your continuing education, you would be wise to become more familiar with one or more of these important sources of information.

Chapter 2
Normalization

Normalization, as defined by leading industry experts, is actually a set of criteria that can be used as a guideline in designing a relational database. In this chapter, we discuss each of the three normal forms. We'll see some examples of designs that violate the three normal forms, along with ways to modify them so that they conform to these standards.

First normal form

The first normal form states that a table's structure cannot contain any repeating data fields. We can best illustrate this with an example. Suppose you are developing a system to track job applicants. During the design phase, you learn that your users want to store two reference phone numbers for each candidate:

Table 2.1   candidates

candidate_id	candidate_name	reference_1	reference_2
1144	Dell'Abate	916 555-2933	714-555-0900
1145	Zanevsky	408 555-9550	602-555-8310

This design violates the first normal form, because the phone numbers repeat. This can cause problems, especially if during production, your users want to track yet another reference phone number. To do this, you must add a new column to the 'candidates' table. You then run the risk of "breaking" existing programs, since they may fail when confronted with a new table layout.

A better design would look like this:

Table 2.2   candidates

candidate_id	candidate_name
1144	Dell'Abate
1145	Zanevsky

Table 2.3   candidates_ref

candidate_id	ref_sequence	ref_phone
1144	1	916 555-2933
1144	2	714 555-0900
1145	1	408 555-9550
1145	2	602 555-8310

Now your users can add as many reference phone numbers as they like without jeopardizing your database design or application code. This new design also conforms to the first normal form, since the records don't contain any repeating data.

Second normal form

The second normal form refers to rows where each column is functionally dependent on the primary key. Let's look at an example that violates the second normal form.

In this example, you are maintaining a property management maintenance system. One of your tables stores profile information for individual properties:

Table 2.4   property_profile

lot_id	address	city
1766	1313 Mockingbird Lane	Paterson
1767	2454 Legion Street	Pattybelle Junction
1768	540 E. 23rd Street	Lynnville
.	.	.

Another table stores data about maintenance procedures:

Table 2.5   maint_procedures

procedure_id	procedure_cost
102	70.99
103	21.00
104	502.54
.	.

You use a third table to track service calls for your properties:

Table 2.6   service_calls

lot_id	procedure_id	address	description	date_of_work
1767	103	2454 Legion Street	Tree trimming	Nov 15 1997
1767	11	2454 Legion Street	Winterize	Dec 01 1997
955	7	707 Condador Rd	Furnace repair	Dec 03 1997
.	.	.	.	.

You identify the primary key on the 'service_calls' table as a combination of the 'lot_id' and 'procedure_id' columns.

Can you see the problem with this design? The 'service_calls' table has at least two columns that are not fully functionally dependent on the primary key. These columns are the 'address' and 'description' fields. Clearly, the address of a property generally doesn't change between service calls. The description of a particular task also usually remains the same, regardless of where you perform the task.

To alleviate this situation, you would move the 'description' column from the 'service_calls' table into the 'maint_procedures' table. The 'address' column in the 'service_calls' table already exists in the 'property_profile' table, so you need only to remove it from 'service_calls.'

The updated tables now conform to the second normal form and look like this:

Table 2.7   maint_procedures

procedure_id	procedure_cost	description
102	70.99	Gutter cleanout
103	21.00	Tree trimming
104	502.54	Weather-strip
.	.	.

Table 2.8   service_calls

lot_id	procedure_id	date_of_work
1767	103	Nov 15 1997
1767	11	Dec 01 1997
955	7	Dec 03 1997
.	.	.

Third normal form

The third normal form refers to records that both conform to the second normal form and do not have any transitive dependencies. A transitive dependence exists when a table contains a particular column that is not a key but still defines other columns. Let's look at this in more detail.

Suppose that you are designing a system to track test grades. One of your tables looks like this:

Table 2.9   test_scores

student_id	class_id	date_of_test	grade	cumulative_avg
3549	CIS091	Oct 17 1997	84	81
8021	MGT100	Oct 17 1997	72	77
1944	CIS091	Oct 17 1997	93	90
.	.	.	.	.

The primary key for this table is the combination of the 'student_id,' 'class_id,' and 'date_of_test' columns. The 'cumulative_avg' column entry represents the student's average for all courses. This column is transitively dependent on the 'student_id' column and therefore violates the third normal form. You should move this column out of the 'test_scores' table and into a table that holds student profile information:

Table 2.10   student_profile

student_id	last_name	first_name	cumulative_avg
1944	Migdal	Sylvia	90
3549	Berson	Mary	81
8021	LaFong	Carl	77
.	.	.	.

Table 2.11   test_scores

student_id	class_id	date_of_test	grade
3549	CIS091	Oct 17 1997	84
8021	MGT100	Oct 17 1997	72
1944	CIS091	Oct 17 1997	93
.	.	.	.

This change benefits you in at least two ways:

- **Reduced space requirements.**   Before, you had to store a student's cumulative average after every test. By moving the column into the 'student_profile' table, you store the information once only.

- **Reduced application complexity.**   Before the change, if you wanted to change a student's cumulative average, you had to update all rows in the 'test_scores' table. After the change, you only need to update a cumulative average in one place.

When not to normalize

Even though you should always try to satisfy each of the three normal forms, there are times when you may need to bend the rules somewhat. In this section, we'll discuss two situations that may require special handling. These situations are:

- Storing calculated values in the database
- Separating historical information into other tables

Calculated values

Normally, a well-designed relational database doesn't store any calculated data such as sums, averages, and maximum and minimum values. Instead, these figures are calculated at runtime, usually by running through the underlying detail data.

There are cases, however, where it may be simpler, faster, and wiser to store a calculated value instead of generating it at runtime. For example, as-

sume that you are developing a frequent-flyer application. Two of your tables
are designed as follows:

Table 2.12   passenger

passenger_id	passenger_first	passenger_last
ETA17094	Dale	Cooper
.	.	.
OLT09334	Leo	Weiser
.	.	.
ZOR00934	Jean	Shepherd
.	.	.

Table 2.13   flights

passenger_id	flight_num	flight_date	miles_credited
OLD09334	11	Nov 8 1997	2490
.	.	.	.
ZOR00934	1794	Nov 11 1997	753
.	.	.	.

As you size the database, you realize that the 'flights' table will grow very
rapidly, eventually reaching a size of several million rows. This presents a potential problem, because customers will be calling your reservations center,
wanting to know how many miles they have in their accounts. The customers
expect to get instant answers, yet it may take several seconds for your lookup
program to run through the 'flights' table and add up all the individual mileage
numbers. Fortunately, there is another way to provide this information more
rapidly.

The method involves storing the sum information with the main records:

Table 2.14   passenger

passenger_id	passenger_first	passenger_last	passenger_miles
ETA17094	Dale	Cooper	18095
.	.	.	
OLT09334	Leo	Weiser	7609

Table 2.14 passenger (Continued)

passenger_id	passenger_first	passenger_last	passenger_miles
.	.	.	
ZOR00934	Jean	Shepherd	753
.	.	.	

To keep the miles count current, you update the totals each night by running a summary program. This change provides you with at least two benefits:

- **Instant access to mileage totals.** Now, when a customer calls in, your telephone representatives can determine the mileage total as soon as they look up the customer's account.

- **Better load balancing.** By running the summary update program at night, you off-load heavy system processing to a time of day when it has less impact on interactive users.

Chances are, in your own applications, there are places where this type of change may help you as well. If you want more instantaneous updates, you can always use a trigger to get the latest data.

Historical information

Suppose you are maintaining a system to track credit card purchases. Customers call in, generally wanting to discuss charges on their most recent statements. Occasionally, however, they want to investigate charges from several months ago. Your largest table in this application is laid out as follows:

Table 2.15 transactions

trans_id	customer_id	date_of_purchase	amount
1093932	4765-095-393	Sep 1 1997	144.44
.	.	.	.
1204955	5099-144-091	Sep 12 1997	56.09
	.	.	.

As you would expect in this type of application, the 'transactions' table quickly grows to many millions of rows. Locating all detail rows for a particular customer account takes several seconds. In fact, both customers and account service representatives are beginning to complain about the response time. How can you improve this situation?

Since customers usually only want to discuss the most recent month's transaction information, you could break up this table into thirteen subtables, for example:

Table 2.16 curr_transactions

trans_id	customer_id	date_of_purchase	amount
1093932	4765-095-393	Sep 1 1997	144.44
.	.	.	.
1204955	5099-144-091	Sep 12 1997	56.09
.	.	.	.
1250444	3303-554-995	Sep 30 1997	1655.32

Table 2.17 prev1_trans

trans_id	customer_id	date_of_purchase	amount
993932	7077-665-992	Aug 1 1997	75.00
.	.	.	.
.	.	.	.
1093900	4455-676-432	Aug 31 1997	753.11
.	.	.	.

Table 2.18 prev12_trans

trans_id	customer_id	date_of_purchase	amount
556709	1122-587-009	Sep 1 1996	4.22
.	.	.	.
.	.	.	.
659321	3390-102-168	Sep 30 1996	90.33

At the end of each month, you run a batch job to delete (or save to a history file or tape) the oldest information from the 'prev12_trans' table. You then move the data from each table "back" one table (e.g., 'prev11_trans' data into 'prev12_trans,' 'prev10_trans' into 'prev11_trans').

Your lookup programs should run much faster now, since they only process one-twelfth of the data that they used to. You don't need to hardcode table names into your application: You locate current data in the 'curr_transactions' table, one-month-old data in 'prev1_trans,' etc.

With all of its benefits, this method is somewhat cumbersome. Fortunately, you can possibly use partitioning in this situation as a more elegant way to solve the problem.

Partitioning

SQL Server, via the replication mechanism, lets you replicate data from one database to another. A major portion of SQL Server's replication technology deals with both horizontal and vertical partitioning. Partitioning lets you keep your normalization strategy intact, yet still control the overall amount of data. We'll discuss replication in more detail later in the book, but at this point, it's a good idea to look at how you can use horizontal and vertical partitioning to streamline data storage. Note that you can also use your physical disk design as a means to partition data. We'll discuss physical disk layout and its effects on performance in Part 3.

Horizontal partitioning

When you partition a table by using a horizontal rule, you're asking SQL Server to make its determination based on certain values within each row. Let's see what this means.

Suppose that you are maintaining an application that tracks sales leads. One of your most important tables tracks the location of sales leads:

Table 2.19 lead_location

lead_id	last_name	...	territory_code
556709	Robinson	...	1002
556710	Schmieding	...	7595
.	.	...	.
602551	Palomino	...	4465

Your systems environment consists of a central location, where inbound sales calls are entered into a database. You then have a number of secondary, read-only systems where your sales representatives run reports to locate new leads. The application uses the 'territory_code' field to determine what information to present to the users. Given this functionality, you realize that there's no need for every site to receive sales leads from other regions. This extra data slows down network traffic and takes up unnecessary space on each system. Conveniently, you can use SQL Server's horizontal replication feature to selectively replicate only those rows that need to be sent to each site. You configure this option when you set up replication, by filling in the restriction clause dialog box. In this case, you would instruct SQL Server to replicate only rows with a 'territory_code' between 0 and 1000 to machine A, 1001 to 2001 to machine B, etc.

Vertical partitioning

In contrast to horizontal partitioning, vertical partitioning lets you restrict which columns you send to other destinations. There may be instances where you want to replicate a limited subset of a table's columns to other machines. For example, assume that the 'lead_location' table described earlier has another column:

Table 2.20   lead_location

lead_id	last_name	...	territory_code	commission_rate
556709	Robinson	...	1002	.75
556710	Schmieding	...	7595	.60
.	.	.	.	.
602551	Palomino	...	4465	1.25

The 'commission_rate' column contains sensitive information that you don't want your users to see. There are many ways to block this: You could create a view that doesn't show the column, or you could be very restrictive with permissions. Another way of blocking user access to this column is to avoid replicating the column in the first place. To do this, you would clear the replication check box for the 'commission_rate' column when configuring replication. Keep in mind that you don't have this option if you are trying to avoid replicating the primary key: SQL Server requires you to replicate primary key columns in all cases.

Combined horizontal/vertical partitioning

One final note regarding horizontal and vertical partitioning: SQL Server lets you combine these two approaches when replicating. Using the examples from above, you could easily restrict replication from the 'lead_location' table based on the 'territory_code' value and also instruct the engine not to replicate the 'commission_rate' column, regardless of the 'territory_code' value. This effectively coalesces the two replication strategies into one combined approach.

Special data types

Of the major relational databases, SQL Server provides the largest potential number of data types for database administrators and developers. Let's look at how some of these data types affect database design and throughput.

Variable-length characters

There are many times when database administrators are unsure of the actual, in-practice size of a particular data element. For example, how can you be sure of the actual length of a city's name? When designing a field to hold city name values, should you allocate 10, 20, or even 30 bytes? What happens if you choose 30 bytes and an operator tries to enter someone from a city that has a name longer than 33 bytes? Given that most city names are far shorter than 30 bytes, wouldn't allocating 30 bytes be a waste of space in most situations?

In cases such as this, you can circumvent the problem by choosing the variable-length character data type, also known as VARCHAR. When you define a field to be of the VARCHAR type, you provide SQL Server with the maximum number of characters that you ever want the field to hold. In the case of city name storage, you decide that the maximum length you ever need to accommodate is 40 characters. You can use this syntax when creating your table:

```
create table locations
(
     city_name varchar(40)
)
```

You could also use:

```
create table locations
(
     city_name character varying (40)
)
```

VARCHAR fields can hold between 1 and 255 bytes of information. You can also define these fields to either accept or reject null values. In this example, we've chosen 40 as the maximum size for the 'city_name' field. If you try to enter a value greater than the defined size of 40 or the VARCHAR maximum of 255 bytes, SQL Server truncates the excess data. In addition, if you store less than the full amount of data, SQL Server doesn't store any extra spaces in a VARCHAR field. On the other hand, if you defined a field as a non-null character type (e.g., you must provide a value), SQL Server appends trailing spaces until the field is full. In either case, you can perform searches without having to worry about trailing blanks. In the case of the 'locations' table, for example, suppose that we entered two rows:

```
insert into locations values ('Albany')
insert into locations values ('Albany              ')
```

We can locate both rows with any of the following SQL statements:

```
select *
from locations
where city_name = 'Albany'

select *
from locations
where city_name = 'Albany           '
```

SQL Server disregards trailing spaces when processing the WHERE clause, except when you use the LIKE operator. For example, assume that the row in question has four trailing spaces in the 'city_name' column. Look at the following two queries and their results:

```
select * from locations where city_name like 'Al%  '
city_name
----------
Albany
(1 row(s) affected)

select * from locations where city_name like 'Al%        '

city_name
----------

(0 row(s) affected)
```

The second query was unable to locate the row, since there were too many trailing spaces in the WHERE clause.

Should you use VARCHARs? The answer partially depends on whether space is a premium. In earlier times, when disk space and disk response were much slower than today, anything that you could do to reduce overall disk usage was helpful. Today's disk subsystems are so fast and inexpensive that saving a few megabytes isn't really a big issue. There is also slightly more overhead for the engine when working with variable-length characters.

In addition, VARCHARs could pose a problem with regard to row size. The maximum row size allowed by SQL Server is 1962 bytes. Anything larger could exceed available page size, and SQL Server doesn't let rows cross page boundaries. When you define a table with fixed-length columns, SQL Server detects and prevents situations where you could overflow the page's boundaries. On the other hand, it's possible that you could successfully create a table with the VARCHAR type that could have problems at runtime. Look at the following set of SQL statements:

```
create table verywide
(
     col1 char(255),
     .    .    .    .
     col9 char(255)
)
Msg 1701, Level 16, State 1
Creating table 'verywide' failed because row size would
be 2297. This exceeds the maximum allowable size of a
row in a table, 1962.
```

Watch what happens when we change the CHAR data type to VARCHAR:

```
create table verywide
(
     col1 varchar(255),
     .    .    .    .
     col9 varchar(255)
)

The total row size, 2318, for table 'verywide' exceeds
the maximum number of bytes per row, 1962.
```

SQL Server let us create the table but exhibited an error message. However, if we ever actually exceed the maximum space of 1962 bytes on an INSERT or UPDATE operation, we'll get an error message:

```
Msg 511, Level 16, State 2
Updated or inserted row is bigger than maximum size
(1962 bytes) allowed for this table.
```

We could never encounter this message if we had defined the table by using regular character fields, since SQL Server wouldn't let us create a table that already exceeded the maximum row size.

One significant argument in favor of using VARCHARs arises when you consider the potential costs of table scans when dealing with fixed-length character columns. It's possible that the engine may have to read dozens, hundreds, or even thousands of extra pages if you choose CHAR columns over VARCHAR columns. For example, suppose that you have a large table that spans 100,000 pages. There are a few CHAR columns in the table that are candidates for conversion to VARCHAR. Assume that this helps reduce the overall table size by 10 percent, which means that the table now fills 90,000 pages. You should now be able to realize measurable table scan performance improvement, since there are simply fewer pages for SQL Server to scan. In addition, the reduction in the number of pages read may also lead to more efficient data caching, since the engine reads fewer pages into memory.

Variable-length binary

Binary data consists of up to 255 bytes of bit information. These fields typically hold information found in bit flags. You can define fixed-length binary fields of up to 255 bytes. In most cases, this should be fine. However, you might decide that you don't know enough about your actual data profile to predict a good size for a binary column. In cases such as this, you can use the variable-length binary type, also known as VARBINARY. This data type lets you store between 1 and 255 characters of binary information and can be defined as either accepting or rejecting null values. You would use this syntax:

```
create table binsample
(
     col1 varbinary(200)
)
```

You can also use a synonym when creating this type:

```
create table binsample
(
     col1 binary varying (200)
)
```

Unlike columns defined as the standard binary type, SQL Server doesn't pad with zeroes any remaining space in a VARBINARY column.

Should you use this data type? The same argument is true in this situation as in the case of variable-length characters. It's nice to save disk space, but this commodity has become cheaper to acquire over time. Variable-length binary fields also require some more engine processing, since their exact size isn't predefined. Therefore, if you have a good idea about how large your typical binary fields are to be, use the standard binary type. On the other hand, if you think that the VARBINARY type might lead to significant space savings on large tables, you might be able to reduce table scan time while improving memory caching by converting to this type. We discussed this concept earlier in our review of VARCHAR versus CHAR considerations.

Text and image

One limitation that database designers continually face is that most database management systems have a restriction on the maximum length of a character string. SQL Server is no different. If you exceed this boundary when creating a table, you receive an error message back from the engine:

```
Msg 131, Level 15, State 2
The size (400) given to the field 'long_string' exceeds
the maximum. The largest size allowed is 255.
```

Another design obstacle deals with the fact that many databases still don't let you store nontraditional data, e.g., pictures, sound clips, and program executables. Happily, SQL Server provides two important data types, TEXT and IMAGE, that enhance your ability to design a robust, real-world database. Let's learn more about these two data types.

Both TEXT and IMAGE data types are stored differently than other SQL Server information. Recall that SQL Server stores all other data types on conventional data pages. The standard data pages limit you to 1962 bytes per row, far less than necessary for the data typically found in TEXT and IMAGE columns. Therefore, SQL Server treats TEXT and IMAGE information as a linked list of data pages. Each page holds two kilobytes of data, and the engine allocates as many pages as necessary for each text or image value. This is how SQL Server lets you accommodate the potentially enormous size of data kept in these columns:

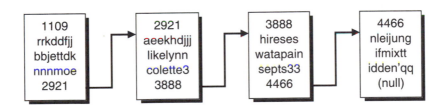

Figure 2.1

This diagram shows a linked list. Each page contains about two kilobytes of information, along with a forwarding pointer to the next page in the list. The last page has a null value for the forwarding pointer.

Limitations

While the TEXT and IMAGE data types can help solve nagging data storage problems, there are several limitations that you should know when working with these types:

- **Indexes.** You can't create an index that includes a column defined as TEXT or IMAGE. We'll discuss this limitation in greater detail in the indexing chapter.

- **WHERE clauses.** You can't search on IMAGE data types in a WHERE clause. For TEXT columns, you have reduced WHERE clause capabilities, limited to the LIKE operator. If you try to search on a TEXT column, you'll receive an error message from the engine:

```
select * from sample_table where
text_column = 'do not try this'
```

```
Msg 306, Level 16, State 1
TEXT and IMAGE datatypes may not be used in the WHERE
or HAVING clause, except with the LIKE predicate and
the IS NULL predicate.
```

- **Variables.** You can't define a local variable as TEXT or IMAGE:

```
declare @@my_text text
```

```
Msg 2739, Level 16, State 1
TEXT and IMAGE datatypes are invalid for local
variables.
```

- **Built-in functions.** You may encounter restrictions with certain built-in functions and the TEXT and IMAGE data types. These restrictions may prevent you from using the function, or you may have to use the CONVERT function to proceed. For example, look at the following SQL:

```
select substring(text_column, 1, 10) from table1
```

```
Msg 256, Level 16, State 1
The data type 'text' is invalid for the substring
function. Allowed types are: CHAR/VARCHAR and
BINARY/VARBINARY.
```

For this function, CONVERT lets you proceed:

```
select substring(convert(char,text_column),1,10)
from darius
```

```
----------
Here is a
```

- **Mathematical operations.** You can't run standard SQL aggregate and numerical operations against TEXT or IMAGE columns:

```
select avg(soundbite) from newsclips
Msg 279, Level 16, State 1
TEXT and IMAGE datatypes are invalid in this
subquery or aggregate expression.
```

If you need to run searches against this type of information, you can always store descriptive keywords in separate columns. These keywords would describe the TEXT or IMAGE data. You can then search the keywords, looking for matches. Once you've found a match, you can retrieve the actual TEXT or IMAGE information.

- **ORDER BY.** You can't place a TEXT or IMAGE column in an ORDER BY clause:

```
select snapshot from pictures order by picture

Msg 420, Level 16, State 1
TEXT and IMAGE datatypes may not be used in an ORDER
BY clause.
```

- **GROUP BY.** You can't place TEXT or IMAGE columns in a GROUP BY clause.

These last three limitations are understandable: How would the engine figure out how to sort, group, or compute on pictures or sound clips?

Examples

Let's look at some examples of where you would use either of these helpful types.

Case 1

In this case, assume that you are designing a problem-tracking system. The users communicate with customers via electronic and surface mail, as well as fax. In the near future, you also expect that customers will communicate by voice mail. Your users want to keep copies of all correspondence; for the purpose of our example, assume that any correspondence (except voice mail) can be represented in plain ASCII.

You expect that you will never need to search through the actual contents of this correspondence. Instead, you plan to maintain other fields that will contain information about the correspondence. Users will use these fields to locate particular rows.

This is a good candidate for either a TEXT or IMAGE data type. The question remains: Which of these two types should you use? If you only plan to store ASCII information, a TEXT field would most likely suffice. However, suppose you know that the users will eventually store voice mail in the database. This cannot be easily represented with the ASCII character set, so you would decide in favor of the IMAGE data type:

```
create table cust_correspond
(
    cust_no         integer,
    mail_type       char(1),
    mail_date       datetime,
    mail_contents   image
)
```

Case 2

In this case, assume that you are creating a system to log customer comments about a product or service that your organization provides. You will receive comments in one of two ways:

- Written on customer response surveys that you have sent out to your customers. These are then keyed into the system by customer service personnel.

- Directly typed in by customer service personnel during phone calls with your customers.

Your users want to be able to search through the actual comments, looking for particular strings, such as "furious," "delighted," "lawsuit," "grateful," etc. This would be a good candidate for the TEXT data type:

```
create table cust_comments
(
    cust_no           integer,
    comment_data      text
)
```

There is one problem with this approach: We learned earlier that SQL Server provides limited search capabilities into TEXT fields. For example, look what happens when you run the following SQL:

```
select * from cust_comments
where comment_data = 'we are so happy with your service'
```

```
Msg 306, Level 16, State 1
TEXT and IMAGE datatypes may not be used in the WHERE or
HAVING clause, except with the LIKE predicate and the IS
NULL predicate.
```

You could change your SQL to use the LIKE clause:

```
select * from cust_comments
where comment_data like '%we are very happy%'
```

As an alternative, you could create a table using the standard character data type:

```
create table cust_comments
(
    cust_no             integer,
    seq_no              integer,
    comment_data        char(80)
)
```

Each line of customer comments would receive a row in this table. You could then search through the 'comment_data' column to find any matches to your keywords.

If your 'cust_comments' table gets large, however, query times could become quite slow. You might consider making one entry per keyword in the following table whenever you insert or update a row in 'cust_comments':

```
create table keyword_locations
(
    keyword             char(10),
    cust_no             integer,
    seq_no              integer,
    primary key (keyword, cust_no, seq_no)
)
```

When users want to find all rows containing a keyword, this table acts as an index into the 'cust_comments' table.

Efficient accessing

If we used traditional SQL access methods to work with the TEXT and IMAGE data types, we would probably see significant performance degradation. This is especially true for operations that update information, since these types of database access are logged by SQL Server. Logging a one-gigabyte image update would be excruciatingly slow, as well as a serious drag on all other users. Fortunately, you can use three useful functions to speed operations on text and image data types. These functions are called READTEXT, WRITETEXT, and UPDATETEXT. We'll cover them in detail in Part 2 on improving database access.

Constraints

Simply expressed, constraints are conditions that you place on tables and/or columns in your database. In this section, we'll discuss several constraints, including:

- Primary key constraints
- Foreign key constraints
- Unique constraints
- Check constraints
- Rules

We'll also examine how defining default values for columns can reduce your application's complexity and workload.

Two system tables exist to service constraints and referential integrity. These tables are 'sysconstraints' and 'sysreferences.' Before beginning our discussion, let's look at how these tables are structured:

Table 2.21   sysconstraints

column name	type	purpose
constid	integer	Constraint identifier assigned by system.
Id	integer	Id of the table owning the constraint.
colid	tinyint	Id of the column on which the constraint is defined. Set to 0 if the constraint is for the table.
spare1	tinyint	Reserved.
status	integer	Constraint type: 1 = PRIMARY KEY constraint 2 = UNIQUE KEY constraint 3 = FOREIGN KEY constraint 4 = CHECK constraint 5 = DEFAULT constraint 16 = Column level constraint 32 = Table level constraint
actions	integer	Reserved.
error	integer	Reserved.

Table 2.22   sysreferences

column name	type	purpose
constid	integer	Constraint identifier assigned by system.
fkeyid	integer	ID of the referencing table.
fkeydbid	smallint	Reserved.
rkeyid	integer	ID of the referenced table.
rkeydbid	smallint	Reserved.
rkeyind	smallint	Reserved.
keycnt	smallint	Number of columns in key.
fkey1	tinyint	Column ID of referencing column.
fkey2	tinyint	Column ID of referencing column.
.	.	.
fkey16	tinyint	Column ID of referencing column.
rkey1	tinyint	Column ID of referencing column.
rkey2	tinyint	Column ID of referencing column.
.	.	.
rkey16	tinyint	Column ID of referencing column.

You can also use the 'sp_pkeys' stored procedure to get more information about a table's primary key, and the 'sp_fkeys' stored procedure to learn about its foreign keys.

Table 2.23   sp_pkeys output

column name	type	purpose
table_qualifier	varchar(32)	Table qualifier. For Microsoft SQL Server, this is the database name.
table_owner	varchar(32)	Name of the user who created the table.
table_name	varchar(32)	The table name.
column_name	varchar(32)	The name of the column.
key_seq	smallint	The column's sequence number.
pk_name	varchar(32)	The name of the primary key.

Table 2.24   sp_fkeys output

column name	type	purpose
pktable_qualifier	varchar(32)	Primary key table qualifier. For Microsoft SQL Server, this is the database name.
pktable_owner	varchar(32)	Name of the user who created the primary key table.
pktable_name	varchar(32)	The primary key table's name.
pkcolumn_name	varchar(32)	The name for each primary key column.
fktable_qualifier	varchar(32)	Foreign key table qualifier. For Microsoft SQL Server, this is the database name.
fktable_owner	varchar(32)	Name of the user who created the foreign key table.
fktable_name	varchar(32)	The foreign key table's name.
fkcolumn_name	varchar(32)	The name for each foreign key column.
key_seq	smallint	The column's sequence number.
update_rule	smallint	The action taken on the foreign key when an UPDATE statement is executed. SQL Server will return 1, whereas Open Data Services gateways can return: 0 = Cascade changes to foreign key. 1 = Restrict changes if there is a foreign key. 2 = Set foreign key to null.
delete_rule	smallint	The action taken on the foreign key when a DELETE statement is executed. SQL Server will return 1, whereas Open Data Services gateways can return: 0 = Cascade changes to foreign key. 1 = Restrict changes if there is a foreign key. 2 = Set foreign key to null.
fk_name	varchar(128)	Foreign key name.
pk_name	varchar(128)	Primary key name.

Primary key constraint

Primary key constraints define a column or columns as the primary identifier of rows within the table. This means that there can be no duplicates between rows within this column or columns. Each of your tables should have a primary key defined. In addition to enhancing data integrity and assisting in data access, primary keys are used by certain SQL Server cursors. You can define primary key constraints in one of two ways:

- Implicitly, by creating a unique index on the column or columns.
- Explicitly, by using the PRIMARY KEY syntax. This method is especially important if you are defining a parent-child relationship. Note that another name for "parent-child" relationships is "master-detail" relationships.

As an example of explicitly defining a primary key constraint, let's use a table from a time and attendance application. In the 'employee_detail' table, you plan to store timecard information. During your analysis, you determine that the combination of the employee number and date of work will be enough to uniquely identify each row. You decide that the system should never allow two records with the same employee number and date of work in the table. You can define this when you create the table:

```
create table employee_detail
(
     employee_num integer,
     date_of_work datetime,
     hours_worked decimal(4,2)
     primary key (employee_num, date_of_work)
)
```

Once you've created this table, there are a number of ways to learn about its primary keys. You can use the 'sp_pkeys' stored procedure, with a parameter of 'employee_detail':

Table 2.25 sp_pkeys sample output

column name	value
table_qualifier	benchmark
table_owner	dbo
table_name	employee_detail
column_name	employee_num
key_seq	1
pk_name	PK__employee__hours__04C4C0F4
table_qualifier	benchmark
table_owner	dbo

Table 2.25   sp_pkeys sample output (Continued)

table_name	employee_detail
column_name	date_of_work
key_seq	2
pk_name	PK__employee__hours__04C4C0F4

The 'sp_helpindex' stored procedure also returns information about a table's primary keys:

Table 2.26   sp_helpindex sample output

column name	value
index_name	PK__employee__hours
index_description	clustered, unique, primary key located on default

You can also use the SQL Enterprise Manager to learn about a table's primary keys:

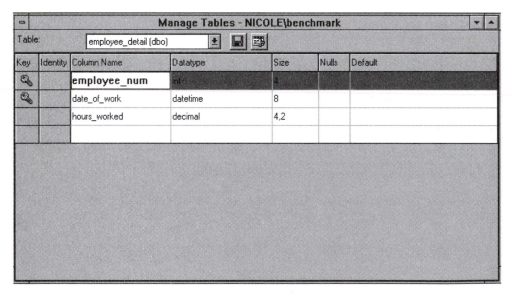

Figure 2.2

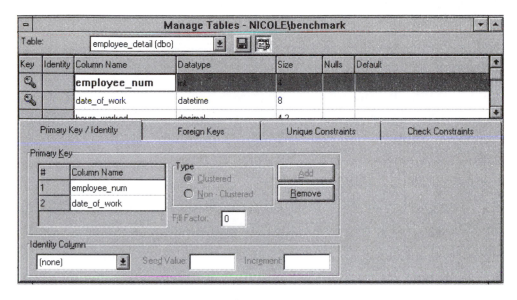

Figure 2.3

SQL Server also creates an entry in the 'sysconstraints' table:

Table 2.27   sysconstraints entry

column name	value
constid	144003544
id	128003487
colid	0
spare1	0
status	133633
actions	4096
error	0

If you wanted to implicitly make these two columns the primary key, you need only create a unique index on the two columns:

```
create unique index emp_dtl1 on employee_detail
(employee_num, date_of_work)
```

Identity attribute

One challenge that developers continually face is how to generate a secure, valid numeric primary key. Fortunately, you can use the IDENTITY property to get around this problem. When you define a column with this property, SQL Server automatically generates a unique number for you. Let's look as some examples that display how to use this feature.

Suppose that you're creating a table that has no explicit, unique numeric information. Your table layout looks like this:

Table 2.28   user_comments

user_id	comment_line	comment_text
sammela	1	I would like to thank the support group for all
sammela	2	their help during my recent operating system
sammela	3	upgrade. Next time, I wait for the 2nd release.
.	.	.
.	.	.
rockyb	1	Please call me for confidential information.

You could make your primary key a combination of the 'user_id' and 'comment_line' fields. While this seems to be the best approach, it may not be as efficient as possible. From a joining and searching perspective, the most efficient primary keys are numeric, which would mean adding an extra field:

Table 2.29   user_comments

comment_id	user_id	comment_line	comment_text
1	sammela	1	I would like to thank the support group for all
2	sammela	2	their help during my recent operating system
3	sammela	3	upgrade. Next time, I wait for the 2nd release.
	.	.	.
	.	.	.
42324	rockyb	1	Please call me for confidential information.

Your problem is deciding how to assign a unique numeric value to each record. This is where the IDENTITY attribute can help. If you define your primary key with the IDENTITY attribute, SQL Server automatically fills in this information for you. You can even specify a starting point, as well as how large the difference should be between generated values. We'll discuss these alternatives later.

To make use of this feature in the case of the 'user_comments' table, your SQL would look like this:

```
create table user_comments
(
      comment_id integer identity primary key,
      user_id char(8),
      comment_line smallint,
      comment_text varchar(80)
)
```

When you insert data into this table, you don't need to concern yourself with providing a value for 'comment_id': SQL Server takes care of this task for you. For example, here's how you could construct your INSERT statement:

```
insert into user_comments
( user_id, comment_line, comment_text)
values
('elarryson',1,'Service was very slow')
```

Notice that we didn't specify a value for the 'comment_id' field. Instead, SQL Server automatically filled in the correct value. Since we defined this field as the primary key, SQL Server takes care of ensuring that the value is unique. To see what value SQL Server assigned to this column, you could check the contents of the @@IDENTITY global variable:

```
select @@identity

-------------
60994
```

Be careful when checking this global variable, since it gets reset by the engine after inserts into other tables that don't have the IDENTITY property set. In addition, when you transfer data from a table that has the IDENTITY property table set into a new table, SQL Server generally keeps the identity value intact. However, if your new table was created by a join, union, or aggregate function, or if you perform math on the IDENTITY column, SQL Server doesn't create the new column with this property.

IDENT_SEED

In most cases, when you define a column with the IDENTITY property, you want SQL Server to start counting from 1. However, there may be times when you want to start generating these identity numbers from a specific value. For example, you may already have manually assigned identity numbers to existing data. In any case, you can specify a starting point, also known as a seed value:

```
create table user_comments
(
      comment_id integer identity(15000,1) primary key,
      .       .       .       .       .
      .       .       .       .       .
)
```

In this example, we've requested that SQL Server start the 'comment_id' column with a value of 15,000. All new rows in this table will have an identity value higher than 15,000:

```
select comment_id from user_comments

comment_id
-----------
15000
15001
15002
```

You can determine what the seed value is for a table by running the 'ident_seed' function:

```
select (ident_seed('user_comments'))


------------------------------------------
15000
```

IDENT_INCR

As we've seen, when you create a table that has an identity column, you can specify what the seed value should be. You can also stipulate what each incremental step should be between new values. For example, you can request that each new identity value be 25 units higher than the previous value:

```
create table user_comments
(
      comment_id integer identity(1,25) primary key,
      .       .       .       .       .
      .       .       .       .       .
)
```

In this example, we're asking SQL Server to start the 'comment_id' value at 1, then increment each new row by 25. If we added three rows to the table, the results would look like this:

```
select comment_id from user_comments

comment_id
-----------
1
26
51
```

You can ask SQL Server to report on what the identity increments are for a table by using the 'ident_incr' function. Here's an example:

```
select (ident_incr('user_comments'))


--------------------------------------------
25
```

You can also use the SQL Enterprise Manager to learn whether a column has been assigned the identity attribute, as well as the identity seed and increment:

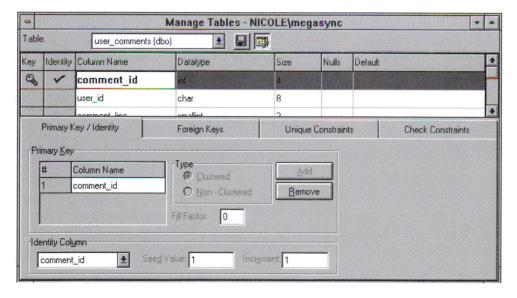

Figure 2.4

TIMESTAMP

At first glance, it appears that you could use the TIMESTAMP data type as a system-generated primary key. However, appearances can be deceptive, and this case is no exception.

Timestamps are unique among SQL Server's roster of data types. When you define a column to be TIMESTAMP, SQL Server automatically updates this column each time you make a change to its row. The value held in these columns isn't a TIMESTAMP in the sense of a particular point-in-time. Instead, it represents a BINARY(8) or VARBINARY(8) value generated by the engine. This value is guaranteed to be unique in the database. For example, look at the following SQL and output:

```
create table timestamp_test (col1 int, col2 timestamp)
insert into timestamp_test (col1) values (1)
insert into timestamp_test (col1) values (2)
insert into timestamp_test (col1) values (5)

select * from timestamp_test

col1          col2
----------    ------------------
1             0x0000000100000a7a
2             0x0000000100000a7d
5             0x0000000100000a80
```

So far, so good. It seems that we could rely on SQL Server to generate a unique primary key by defining the column as a TIMESTAMP. However, watch what happens after the next SQL statement:

```
update timestamp_test set col1 = 6 where col1 = 5

select * from timestamp_test

col1          col2
----------    ------------------
1             0x0000000100000a7a
2             0x0000000100000a7d
6             0x0000000100000a8a
```

Observe what happened to the data held in 'col2' for the row that changed. As promised, SQL Server automatically updated the timestamp value when the row changed. Primary keys are one item that you definitely don't want to change during the life of the row. Continually changing primary key values would play havoc with the referential integrity of your database, since all joins to other tables on this value would cease to exist after the first automatic update. With this in mind, use the TIMESTAMP type for circumstances when you want to track whether or not a row has changed, not for an automatic key generator.

Foreign key constraint

Foreign key constraints define relationships among tables. Typically, these are known as "parent-child" or "master-detail" relationships. Using our example from above, let's say that each employee has a profile record that holds information about the employee's name, address, etc.:

```
create table employee_header
(
      employee_num    integer,
      employee_first char(10),
      employee_last   char(20),
      primary key (employee_num)
)
```

The 'employee_detail' table holds timecard information. An employee can have only one 'employee_header' record but can have many 'employee_detail' records. This is a classic "parent-child" relationship, where the 'employee_header' table is the parent and the 'employee_detail' table is the child.

You can define a foreign key in the 'employee_detail' table, which helps you avoid having child records without corresponding parent records. Remember that you must also define a primary key constraint for the parent record.

For example, suppose that you first define a primary key for the 'employee_header' table and then define a foreign key for the 'employee_detail' table. If you attempt to add an employee's time stamp data without first creating an 'employee_header' record, your application receives an error from the database server:

```
Msg 547, Level 16, State 2
INSERT statement conflicted with COLUMN FOREIGN KEY
constraint 'FK__employee___emplo__0F424F67'. The
conflict occurred in database 'benchmark', table
'employee_header', column 'employee_num'
Command has been aborted.
```

You'll also receive an error if you try to delete a parent without first deleting all affected children:

```
Msg 547, Level 16, State 2
DELETE statement conflicted with COLUMN REFERENCE
constraint 'FK__employee___emplo__0F424F67'. The
conflict occurred in database 'benchmark', table
'employee_detail', column 'employee_num'
Command has been aborted.
```

The SQL to define a foreign key looks like this:

```
create table employee_detail
(
      employee_num integer,
      date_of_work datetime,
      hours_worked decimal(4,2)
      primary key (employee_num, date_of_work),
      foreign key (employee_num) references
      employee_header (employee_num)
)
```

You can learn about this foreign key by running 'sp_fkeys' with a parameter of 'employee_header':

Table 2.30   sp_fkeys sample output

column name	value
pktable_qualifier	benchmark
pktable_owner	dbo
pktable_name	employee_header
pkcolumn_name	employee_num
fktable_qualifier	benchmark
fktable_owner	dbo
fktable_name	employee_detail
fkcolumn_name	employee_num
key_seq	1
update_rule	1
delete_rule	1
fk_name	FK__employee___emplo__0F424F67
pk_name	PK__employee_header__0B71BE83

An additional way to discover more about foreign keys is to use the SQL Enterprise Manager:

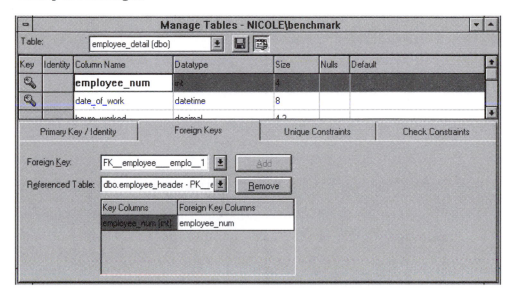

Figure 2.5

Unique constraint

Let's say that you have another column in the 'employee_header' table that is unique, but you don't want to use it as a primary key. You can set up a unique constraint instead.

If you defined a unique constraint during table creation, your SQL would look like this:

```
create table employee_header
(
      employee_num   integer,
      employee_first char(10),
      employee_last  char(20),
      employee_ssn   char(9),
      unique (employee_ssn)
)
```

This automatically places a unique index on the 'employee_ssn' column. Since you didn't provide a name for the constraint, the engine generated one for you.

If you want to remove a constraint, it's a good idea to drop the constraint, rather than simply deleting the index. You use the ALTER TABLE statement to drop constraints:

```
ALTER TABLE <table name>
DROP CONSTRAINT <constraint name>
```

If you want to alter an existing constraint, it's best to first drop it, then re-create it.

Check constraint

Suppose you want to prevent application programs or users from entering dates outside a specified boundary. By using a check constraint, you can protect domain integrity and safeguard your database from these types of data errors. Using our payroll example, we place a check constraint on the 'date_of_work' column:

```
create table employee_detail
(
        employee_num integer,
        date_of_work datetime,
        hours_worked decimal(2),
        primary key (employee_num, date_of_work),
        foreign key (employee_num) references
            employee_header(employee_num),
        check (date_of_work between
            "1996-01-01" and "1996-12-31")
)
```

This sample places a check constraint at the table level. You can define only one table-level constraint. If you had more columns that required constraints, you could define the check constraint at the column level:

```
create table employee_detail
(
        employee_num integer,
        date_of_work datetime check (date_of_work
            between "1996-01-01" and "1996-12-31"),
        hours_worked decimal(2) check (hours_worked
            between 0 and 24),
```

```
        primary key (employee_num, date_of_work),
        foreign key (employee_num) references
            employee_header(employee_num)
)
```

If you try to insert a row into this table with a value outside the legal date range, you'll get an error message back from SQL Server:

```
Msg 547, Level 16, State 2
INSERT statement conflicted with TABLE CHECK constraint
'CK__employee_detail__25319086'. The conflict occurred
in database 'benchmark', table 'employee_detail'
Command has been aborted.
```

You can learn about a table's constraints by running the 'sp_helpconstraint' stored procedure:

```
Object Name
---------------
employee_detail
```

constraint_type	constraint_name	constraint_keys
---------------	---------------------	--------------
PRIMARY KEY (clustered)	PK__employee_detail__39388933	employee_num, date_of_work
FOREIGN KEY	FK__employee_emplo__3C14F5DE	employee_num REFERENCES benchmark.dbo. employee_header (employee_num)
CHECK on column date_of_work	CK__employee___date___3A2CAD6C	(date_of_work >= '1996-01-01' and (date of work <= '1996-12-31'))
CHECK on column	CK__employee___hours___3B20D1A5	(hours_worked >= 0 and hours_worked (hours_worked <= 24))

```
No foreign keys reference this table.
```

You can also use the SQL Enterprise Manager to learn about a table's constraints:

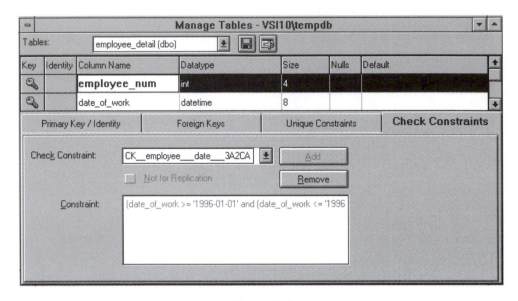

Figure 2.6

If you learn that you need more constraints, you can always add them later, using the ALTER TABLE syntax:

```
alter table awards
    add check ((mileage_level % 1000) = 0)
```

Rules

Another way to protect domain integrity is to create data-checking rules. For example, suppose that you want to ensure that users never enter a 'mileage_level' value less than 5000 in the 'awards' table. You could take these steps to enforce this rule:

1. Create a rule, using this syntax:

    ```
    create rule minimum_award as @mileage_level >= 5000
    ```

2. Bind the rule to the table's column:

    ```
    sp_bindrule minimum_award, 'awards.mileage_level'
    ```

Once you've created the rule, if you attempt to insert an out-of-range value, you'll get an error message back from SQL Server:

```
insert into awards values
    ("H2A", 2000, "Free night in hourly hotel")
```

```
Msg 513, Level 16, State 1
A column insert or update conflicts with a rule imposed
by a previous CREATE RULE command. The command was abort-
ed. The conflict occurred in database 'benchmark', table
'awards', column 'mileage_level'
```

Keep in mind that although you can only have one rule per column, you can define multiple check constraints for the same entity. This means that it's probably a better idea to use check constraints over rules if you think that you might need to define multiple domain integrity safeguards.

You can list the defined rules by running the 'sp_help' stored procedure:

```
Name                  Owner                     Object_type
-----------           ----------------          -----------

. . .                 . . .                     . . .
minimum_award         dbo                       rule¶
. . .                 . . .                     . . .
```

You can then learn about the exact syntax of a particular existing rule by running the 'sp_helptext' stored procedure:

```
text
-------------------------------------------------------
create rule minimum_award as @mileage_level >= 5000
```

Another way to work with rules is to use the **SQL Enterprise Manager:**

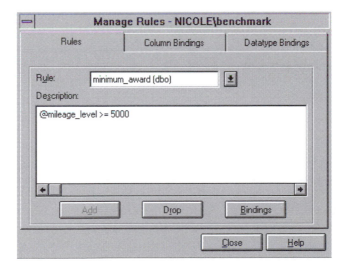

Figure 2.7

In this figure, we've created a rule that we've called 'minimum_award.' This rule states that the 'mileage_level' value must be greater than or equal to 5000.

Next, we're binding this rule to a column within a particular table.

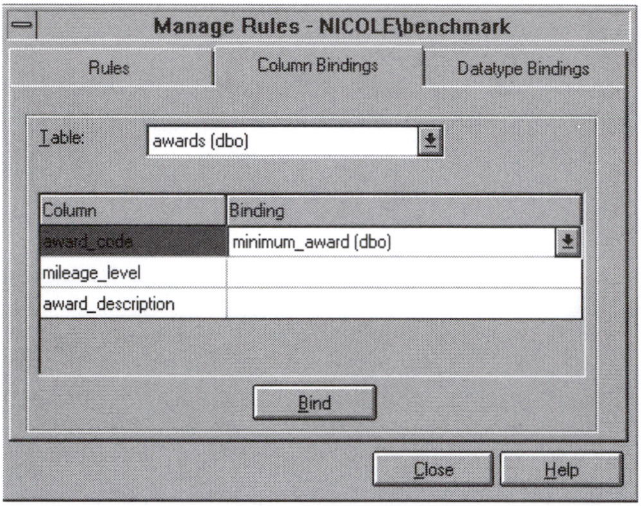

Figure 2.8

One final note regarding rules: You can also bind a rule to a user-defined data type. We'll explore this in more detail later in this chapter.

Default values

SQL Server lets you specify default values for a table's columns. This can be very useful. Let's look at an example of a personnel application. As part of the system, you maintain a table to store salary adjustments:

Table 2.31   salary_adjust

employee_id	adjust_date	adjust_amount
1109	Jun 10 1997	4.250
445	Jun 10 1997	5.250
1380	Jun 10 1997	3.000
.	.	.

You can simplify your application code and improve performance by instructing the database engine to use default values for certain columns if they are not provided by the user. In this case, you learn from your users that they want to use today's date as a default, as well as an adjustment amount of three percent. The SQL to create the table would look like this:

```
create table salary_adjust
(
      employee_id    integer,
      adjust_date    datetime default current_timestamp,
      adjust_amount decimal(5,3)   default 3.000
)
```

If your users expect to use these values most of the time, you can reduce the size and complexity of your application. For these cases, your insertion logic would look like this:

```
insert into salary_adjust(employee_id) values (nnnn)
```

where "nnnn" is an employee ID supplied at runtime.

The two biggest benefits of default values are increased data integrity and reduced traffic between the front-end process and the database server. This traffic reduction is especially important in client/server configurations, where the client and server may be separated by long distances.

You can use the SQL Enterprise Manager to define defaults that you can then use in a variety of situations. To do this, you first define a default value:

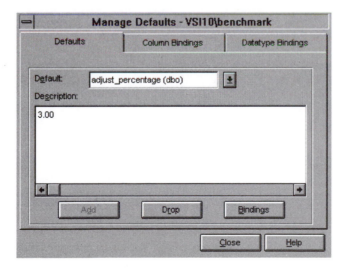

Figure 2.9

Then, apply the value to a column:

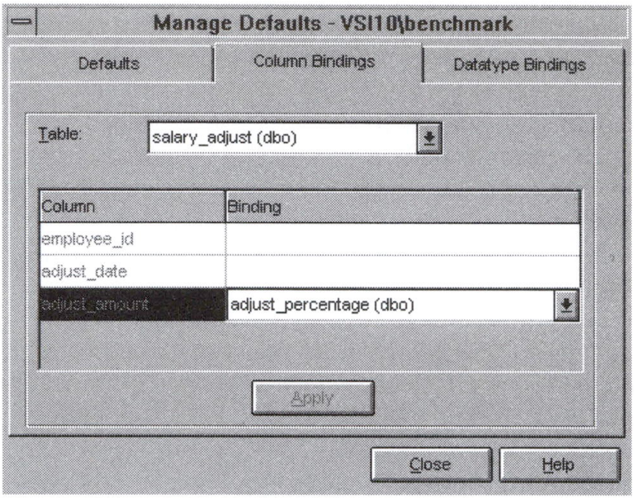

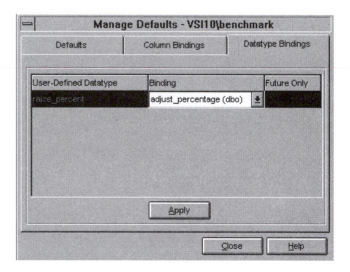

Figure 2.10

You can even specify a default value for a particular user-defined data type:

Figure 2.11

User-defined data types

One helpful feature that SQL Server provides developers and administrators is the ability to create custom, user-defined data types. Let's look at how you can incorporate this innovation into your environment to help improve application development and maintenance.

Suppose that you are the database analyst on a team developing a quality assurance tracking system. One of your important data elements is the customer's account number, which contains numeric information with a range between 0 and 1,000,000, and is found in a number of important tables and programs. As we'll see later in this chapter, it's very important to be consistent when defining data types. Unfortunately, you've noticed that your developers are defining this data type with a variety of values, from SMALLINT to INTEGER to CHAR to VARCHAR. This is causing a number of unnecessary conversion problems in stored procedures, as well as causing all your database tables to have different layouts. How can you stop this from happening? One way is to publish an internal data dictionary that explains what the correct data types should be for all system elements. You could then instruct all developers and administrators to make sure that they follow these rules when creating tables or defining host variables. Another way to achieve your desired results would be to create a custom, user-defined data type. When you create a user-defined data type, you essentially create a synonym between a name of your choice and an underlying data type. Administrators and developers then use this type, rather than deciding on their own how to define columns and variables that contain that type of information. This can be very useful, especially on large, decentralized projects where you may observe ten different ways of defining the same element.

In this example, you know that the customer account number field is supposed to be an INTEGER, yet your developers are using all different combinations of data types. The correct approach is to define a user-defined data type that maps to an INTEGER and give it a meaningful name. You decide on 'account_type' to be the new data type that maps to any field that contains an account number. Regardless of the naming method you follow, it's a good idea to be consistent with these names. For example, you might append '_type' to the end of the user-defined data type name. It's also a good idea to notify everyone who might create tables or views or write stored procedures and other applications. As a rule, try to limit the number of people who have the permission to create new user-defined data types.

To create a user-defined data type, you have two choices. First, you can use the 'sp_addtype' stored procedure:

```
sp_addtype account_type, 'integer', 'not null'
```

Another way is to use the SQL Enterprise Manager dialog box:

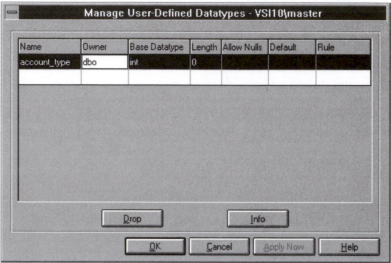

Figure 2.12

You can also get a report of locations where the data type has been used:

Figure 2.13

If you want to associate a rule with the newly formed data type, you can use the SQL Enterprise Manager:

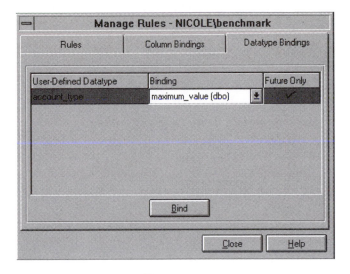

Figure 2.14

Whichever method you use, once you've created the user-defined data type, you can use it when you create tables and define stored procedure variables:

```
create table clients
(
     account_number account_type
     .      .      .
     .      .      .
)
create table contacts
(
     contact_number integer,
     account_number account_type,
     .      .      .
     .      .      .
)


.      .      .
.      .      .
declare @@lookup_number account_type

select @@lookup_number = 123

select * from clients
where account_number = @@lookup_number
.      .      .
.      .      .
```

In addition to setting up a standard data profile, there are other benefits to creating and employing these user-defined data types, including:

- **Data integrity.** In the example above, notice how we informed SQL Server that the 'account_type' value was not allowed to be null. This is one way that you can enforce data integrity rules without requiring all developers to be aware of them.

- **Default values**. By employing the SQL Enterprise Manager, you have the option of stipulating a default value for the user-defined data type. Another way to do this is to use the 'sp_binddefault' stored procedure. In either case, programmers can take advantage of this default value when inserting data into any columns that are defined with this type.

- **Rules**. As we saw earlier in this chapter, rules can be a powerful device to help guarantee that data meets organizational requirements before it is placed into the database. The SQL Enterprise Manager user-defined data type dialog lets you assign a rule to these data types. You can also use the 'sp_bindrule' stored procedure.

- **Space control**. Developers and administrators often make the mistake of allocating too much space to database fields. By creating and employing user-defined data types, you can map commonly used fields to more appropriate data types. For example, you can use these user-defined data types to associate certain character information with the VARCHAR type instead, or particular numeric information with SMALLINTs. This has the potential to save space.

Note that when you create a user-defined data type, it's usually limited to the database where you issued the command. However, if you want the data type to apply to all databases, simply issue the request while connected to the 'model' database. Also, choose your user-defined data type names and mappings carefully: If you later decide to drop the data type (either via SQL Enterprise Manager or the 'sp_droptype' procedure) and the type is already referenced in a table, you'll get an error message:

```
sp_droptype account_type

Msg 15180, Level 16, State 1
Type is being used. You cannot drop it.
object          type owner      column          datatype
-----------     ---- -----      -----------     -----------
clients         U    dbo        account_number  account_type
contacts        U    dbo        account_number  account_type
```

To learn more about the user type status for your environment, you can run the 'sp_datatype_info' stored procedure. This procedure returns a large assortment of helpful information:

Table 2.32 sp_datatype_info

column name	type	purpose
type_name	varchar	The data type name.
data_type	smallint	The ODBC code that maps to this type.
Precision	integer	The maximum precision for this type, or NULL if not appropriate.
literal_prefix	varchar	The special character used to denote the start of a literal. An example of this is a quote prior to a character literal.
literal_suffix	varchar	The special character used to denote the end of a literal. An example of this is a quote after a character literal.
create_params	varchar	The parameters necessary when creating this data type.
Nullable	smallint	A flag that denotes whether this type can be created to allow nulls. 1 means that it can; 0 means that it cannot.
case_senstive	smallint	A flag that shows whether data stored in this type is case sensitive. This is important when SQL Server is trying to sort data. 1 means that data is case sensitive; 0 means that it is not.
Searchable	smallint	A flag stating whether data stored in columns of this type can be placed in a WHERE clause.
unsigned_attribute	smallint	A flag showing whether this data type is unsigned. 1 means that it is; 0 means that it is not.
Money	smallint	A flag determining whether this data type corresponds to money. 1 means that it is; 0 means that it is not.
auto_increment	smallint	A flag signifying if this data type auto-increments. 1 means that it does; 0 means that it does not. NULL means that the type isn't numeric and therefore won't ever be able to auto-increment.

Table 2.32   sp_datatype_info (Continued)

column name	type	purpose
local_type_name	varchar	The language-dependent name for this data type.
minimum_scale	smallint	The minimum scale of the data type. NULL if this isn't applicable.
maximum_scale	smallint	The maximum scale of the data type. NULL if this isn't applicable.
sql_data_type	smallint	The actual value of the SQL data type, which corresponds to the earlier data_type column, except when the type in question is datetime or interval. This was added in SQL Server 6.5.
sql_datetime_sub	smallint	If the previous column is SQL_DATETIME or SQL_INTERVAL, this column provides the subcode for these types. This was added in SQL Server 6.5.
num_prec_radix	integer	This column holds an indicator stating that the column_size column holds the number of bits for the data type. This is only true for data types of approximate numeric value: for precise numeric data types, this column holds 10, indicating that column_size holds decimal digits. This was added in SQL Server 6.5.
usertype	smallint	The identification number for this data type.

Here's some sample output for this stored procedure. To aid in readability, we've displayed the information in columnar form:

Table 2.33   sp_datatype_info sample output

column name	sample1	sample2	sample3	sample4
type_name	char	numeric	datetime	account_type
data_type	1	2	11	4
precision	255	28	23	10
literal_prefix	'	(null)	'	(null)
literal_suffux	'	(null)	'	(null)
create_params	length	precision,scale	(null)	(null)

Table 2.33 sp_datatype_info sample output (Continued)

column name	sample1	sample2	sample3	sample4
nullable	1	1	1	0
case_senstive	0	0	0	0
searchable	3	2	3	2
unsigned_attribute	(null)	0	(null)	0
money	0	0	0	0
auto_increment	(null)	0	(null)	0
local_type_name	char	numeric	datetime	account_type
minimum_scale	(null)	0	3	0
maximum_scale	(null)	28	3	0
sql_data_type	1	2	9	4
sql_datetime_sub	(null)	(null)	3	(null)
num_prec_radix	(null)	10	10	10
usertype	1	25	12	101

ANSI specification behavior and SQL Server

Each major relational database management system treats nulls and various processing exceptions in a slightly different way. This can be very confusing when designing and maintaining an SQL-based application, since you could easily get different results running against the exact same data: The only difference is that you're running on diversified database systems. Luckily, the American National Standards Institute (ANSI) has defined a standard set of behaviors for handling nulls and these processing exceptions. Beginning with SQL Server version 6.5, you can now direct the database engine to treat nulls and processing exceptions according to the ANSI specification. This means that if you follow the ANSI specification across all of your database environments, you can expect similar behavior, regardless of your choice of database engine. Let's look at how SQL Server treats nulls and these exceptions in a number of situations, then compare this with the ANSI standard. Before beginning, let's create a small table that we'll use for these examples. The table has the following layout and contents:

Table 2.34   demo_ansi

record_id	numeric_value	character_value
1	10	This
2	15	column
3	<null>	has
4	25	only
5	30	10 bytes

Retrieving all rows from this table produces this output:

```
record_id    numeric_value character_value
-----------  ------------- ---------------
1            10            This
2            15            column
3            (null)        has
4            25            only
5            30            10 bytes

(5 row(s) affected)
```

In the first example, we want to get the average of the data in the 'numeric_value' column:

```
select avg(numeric_value) from demo_ansi


-----------
20


(1 row(s) affected)
```

In this case, SQL Server discarded the null value in row 3 and calculated the average based on the remaining values. However, the ANSI specification says that any mathematical evaluation that contains a null should evaluate to a null. Setting the new SQL Server global variable, ANSI_WARNINGS, would therefore slightly change the results of our previous example:

```
set ANSI_WARNINGS on

select avg(numeric_value) from demo_ansi

Warning, null value eliminated from aggregate.
```

```
-----------
20

(1 row(s) affected)
```

In addition, the ANSI_WARNINGS variable produces error messages when your program encounters any of the following situations:

- **Character truncation.** There are times when you inadvertently try to add more data into a column than is allowed. For example, look at the following SQL:

  ```
  insert into demo_ansi
  (numeric_value, character_value)
  values
  (35, "A very long string that is truncated")

  select * from demo_ansi where numeric_value = 35

  record_id   numeric_value character_value
  ----------- ------------- ---------------
  6           35            A very lon

  (1 row(s) affected)
  ```

  SQL Server accepted the data and simply truncated the excess. After setting ANSI_WARNINGS on, the same sequence produces this message:

  ```
  Msg 8152, Level 16, State 1
  Column 'character_value' of table
  'demonstrate.dbo.demo_ansi' cannot accept
  36 bytes (10 max).
  ```

- **Divide by zero.** If you don't enable ANSI_WARNINGS and you attempt to divide by zero in an expression, SQL Server attempts to satisfy your request. However, enabling this variable halts execution of your query and produces this message:

  ```
  Msg 8134, Level 16, State 1
  Divide by zero error encountered
  ```

SQL Server then uses NULL as the result of the arithmetic expression.

Other areas of ANSI behavior deal with how SQL Server pads certain types of fields, arithmetic aborts, implicit transactions, and cursor response. We'll cover transactions and cursors in our chapters on enhancing database access. At this point, let's focus on padding and arithmetic aborts.

When you enable the ANSI_PADDING global variable, SQL Server pads all VARBINARY and VARCHAR fields with nulls. In addition, if this variable is turned on and you attempt to enter a null value into any other fixed length column, SQL Server replaces the null with spaces.

Setting the ARITHABORT parameter tells SQL Server to abort your SQL operations whenever the engine encounters an arithmetic overflow or a divide-by-zero error happens. On the other hand, setting ARITHIGNORE lets the engine know that you want a null to be returned in the event of this type of error. Which should you use? For operations that require precision and extreme accuracy, it's better for your query to fail if it encounters an overflow or a divide-by-zero, so setting ARITHABORT is the correct course of action. Conversely, for procedures that are not essential, returning NULL should not be much of a problem; you can comfortably turn on ARITHIGNORE.

Two final points regarding all of these ANSI options:

1. By setting the ANSI_DEFAULTS global variable, you can tell SQL Server to use all of these options. This is much easier and faster than individually setting each variable. These settings remain in effect until the user logs off or the stored procedure completes.

2. If you've just upgraded from an earlier version of SQL Server, be careful when using this new feature, since it's possible that your older applications may not have been designed with ANSI behavior in mind. Consequently, these applications might fail when confronted with the new ANSI options.

Disabling constraints

As we've seen, constraints are useful tools that help maintain database integrity. There are occasions, however, when it's wise to consider bypassing the constraint checking mechanisms. Let's look at some of these situations, along with several methods that you can use to temporarily disable constraints.

Assume that you are replicating a table between two systems. On the source system, you perform a variety of primary and foreign key referential integrity checks. In addition, you also check to make sure that certain values in the table fall within acceptable ranges. Your SQL that creates the table looks like:

```
create table transactions
(
      transaction_id integer identity primary key,
      .    .    .
```

```
transaction_amount decimal(8,2)
check (transaction_amount between
    0 and 999999.99)
)
```

You also used the same SQL to define the destination table. Can you see the potential unnecessary performance barrier? Since you are already checking the 'transaction_amount' value on the source database, why check it again on the destination database? With SQL Server 6.5, you can prevent the destination server from performing this extraneous check, by specifying NOT FOR REPLICATION when you create the constraint. We'll discuss replication in more detail later in the book, in Chapter 16.

Another example of why you might want to disable constraint checking happens when you're running a large number of complex transactions. Some types of transactions briefly and intentionally violate a constraint. By the time the transaction finishes, the user's program may have corrected the constraint violation. These types of temporary constraint issues are known as interim-deferred violations. When SQL Server is searching for and reporting these violations, it creates work tables. These work tables can consume important disk and CPU resources and may be entirely unnecessary in your environment, especially if you don't plan on needing this type of engine review. Beginning with SQL Server version 6.5, you can instruct the engine not to take these steps, by setting the DISABLE_DEF_CNST_CHK option. When this preference is enabled, SQL Server skips these steps, thereby bypassing the temporary table creation work. However, if your application does cause an interim-deferred violation, SQL Server won't gracefully continue: Your application receives an error instead, and the database operation is halted.

Finally, suppose that you're performing a massive update on an existing table. Speed is of the essence during this procedure. You're absolutely sure that your application is of the highest caliber: No constraint violations can possibly be part of your code. In this case, it may pay to remove these constraints until after your program has completed. You can do this by using the ALTER TABLE statement, with the NOCHECK keyword. Once your program has finished, remember to add the constraints back into the table schema. Keep in mind that you should only take this type of step if you feel that:

- The constraint checking is taking too much time.

- Your program won't violate the constraints anyway.

- You remember to add the constraints back on the table after completing your work.

- Other processes don't update the table during the time that constraints are removed.

Using views

As a database administrator or developer, you can use views to present a simpler, more secure appearance of your data. In this section, we examine how you can make the most efficient use of this powerful tool. To create views, you provide the SQL necessary to construct the view. You can enter this SQL via the SQL Enterprise Manager Create View dialog box:

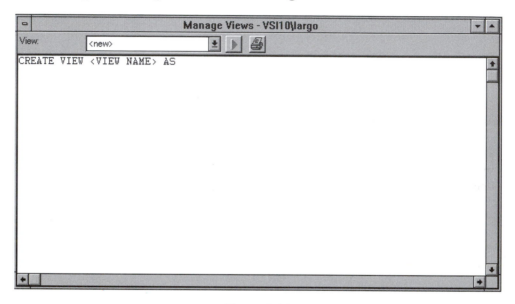

Figure 2.15

You can create views with any other tool that lets you specify SQL statements. For the purpose of our upcoming examples, let's use the following two tables:

Table 2.35   sales_representatives

representative_id	last_name	first_name	user_id	...
.	.	.	.	.
9043	Sierra	Colette	sierra	...
9044	Glenn	Gerry	gglenn	...
9045	Fitzgerald	Susan	sufitz	...
.	.	.		.

Table 2.36   transactions

transaction_id	representative_id	transaction_date	amount	commission
.	.	.	.	.
334933	9044	Aug 19 1997	590.33	5.90
334934	9044	Aug 19 1997	1255.02	15.05
334935	9045	Aug 19 1997	218.94	1.75
.	.	.	.	.

One of your goals is to create a sales reporting report that provides a variety of information to all users. However, the 'commission' column in the 'transaction' table is confidential and should only be presented to the sales representative or her manager. How can you present all of the required information, yet keep this data confidential? You could do it programmatically, but that would be very inefficient to design and maintain. In addition, a programmatic approach could lead to excessive network traffic, as the client itself would decide which data to present and which data to discard. You could also try manipulating security so that certain users could see only particular columns, but this technique requires a great deal of administrative effort.

A better formula to follow would be to create views that meet your needs. First, let's create a simple view that automatically performs the joins between the table:

```
create view V_sales_detail as
select *
from    sales_representatives,
        transactions
where   sales_representatives.representative_id =
        transactions.representative_id
```

This view gives us all information from both tables, joined on the 'representative_id' column. Developers and users can then simply query from the view without needing to know how the tables are related. Next, let's build a new view that shows more selective information:

```
create view V_partial_detail as
select a.representative_id,
       a.last_name,
       a.first_name,
       b.transaction_date,
       b.amount
```

```
from    sales_representatives a,
        transactions b
where   a.representative_id = b.representative_id
```

Finally, let's build a view that meets our original need for secure access to the 'commission' field:

```
create view V_secure
as
select a.representative_id,
       a.last_name,
       a.first_name,
       b.transaction_date,
       b.amount,
       b.commission
from    sales_representatives a,
        transactions b
where   a.representative_id = b.representative_id
and     (a.user_id = CURRENT_USER or
        CURRENT_USER = "manager")
```

We've told SQL Server not to allow anyone access to this information unless their login either matches the 'user_id' column in the 'sales_representatives' table or is the "manager." This helps strengthen data security (although it's ineffective if users don't safeguard their logins).

A few final notes regarding views. First, there are a number of actions that you can't perform with views, such as:

- You can't place a view on a temporary table. If you make this request, SQL Server returns an error:

  ```
  Msg 4508, Level 16, State 1
  Views are not allowed on temporary tables. Table
  names that begin with '#' denote temporary tables.
  ```

- You can't insert or update columns from different tables within a view that references multiple tables. If you try, you'll get this message:

  ```
  Msg 4405, Level 16, State 2
  View 'V_test' is not updatable because the FROM
  clause names multiple tables.
  ```

- You can't build triggers or assign defaults or rules on views.

- You can't create views in other databases: you must be connected to the database to create a view.

Finally, while views are helpful aids in data access, there can be occasions where you should use base tables instead. We'll cover these situations in our chapters on improving database access.

Viewing dependencies

As we've seen, SQL Server lets database administrators create and assign numerous types of constraints and rules. These constraints and rules create dependencies among various tables, however. By dependency, we mean any reliance by one object on another. It's important to know what dependencies are in place on your system at any point in time, since removing or even changing one object might have unforeseen effects elsewhere. How can you learn about these dependencies? SQL Server provides several valuable methods that you can employ to gain this understanding.

The simplest technique would be to use the SQL Enterprise Manager's object dependencies dialog box. You can request this screen for any table, view, rule, stored procedure, or trigger. For example, we created a few demonstration tables, triggers, views, and stored procedures. One of the tables was called 'orders.' The following shows the object dependencies dialog box for this table:

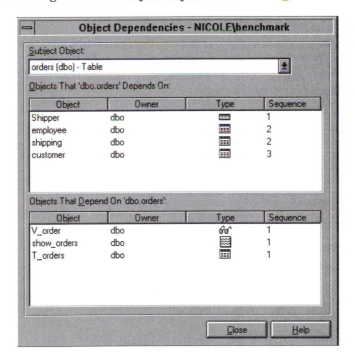

Figure 2.16

SQL Server furnishes some very useful information on this screen. We can see which tables, views, stored procedures, and triggers depend on this table, as well as what this table in turn depends upon.

Another method would be to use the 'sp_depends' stored procedure. This procedure shows what objects depend on the object:

```
sp_depends orders

In the current database the specified object is
referenced by the following:
name                                 type
------------------------------   ---------------
dbo.show_orders                      stored procedure
dbo.T_orders                         trigger
dbo.V_order                          view
```

This output corresponds to the lower half of the object dependencies dialog box shown earlier.

Speaking of dependencies, the 'sp_depends' procedure, as well as the object dependencies dialog box both depend on the 'sysdepends' system table for important information:

Table 2.37 sysdepends

column name	type	purpose
id	integer	The object ID.
Number	smallint	The stored procedure number.
depid	int	The dependent object's ID number.
depnumber	smallint	The dependent stored procedure number.
depdbid	smallint	Reserved.
depsiteid	smallint	Reserved.
status	smallint	SQL Server's internal status indicator.
selall	bit	Enabled if the object is a SELECT * statement.
resultobj	bit	Enabled if the object gets updated.
readobj	bit	Enabled if the object is read.

Chapter 3
Indexing Strategies

With the exception of correctly defined primary and foreign keys, there is no right or wrong way to index a database. Different applications have different data access profiles. An indexing strategy that works for one application may not work for another.

For example, some applications require instantaneous access to data, using numerous search columns and sort combinations. Other systems are more rigidly defined, with only a few possible search columns and sort combinations. While the SQL Server query optimizer can choose the most efficient query plan even if the underlying data changes, your users may request completely new queries and reports: What satisfied them in January may not suffice in October. Therefore, it is up to each administrator and analyst to continually analyze their index strategy and make modifications as necessary.

Ideally, you analyze your database and generate your indexes before bringing your application into production. However, if you miss something before you go into production, don't worry. It is very easy to put the proper indexes in place on a production system, because adding, altering, or dropping indexes generally does not require you to alter existing source code. One exception to this rule occurs when you drop either a unique index or primary key that was relied on by one or more of SQL Server's cursors. With that said, you still have a great deal of flexibility regarding indexes once your system is up and running.

This chapter addresses some of the methods you can use to create effective indexes or to make existing indexes more efficient.

Before beginning our discussion, let's look at a few sample tables that we'll use for our examples. In this case, we're building an airline frequent flier application, which partially consists of these tables:

Table 3.1   customer_master

account_number	last_name	first_name	street	...	account_balance
344484454	Bockwinkle	Terry	11 Jeeves Way		24998
344484455	Okerlund	Nick	5654 Jacques St.		105660
344484456	Blassie	George	9 Mariner Rd.		3004
...	...	...	...	...	...

Table 3.2   customer_flights

account_number	flight_date	miles	origin	destination
344484454	Dec 15 1996	5609	SFO	LHR
119009887	Dec 15 1996	500	LAX	PHX
559449332	Dec 15 1996	1106	MIA	EWR
...	...	...	...	...

Table 3.3   awards

award_code	mileage_level	award_description
F25A	25000	Roundtrip within North America
F25B	25000	Roundtrip within Europe
F50A	50000	Roundtrip between US and South America
F50B	50000	Roundtrip between US and Australia
H10A	10000	One night at a participating hotel
H25A	25000	Three nights at a participating hotel
...	...	...

Table 3.4   partners

partner_code	partner_description
AR	Arizona Airlines
BL	Big Leisure Cruises
IH	International Hotels
PC	Polynesian Rent-a-Car
ZK	Zlotnick Kruises for Kidz
...	...

Index structure

Before we discuss specific index suggestions, let's look at how SQL Server structures indexes. The engine stores index information on disk pages. This information helps SQL Server rapidly locate appropriate rows when searching for data. Indexes can be clustered or non-clustered, and this classification makes a great deal of difference for a number of operations, including the index structure itself.

Clustered indexes

When you define an index as a clustered index, SQL Server arranges the actual data in the base table in the order of the index. When you define a primary key for a table, SQL Server creates a unique, clustered index on the primary key column(s), unless you direct the engine to create the primary key index as non-clustered. In the case of the 'awards' table described earlier, the table is physically ordered by the 'award_code' column, since this column is the primary key. Whenever you insert a row into the 'awards' table, SQL Server checks to see if there are any existing rows with the same 'award_code' value. If there are, you receive the following error message:

```
Msg 2627, Level 14, State 1
Violation of PRIMARY KEY constraint
'PK__awards__award_co__06AD0966': Attempt to insert
duplicate key in object 'awards'.
```

You can only have one clustered index per table. In most cases, the primary key is the best candidate for a clustered index. There may be occasions, however, where you want to physically order the table by another column(s). How can you achieve this ordering, yet maintain the safety that a primary key provides? You have at least two choices:

1. You can create the table with a primary key but request that SQL Server not treat the primary key index as clustered. This technique is not portable, however: other database engines may not support this syntax.

2. You can create the table with a unique index on the primary key, and a clustered index on the columns that you want physically ordered. This approach ensures data integrity of your primary key, since SQL Server checks for duplicates on any unique indexes.

Using the 'awards' table as an example, suppose that you want the table physically stored by the 'mileage_level' column, with the 'award_code' column still treated as a unique primary key. You can use either of the following two statements to create the table and its indexes:

```
create table awards
(
      award_code    char(4) primary key nonclustered,
      mileage_level integer,
      award_description varchar(255)
)
create clustered index aw_mileage_level_ix on
      awards(mileage_level)
```

—or—

```
create table awards
(
      award_code    char(4) unique,
      mileage_level integer,
      award_description varchar(255)
)
create clustered index aw_mileage_level_ix on
      awards(mileage_level)
```

Running 'sp_helpindex' on this table produces:

Table 3.5   sp_helpindex output for non-clustered primary key

column_name	value
index_name	aw_mileage_level_ix
index_description	clustered located on default
index_keys	mileage_level
index_name	PK__awards__award_co
index_description	non-clustered, unique, primary key located on default
index_keys	award_code

Table 3.6 sp_helpindex output for unique index pseudo primary key

column_name	value
index_name	aw_mileage_level_ix
index_description	clustered located on default
index_keys	mileage_level
index_name	UQ__awards__award_co
index_description	nonclustered, unique located on default
index_keys	award_code

Regardless of which tactic you follow, the table is now stored in the order of 'mileage_level.' If you try to insert a duplicate value for 'award_code' and you've chosen the second clustering mode, you receive this error:

```
Msg 2615, Level 14, State 1
Attempt to insert duplicate row in table 'awards' with in
dex 'aw_mileage_level_ix' in database 'benchmark'. Could
drop and recreate index with ignore duprow or allow   du-
prow.
```

When there is a clustered index in place on a table and you insert a new row, SQL Server attempts to fit the new row on the appropriate existing page. If there is no room, the engine performs a page split operation. This operation entails the following steps:

1. Locate an available page.
2. If no pages are available, allocate a new extent.
3. Split the data from the previously full page onto two pages.
4. Adjust previous and next page pointers on appropriate neighboring pages.

While these steps happen very quickly, there still is the potential for some overhead, especially if there are many other indexes in place, because these other indexes may need updating as well. With all of this said, for most applications this extra work would probably go unnoticed. However, if you are writing an entry-intensive program, you might wish to reconsider your use of clustered indexes if you observe degraded response during insert or delete operations. As an alternative strategy, you could reevaluate the index fill factor on all affected tables. We'll discuss the importance of index fill factor later in this section.

Note that update operations would most likely be unaffected, since you're probably not changing primary key values. Note that it still is possible to see decreased update performance if the clustered index is on a column other than the primary key.

Non-clustered indexes

A table can have only one clustered index, but many non-clustered indexes. When you create a non-clustered index, SQL Server still reads all the rows and constructs index pages. The major difference between clustered and non-clustered indexes is that SQL Server leaves the underlying rows unchanged for non-clustered, instead of physically reordering the data. This means that unlike clustered indexes, you don't have to be concerned about the potential for the engine resequencing all data pages if you insert a new row in the middle of existing rows.

Leaf vs. non-leaf pages

Two important terms to know when discussing indexes are leaf pages and non-leaf pages. In addition, these terms are affected by the type of index in question. For clustered indexes, leaf pages correspond to actual data pages, and non-leaf pages make up the index and point to various leaf pages. For non-clustered indexes, SQL Server uses both leaf and non-leaf pages to hold index information. This means that there may be situations where SQL Server never needs to look at actual data pages if the information in the query can be found on the index leaf page. Let's look at some examples to illustrate these concepts.

In the following diagram, we've created an index on the 'customer_master' table's 'last_name' column. This index is not clustered, since the table already has a clustered index on the 'account_number' column. The index structure looks like this:

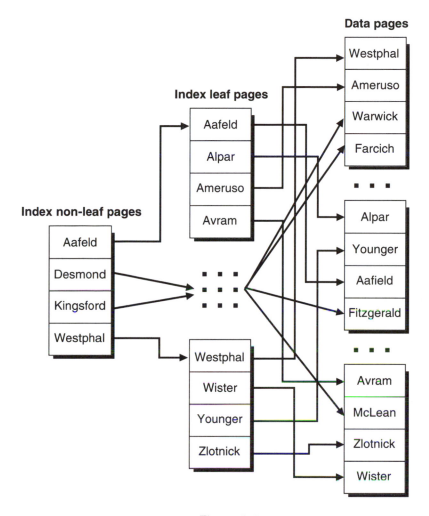

Figure 3.1

There are three different data structures in this diagram. The non-leaf index pages are stationed at the root of the index and contain widely varying entries. Each entry in a non-leaf index page then points to a leaf index page, which contains all the values between the two index keys found on the higher-level, non-leaf index page. Finally, the leaf index pages point to the actual data pages. If you are selecting only the indexed column, SQL Server can satisfy your request without having to read the data page: Simply reading the index gives the engine the required data.

In another example, let's look at a diagram of the 'customer_master' table's primary key column, 'account_number.' Recall that this index is clustered, which produces an index structure like this:

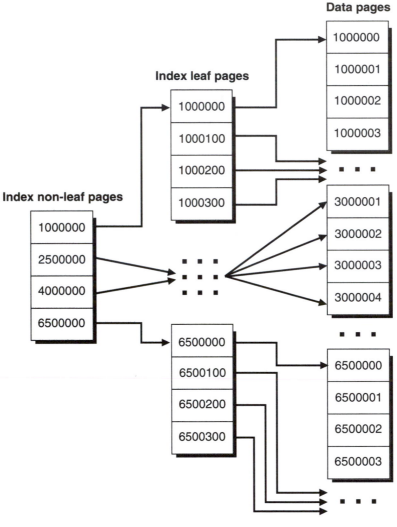

Figure 3.2

Notice how the table's pages are sequenced in the same order as the index. When you request a clustered index, SQL Server reorders the physical data pages to match the index. Keep in mind that this is true for the life of the table: All pages must fit the correct cluster order for all new rows.

Primary keys

Each table should have an index on the primary key. The SQL Server engine automatically performs this task for you if you use the following syntax:

```
create table customer_master
(
      account_number  integer primary key,
      last_name       varchar(30),
         .         .
         .         .
)
```

For tables that have composite primary keys, use this syntax:

```
create table customer_flights
(
      account_number integer,
      flight_date datetime,
      origin char(3),
      destination char(3)
      primary key (account_number, flight_date, origin)
)
```

If do not wish to use this syntax, you should still create a unique index on the column or columns that make up your primary key. Doing so speeds access to the table by allowing the engine to make only one read to determine if a particular row exists. In addition, sorting the table on the primary key (to create a report, for example) is much faster.

When you instruct SQL Server to create a primary key on a column or columns, SQL Server creates an index and also physically orders the table in the primary key's sequence. This is known as a clustered index.

For example, when we created the 'customer_master' table and defined the 'account_number' column as the primary key, SQL Server built an index on that column and also physically ordered the table in 'account_number' sequence.

Filter columns

If you frequently search a table, based on a particular value in a column, you should place an index on that column. This is especially true in cases where the table has many rows and the values within the column are diverse (e.g., not highly duplicated). Let's use an example from the airline mileage system described earlier. Suppose that the 'customer_master' table has 50,000 rows, with numerous distinct last names. Users continually wish to retrieve information with the following query:

```
select * from customer_master
where last_name  = (value entered by user)
```

If there is no index on the filter column, this query requires a sequential scan of the table:

```
STEP 1
The type of query is SELECT
FROM TABLE
customer_master
Row estimate:  4998
Cost estimate: 28608
Nested iteration
Table Scan
Table: customer_master    scan count 1,    logical reads:
1788,physical reads: 117
```

The Statistics I/O screen demonstrates how many read operations this query requires:

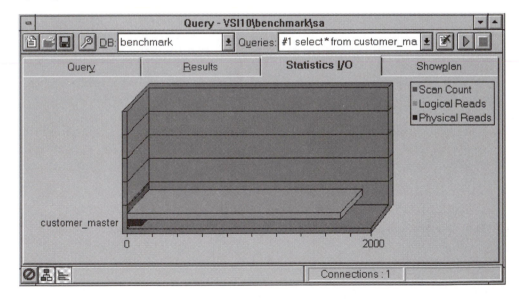

Figure 3.3

In this case, you would benefit by creating the following index:

```
create index cm_lastname_ix1 on customer_master(last_name)
STEP 1
The type of query is SELECT
FROM TABLE
customer_master
Row estimate:  1
Cost estimate: 64
Nested iteration
  Index : cm_lastname_ix
Table: customer_master   scan count 1,  logical reads: 4,
physical reads: 3
```

with this result:

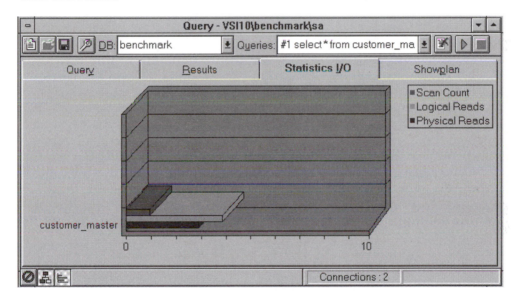

Figure 3.4

Note how many fewer logical and physical reads the SQL Server engine performs in the second version of the query. The engine can now use the 'cm_lastname_ix' index to process the previous query much more rapidly. The only exception to this rule would be if the engine is already using another index on the table to satisfy a join or another filter. Since the previous query doesn't have another filter condition or a join to another table, the new index should help.

Join columns

Wherever possible, you should create indexes on both sides of a frequently used join relationship. Using the airline mileage example, suppose that we want to create a report showing all flights taken by a particular customer:

```
select  cm.account_number,
        cm.last_name,
        cm.first_name,
        cm.street,
        cm.city,
        cf.flight_date,
        cf.origin,
        cf.destination,
        cf.miles
from    customer_master cm,
        customer_flights cf
where   cm.account_number = cf.account_number
and     cm.last_name = "Culpepper"
```

In this case, assume that the report is first reading the 'customer_master' table (to get the first and last names and account_number of each customer) and then reading the 'customer_flights' table (to get information about each customer's flights). If there is no index on 'customer_flights.account_number,' the engine is forced to sequentially read all rows in the 'customer_flights' table to find matches based on 'customer_master.account_number':

```
STEP 1
The type of query is SELECT
FROM TABLE
customer_master cm
Row estimate:   1
Cost estimate: 64
Nested iteration
Index : cm_lastname_ix
FROM TABLE
customer_flights cf
JOINS WITH
customer_master cm
Row estimate:   4
Cost estimate: 43696
Nested iteration
Table Scan
Table: customer_master  scan count 1,   logical reads: 4,
```

```
physical reads: 1
Table: customer_flights  scan count 1,  logical reads:
2731,  physical reads: 94
```

We can also get a graphical representation of the I/O costs:

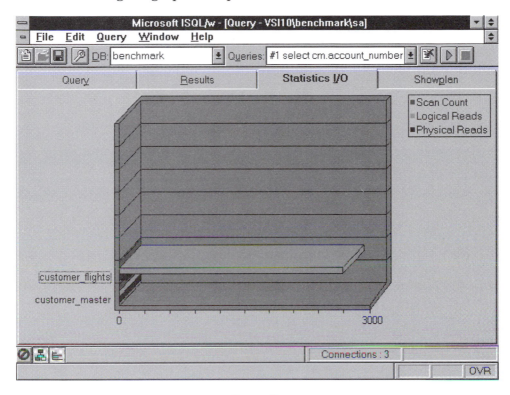

Figure 3.5

In this case, it's a good idea to create an index on the 'customer_flights.account_number' column. After making this change, we get a different query plan:

```
STEP 1
The type of query is SELECT
FROM TABLE
customer_master cm
Row estimate:  1
Cost estimate: 64
Nested iteration
Index : cm_lastname_ix
FROM TABLE
```

```
customer_flights cf
JOINS WITH
customer_master cm
Row estimate:  1
Cost estimate: 80
Nested iteration
```

```
 Index : cf_account_number_ix
```
```
Table: customer_master  scan count 1,  logical reads: 4,
physical reads: 0
Table: customer_flights  scan count 1, logical reads: 3,
physical reads: 2
```

Once again, a different index strategy greatly reduces costly I/O:

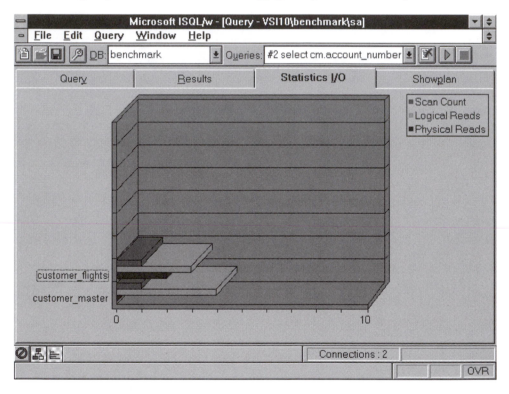

Figure 3.6

In the absence of indexes on join columns, the optimizer may use other techniques to speed information retrieval. For more information about the various techniques that the optimizer uses to retrieve information, see Chapter 4, "Understanding the SQL Server Optimizer." Despite these sophisticated alternative join methods, you should always investigate the performance impact of placing indexes on join columns.

Wide vs. narrow index keys

An index is considered wide when it contains a large amount of data. This can be composed of either numerous small columns or several big columns. On the other hand, a narrow index simply consists of less data. For example, an index made up of a single char(255) column is wider than an index made up of five char(4) columns.

Why are narrow indexes generally better? To answer this question, it helps to understand that when you create an index, SQL Server stores the index' key values and record locations on index pages. With narrow indexes, SQL Server can fit more key values and pointers on each index page. This means that the optimizer can find your data more quickly, since it can usually perform fewer index page reads before encountering your data. In addition, since there are more index keys and pointers per page, the optimizer can also churn through this information more effectively than if it had to read in dozens of pages before making a decision. Conversely, when your index keys are wide, the engine is able to fit only a relatively few number of key value and data pointers on each page. The index structure also tends to be deeper with wide keys, forcing the optimizer to carry out even more computations.

Using the 'customer_master' table as an example, suppose that you place a composite index on the 'last_name,' 'first_name,' 'address1,' 'address2,' and 'city' columns. This index can be thought of as wide, since it contains a relatively high number of columns, as well as a great deal of data. In situations like this, you should always analyze why you've created this kind of index. Perhaps the users have asked to search on all of these fields together. It's also possible that they want to sort on all of these fields. It's more likely, however, that this index represents a "kitchen sink" approach to indexing, whereby you add as many columns into the index as possible. This isn't as effective as you might think, for a number of reasons. In particular, the width of the index means that SQL Server is able to fit only a fairly small number of key values and pointers on each page. The index structure itself needs to be deeper as well. The performance obstacle really becomes painfully obvious when you ask the optimizer to search on only one or two of the index' columns. In this example, suppose that you wanted to find all rows that had a 'last_name' value between "Hank" and "Hendrix." The optimizer selects this index, since there is no better candidate in place. Unfortunately, the optimizer now needs to read potentially hundreds of index pages to locate the appropriate information, since the width of the index means that the index itself is very deep. Contrast this with what would happen if you had a single index on 'last_name.' The number of keys per index page would be substantially greater, which would let the optimizer find the correct information much more quickly, and with many fewer reads.

Another problem with this index deals with how SQL Server uses a composite index to satisfy searches and sorts. This index may not be as useful as you would imagine. We'll discuss ways that you can create better composite indexes later in this chapter.

With all of these warnings about wide indexes, there is one mitigating factor. As we saw earlier, if you are only requesting columns from a particular non-clustered index itself, SQL Server can bypass reading the actual data and get its information from the index keys. For example, suppose that you run the following query:

```
select  cf.account_number,
        last_name,
        first_name,
        flight_date
from    customer_master cm,
        customer_flights cf
where   cm.account_number = cf.account_number
and     cf.account_number = 4993302

STEP 1
The type of query is SELECT
FROM TABLE
customer_flights cf
Nested iteration
Index : cf_acct_flight_ix
FROM TABLE
customer_master cm
Nested iteration
Using Clustered Index
```

We're only asking for the 'account_number' and 'flight_date' columns from the 'customer_flights' table. Since both of these columns are present in the 'cf_acct_flight_ix' index and the index is non-clustered, SQL Server can satisfy this request without reading the table's data pages. If we were retrieving large blocks of data, this might have an effect on performance, especially when you remember that disk I/O can add a great deal of overhead to a query. Eliminating disk access wherever possible can be very beneficial. Keep this last caveat in mind as you examine your indexes: Wide indexes are not always performance wreckers.

Unique vs. non-unique

A unique index guarantees that there will be only one row with a particular column or group of columns value within a table. This enables the SQL Server engine to rapidly locate and retrieve the row, since one index read is all that is necessary to find the information. Additionally, a unique index on a column prevents users from entering duplicate values and possibly damaging the integrity of the database through applications or direct data entry.

If you create an index on a column or group of columns that you know will be unique, consider making the index unique. If you are unsure of whether the columns are unique or not, you can always run a simple query to help you decide:

```
declare @@total_count integer
declare @@unique_count integer

select @@total_count = count(*) from beverage
select @@unique_count = count(distinct(test_column))
from test_table

if @@total_count = @@unique_count
    raiserror ('Total count = Unique count',1,2)
else
    raiserror ('Warning: Total count is different than
    unique count',1,2)
```

Another approach is simply to attempt to create the index. If there is indeed duplicate data in the column, SQL Server returns the following error message:

```
Msg 1505, Level 16, State 1
Create unique index aborted on duplicate key. Primary
key is '65.43'
```

Note that using the PRIMARY KEY syntax in the CREATE TABLE statement automatically generates a unique index.

Character vs. numeric

If you have an indexed character column that is composed solely of numeric information, you should consider changing the column's data type to:

- **TINYINT.**   If you are certain that the maximum numeric value for this column won't ever exceed 255, you can create the column with a type of TINYINT. This data type only requires one byte of storage.

- **SMALLINT.**   If the maximum numeric value to be stored in the column won't exceed 32,767, you can choose a SMALLINT. A SMALLINT requires only two bytes of storage.

- **INTEGER.**   If the maximum numeric value that you expect to place in the column will be greater than 32,767, use a 4-byte integer to hold the data.

- **DATETIME.**   If the column's data holds date and time information in the range of January 1, 1753, through December 31, 9999, you can use this variable, which is composed of two 4-byte integers. The first integer holds the number of days either before or after January 1, 1900, and the second integer holds the number of milliseconds past midnight on that particular date.

- **SMALLDATETIME.**   If you don't need as wide a date spectrum as supported by the DATETIME type, try using this type instead. You can store any date between January 1, 1900, and June 6, 2079, in this kind of column. Along with each date, you can supply a time value. These time values provide granularity to the minute. Due to the reduced range of dates supported by SMALLDATETIME, SQL Server is able to use only one 4-byte integer to hold these values. This integer is actually made up of two small integers (one for the date, one for the time).

For example, assume that you have a column that has been defined as a CHAR(10) and holds only numeric values that range between 0 and 100. By defining the column as a CHAR(10), you use ten bytes of storage for this column in each row and index. By changing the data type of the column to a TINYINT, (since no value exceeds 255), you use only one byte of storage within each row and index. This is a substantial saving of space, especially when multiplied by the number of rows in a large table. If you feel that you will need to exceed 255 but will never go over 10,000, you can always choose a data type of SMALLINT.

In terms of indexing, if the column is defined as a CHAR(10), the SQL Server engine needs to read all ten bytes when traversing the index tree, versus only two bytes if the column is changed to a SMALLINT. Joins are also much faster between INTEGER columns than between CHAR columns.

In all of the above cases, you must be sure that the data to be stored in the column won't contain any decimal values. For circumstances where you need to store decimal values, consider using an alternative numeric type, such as NUMERIC, DECIMAL, MONEY, or SMALLMONEY.

Composite index issues

There are probably many times that you want to retrieve or sort information from a table based on more than one column. Using the airline mileage example described earlier, suppose that you want to locate all customers within a city who aren't actively participating in the program. Your query could look like this:

```
select *
from customer_master
where city  = "Singapore"
and   account_balance < 5000
```

If there are no indexes on the appropriate columns, SQL Server produces this query plan:

```
STEP 1
The type of query is SELECT
FROM TABLE
customer_master
Row estimate:  62
Cost estimate: 1104
Nested iteration
Table Scan
```

The 'table scan' message is discouraging: it means that SQL Server is going to read all of the rows in the table in sequence to find any rows that match our query. You decide to add a composite index on the 'customer_master' table. This composite index contains the 'city' and 'account_balance' fields:

```
STEP 1
The type of query is SELECT
FROM TABLE
customer_master
Row estimate:  1
Cost estimate: 48
Nested iteration
Index : cm_citybalance_ix
```

This query plan is much more encouraging. Notice the difference in SQL Server's cost estimate. Previously, the optimizer estimated a cost of 1104 using the table scan. Now, after the composite index, the optimizer estimates a cost of 48. Remember that these numbers have no significance when taken alone; comparing them yields useful information, however.

When constructing queries that use a composite index, you need to make sure that your queries are anchored from the leftmost column. If you don't do this, you actually may not use the index when you think that you are. Let's look at some examples that illustrate this point.

In this case, your query uses both columns that make up the composite index:

```
select *
from customer_master
where city  = "Singapore"
and    account_balance < 5000

STEP 1
The type of query is SELECT
FROM TABLE
customer_master
Row estimate:  1
Cost estimate: 48
Nested iteration
Index : cm_citybalance_ix
```

Next, you construct a query that only uses the first column in the composite index:

```
select *
from customer_master
where city = "Singapore"

STEP 1
The type of query is SELECT
FROM TABLE
customer_master
Row estimate:  1
Cost estimate: 48
Nested iteration
Index : cm_citybalance_ix
```

SQL Server is still able to use the composite index, since you're asking for the leftmost column in the WHERE clause. In the next case, however, you're searching on a column that exists later in the index:

```
select *
from customer_master
where  account_balance = 20000
```

```
STEP 1
The type of query is SELECT
FROM TABLE
customer_master
Row estimate:  190
Cost estimate: 1104
Nested iteration
Table Scan
```

SQL Server is unable to use the composite index in this case. If you really need to search on the 'account_balance' field by itself, consider adding an index. Doing this produces this query plan:

```
STEP 1
The type of query is SELECT
FROM TABLE
customer_master
Row estimate:  1
Cost estimate: 64
Nested iteration
Index : cm_balance_ix
```

Our index change puts us back on track: the query should now perform acceptably.

In your composite index research, remember what we discussed earlier in this chapter regarding wide versus narrow index keys: It's better to define several narrow indexes than to define one wide index. You can use SQL Server's SHOWPLAN output to see if your indexes are truly being utilized like you think they are. We'll cover this important topic in Chapter 4.

One final note regarding composite indexes: SQL Server 6.5 raises the limitation on the total length of all the column names that make up the composite index. It is now 900 bytes, which means that if you add up the length of each of the column names in the index, it can now be up to 900 bytes.

Avoiding highly duplicate indexes

A highly duplicate index is one where there are a limited number of unique values contained in the index. For example, if you place an index on a column that contains no more than two or three values, you have a highly duplicate index. It is worse to have a highly duplicate index on a column than not have one at all, because the engine must perform a great deal of work to process the index during important operations such as inserting, updating, or deleting data.

For example, assume you have the following table that tracks participation in a special bonus program for your customers:

Table 3.7   bonus

account_number	participated	...
55095543	Y	...
55095544	Y	...
55095545	N	...
55095546	Y	...
55095547	N	...
55095548	Y	...
.	.	...

If you place an index on the 'participated' column, you will only have two possible values: (Y)es or (N)o. When you add a new row into this table, the engine must add the new value into the existing index. This may cause the undesired side effect of internal index restructuring to handle the additional value. Deleting, querying, or sorting based on the index also causes the engine excess work. This adds a great deal of unnecessary I/O operations to your system and can actually degrade performance. It also doesn't make much sense to ask the database engine to use an index to find such heavily duplicated data, since it's probably faster and simpler for the engine to go directly to the data and read it sequentially. You can determine if an index is highly duplicate by running the DBCC SHOW_STATISTICS command or by using the 'Index Distribution Statistics' option on the 'Index Information' screen in the SQL Enterprise Manager utility, as shown in Figure 3.7.

Among other information, this utility reports on the index' selectivity, which refers to the relative number of distinct values. In this case, there are only two possible values, which yields a very poor degree of selectivity. When confronted with such a poor degree of selectivity, SQL Server may not even use the highly duplicate index at all to retrieve information. Unfortunately, the overhead found during inserts, updates, and deletes still remains, however.

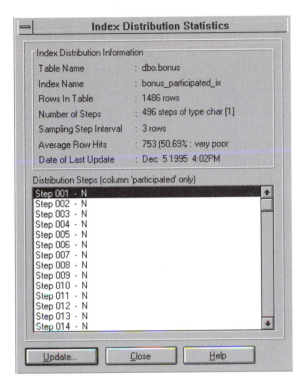

Figure 3.7

In those cases where you must sort or search on a highly duplicate value, combine the column in question with a *more selective* column to make up a composite index. In the previous example, the correct composite index would be:

```
create index bonus_acct_participated_ix on
        bonus(account_number, participated)
```

The 'account_number' column is much more selective than the 'participated' column. Combining these two columns yields a more selective and efficient index:

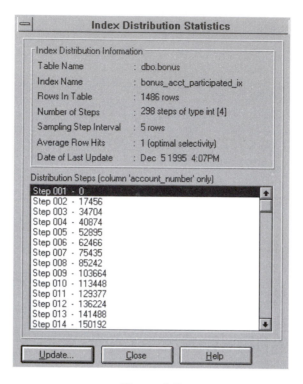

Figure 3.8

You can now use this index to search for and sort by 'account_number' all customers who have participated in the bonus plan. Don't forget that to use a composite index in filtering or sorting data, you must always start from the left and work to the right. We'll discuss efficient use of composite indexes later in this chapter.

Clustered indexes and presorted data

If you're creating a clustered index and you know that the underlying table's data is already sorted, you can speed up the index creation by telling the optimizer to skip the data sorting step. However, if the optimizer encounters a non-sorted row, it stops the index build:

```
create clustered index sort_sample_ix
    on table1 (col1) with sorted_data

Msg 1530, Level 16, State 1
Create index with sorted_data was aborted because of row
```

```
out of order. Primary key of first out of order row is
'industrial    '
```

Clustered indexes and data reorganization

SQL Server's default behavior when building a clustered index is to reorganize the table's data. As we saw earlier, if you know that your table is already in sorted order, you can skip the physical table reordering. However, there are times where this operation is still a good idea, including these cases:

- **Data fragmentation.** If you know that the table's data is not contiguous, consider asking for a sorted data reorganization when you build the clustered index. You can learn more about table fragmentation in Chapter 11, "Disk Management."

- **Index fill factor changes.** If you want to change the density of your index and data pages with the FILLFACTOR parameter, you'll need to ask for data reorganization.

The syntax for sorted data reorganization is:

```
CREATE INDEX <name> on <table>(<column>,...)
    WITH SORTED_DATA_REORG
```

Sort columns

In general, it's a good idea to place indexes on sort columns (e.g., columns used in the ORDER BY clause). However, the SQL Server optimizer may not choose these indexes if a table scan or other index is more efficient for the overall database operation.

If you want to sort on a clustered index, there is no need to explicitly provide an ORDER BY clause, since the table's data is already physically ordered according to the clustered index. For example, remember that the 'customer_master' table is clustered on the primary key (account_number). This means that if you run this query:

```
select * from customer_master
where account_number between 500000 and 550000
```

the engine returns the data as if you had issued this statement:

```
select * from customer_master
```

```
where account_number between 500000 and 550000
order by account_number
```

Keep in mind that once you start sorting on columns from different tables within the same statement, SQL Server won't be able to take full advantage of indexes. For example, look at this query and query plan:

```
select  cm.account_number,
        cf.flight_date
from    customer_master cm,
        customer_flights cf
where   cm.account_number between 500000 and 550000
and     cm.account_number = cf.account_number
order by cm.account_number, cf.flight_date


STEP 1
The type of query is INSERT
The update mode is direct
Worktable created for ORDER BY
FROM TABLE
customer_master cm
Row estimate:  12495
Cost estimate: 1024
Nested iteration
Using Clustered Index
FROM TABLE
customer_flights cf
JOINS WITH
customer_master cm
Row estimate:  12536
Cost estimate: 582624
Nested iteration
Index : cf_account_number_ix
TO TABLE
Worktable 1
STEP 2
The type of query is SELECT
This step involves sorting
FROM TABLE
Worktable 1
Row estimate:  12536
Cost estimate: 1514
Using GETSORTED Table Scan
```

The optimizer is able to use indexes on both tables to locate appropriate records. It can't use either index for sorting, however, since we've asked it to sort on data from two tables. If you expect this type of operation to be common, contemplate explicitly creating and populating your own work table that is built from the joined data. You can then create and use indexes on these tables, which should help speed up data sorting. This extra step may cost more time than it saves; there is no harm in experimenting, however.

Indexing and special data types

As we saw earlier, SQL Server provides database administrators and developers with a broad array of available data types. In this section, we examine how you most effectively create and maintain indexes on some of SQL Server's special data types.

By special data types, we mean those data types not typically found in traditional relational database environments. Traditional data types for relational databases have included CHAR, NUMERIC, DECIMAL, etc. Contrast this with some of the newer data types, including BIT, IMAGE, TIMESTAMP, BINARY, etc. Let's describe how SQL Server indexes each of these special data types, along with how you can use indexes to speed retrieval for these types:

- **BINARY.** Binary data consists of up to 255 bytes of bit information. You can create indexes on columns defined as this data type. When searching for data, or joining between tables, the optimizer can then make use of the index. However, before creating indexes on columns of this type, make sure that the underlying data is not highly duplicate.

- **BIT.** This data type lets you hold one of two values: 0 or 1. Columns defined with this type require one byte of storage and must not be null. SQL Server doesn't let you create indexes on bit columns. Even if you could, the index would only have two possible values, which would make it highly duplicate and therefore not very effective. If you attempt to create an index, you'll get this error message:

```
Msg 1901, Level 16, State 1
Column 'col1' -- Can't create index on a column of
BIT data type.
```

- **IMAGE.** SQL Server users typically employ the IMAGE data type when storing binary data, such as pictures, sound files, program executables, etc. SQL Server sets a limit of approximately two gigabytes for columns defined as IMAGE. However, you cannot create indexes on IMAGE fields. This makes sense: How would the engine be able to

construct an image on the type of information typically stored in IM-
AGE fields? If you attempt to create an index, you'll get this error
message:

```
Msg 1919, Level 16, State 1
Column 'col1' -- Can't create index on a column of
TEXT or IMAGE data type.
```

- **TEXT.**   The TEXT data type is typically used to hold blocks of text
  data, especially when you're not sure of the actual size of the stored
  information. TEXT fields can hold over two gigabytes of data, so
  chances are that you'll have enough space to hold your text. There is
  one drawback shared by both TEXT and IMAGE fields: You can't create indexes on columns defined with these types.

- **TINYINT.**   TINYINT columns can hold numeric values up to 255.
  You can create unique or non-unique indexes on these types of columns. However, there is one caveat to remember: Given the relatively
  low limit on the numeric values that you can store, you have a fairly
  good chance of having a highly duplicate index on TINYINT columns.
  For this reason, carefully evaluate whether a TINYINT column truly
  benefits from having an index.

- **TIMESTAMP.**   We discussed this special type earlier in the chapter. SQL Server lets you create and utilize indexes on columns of this
  type:

```
create index timestamp_index on
timestamp_test (col2)


select * from timestamp_test
where col2 = 0x0000000100000a8a


STEP 1
The type of query is SELECT
FROM TABLE
test1
Nested iteration
Index : timestamp_index
```

- **User-defined.**   As we saw earlier in this chapter, SQL Server provides you with the power to define your own data types and then map
  them to existing data types. With regard to indexing, the user-defined
  type is treated no differently than the underlying data type.

- **VARCHAR.**   Variable-length character fields hold the same kinds of
  information as standard character fields. Unlike fixed-length charac-

ter fields, however, VARCHARs provide added flexibility, letting you use only as much space as you need. With regard to indexes, you can create the same kinds of indexes on variable-length character fields as you can on fixed-length character fields.

- **VARBINARY.** This data type is identical to the BINARY data type in that it holds binary information. The major difference between this type and the BINARY type is similar to the difference between the CHAR and VARCHAR data types. When you're unsure of the typical size of the data that you'll be holding in a BINARY field, you can choose the VARBINARY type and define the column to be up to 255 characters in length. Access to data is slightly faster for the BINARY type, however, since the engine knows exactly how long a BINARY column will be. From an indexing perspective, you can create indexes on VARBINARY columns just like you can for BINARY columns.

Indexing and work tables

Work tables (also known as temporary tables) are temporary storage locations used by SQL Server to satisfy processing demands. They can be explicitly created by the user or implicitly created by the engine. In this section, we examine how developers and database administrators can apply good indexing practice to work tables to help expedite response.

As a developer, there are times when SQL Server automatically creates work tables for you. Aside from reworking your queries or altering database index structure, you don't have much control over these work tables. This also means that you can't create indexes on these work tables. However, SQL Server often builds its own indexes on the key columns of these implicitly created work tables.

On the other hand, when you explicitly create a work table, you have a large degree of control over how that table is indexed, if at all. At this point, an example is in order.

Let's propose that you are developing a trend analysis query program to retrieve and manipulate information from the 'customer_master' and 'customer_flights' tables. Users of this program will make many "what if" changes to the underlying data and then will run more queries and analysis routines. Since this is your production database, you certainly don't want the users changing actual data. Instead, you elect to extract what you need into a work table:

```
create table #analyze
(
    city char(20),
```

```
        miles smallint,
        origin char(5)
)

insert into #analyze
select cm.city,
       cf.miles,
       cf.origin
from   customer_master cm,
       customer_flights cf
where  cm.account_number = cf.account_number
and    cm.account_balance < 10000
```

You could also use a SELECT INTO statement to build and populate a temporary table.

Are you ready to start running queries and reports against this table? If the table holds only a few dozen rows, the answer is probably yes. However, if you expect that you'll have significant amounts of data in this work table, it's wise to create indexes where appropriate. For example, look at the query plans for this next SQL statement, both before and after an index:

```
select * from #analyze
where city in ('Lisboa', 'Lexington')

STEP 1
The type of query is SELECT
FROM TABLE
#analyze
Nested iteration
Table Scan
Table: #analyze   scan count 1,   logical reads:
2550,   physical reads: 423,   read ahead reads: 8664
```

This query took about 30 seconds to return information. We'll cover the query optimizer and its output in much greater detail later. At this point, accept that table scan operations generally take much more time than indexed operations. Therefore, adding an index to the '#analyze' table greatly speeds up the query:

```
create index analyze_city_ix on #analyze(city)

select * from #analyze
where city in ('Lisboa', 'Lexington')
```

```
STEP 1
The type of query is SELECT
FROM TABLE
#analyze
Nested iteration
Index : analyze_city_ix
FROM TABLE
#analyze
Nested iteration
Index : analyze_city_ix
FROM TABLE
#analyze
Nested iteration
Using Dynamic Index
Table: #analyze  scan count 3,  logical reads: 9,
physical reads: 0,  read ahead reads: 0
Table: Worktable  scan count 4,  logical reads: 2553,
physical reads: 64,  read ahead reads: 13326
```

After the index was added, the query returned data in less than one second. In summary, try to determine the number of explicit work tables that your application uses. If you expect these tables to hold abundant data, carefully evaluate good candidate columns for indexes. One additional point: If you do decide to create indexes, it's a good idea to wait until after you've finished loading the table before you launch the index build operation. We'll consider this point in more detail in our chapters on efficient database access.

Excess indexing

It is possible to have too much of a good thing. Some database administrators, in an effort to anticipate every possible sort and search combination, create indexes on practically every column in every table. Obviously, this is an extreme example. Nevertheless, there are cases where you can have too many indexes, such as when programmers create "test" indexes on tables and forget to drop them later.

Having too many indexes hurts your system in many ways:

- Every time you perform an insert or delete, the indexes and the data need to be modified.

- When you update an indexed column, the SQL Server engine updates all affected indexes. This can have the added undesirable effect of causing the engine to restructure the index trees. This update operation could act as a drag on performance for all applications accessing the table. It could even briefly degrade response across the entire system. You, as an administrator, would have no way of knowing if and when this would occur.

- Excess indexes consume more disk space, and as with any resource, there is usually never enough disk space to spare.

- When confronted with too many indexes, the optimizer may choose a less-qualified index. Your database operation may actually run more slowly than if you had fewer indexes in place.

The best way to know if you have too many indexes is to test your application with the SHOWPLAN command. Try to simulate a typical work day. When you are finished, remember to remove the SHOWPLAN command from your application, then review the output. You should be able to quickly determine which of your indexes are being used. You can then remove any indexes that are not commonly referenced. We'll look at how you can interpret the SHOW-PLAN output to learn more about index utilization in Chapter 4.

There are times when you need additional indexes to handle specific, easily identifiable tasks, such as an end-of-month processing suite. In these cases, you can simply create the indexes immediately before they are needed and drop them as soon as you finish.

Index fill factor

Before considering this topic, let's first understand what the index fill factor is. Index information is stored on pages. Each page holds up to two kilobytes of this data. The fill factor is simply a measure of how full SQL Server makes each page when building or rebuilding an index. Look at the following sets of simple diagrams demonstrating an index on the 'city' column:

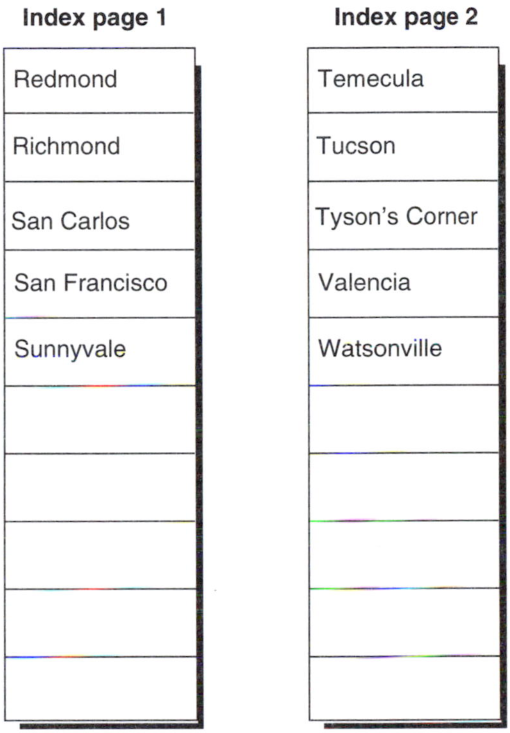

Index page 1	Index page 2
Redmond	Temecula
Richmond	Tucson
San Carlos	Tyson's Corner
San Francisco	Valencia
Sunnyvale	Watsonville

Figure 3.9

   In the first case, SQL Server has used a 50 percent fill factor. This means that each index page is only half-filled when the index is created. SQL Server therefore needed two pages to hold the information. A fill factor of 100 percent produces an index diagram like this:

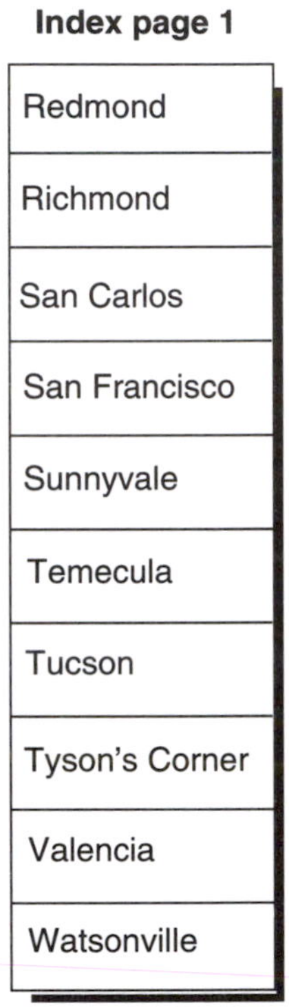

Index page 1

| Redmond |
| Richmond |
| San Carlos |
| San Francisco |
| Sunnyvale |
| Temecula |
| Tucson |
| Tyson's Corner |
| Valencia |
| Watsonville |

Figure 3.10

SQL Server completely fills all index pages when the fill factor is 100 percent; there is no more room on the existing pages for new index entries. What happens if you add a row to a table that has a fill factor of 100 percent? SQL Server creates a new index page and divides the data between the existing and new index page:

Original index page	New index page
Redmond	Tucson
Richmond	Tyson's Corner
San Carlos	Valencia
San Francisco	Walden
Sunnyvale	Watsonville
Temecula	

Figure 3.11

When you create an index, you have the option of setting the index fill factor by setting the FILLFACTOR parameter. You can set this value between 0 and 100. You can set a default, system-wide FILLFACTOR by using the 'sp_configure' stored procedure. If you don't explicitly set a FILLFACTOR value when creating an index, SQL Server then uses this default.

If you decide to set a value for FILLFACTOR, remember that the following conditions should be in effect:

- **Existing data.**   FILLFACTOR is significant only if there is existing data in the column(s) that you are indexing. Setting this on a new, empty table has no effect.

- **Data content predictability.**   To effectively set this parameter, you need to have some idea about how the indexed data will change in the future.

In addition, fill factor is only significant when you create the index. As time passes, and users make changes to the table's data as well as insert new rows and delete existing rows, the fill factor that you chose will no longer be true. For this reason, it's a good idea periodically to rebuild your indexes with your desired fill factor.

As we just saw, creating an index with a FILLFACTOR of 100 means that SQL Server completely fills each index page. You would use only this FILL-FACTOR if you never planned to add or change any data. Good candidates for this setting are lookup tables, since they typically don't change very often.

How can you learn what the current fill factor is for your indexes? Let's look at some examples taken from the SQL Enterprise Manager's 'Manage Indexes' screen. In the first case, we've requested a fill factor of 25 percent for the index on the 'customer_master' table's 'account_balance' field:

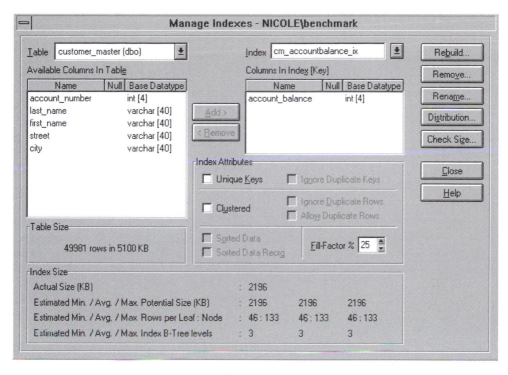

Figure 3.12

SQL Server tells us several important pieces of information about our new index. First, it reports the amount of disk space needed to hold the index, which is 2.196 megabytes in this case. Next, we learn the estimated minimum, average, and potential size for the index, which corresponds to the 2.196 megabyte figure we just saw. This is always true on indexes that operate on fixed data types, such as integer. The next statistic is the estimated, average, and maximum rows per index leaf and node page. Finally, SQL Server reports on how deep the B-tree is for this index.

This screen becomes more interesting for variable-length character field indexes, such as the one on the 'customer_master' table's 'last_name' column:

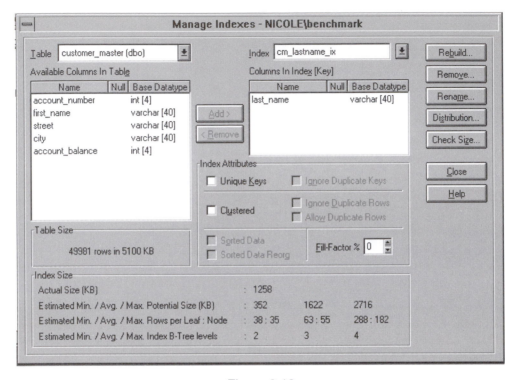

Figure 3.13

Why is there such a wide diversity among the estimated minimum, average, and maximum values for the potential size, rows per leaf and node, and B-tree levels statistics? Since this column was defined as variable length, SQL Server uses the following estimates:

- **Minimum.** For the minimum values, SQL Server operates on the assumption that the variable-length column is completely empty.

- **Average.** For the average value, the engine assumes each variable-length column's data is 50 percent full.

- **Maximum.** For this estimate, SQL Server calculates based on all variable length columns being totally full.

Returning to the 'account_balance' column index, let's see what happens when we change the fill factor. One nice feature of this screen is that you can experiment with alterations to the fill factor, and SQL Server reports what these numbers should look like after such a change. For example, we've raised the fill factor to 40 percent. Notice how the values change. Keep in mind that these numbers are estimates: SQL Server won't be able to report the actual numbers until we execute the change:

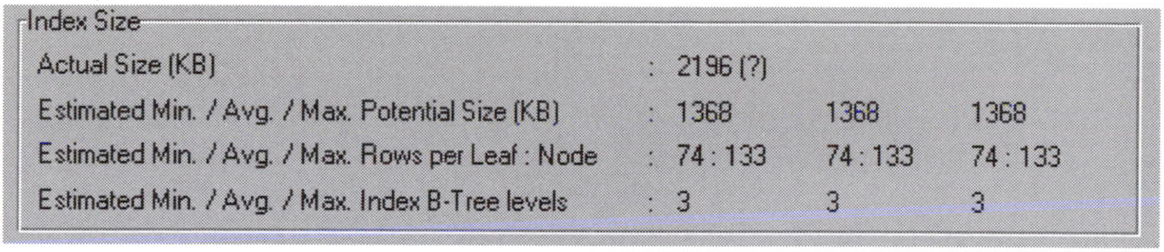

Index Size			
Actual Size (KB)	: 2196 (?)		
Estimated Min. / Avg. / Max. Potential Size (KB)	: 1368	1368	1368
Estimated Min. / Avg. / Max. Rows per Leaf : Node	: 74 : 133	74 : 133	74 : 133
Estimated Min. / Avg. / Max. Index B-Tree levels	: 3	3	3

Figure 3.14

In the next example, we've actually changed this value to 50 percent and then requested that SQL Server rebuild the index:

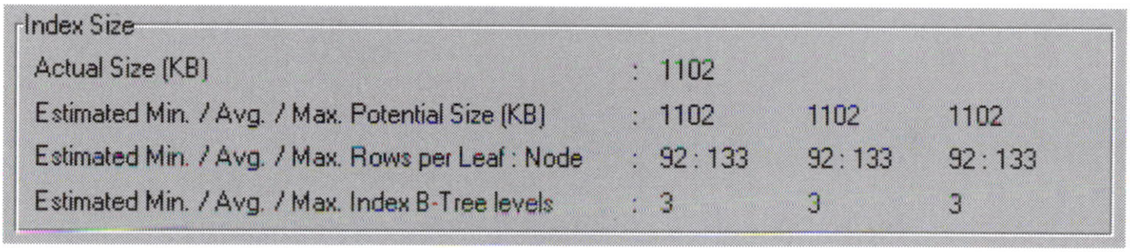

Index Size			
Actual Size (KB)	: 1102		
Estimated Min. / Avg. / Max. Potential Size (KB)	: 1102	1102	1102
Estimated Min. / Avg. / Max. Rows per Leaf : Node	: 92 : 133	92 : 133	92 : 133
Estimated Min. / Avg. / Max. Index B-Tree levels	: 3	3	3

Figure 3.15

Observe how many of the index statistics changed: the index has a different size, along with different rows per leaf and node pages. This is understandable, since we've radically changed the structure of each index page. In particular, watch how the actual and potential index size values have greatly diminished. With a fill factor of 50 percent, SQL Server is able to fit many more rows on each index page, thereby conserving space.

Finally, we've raised the fill factor to 100 percent, which would be appropriate for a lookup table that was fairly static:

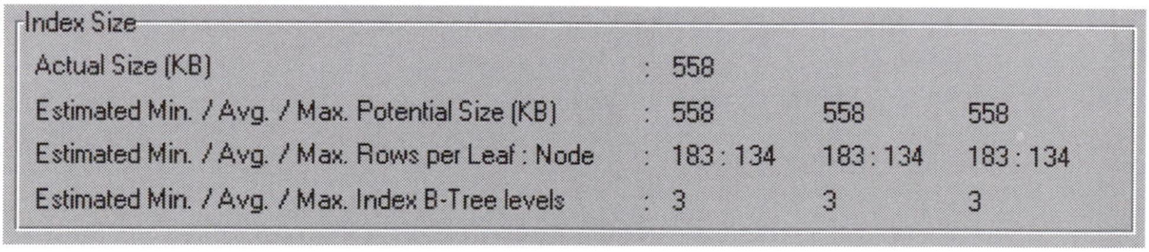

Index Size			
Actual Size (KB)	: 558		
Estimated Min. / Avg. / Max. Potential Size (KB)	: 558	558	558
Estimated Min. / Avg. / Max. Rows per Leaf : Node	: 183 : 134	183 : 134	183 : 134
Estimated Min. / Avg. / Max. Index B-Tree levels	: 3	3	3

Figure 3.16

The index size has gotten still smaller, since we're asking SQL Server to fill all pages to the maximum. In addition, there will be many more rows per leaf and node page.

PAD_INDEX option

With SQL Server 6.5, you can specify whether you want your the engine to apply your fill factor to both node and data pages by providing a parameter of PAD_INDEX when you create the index. For example, in the following statement, we've asked SQL Server to use a fill factor of 35 for our index data and node pages:

```
create index cm_city_ix on customer_master(city)
with pad_index, fillfactor = 35
```

This means that data pages, as well as node pages, will be created with 65 percent of their space available.

Index location

One way that you can potentially improve performance is to place the indexes for a table on a different device than the table's data. Let's look at an example of how you could follow this strategy. In this example, we'll use the 'isql' utility, rather than the graphical SQL Enterprise Manager, although it would probably be simpler and safer to use the latter. Keep in mind that you have the freedom to use either tool when performing database administration tasks. For the purposes of our example, assume that you have just installed a new disk drive and have assigned it to drive letter J:

1. Create a new database device that uses this new drive:
    ```
    disk init
    name = "dbspace3",
    physname = "J:\data\dbspace3.dat",
    vdevno = 25,
    size = 10240
    ```
    The 'vdevno' value is the virtual device number that you want to assign to this device; it can be between 1 and 255. Virtual device number 0 is reserved for the MASTER database device.

    The 'size' value is the number of 2-kilobyte blocks that you want assigned to the device. In this case, we've requested a total device size of 20 megabytes.

2. Alter your database to use this new device. Make sure that you run this command from the MASTER database:

```
alter database benchmark on dbspace3 = 20
```

In this case, we've asked that the database use the full 20 megabytes that we just created.

3. Add a segment that uses this new device. Think of the segment name as a logical name for the device. Therefore, make the name meaningful:

```
sp_addsegment benchmark_index, dbspace3
```

4. You can now place indexes or data on the new segment:

```
create index cf_flight_date_ix on
customer_flights(flight_date)
on benchmark_index
```

Since the disk drives are often the biggest bottleneck when retrieving data, separating the index onto a separate drive lets SQL Server minimize the potential impact of disk I/O, especially given SQL Server's multithreaded architecture.

Chapter 4

Understanding the Microsoft SQL Server Optimizer

Whether you're a database administrator, application designer, or developer, it's a good idea to understand how Microsoft SQL Server processes database requests. In this chapter, we spend some time learning about this important subject. We begin by learning about what an optimizer is, its role, and important optimizer features and algorithms. We continue by examining how to use the SHOWPLAN command to determine the particular course of action the optimizer is taking as it processes our database requests. There are many ways that you can control the optimizer's behavior. We close out the chapter by reviewing how you can programmatically alter the optimizer's data processing strategy.

What is an optimizer?

Data normalization is one of the most important advantages that relational databases provide over older data models. When you design a normalized database, you frequently place different data entities in separate tables. For example, in our sample airline mileage tracking system, we store customer profile information in the 'customer_master' table, and customer flight information in the 'customer_flights' table. If a user wants to see the name of a customer who took a flight on a particular date, we need to retrieve information from both tables and somehow combine and present this data. In other cases, we may want to search in a single table for a particular value, or sort results from a more complex query. In all cases, it's important to retrieve and present this data, but we want to do it as efficiently as possible. This is where the optimizer enters the scene. The optimizer's job is to determine the best course of action to get us what we want. The best course of action is usually defined as the most efficient technique to produce the desired result.

Optimizer features and algorithms

Beginning with version 6.0, the SQL Server optimizer includes a variety of new and updated features and algorithms. These include:

- **Bidirectional index processing.** You can use the same index if you're sorting in either ascending or descending order.

- **Subquery optimization.** SQL Server now examines subqueries, as well as other portions of the query, for cost. This can greatly reduce processing time, since the optimizer may find better data access paths.

- **Asynchronous read-ahead.** The optimizer uses algorithms to determine if queries and other large database operations will benefit from parallel reading of data and indexes. SQL Server uses the multithreading features of the NT platform to aid in these parallel scans. These parallel operations can greatly improve performance in certain cases.

- **Binary AND/OR sorting.** In older versions of SQL Server, you could not have more than 250 AND/OR combinations. SQL Server no longer has this limitation. In addition, the optimizer performs binary sort on these Boolean operators, providing better overall response.

- **DISTINCT function improvements.** If you request a SELECT DISTINCT on an indexed column, SQL Server now takes advantage of the index to speed completion of this task.

- **Index distribution information.** SQL Server now tracks key value distribution for all indexes on a table, including composite indexes. This information helps the optimizer to make the best possible decision when selecting among indexes.

Optimizer diagnostics

The easiest way to learn about the optimizer's choices for data processing are to monitor the results of the SHOWPLAN command. If you're using a character-based tool, such as isql, you can request SHOWPLAN output by entering SET SHOWPLAN ON. If you're using a graphical query tool, such as the query tool from the SQL Enterprise Manager, or isql/w, you can set a configuration option to provide this information. Once you've requested SHOWPLAN output, you'll receive it after every database operation.

Using SHOWPLAN

Let's look at some sample output from the SHOWPLAN command. We'll run a number of queries that illustrate the different types of information that this useful utility provides. Before looking at the output from this command, we first discuss situations where it provides data.

SHOWPLAN and SQL statements

The SHOWPLAN command displays important optimizer and engine statistics for all SQL operations. Since queries are often the most time-consuming database operation, chances are that you'll use SHOWPLAN primarily to research what choices the optimizer is making to process your query. If you find that UP-DATE, DELETE, and other nonquery operations are taking longer than expected, it's not a bad idea to review the SHOWPLAN output for these types of database access as well.

SHOWPLAN and stored procedures

The SHOWPLAN command also shows optimizer diagnostics for stored procedures. For example, look at the following stored procedure definition, along with the query plan for one call to the procedure:

```
create procedure show_long_flights
  (@account_number integer) as
select  cm.account_number,
        cm.last_name,
        cm.first_name,
        cf.flight_date,
        cf.origin,
        cf.destination,
        cf.miles
from    customer_master cm,
        customer_flights cf
where   cm.account_number = @account_number
and     cf.account_number = cm.account_number
and     cf.miles > 3000
go

STEP 1
The type of query is EXECUTE
```

```
SQL Server Parse and Compile Time:
   cpu time = 0 ms.
STEP 1
The type of query is DECLARE
STEP 1
The type of query is SELECT
FROM TABLE
customer_master cm
Nested iteration
Using Clustered Index
FROM TABLE
customer_flights cf
Nested iteration
Index : cf_account_number_ix
```

The query plan is nearly identical to the one that would be generated if you ran the query outside a stored procedure:

```
STEP 1
The type of query is SELECT
FROM TABLE
customer_master cm
Nested iteration
Using Clustered Index
FROM TABLE
customer_flights cf
Nested iteration
Index : cf_account_number_ix
```

The main difference between the two query plans is that the stored procedure's query plan also shows the engine steps necessary to load and run the procedure itself. Incidentally, you can learn a great deal about the structure of the SQL Server system tables and internal processes by studying the SHOW-PLAN output of any of the over 150 various system stored procedures.

SHOWPLAN and detailed query plans

The examples that we'll review in this section show the basics of SHOWPLAN's output. You have the option, however, of seeing a much higher degree of optimizer detail. These details include information about all of the query plans evaluated by the optimizer, potential join paths, and other statistics that the optimizer used when making its decisions. You can request this level of detail by setting special trace flags that tell the optimizer that you want as much information as possible. We'll cover trace flags in much more detail in Part 3. At this point, let's look at an example of the kinds of information that these trace flags provide.

Suppose that a user wants a report showing the possible awards for customers living in a range of cities, who have flown at least five times in the last seven years. You pass the following somewhat complex query to the engine:

```
select cm.account_number,
       cm.last_name,
       cm.first_name,
       aw.award_description
from customer_master cm,
     customer_flights cf,
     awards aw
where cm.account_number = cf.account_number
and   cm.city between "Aldwin" and "Bellmore"
and   cm.account_balance >= aw.mileage_level
and   cf.flight_date >= "01/01/1990"
group by cm.account_number,cm.last_name,
         cm.first_name, aw.award_description
having count(cf.flight_date) >= 5
```

The normal SHOWPLAN output looks like this:

```
STEP 1
The type of query is INSERT
The update mode is direct
Worktable created for REFORMATTING
FROM TABLE
customer_master
Nested iteration
Index : cm_city_ix
FROM TABLE
awards
Nested iteration
Table Scan
TO TABLE
Worktable 1
STEP 2
The type of query is SELECT (into a worktable)
GROUP BY
Vector Aggregate
FROM TABLE
Worktable 1
Nested iteration
Table Scan
```

```
FROM TABLE
customer_flights cf
Nested iteration
Index : cf_acct_flight_ix
TO TABLE
Worktable 2
STEP 3
The type of query is SELECT
FROM TABLE
Worktable 2
Nested iteration
Table Scan

Table: customer_master  scan count 1,  logical reads:
1434,  physical reads: 1075,  read ahead reads: 43
Table: customer_flights  scan count 1999,  logical
reads: 8047,  physical reads: 989,  read ahead reads: 0
Table: awards  scan count 1414,  logical reads: 1414,
physical reads: 1,  read ahead reads: 0
Table: Worktable  scan count 1,  logical reads: 24,
physical reads: 1,  read ahead reads: 0
Table: Worktable  scan count 1,  logical reads: 78,
physical reads: 78,  read ahead reads: 0
```

You can set a number of SQL Server trace flags to get even more detail about the optimizer's choice of query plans. For example, if we set trace flags 302 (statistics), 310 (join order), 325 (ORDER BY costs), 326 (sort costs), and 3604 (send trace output to client), the optimizer's SHOWPLAN output expands enormously. We'll cover a number of trace flags later in the book. At this point, let's look at some added optimizer output:

```
******************************
Leaving q_init_sclause() for table 'customer_master' (varno 0).
The table has 49981 rows and 2550 pages.
Cheapest index is index 0, costing 2550 pages per scan.
I_COVERS(1): 2

******************************

. . . .
. . . .

******************************
Leaving q_init_sclause() for table 'awards' (varno 2).
The table has 6 rows and 1 pages.
Cheapest index is index 0, costing 1 pages per scan.
```

```
* * * * * * * * * * * * * * * * * * * * * * * * * * * * * *
. . . .
. . . .

* * * * * * * * * * * * * * * * * * * * * * * * * * * *
Entering q_score_index() for table 'customer_flights' (varno 1).
The table has 402692 rows and 6042 pages.
Scoring the search clause:
AND (!:0xd7d26a)  (andstat:0xa)
  GE (L:0xd7d300)  (rsltype:0x3d rsllen:8 rslprec:23 rslscale:3
  opstat:0x0)
    VAR (L:0xd7df60)  (varname:flight_date varno:1 colid:3
    coltype(0x3d):DATETIME colen:8 coloff:10 colprec:23 colscale:3
    vartypeid:12 varusecnt:2 varstat:0x1 varlevel:0 varsubq:0)
    DATETIME (R:0xd7d2e0)  (left:0xd7d2e8 len:8 maxlen:10 value:'Jan
    1 1990 12:00AM')

Cheapest index is index 2, costing 3798 pages and generating 132888
rows per scan.
Search argument selectivity is 0.330000.
* * * * * * * * * * * * * * * * * * * * * * * * * * * * * *
. . . .
. . . .

* * * * * * * * * * * * * * * * * * * * * * * * * * * *
Entering q_score_join() for table 'customer_master' (varno 0).
The table has 49981 rows and 2550 pages.
Scoring the join clause:
AND (!:0xd7d320)  (andstat:0x2)
  GE (L:0xd7d256)  (rsltype:0x38 rsllen:4 rslprec:10 rslscale:0
  opstat:0x0)
    VAR (L:0xd7e004)  (varname:account_balance varno:0 colid:6
    coltype(0x38):INT4 colen:4 coloff:6 colprec:10 colscale:0
    vartypeid:7 varnext:d7df24 varusecnt:1 varlevel:0 varsubq:0)
    VAR (R:0xd7e042)  (varname:mileage_level varno:2 colid:2
    coltype(0x38):INT4 colen:4 coloff:6 colprec:10 colscale:0
    vartypeid:7 varnext:d7de74 varusecnt:1 varlevel:0 varsubq:0)

Cheapest index is index 0, costing 2550 pages and generating 24990
rows per scan.
Join selectivity is 2.
* * * * * * * * * * * * * * * * * * * * * * * * * * * * * *
. . . .
. . . .

* * * * * * * * * * * * * * * * * * * * * * * * * * * *
Entering q_score_join() for table 'awards' (varno 2).
The table has 6 rows and 1 pages.
```

```
Scoring the join clause:
AND (!:0xd7d320) (andstat:0x2)
  LE (L:0xd7d256) (rsltype:0x38 rsllen:4 rslprec:10 rslscale:0
  opstat:0x0)
    VAR (L:0xd7e042) (varname:mileage_level varno:2 colid:2
    coltype(0x38):INT4 colen:4 coloff:6 colprec:10 colscale:0
    vartypeid:7 varnext:d7de74 varusecnt:1 varlevel:0 varsubq:0)
    VAR (R:0xd7e004) (varname:account_balance right:d7e042 varno:0
   colid:6 coltype(0x38):INT4 colen:4 coloff:6 colprec:10 colscale:0
    vartypeid:7 varnext:d7df24 varusecnt:1 varstat:0x894 varlevel:0
    varsubq:0)

Cheapest index is index 0, costing 1 pages and generating 3 rows per
scan.
Join selectivity is 2.
*******************************


QUERY IS CONNECTED

J_OPTIMIZE: Remaining vars=[0,1,2]

permutation: 0 - 1 - 2

NEW PLAN (total cost = 58864720):
JPLAN (0x26df664) varno=0 indexid=3 totcost=20096 pathtype=sclause
class=join optype=? method=NESTED ITERATION outerrows=1 rows=1220
joinsel=1 lp=1256 pp=1256 cpages=1256 ctotpages=1315 corder=5
cstat=0x0 matcost=13329 matpages=56 crows=1220 cjoinsel=0
. . . .
. . . .
WORK PLAN (total cost = 58877207):
JPLAN (0x26df664) varno=0 indexid=3 totcost=20096 pathtype=sclause
class=join optype=? method=NESTED ITERATION outerrows=1 rows=1220
joinsel=1 lp=1256 pp=1256 cpages=1256 ctotpages=1315 corder=5
cstat=0x0 matcost=13329 matpages=56 crows=1220 cjoinsel=0

JPLAN (0x26df6c0) varno=1 indexid=2 totcost=58842170
pathtype=sclause
class=join optype=? method=NESTED ITERATION outerrows=1220 rows=1220
joinsel=1220 lp=4633560 pp=3541075 cpages=3798 ctotpages=3798
corder=1 cstat=0x10 matcost=13755 matpages=65 crows=132888
cjoinsel=1
joinmap=[0]
. . . .
. . . .
JPLAN (0x26df71c) varno=2 indexid=0 totcost=2454 pathtype=sclause
class=join optype=? method=NESTED ITERATION outerrows=1220 rows=3660
joinsel=2 lp=1220 pp=1 cpages=1 ctotpages=1 corder=1 cstat=0x20
crows=6 cjoinsel=1 joinmap=[0]
```

```
WORK PLAN (total cost = 122003):
WORK PLAN (total cost = 162583):
WORK PLAN (total cost = 175070):
WORK PLAN (total cost = 117202):
WORK PLAN (total cost = 129689):
.  .  .  .

.  .  .  .
FINAL PLAN (total cost = 11728):
JPLAN (0x26deac4) varno=3 indexid=0 totcost=11728 pathtype=sclause
class=join optype=SUBSTITUTE method=NESTED ITERATION outerrows=1
rows=1207 joinsel=1 lp=733 pp=733 cpages=733 ctotpages=0 corder=0
cstat=0x1 crows=1207 cjoinsel=1
```

At the end of all of this output, SQL Server still displays the original SHOWPLAN output as well.

Given the massive amount of information that these trace flags furnish, is it worthwhile asking for this much detail on a regular basis? There is value in understanding how the optimizer works, so if you find yourself with some spare time, it is instructive to delve into this output. However, for normal, day-to-day operations, the answer is no. As an administrator, your goal should be to make sure that your tables are well designed and indexed. You should check optimizer query plans in great detail only in those cases where you are certain that SQL Server is missing some important fact about your particular environment. Armed with this information, you can then pass "hints" to the optimizer to change its behavior when generating query plans.

SHOWPLAN topics

The SHOWPLAN command provides copious information about what steps the optimizer is taking to process a query. In this section, we examine the various components of SHOWPLAN output. As part of this discussion, we also review some new SHOWPLAN features found in SQL Server 6.5.

Step

When the optimizer processes a query or operation, it first breaks down the procedure into a number of individual tasks. For example, in the following query, we're trying to get a count of customers by city, along with their average account balance. In addition, we only want to see those customers that have more than enough miles in their accounts to qualify for the average award:

```
select city, count(*) Customer_Count,
       avg(account_balance) Average
into tempdb.dbo.vips
from   customer_master
```

```
where   account_balance >=
(select avg(mileage_level)
 from    awards)
group by city
```

STEP 1

```
The type of query is SELECT
Scalar Aggregate
FROM TABLE
awards
Row estimate:  6
Cost estimate: 16
Nested iteration
Table Scan
```

STEP 2

```
The type of query is SELECT (into a worktable)
GROUP BY
Vector Aggregate
FROM TABLE
customer_master
Row estimate:  4123
Cost estimate: 40800
Nested iteration
Table Scan
TO TABLE
Worktable 1
```

STEP 3

```
The type of query is TABCREATE
```

STEP 4

```
The type of query is INSERT
The update mode is direct
Worktable created for SELECT INTO
FROM TABLE
Worktable 1
Row estimate:  4123
Cost estimate: 2064
Nested iteration
Table Scan
TO TABLE
tempdb.dbo.vips
```

We'll discuss how to decipher query plans throughout this chapter. For our discussion at this point, notice how the optimizer broke the query into a number of small steps. This is the case with many queries and operations.

Row and cost estimate

As you may have noticed, each SHOWPLAN sample comes with row and cost estimate information. What do these numbers mean, and how should you make use of them? In a nutshell, think of the row estimate as the engine's best guess, based on available information, of how many rows it expects to return for your query or database operation. The optimizer uses statistical and index information to arrive at this number, which may or may not be correct. Notice the difference in row estimates between query plans that use indexes versus query plans that require table scans. The index's statistical information is of great help to the optimizer in calculating its row estimate. Given this high degree of variability, there's no need for you to make any query alterations or other modifications based solely on this number.

The cost estimate, on the other hand, does have significance. This number represents the optimizer's most accurate calculation about the amount of resources necessary to satisfy your request. You don't need to be concerned about the unit of measure when evaluating cost estimates. Instead, use the cost estimate value to compare different queries. For example, suppose that you have a choice of expressing a query in two ways. The first query plan shows a cost estimate of 6005, while the second shows a cost estimate of 43. In situations like this, it's always better to pick the query plan with a lower cost estimate, since it means that the engine will have less work to do.

Table scan

A table scan means that the SQL Server engine is reading every row of the table to satisfy the query requirements.

```
select *
from    customer_master
where   city = "Sao Paolo"

STEP 1
The type of query is SELECT
FROM TABLE
customer_master
Row estimate:  4998
Cost estimate: 40800
Nested iteration
Table Scan
```

In this case, there is no index on the 'city' column in the 'customer_master' table. This means that the engine must read every row in the table to locate all matches for the query criteria. This is very expensive and slow; if many of your most sluggish queries involve table scans, you may wish to consider adding indexes where appropriate. Notice what happens when we add an index to the 'city' column and then rerun the query:

```
STEP 1
The type of query is SELECT
FROM TABLE
customer_master
Row estimate:  1
Cost estimate: 64
Nested iteration
    Index : cm_city_ix
```

Let's spend some more time focusing on the important topic of indexes.

Indexes

Indexes are the biggest factors in database performance. The Microsoft SQL Server optimizer tells us which indexes (if any) it uses to rapidly locate and retrieve information. In this section, we examine how to interpret index output from the SHOWPLAN command.

Clustered index

When a table has a clustered index, it means that the physical table is written in the order of the index. The most common clustered indexes are created by SQL Server when you create a table with a primary key. For example, we created the 'customer_master' table with the 'account_number' column defined as the primary key. Running 'sp_helpindex' on this table produces this output:

Table 4.1   sp_helpindex output

column_name	value
index_name	PK__customer___account
index_description	clustered, unique, primary key located on default
index_keys	account_number
index_name	cm_lastname_ix
index_description	non-clustered located on default
index_keys	last_name
index_name	cm_city_ix
index_description	non-clustered located on default
index_keys	city

You can have only one clustered index on a table (since you can only physically order a table in one way). You can also have up to 249 non-clustered indexes.

As part of the SHOWPLAN output, SQL Server reports on whether the chosen index is clustered or not:

```
select *
from    customer_master
where   account_number = 90554303

STEP 1
The type of query is SELECT
FROM TABLE
customer_master
Row estimate:   1
Cost estimate: 32
Nested iteration
Using Clustered Index
```

Index name

When you examine a query plan, there's no doubt about which indexes the optimizer is using, because SQL Server reports the name of any selected indexes
as part of the SHOWPLAN output:

```
select account_number,
       flight_date,
       miles
from    customer_flights
where   account_number between 1000000 and 2000000
and     flight_date between "04/01/96" and "06/30/96"

STEP 1
The type of query is SELECT
FROM TABLE
customer_flights
Row estimate:   302
Cost estimate: 1264
Nested iteration
Index : cf_acct_flight_ix
```

The optimizer chose the 'cf_acct_flight_ix' index because it provides the
best path to rapidly retrieve information. It's a good idea to periodically examine the SHOWPLAN output, since there may be a difference between the indexes that you expect the optimizer to use and the ones that it actually favors.

Dynamic index

Sometimes, SQL Server finds it easier to make multiple indexed passes through a table rather than retrieving all rows through a table scan:

```
select  *
from    customer_master
where   last_name       = "Tipton"
or      account_number  = 78588559


STEP 1
The type of query is SELECT
FROM TABLE
customer_master
Nested iteration
Index : cm_lastname_ix
FROM TABLE
customer_master
Nested iteration
Using Clustered Index
FROM TABLE
customer_master
Nested iteration
Using Dynamic Index
```

Each 'FROM TABLE' on the 'customer_master' table indicates another pass through the table. SQL Server uses the appropriate index for each candidate column to quickly locate data. In this case, the first pass is through the 'customer_master' table, using the index on the 'last_name' column. The next pass is through the 'customer_master' table, using the index on 'account_number.' This index is clustered, so the underlying table's data is sequenced on this value. For each pass, the engine writes the row ID values for the results into a work table. This is known as a "dynamic index." Once the engine has finished making all passes through the table, it uses the dynamic index to rapidly retrieve and present the actual information from the base table.

Dynamic indexes are also helpful in situations where you've asked to use the IN clause:

```
select  *
from    customer_master
where   account_number in (5945949,7606060,7223993)

STEP 1
The type of query is SELECT
```

```
FROM TABLE
customer_master
Nested iteration
Using Clustered Index
FROM TABLE
customer_master
Nested iteration
Using Clustered Index
FROM TABLE
customer_master
Nested iteration
Using Clustered Index
FROM TABLE
customer_master
Nested iteration
Using Dynamic Index
```

Typically, SQL Server uses dynamic indexes only if all three of these conditions are met:

1. The optimizer can't determine a faster retrieval strategy.

2. No part of the query requires a table scan. If this was so, the optimizer would simply use the table scan to satisfy all query conditions.

3. All of the query criteria found in the IN or OR clause are part of the same table.

Nested iteration

In many queries, the optimizer decides that the engine should retrieve data from a table from inside a processing loop, using this type of logic:

```
While (not end-of-data)
    Fetch a row from the table
    Decide if the row matches the query criteria
    If the row matches the query criteria
        Return the row
    End if
End while
```

This is known as a nested iteration and is often independent of the state of indexes on the table. For example, examine the following two queries and query plans:

Example 1:

```
select flight_date,
```

```
        miles,
        origin,
        destination
from    customer_flights
where   origin in ("PHX", "SJC")


STEP 1
The type of query is SELECT
FROM TABLE
customer_flights
Row estimate:  200000
Cost estimate: 47776
Nested iteration
Table Scan
```

Example 2:

```
select flight_date,
       miles,
       origin,
       destination
from    customer_flights
where   account_number = 34995953


STEP 1
The type of query is SELECT
FROM TABLE
customer_flights
Row estimate:  1
Cost estimate: 80
Nested iteration
Index : cf_acct_flight_ix
```

In the first case, there is no available index to speed the query, yet the optimizer still chose a nested iteration. In the second case, the optimizer used the 'cf_acct_flight_ix' to quickly locate data, yet still performed a nested iteration.

Update modes

When SQL Server writes into a table, it has a choice of two ways to accomplish this operation: deferred update or direct update. In this section, we examine both methods. The UPDATE statement has some special considerations regarding these procedures; we explore this after we've discussed both techniques.

Deferred update

When SQL Server modifies data via a deferred update, it follows these steps:

1. The engine updates all transaction log records, reflecting the upcoming changes that are to be made to data. For INSERT statements, this means that the transaction log shows the new values to be added to the table. For UPDATE statements, the transaction log shows the old and new values. For DELETE statements, the transaction log holds the values that are to be deleted.
2. Once the engine finishes writing all of the log records, it applies the changes to the table in one pass.

Why would SQL Server choose this approach when modifying data? There are several situations where this is the best technique, but the most common cause of a deferred update is when there is an uncertain scope of information. Let's learn more about this condition.

Since SQL databases are set-oriented, there are several types of procedures that cannot be determined until the entire set has been identified. For example, suppose that you want to duplicate all the rows within a table:

```
insert into sample_awards
select *
from sample_awards

STEP 1
The type of query is INSERT
The update mode is deferred
FROM TABLE
sample_awards
Nested iteration
Table Scan
TO TABLE
sample_awards
```

If SQL Server didn't use a deferred update, it would never finish the INSERT statement, since the table would continually be growing. Performing a deferred update lets the engine first gather all the rows in the table into the transaction log and then apply the log to the table.

SQL Server can have this uncertainty for UPDATE and DELETE statements as well. For example, suppose that you ask the engine to perform this operation:

```
delete from customer_flights
```

```
where account_number = 76005544

STEP 1
The type of query is DELETE
The update mode is deferred
FROM TABLE
customer_flights
Row estimate:  1
Cost estimate: 80
Nested iteration
Index : cf_acct_flight_ix
TO TABLE
customer_flights
```

Although there is an index on the 'account_number' column in the 'customer_flights' table, the optimizer cannot determine how many rows might have the account_number value specified in the DELETE statement. This uncertainty causes a deferred update. In the section on direct updates, we'll run nearly the same query, except in this case the optimizer can use a unique index to determine the exact number of affected rows. In that case, the engine chooses a direct update.

Direct update

When the optimizer chooses a direct update, it immediately makes the change to the table. This is the default method, since it is generally more rapid and also does not consume the amount of transaction log overhead as the deferred update approach. As we discussed in the deferred update section, here is an SQL statement and query plan where there is a unique index on the WHERE clause criteria:

```
delete from customer_master
where account_number = 76005544

STEP 1
The type of query is DELETE
The update mode is direct
FROM TABLE
customer_master
Row estimate:  1
Cost estimate: 32
Nested iteration
Using Clustered Index
TO TABLE
customer_master
```

In this case, the optimizer was able to ensure that there was either 0 or 1 record with this profile in the 'customer_master' table, since the 'account_number' column is the primary key. Contrast this query plan with the 'customer_flights' plan described in the deferred update section.

Special UPDATE statement considerations

When you ask SQL Server to update data, it has a choice between performing a direct update (also known as an update-in-place operation) or a deferred update. When SQL Server performs a direct update, the engine acts directly on the table's data. In the case of a deferred update, SQL Server first deletes the original row, then inserts a new row in its place. SQL Server performs a direct update as long as all of the following are true:

Table-specific attributes

- The table does not have an UPDATE trigger.
- The table is not replicated.

Single row update attributes

- The column, after updating, must fit on the original data page.
- If the column is part of a non-unique, non-clustered index, the column is of fixed length.
- If the column is part of a unique, non-clustered index, the column is of fixed width, and the row can be located as an exact match.
- The updated row is no more than 50 percent different from the original row and no more than 24 adjacent bytes have changed.

Multirow update attributes

- The column is not part of a unique, non-clustered index.
- The table has no timestamp data type columns.
- The updated column is of fixed length.

Keep in mind that the rules for direct UPDATE have been evolving over time and may change again in future releases.

FROM TABLE

Each step of the query plan itemizes the table that is being consulted by the SQL Server engine. For example, review the following query and query plan:

```
select cm.last_name,
       cm.first_name,
       cf.flight_date,
       pa.partner_description
```

```
from    customer_master cm,
        customer_flights cf,
        partners pa
where   cm.account_number = cf.account_number
and     cf.partner = pa.partner_code
and     cm.city between "Paris" and "Podunk"

STEP 1
The type of query is SELECT
FROM TABLE
customer_master cm
Row estimate:  1
Cost estimate: 80
Nested iteration
Index : cm_city_ix
FROM TABLE
customer_flights cf
JOINS WITH
customer_master cm
Row estimate:  1
Cost estimate: 80
Nested iteration
Index : cf_acct_flight_ix
FROM TABLE
partners pa
JOINS WITH
customer_flights cf
Row estimate:  1
Cost estimate: 16
Nested iteration
Table Scan
```

Notice how the optimizer reports on each table that it is examining in the query. Some of these FROM TABLE clauses are actual database tables; some can be work tables as well.

TO TABLE

The SQL Server engine reports on destination tables for operations that modify data, such as INSERT, UPDATE, DELETE, SELECT INTO, or work table queries:

```
update customer_master
set    account_balance = account_balance * 1.1
where  account_balance > 50000
```

```
STEP 1
The type of query is UPDATE
The update mode is direct
FROM TABLE
customer_master
Row estimate:  16493
Cost estimate: 40800
Nested iteration
Table Scan
TO TABLE
customer_master
```

In this case, we're updating the 'account_balance' column in the 'customer_master' table.

Query type

The optimizer lists, by step, the actual database operation that it is performing. Some of the more common query types include:

Table 4.2 Query types

Query Type	Description
ABORT	Stop a transaction.
ALTERTAB	Alter a table.
BEGINXACT	Start a transaction.
DELETE	Delete data.
ENDXACT	Commit a transaction.
GRANT	Grant permission.
INDCREATE	Create an index.
INDDESTROY	Drop an index.
INSERT	Insert data.
SELECT	Retrieve data.
TABCREATE	Create a table.
TABDESTROY	Drop a table.
TRUNCATETABLE	Delete all rows from a table.
UPDATE	Update data.
UPDATESTATS	Update data distribution statistics.

These are only a few of the existing query types; all other database operations have corresponding query type descriptions.

GROUP BY

The GROUP BY clause is a useful component for queries that tabulate information. For example, in this query, we want to get a count of flights, grouped by origin city:

```
select origin, count(*)
from   customer_flights
group by origin

STEP 1
The type of query is SELECT (into a worktable)
GROUP BY
Vector Aggregate
FROM TABLE
customer_flights
Row estimate:  200000
Cost estimate: 47776
Nested iteration
Table Scan
TO TABLE
Worktable 1
STEP 2
The type of query is SELECT
FROM TABLE
Worktable 1
Row estimate:  200000
Cost estimate: 15936
Nested iteration
Table Scan
```

When you request a GROUP BY, SQL Server breaks the query down into at least two steps. The first step locates all appropriate rows and inserts them into a work table. The second part of the query tabulates and returns the rows from the work table.

GROUP BY WITH ROLLUP

SQL Server 6.5 introduces a new GROUP BY option, known as GROUP BY WITH ROLLUP. This new capability lets you easily create and maintain running averages or totals. We'll look at ways that you can incorporate this new feature into your queries in our chapters on efficient database access. For our discussion here, let's look at a query and query plan that uses this alternative:

```
select last_name, city, sum(account_balance)
from customer_master
where city between "Hightown" and "Hiore"
group by last_name, city
with rollup

STEP 1
The type of query is INSERT
The update mode is direct
FROM TABLE
customer_master
Nested iteration
Index : cm_city_ix
TO TABLE
Worktable 1
STEP 2
The type of query is SELECT
FROM TABLE
Worktable 2
  Vector Aggregate
GROUP BY WITH ROLLUP
  FROM TABLE
  Worktable 1
  Using GETSORTED Table Scan
  TO TABLE
  Worktable 2
```

GROUP BY WITH CUBE

In addition to GROUP BY WITH ROLLUP, SQL Server 6.5 also introduces the GROUP BY WITH CUBE option, which can improve summary information for your queries. We'll discuss this added feature in Part 2. At this point, let's examine a query and query plan that take advantage of this new facility:

```
select last_name, city, sum(account_balance)
from customer_master
where city between "Hightown" and "Hiore"
group by last_name, city
with cube

STEP 1
```

```
The type of query is INSERT
The update mode is direct
FROM TABLE
customer_master
Nested iteration
Index : cm_city_ix
TO TABLE
Worktable 1
STEP 2
The type of query is SELECT
FROM TABLE
Worktable 2
```

```
  GROUP BY WITH CUBE
  Vector Aggregate
  FROM TABLE
  Worktable 1
  Using GETSORTED Table Scan
  TO TABLE
  Worktable 2
```

Work table

Work tables are an important storage location for SQL Server. In this section, we explore a number of scenarios where SQL Server constructs and utilizes these important objects.

For SELECT INTO

There are certain times where you may want a query to create a new table. For example, suppose that you want to extract a listing of your best customers into a new table:

```
select  *
into    top_customers
from    customer_master
where   account_balance > 300000

STEP 1
The type of query is TABCREATE
STEP 2
The type of query is INSERT
The update mode is direct
```

```
Worktable created for SELECT INTO
FROM TABLE
customer_master
```

```
Row estimate:  16493
Cost estimate: 28608
Nested iteration
Table Scan
TO TABLE
top_customers
```

In this case, the first step for the optimizer is to create the new table. Next, the engine directly inserts qualifying data into this new table from the 'customer_master' table. In this case, the optimizer read all rows from the 'customer_master' table, since there is no index on 'account_balance.' If there was an index on this column, the optimizer would still take the same steps; the operation would be faster, however.

For DISTINCT

Suppose that you want to retrieve a unique list of customer names:

```
select distinct(last_name)
from   customer_master

STEP 1
The type of query is INSERT
The update mode is direct
Worktable created for DISTINCT
FROM TABLE
customer_master
Row estimate:  49981
Cost estimate: 21040
Nested iteration
Index : cm_lastname_ix
TO TABLE
Worktable 1
STEP 2
The type of query is SELECT
This step involves sorting
FROM TABLE
Worktable 1
Row estimate:  49981
Cost estimate: 21734
Using GETSORTED Table Scan
```

The optimizer breaks down this query into a number of steps. First, it creates a temporary table to hold intermediate query results. It then inserts all customer last name information (including duplicates) from 'customer_master' into this temporary table. Since there is an index on this column, the engine is able to use it to speed up this step. Once the temporary table has been finished, the optimizer sorts the data in the table, removes duplicates, and returns the unique list of customer last names to the user.

For ORDER BY

Sorting is an important part of information retrieval. If you ask SQL Server to sort information and there is no appropriate index, the optimizer creates a work table to speed the sorting operation.

```
select *
from    customer_flights
order by origin, flight_date

STEP 1
The type of query is INSERT
The update mode is direct
Worktable created for ORDER BY
FROM TABLE
customer_flights
Row estimate:  200000
Cost estimate: 48016
Nested iteration
Table Scan
TO TABLE
Worktable 1
STEP 2
The type of query is SELECT
This step involves sorting
FROM TABLE
Worktable 1
Row estimate:  200000
Cost estimate: 59082
Using GETSORTED Table Scan
```

Once the optimizer has created and populated the temporary work table (step 1), it then sorts the work table and returns the information to the user (step 2).

For REFORMATTING

There may be times when you attempt to join two large tables without appropriate indexes. If SQL Server has no other options to speed information retrieval, it may create a work table to process the results of your query:

```
select  cm.account_number,
        cm.last_name,
        cm.first_name,
        cf.flight_date,
        cf.miles
from    customer_master  cm,
        customer_flights cf
where   cm.account_balance = cf.miles
and     cm.account_number  = cf.account_number
and     cf.miles < 1000

STEP 1
The type of query is INSERT
The update mode is direct
Worktable created for REFORMATTING
FROM TABLE
customer_flights
Row estimate:  0
Cost estimate: 0
Nested iteration
Table Scan
TO TABLE
Worktable 1
STEP 2
The type of query is SELECT
FROM TABLE
customer_master cm
Row estimate:  49981
Cost estimate: 28608
Nested iteration
Table Scan
FROM TABLE
Worktable 1
JOINS WITH
customer_master cm
Row estimate:  49981
Cost estimate: 606213
Nested iteration
Using Clustered Index
```

The first step to return data is for SQL Server to create the work table that will hold the intermediate query results. SQL Server inserts rows from the smaller of the two tables (the 'customer_flights' table, in this case) into the work table.

Next, SQL Server constructs a clustered index on the work table. This clustered index is now used to join the work table to the original table and to retrieve all appropriate rows.

If you find that many of your queries are producing work tables for reformatting, it's a good idea to carefully evaluate your indexing strategy.

Scalar aggregate

One of the many powerful features of SQL is its built-in functions, which are known as aggregate functions. These functions use the engine's capabilities to perform a wide variety of data summation operations. Aggregate functions include:

- AVG()
- COUNT()
- COUNT(*)
- MAX()
- MIN()
- SUM()

When you use one of these functions in a SELECT statement without a GROUP BY clause, SQL Server returns a single value. This is true no matter how many rows you're examining. When one of these functions brings back a single value, the operation is known as a "scalar aggregate." Here's a sample scalar aggregate query, along with the SHOWPLAN output:

```
select  avg(account_balance)
from    customer_master
where   city = "Springfield"

STEP 1
The type of query is SELECT
Scalar Aggregate
FROM TABLE
customer_master
Row estimate:   4998
Cost estimate: 40800
Nested iteration
Table Scan
STEP 2
The type of query is SELECT
```

Here's what happens when we add an index on the 'city' column:

```
STEP 1
The type of query is SELECT
Scalar Aggregate
FROM TABLE
customer_master
Row estimate:  10
Cost estimate: 640
Nested iteration
  Index : cm_city_ix
STEP 2
The type of query is SELECT
```

Adding the index speeds up this query; it does not, however, change the number of steps that SQL Server takes to return data. The first step in processing this query is for the engine to locate all rows in the 'customer_master' table that have a 'city' value of 'Springfield.' If there is no index in place on this column (example 1), the engine performs a table scan. If there is an applicable index on the column (example 2), the engine locates the appropriate rows via this index. Since we've asked for the average of all applicable account balances, the engine keeps a running average in an internal variable. Once the engine finishes tabulating these numbers, it retrieves the contents of this variable as step 2.

Vector aggregate

A vector aggregate is similar to a scalar aggregate function. The difference between these two operations occurs when you include a GROUP BY in the same query that has the scalar aggregate:

```
select city, avg(account_balance)
from    customer_master
group by city

STEP 1
The type of query is SELECT (into a worktable)
GROUP BY
Vector Aggregate
FROM TABLE
customer_master
Row estimate:  49981
Cost estimate: 28608
Nested iteration
Table Scan
TO TABLE
Worktable 1
```

```
STEP 2
The type of query is SELECT
FROM TABLE
Worktable 1
Row estimate:  49981
Cost estimate: 23536
Nested iteration
Table Scan
```

In step 1, the engine retrieves 'city' and 'account_balance' information for all rows in the 'customer_master' table. It then places this data into a temporary work table. The next step is for the engine to scan the work table to tabulate the average account balances and group them by city. The engine may make multiple passes in both steps of this operation.

Sorting

See the "Work table" section earlier in this chapter for more details on sorting-created work tables.

Joins

Joins are an integral component of relational database design and usage. We'll cover joins in much more detail in Chapter 5. At this point, however, let's look at how the SQL Server optimizer's SHOWPLAN command reports about joins.

Standard join

Here's a query and query plan that demonstrates a standard join:

```
select * from customer_flights f, partners p
where f.partner = p.partner_code
and f.account_number between 1000000 and 1100000

STEP 1
The type of query is SELECT
FROM TABLE
customer_flights f
Nested iteration
Index : cf_acct_flight_ix
FROM TABLE
partners p
Nested iteration
Table Scan
```

Cross join

A cross join produces all possible combinations among the tables in the query. This is also known as a "Cartesian product":

```
select last_name, first_name, flight_date
from customer_master, customer_flights

STEP 1
The type of query is SELECT
FROM TABLE
customer_master
Nested iteration
Table Scan
FROM TABLE
customer_flights
Nested iteration
Index : cf_acct_flight_ix
```

Inner join

An inner join, while slightly different in syntax than the standard join, still produces the same output as a standard join:

```
select * from customer_flights f inner join partners p
on f.partner = p.partner_code
and f.account_number between 1000000 and 1100000

STEP 1
The type of query is SELECT
FROM TABLE
customer_flights f
Nested iteration
Index : cf_acct_flight_ix
FROM TABLE
partners p
Nested iteration
Table Scan
```

Left outer join

Beginning with SQL Server 6.5, the SHOWPLAN output for left outer joins has been enhanced. Recall that when processing a left outer join, the optimizer returns rows from the left table, even if there is no corresponding join match to the right table:

```
select *
from customer_master c left join customer_flights f on
c.account_number = f.account_number
```

You can also use this syntax to request a left outer join:

```
select * from customer_master c, customer_flights f
where c.account_number *= f.account_number

STEP 1
The type of query is SELECT
FROM TABLE
customer_master c
Nested iteration
Table Scan
LEFT OUTER JOIN : nested iteration
    FROM TABLE
    customer_flights f
    Nested iteration
    Index : cf_acct_flight_ix
```

To satisfy the left outer join, SQL Server first obtains a row from the left table, then performs the right table's query plan.

Right outer join

A right outer join is similar to a left outer join: The only difference is that the order of the tables is reversed. SQL Server automatically converts right outer joins into left outer joins by switching the tables:

```
select *
from customer_master c right join customer_flights f on
c.account_number = f.account_number
```

You can also use this syntax to request a right outer join:

```
select * from customer_master c, customer_flights f
where c.account_number =* f.account_number

STEP 1
The type of query is SELECT
```

```
FROM TABLE
customer_flights f
Nested iteration
Table Scan
```

LEFT OUTER JOIN : nested iteration

```
  FROM TABLE
  customer_master c
  Nested iteration
  Using Clustered Index
```

Full outer join

A full outer joins produces the same rows as the left and right outer joins. The main difference between full outer and these other joins is that SQL Server constructs the query plan differently, as well as saving all nonmatched rows until the end of the output stream:

```
select *
from customer_master c full outer join
customer_flights f on
c.account_number = f.account_number

STEP 1
The type of query is INSERT
The update mode is direct
Worktable created for REFORMATTING
FROM TABLE
customer_master
Nested iteration
Table Scan
TO TABLE
Worktable 1
STEP 2
The type of query is SELECT
FROM TABLE
customer_flights f
Nested iteration
Table Scan
```

FULL OUTER JOIN : nested iteration

```
  FROM TABLE
  Worktable 1
  Nested iteration
  Using Clustered Index
```

Subqueries

One of SQL's most powerful capabilities lies in its abilities to handle subqueries. Let's look at some typical subqueries, along with their respective SHOWPLAN output.

In this example, we're using a subquery to locate a record in the 'customer_master' table. If we find this information, then we can use it to accomplish the rest of our search:

```
select flight_date, miles
from customer_flights
where account_number in
(select account_number
from customer_master
where last_name = "Monsoon")

STEP 1
The type of query is SELECT
FROM TABLE
customer_flights
Nested iteration
Table Scan
EXISTS : nested iteration
  FROM TABLE
  customer_master
  Nested iteration
  Index : cm_lastname_ix
```

We can also request that SQL Server discard data if it matches a subquery:

```
select flight_date, miles
from customer_flights
where account_number not in
(select account_number
from customer_master
where last_name = "Monsoon")

STEP 1
The type of query is SELECT
FROM TABLE
customer_flights
Nested iteration
Table Scan
NOT EXISTS : nested iteration
  FROM TABLE
```

```
customer_master
Nested iteration
Index : cm_lastname_ix
```

Another helpful use for subqueries is to use them in conjunction with aggregate functions. In this next example, we're looking for customers who have a balance less than or equal to the shortest flight in the 'customer_flights' table:

```
select last_name, first_name
from customer_master
where account_balance <=
(select min(miles) from customer_flights)

STEP 1
The type of query is SELECT
Scalar Aggregate
FROM TABLE
customer_flights
Nested iteration
Index : cf_miles_ix
STEP 2
The type of query is SELECT
FROM TABLE
customer_master
Nested iteration
Table Scan
```

EXISTS

As we saw in the earlier discussion on subqueries, searching for the existence of a record in a subquery causes the engine to perform a nested iteration on the subquery's table. We can also explicitly request an EXISTS nested iteration:

```
select flight_date, miles
from customer_flights cf
where exists
(select *
from customer_master cm
where last_name = "Monsoon"
and cm.account_number = cf.account_number)

STEP 1
The type of query is SELECT
FROM TABLE
customer_flights cf
```

```
Nested iteration
Table Scan
EXISTS : nested iteration
  FROM TABLE
  customer_master cm
  Nested iteration
  Index : cm_lastname_ix
```

In this case, all that we've done is move the join condition into the subquery.

NOT EXISTS

Just as positive subqueries correspond with EXISTS, negative subqueries correspond with NOT EXISTS:

```
select flight_date, miles
from customer_flights cf
where not exists
(select *
from customer_master cm
where last_name = "Monsoon"
and cm.account_number = cf.account_number)

STEP 1
The type of query is SELECT
FROM TABLE
customer_flights cf
Nested iteration
Table Scan
NOT EXISTS : nested iteration
  FROM TABLE
  customer_master cm
  Nested iteration
  Index : cm_lastname_ix
```

UNION ALL

The SQL Server 6.5 optimizer presents its SHOWPLAN output a little differently when you request a UNION ALL that operates on a view or derived table. For example, look at the following query and query plan. The 'sample1' and 'sample2' tables have identical layouts:

```
select * from sample1
union all
select * from sample2
```

```
STEP 1
The type of query is SELECT
FROM TABLE
sample1
Nested iteration
Table Scan
STEP 2
The type of query is SELECT
FROM TABLE
sample2
Nested iteration
Table Scan
```

The change occurs when we create a view that incorporates the above two tables and then retrieve data from it:

```
create view V_1 as
select * from sample1
union all
select * from sample2

select * from V_1

STEP 1
The type of query is SELECT
FROM TABLE
sample1
Nested iteration
Table Scan
UNION ALL
  FROM TABLE
  sample2
  Nested iteration
  Table Scan
```

Compare the two query plans. The optimizer now indents the query plan for the second table when we're examining a derived table or view.

CONSTRAINT

Another SQL Server 6.5 optimizer enhancement relates to queries that reference constraints. Recall that you can set constraints to enforce referential and data integrity, as well as business rules. SQL Server now reports situations where the engine needs to perform constraint checking to satisfy a database operation. For example, suppose that you have two tables that have a parent-child relationship, defined by a foreign key. If we attempt to delete a parent record before deleting appropriate child records, SQL Server returns an error:

```
STEP 1
The type of query is DELETE
The update mode is deferred
FROM TABLE
parent
Nested iteration
Using Clustered Index
FROM TABLE
child
CONSTRAINT : nested iteration
Table Scan
TO TABLE
parent
Msg 547, Level 16, State 2
DELETE statement conflicted with COLUMN REFERENCE
constraint 'FK__child__parent_id__13D1FA5A'. The
conflict occurred in database 'db51', table 'child',
column 'parent_id'
Command has been aborted.
```

If there is no corresponding child record, the delete operation proceeds normally:

```
STEP 1
The type of query is DELETE
The update mode is deferred
FROM TABLE
parent
Nested iteration
Using Clustered Index
FROM TABLE
child
CONSTRAINT : nested iteration
Table Scan
TO TABLE
parent
```

In both cases, notice the new part of the query plan that deals with the constraint evaluation.

Programming considerations

Application developers have a degree of control when it comes to the methods that the optimizer chooses to process database requests. In this section, we examine a variety of techniques that you can use to suggest courses of action. These include optimizer hints and query processing options.

Giving hints to the optimizer

Index suggestions

One of the advantages of using a database engine with an advanced query optimizer is that it frees the developer from having to choose the database access method. Normally, the SQL Server optimizer chooses the most efficient query plan; there's generally no need for the programmer or DBA to second-guess the optimizer. There are times, however, where you may want to fine-tune a query. In this section, we look at two indexing hints that you can provide to the optimizer.

INDEX

You can override the indexing choice that SQL Server would make by providing an index name when you issue your SELECT statement. For single-table queries, this generally isn't necessary. For example, in the following query, there are two good candidate indexes in place on the 'customer_master' table. Notice how the optimizer makes two passes through the table, using the 'cm_lastname_ix' index to locate records that match the 'last_name' criteria, and the 'cm_city_ix' index to find 'city' matching records:

```
select  *
from    customer_master
where   last_name = "Norton"
or      city = "Brooklyn"

STEP 1
The type of query is SELECT
FROM TABLE
customer_master
Nested iteration
Index : cm_lastname_ix
FROM TABLE
customer_master
Nested iteration
```

```
Index : cm_city_ix
FROM TABLE
customer_master
Nested iteration
Using Dynamic Index
```

For multiple table queries, there can be situations where overriding the op-timizer's index choice is worth investigating. For example, look at the following query and query plan. Note that the tables in this query have indexes as fol-lows:

```
customer_master:
     primary key:            account_number
     cm_lastname_ix:         last_name
customer_flights:
     cf_account_number_ix:  account_number
     cf_miles_ix:            miles
```

```
select  cm.last_name,
        cf.flight_date
from    customer_master cm,
        customer_flights cf
where   cm.account_number = cf.account_number
and     cf.flight_date between "07/01/97" and "12/31/97"
and     cf.miles between 500 and 1000
```

```
STEP 1
The type of query is SELECT
FROM TABLE
customer_flights cf
Row estimate:   754
Cost estimate: 47776
Nested iteration
Table Scan
FROM TABLE
customer_master cm
JOINS WITH
customer_flights cf
Row estimate:   754
Cost estimate: 24128
Nested iteration
Using Clustered Index
```

The optimizer did not choose to use the index on the 'miles' column in the 'customer_flights' table. After examining the query and query plan, you decide that this index might yield better response than the table scan. You alter the query as follows:

```
select  cm.last_name,
        cf.flight_date
from    customer_master cm,
        customer_flights cf (index=cf_miles_ix)
where   cm.account_number = cf.account_number
and     cf.flight_date between "07/01/97" and "12/31/97"
and     cf.miles between 500 and 1000

STEP 1
The type of query is SELECT
FROM TABLE
customer_flights cf
Row estimate:  754
Cost estimate: 48624
Nested iteration
Index : cf_miles_ix
FROM TABLE
customer_master cm
JOINS WITH
customer_flights cf
Row estimate:  754
Cost estimate: 24128
Nested iteration
Using Clustered Index
```

This modification greatly improved query response time, since the engine was now easily able to find records in the 'customer_flights' table that matches the 'miles' requirement.

You can also force the optimizer to perform a table scan, regardless of indexes, by setting the 'index' value equal to 0. For example, this query tells the optimizer to use a table scan:

```
select  *
from    customer_master (index=0)
where   account_number = 4499554

STEP 1
The type of query is SELECT
FROM TABLE
customer_master
Nested iteration
Table Scan
```

Of course, in this case, requesting a table scan would lead to disastrous performance. You can ensure that the optimizer selects a clustered index (if one exists), by setting 'index' equal to 1:

```
select *
from    customer_master (index=1)
where   account_number = 4499554

STEP 1
The type of query is SELECT
FROM TABLE
customer_master
Nested iteration
Using Clustered Index
```

FASTFIRSTROW

Microsoft SQL Server 6.0 includes new, asynchronous, read-ahead functionality. This means that there are situations when the optimizer picks table scans and sorting over non-clustered indexes when processing an ORDER BY, because the new functionality can actually sort data faster performing table scans than using non-clustered index sorts. You can override this feature and force the optimizer to use the non-clustered index by providing a FASTFIRSTROW optimizer hint. Setting this value tells the optimizer to use a non-clustered index on the ORDER BY column, instead of performing a table scan and building a work table. FASTFIRSTROW tends to bring the first rows back more quickly but takes longer to return the rest of the result set. This may be helpful for applications where users want the first screenful of information as quickly as possible and are willing to wait for the rest of the data.

Like many of the optimizer hints, you should carefully evaluate asking SQL Server to disregard the results of its query optimization calculations regarding asynchronous read-ahead and indexes: Your suggestions may actually hurt overall performance. For example, look at the following two queries and query plans:

Query 1:

```
select *
from    customer_master
where   account_balance between 35000 and 40000
order by last_name
```

```
STEP 1
The type of query is INSERT
The update mode is direct
Worktable created for ORDER BY
FROM TABLE
customer_master
Row estimate:  12495
Cost estimate: 28608
Nested iteration
Table Scan
TO TABLE
Worktable 1
STEP 2
The type of query is SELECT
This step involves sorting
FROM TABLE
Worktable 1
Row estimate:  12495
Cost estimate: 24897
Using GETSORTED Table Scan
```

Query 2:

```
select *
from   customer_master (fastfirstrow)
where  account_balance between 35000 and 40000
order by last_name

STEP 1
The type of query is SELECT
FROM TABLE
customer_master
Row estimate:  12495
Cost estimate: 249116
Nested iteration
Index : cm_lastname_ix
```

On first examination, query 2's query plan, which uses FASTFIRSTROW, appears simpler: The optimizer isn't creating a work table, and it is using the 'cm_lastname_ix' index to sort. However, query 2 took four minutes to complete; query 1 finished in less than ten seconds. Look at the difference in I/O operations:

Query 1:

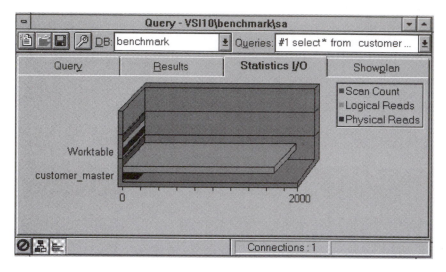

Figure 4.1

Query 2:

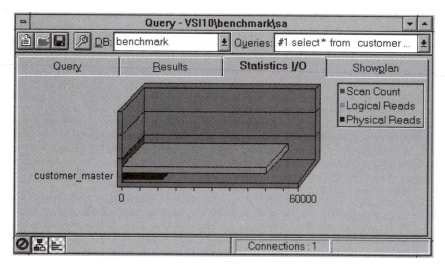

Figure 4.2

The second query plan required a much higher number of I/O operations. This was also reflected in the huge increase in the amount of time necessary to return results. This demonstrates the potential danger of FASTFIRSTROW. In most cases, it's probably best let the optimizer do its job and choose the best plan.

Join suggestions

SET FORCEPLAN

When you request a table join, the optimizer may not process the tables in the order that you specify. Since the optimizer is costbased, it may be able to find a faster join sequence. In most cases, it's best to let the optimizer make this decision. However, you can force the optimizer to process tables in the exact order that you specified in your query, by setting the FORCEPLAN option:

```
SET FORCEPLAN ON
```

This setting remains in effect for your session; it does not affect any other users. As with any optimizer setting, it's a good idea to research the performance impact of parameter settings before committing them to production.

Locking suggestions

You can request a variety of locking modes from within an SQL statement. In the following section, we briefly examine each of these locking modes. For more information about this subject, see the "Concurrency" section in Chapter 7.

Insert row-level locking

Prior to version 6.5, SQL Server only supported page-level locking. For many data access operations, this was not an issue. However, certain situations could pose a performance problem. Let's examine one of the most common of these situations, along with how SQL Server's new Insert Row-Level locking feature now helps eliminate this possible obstacle.

In this case, imagine that you have a number of users or processes all inserting data into one table at the same time. If the table had a clustered index (meaning that its data was ordered by its primary key), chances are that users would be entering data onto different pages, since it's unlikely that all users would be typing in sequential primary keys. Since the users would be working on different data and index pages, there would be little chance of two or more users hitting the same page at the same time. Things become a little more complicated, however, if any of these conditions apply:

- **The primary key is defined with the identity attribute.**   By definition, identity column's values increase sequentially, usually by one (although you can set this to be a different number). In cases such as this, SQL Server stores each new row on the same page as the previous row until the engine determines that it needs a new page to hold additional rows.

- **The table has indexes, but none are defined as clustered.**   When there are non-clustered indexes on a table, SQL Server uses the last page of the table as the location for new rows.

- **The table has no indexes.**   When a table has no indexes, SQL Server also adds new rows onto the last page of the table.

In all three of these circumstances, there is a potential for a "hotspot" to develop. You can best think of a hotspot as a location that many users or processes need to access at the same time. This forms a bottleneck, which leads to degraded performance, as users are forced to wait until the resource (in this case, the last page of a table) is available.

Version 6.5 addresses this problem with a feature known as Insert Row-Level locking (IRL). IRL lets multiple users lock different rows on the same page at the same time. This helps increase concurrency by eliminating the page-level hotspot. Administrators use the 'sp_tableoption' stored procedure to enable or disable the IRL feature for a particular table. For example, the following call turns on IRL for the 'customer_flights' table:

```
sp_tableoption 'customer_flights', 'insert row lock','true'
```

To disable IRL, simply change the last parameter from 'true' to 'false.' You can also use this stored procedure to learn what the current IRL status is for all tables:

```
sp_tableoption '%.%', 'insert row lock'
```

Option Status	Table Name	Owner Name
False	customer_master	dbo
True	customer_flights	dbo
.	.	.
.	.	.
True	partners	dbo

IRL introduces two new lock modes:

- **Insert_page.**   This lock signifies that a user is inserting data onto a particular page within a table that has been IRL-enabled. Multiple users can hold this lock at the same time on a page.

- **Link_page.**   As pages fill, SQL Server directs new data onto additional pages. Part of this operation requires that these pages be linked to the table. If IRL is enabled for the table, the engine grants a link_page lock to the first transaction that uses one of these newly linked pages. The link_page lock is actually an upgrade of the trans-action's insert_page lock. No other users or processes can then receive an insert_page lock on the table until the link_page lock is released.

Should you take advantage of IRL? We'll discuss this in more detail later, but for now, the answer to this question is heavily dependent on your application profile, user load, and database design. Generally, if you have an already-running application that performs well, there's no need to introduce a new locking scheme. IRL provides some nice benefits, but at a cost of potential deadlocks as well as additional transaction log consumption. On the other hand, if you are designing a new application that should see many users adding data at the same time into the same tables, then you might consider trying IRL to see what impact it has on performance. As is the case with any anticipated performance benefit, keep careful records of system response before and after any changes.

HOLDLOCK

Normally, SQL Server releases shared locks when it has finished processing the desired table or page. Setting an optimizer hint of HOLDLOCK forces SQL Server to hold the lock until the entire transaction has completed. This setting can greatly reduce concurrency, so use it carefully. Let's look at a situation where this lock level would be justified.

If you're running an automatic data update process that reads rows from a table and then modifies these rows based on their original values, your goal should be to preserve these rows for the duration of the entire transaction. You could lock the entire table, but a less restrictive approach would be to use the HOLDLOCK option:

```
begin transaction
select * from table_a (holdlock)
where lookup_value between 0 and 2000
  . . .
  . . .
update table_a set numeric_data = 25
where lookup_value between 0 and 2000
  . . .
  . . .
```

Your reason for using HOLDLOCK is that you don't want anyone changing the values that you've read (for those rows with a 'lookup_value' between 0 and 2000). You haven't even touched this information, but you will later in the transaction. If someone were to modify one or more of the rows you read, your program might make an incorrect decision during the UPDATE statement.

NOLOCK

If you pass an optimizer hint of NOLOCK to SQL Server, you are asking the engine not to shield you from a potential "phantom" row. This means that your query operates in "dirty read" mode. Your program may see data that is uncommitted or data that may eventually be rolled back. The benefit of this optimizer hint is that it increases concurrency, but it has the potential to reduce data consistency. Suppose that two users are working with the same table. User 1 begins a transaction and inserts a row into a table. Normally, user 2 won't see this row until user 1 commits her transaction. This is SQL Server's default behavior. However, if user 2 ran the following query, he will have access to user 1's not-yet-committed data:

```
select * from sample_table (nolock)
```

Take care when requesting this option, since you might end up seeing (and making decisions on) data that is not stable. However, there are times when this setting does have its uses. For instance, you might want to run a "quick-and-dirty" report that can tolerate uncommitted information.

PAGLOCK

An optimizer hint of PAGLOCK tells SQL Server to request share locks at the page level, instead of at the table level. Since this can greatly increase the number of locks within a transaction, it's possible that you may run out of this resource. However, this does increase concurrency, since you will be able to modify other, nonlocked pages within the table. This is the default method chosen by SQL Server and corresponds to an isolation level of read committed.

TABLOCK

The optimizer hint of TABLOCK does the exact opposite of PAGLOCK: This hint instructs SQL Server to place one shared lock on the entire table. The lock is held until the transaction completes. This reduces the overall number of potential locks, from one per affected page to one for the entire table. However, other users will not be able to update other parts of the table if there is a shared lock on the entire table.

```
begin transaction
select * from awards (tablock)
 . . .
 . . .
```

Other users can read information from this table, but if they try to perform an update operation, their programs will block until you've released the table lock.

TABLOCKX

The TABLOCKX optimizer hint is identical to the TABLOCK hint, with one exception: TABLOCKX places an exclusive lock on the table for the duration of the entire transaction. If you are attempting this operation in a multiuser environment, it's possible that you may never successfully achieve the exclusive lock, since other users or processes may already be accessing the table.

When would this type of access be necessary? Generally, you would only request an exclusive lock when updating all rows in a table:

```
begin transaction
declare upd_cur cursor for
select account_balance from customer_master (tablockx)
for update
open upd_cur
fetch upd_cur
update customer_master
set account_balance = account_balance + 500
where current of upd_cur
. . .
. . .
```

Your program now has exclusive control of the whole 'customer_master' table. You relinquish this control only when you commit or roll back the transaction. No one else on the system can update, or even view, any data from this table until you finish.

UPDLOCK

An optimizer hint of UPDLOCK tells SQL Server to hold update locks instead of shared locks while accessing data in the table. In addition, SQL Server holds these locks until the transaction has finished. You are most likely to reap the benefits of this optimizer hint when you are reading information from a table that you intend to update after the query:

```
begin transaction
select account_number, account_balance
from customer_master (updlock)
where city = "Paterson"
. . .
. . .
update customer_master
set account_balance = account_balance * 1.25
where city = "Paterson"
commit transaction
```

Setting the UPDLOCK option forces SQL Server to use update locks on all appropriate pages, instead of the less-restrictive shared lock, which is the default. This setting lets you proceed with the transaction, knowing that others can look at these rows, but no one can change them until you complete your work.

Query processing options

When you're developing a new application or maintaining an existing system, there are several query processing options that you can set to speed up your development and testing efforts.

SET FMTONLY

You can ask the optimizer to return only metadata information to the client by setting the FMTONLY option to ON. When you've selected this option, the engine does not process any rows or return them to the application. This is very useful when you want to see exactly which columns would be returned by a query without actually running the query.

SET NOEXEC

When you submit a database request, the engine performs two tasks: compiling the request and then executing the request. During development and research, there are many times where you may only want to see the query plan; it's not actually necessary to run the query. For example, suppose that you are testing some complex queries on a production system. Your goal is to determine the most efficient methods of issuing these queries, but you face a problem: If you let these complex queries run, you may bog down the system and irritate your users. How can you complete your research while avoiding this problem? You can ask the engine not to execute the query by setting the NOEXEC query option. You would use the following syntax to request query compilation without execution:

```
SET NOEXEC ON
```

This setting affects only your session; other users continue to work normally. Once you're satisfied with the query plan, you can resume normal processing by issuing:

```
SET NOEXEC OFF
```

SET PARSEONLY

You can go one step further in reducing the amount of processing that SQL Server performs on your SQL statements: You can request that the optimizer only check syntax, skipping compilation and execution. This is helpful when you only want to ensure that your statement is syntactically correct. You can request this syntax validity check by running:

```
SET PARSEONLY ON
```

Like most other SET options, this parameter affects only your session.

SET ROWCOUNT

SQL Server lets you limit the number of rows sent from the database engine to the front-end process, by setting the ROWCOUNT parameter. There are a number of situations where this can be very helpful, including:

- **Controlling user queries.** End users have a way of issuing long, complex queries and then complaining when the queries take a long time to return all rows. You can block these enormous result sets by setting ROWCOUNT to a reasonable number.

- **Reducing client/server traffic.** One way to bog down a network is to send huge volumes of unnecessary data from the server to the clients. You can govern the number of rows sent over the network by providing a value for the ROWCOUNT parameter. However, setting this parameter doesn't attack the root cause of excessive client/server traffic, which is usually tied to some aspect of the database design or processing environment. With this in mind, don't forget to analyze your client/server and database environment to determine instances where you can minimize this traffic.

- **Streamlining development.** When you're developing or maintaining an application, you probably don't need to run your long queries all the way to completion. You can halt processing after a few rows.

To limit the number of rows affected by database operations, use this syntax:

```
SET ROWCOUNT n
```

where n is the maximum number of rows that you want to be affected by the operation. You can reset this value by setting ROWCOUNT equal to 0.

Be careful when using SET ROWCOUNT, because this setting affects *all* database operations, including INSERT, UPDATE, and DELETE. SQL Server will stop processing data when the number of affected rows equals or exceeds the ROWCOUNT setting, regardless of where the database operation stands. Therefore, it's conceivable that a user could mistakenly believe that a database operation has successfully completed, when it has in fact halted. For example, look at the following operation, where we're trying to update all rows in the 'customer_master' table, raising each customer's account balance for those who have more than 30,000 miles in their account. Before running the operation, we've set the ROWCOUNT parameter to 1000:

```
set rowcount 1000

STEP 1
The type of query is SETRCON

update customer_master
set account_balance = account_balance * 1.10
where account_balance > 30000

STEP 1
The type of query is UPDATE
The update mode is direct
FROM TABLE
customer_master
Nested iteration
Table Scan
TO TABLE
customer_master
(1000 rows affected)
```

Notice how the update operation finished after exactly 1000 rows. There were probably many more eligible customers, but they won't receive their bonus. With this in mind, consider using the ROWCOUNT setting only in circumstances where users are retrieving information from the database.

The UPDATE STATISTICS command

To process indexed database operations as efficiently as possible, SQL Server keeps track of index key values, including distribution and values. This information helps the optimizer to make the best possible decisions. SQL Server runs UPDATE STATISTICS whenever you create an index or re-create an index. If you expect that your index key values will change over time, you should periodically rerun this important command. If your key values change and you don't refresh the key distribution statistics, it's possible that the optimizer might make a wrong query-processing decision based on this old information. While this won't affect the actual data that the engine returns, it could substantially slow down system performance.

The syntax for UPDATE STATISTICS is:

```
UPDATE STATISTICS
        [[database.]owner.]table_name [index_name]
```

This command has a high degree of granularity. This means that you can be very selective when reconstructing index statistics. Since UPDATE STATISTICS is a very time-consuming process, it's a good idea to run it during off-hours. This helps to minimize any potential negative impacts on user processes. You can use the task scheduling features of SQL Server to plan for these important operations. For example, suppose that we want to schedule a one-time UPDATE STATISTICS request on the 'customer_flights' table:

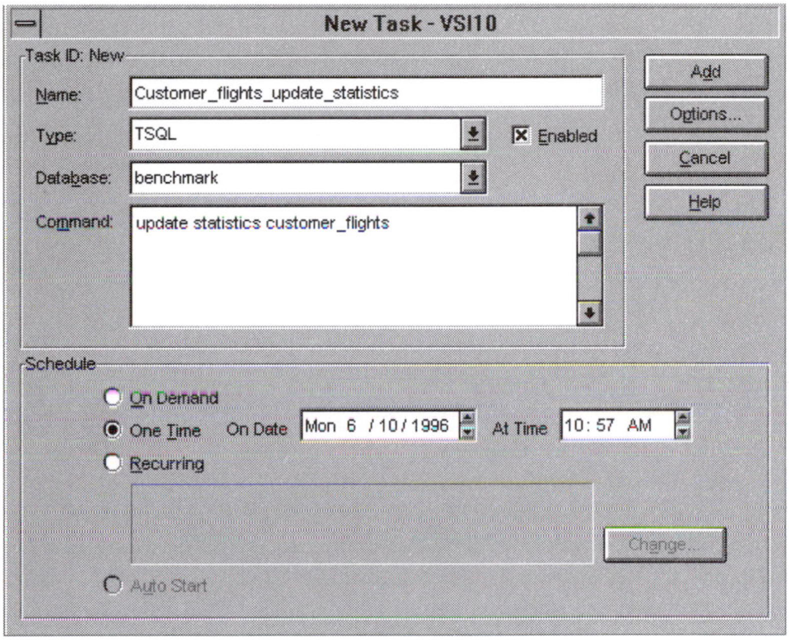

Figure 4.3

DBCC SHOW_STATISTICS

To learn about an index' existing distribution, you can run the DBCC SHOW_STATSTICS command:

```
dbcc show_statistics(customer_master, cm_lastname_ix)

STEP 1
The type of query is DBCC_CMD
```

```
SQL Server Parse and Compile Time:
   cpu time = 0 ms.
Updated                 Rows      Steps      Density
-------------------- --------- ---------- -----------
Mar 19 1996 10:37PM  49981        41         .000054


(1 row(s) affected)

All density             Columns
---------------------- -----------------------------
.000054                 last_name


(1 row(s) affected)

Steps
-----------------------------------------
Aaron
Aquilas
Bixby
 .  .  .
 .  .  .
 .  .  .
Yancy
Yugovitz
Zlotnick


(41 row(s) affected)
```

How can you interpret this information? Generally, the lower the "density," the more selective the index. Multiplying the 'density' value by the number of rows in the table tells you how many duplicates you can expect to find. In this example, multiplying these two values yields 2.69. This means that there are only 2.69 potential duplicates based on 'last_name.'

You can also use the SQL Enterprise Manager tool to get the same information. In this example, we're looking at the 'customer_master' table's primary key:

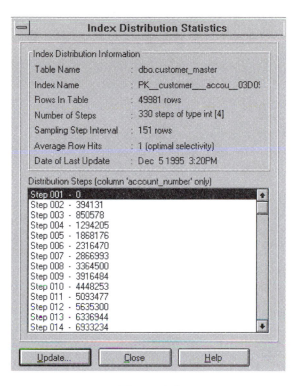

Figure 4.4

Part 2

Improving Database Access

In Part 2, we explore how to design, develop, and maintain your applications so that they perform as efficiently as possible. Since Structured Query Language (SQL) is the primary means of communicating with an SQL Server database, we devote the first section to a discussion about optimizing your application's SQL code. Many developers choose to streamline database access by using stored procedures and triggers, so we then spend some time reviewing these important features. Next, we cover some general areas of interest, including transactions, cursors, and concurrency. Finally, we close out Part 2 by examining how to boost client/server performance.

We've deliberately steered clear of reviewing individual client-based development tools or languages. There are many different languages and tools on the market that incorporate database access capabilities. To cover even a small sample of these products could fill several books. Fortunately for developers, there are several books on the market for most of these languages and tools. To get the finest SQL Server performance from any of these products, your best bet is to combine the knowledge that you can get from these language- or tool-specific books with the efficient relational database design, SQL, stored procedures, and engine management techniques that we cover in this book.

Chapter 5
SQL Tips

With the exception of your database design, your SQL statements have the most impact on system performance. Consequently, it is a good idea to carefully examine your SQL during development as well as during production.

In this chapter, we focus on some of the most common areas for SQL performance improvement. We begin by getting a better understanding of joins, including some of the new join concepts introduced in SQL Server 6.5. Data types can affect performance, so we'll explore the costs of non-numeric versus numeric joins and filters, as well as character substring searches. Temporary tables are capable of having a big effect on performance too, so we'll learn where and when to use them. Views, embedded SQL math, subqueries, and unions are all helpful features, but each of them has a cost that you should consider. We'll also look at the new ROLLUP and CUBE operators that are part of SQL Server 6.5. We close out the chapter by examining how to improve large data modification operations, including INSERT and DELETE.

If your system is in production and you have a large volume of data, consider creating a small scale test case before you implement any of the schema or SQL changes suggested in this chapter. This would involve the following steps:

1. Create copies of the existing tables' schema, including indexes, constraints, triggers, and rules.

2. Populate the new tables. Keep in mind that if you underpopulate these tables, you run the risk of the optimizer choosing different query plans in the test environment than it would in the production environment. For this reason, once you finish your schema or query changes, it's a good idea to test them in the production environment as well.

3. Turn on SHOWPLAN.

4. Make your schema or SQL alterations.

5. Analyze the new schema or SQL statement in the test environment.

6. Adjust the query or database design to improve the query plan.

7. Verify the new schema or SQL statement in the production environment.

You should modify your production environment only if you are convinced that your change improves performance.

Types of joins

Joins let you match data from multiple tables, based on significant key information. Prior to SQL Server 6.5, the engine supported several kind of joins. Beginning with SQL Server 6.5, Microsoft has enhanced the engine to cover ANSI standard joins as well. In this chapter, we cover a number of topics that relate to joins. Therefore, before getting much further, let's look at the various types of joins that SQL Server provides.

Before beginning our discussion on all of the diversified types of joins, let's create and populate two simple, model tables that will help illustrate our examples:

Table 5.1   cities

city_id	city_name
1	Geneva
2	Singapore
3	Phoenix
4	Sao Paolo
5	Tangier

Table 5.2 weather_reports

report_id	city_id	report_date	report_temperature
1	1	Jan 30 1997	16
2	1	Jan 31 1997	19
3	1	Feb 01 1997	22
4	3	Jan 30 1997	45
5	3	Jan 31 1997	51
6	4	Jan 30 1997	75
7	4	Jan 31 1997	77

Standard join

When we request a standard join, we're asking the engine to concatenate the results from two (or more) tables that match on a certain key value. This is the simplest, and most common type of join operation. Using the model tables and data listed above, look at the following query, along with its output:

```
select city_name, report_date, report_temperature
from cities c, weather_reports w
where c.city_id = w.city_id

city_name              report_date      report_temperature
------------------     ---------------  ------------------
Geneva                 Jan 30 1997      16
Geneva                 Jan 31 1997      19
Geneva                 Feb 1 1997       22
Phoenix                Jan 30 1997      45
Phoenix                Jan 31 1997      51
Sao Paolo              Jan 30 1997      75
Sao Paolo              Jan 31 1997      77
```

In this case, we want SQL Server to return only those rows where a match exists between the 'city_id' columns in both tables. Consequently, we won't see anything about cities that haven't had a corresponding entry in the 'weather_reports' table. We also won't see any rows in the 'weather_reports' table that don't have a match in the 'cities' table.

Cross join

A cross join concatenates all rows from the first table with all rows from the second table. This is also known as a "Cartesian product." Chances are, you won't make much use of this type of join, since it doesn't normally yield very helpful information. The only times when you may actually need this operation is when you want to see all possible combinations of two or more tables:

```
select city_name, report_date, report_temperature
from cities c cross join weather_reports w
```

```
city_name                report_date          report_temperature
-------------------      ---------------      ------------------
Geneva                   Jan 30 1997          16
Geneva                   Jan 31 1997          19
Geneva                   Feb 1 1997           22
Geneva                   Jan 30 1997          45
Geneva                   Jan 31 1997          51
Geneva                   Jan 30 1997          75
Geneva                   Jan 31 1997          77
  .                          .                   .
  .                          .                   .
  .                          .                   .
Tangier                  Jan 30 1997          16
Tangier                  Jan 31 1997          19
Tangier                  Feb 1 1997           22
Tangier                  Jan 30 1997          45
Tangier                  Jan 31 1997          51
Tangier                  Jan 30 1997          75
Tangier                  Jan 31 1997          77
```

Inner join

An inner join, while slightly different in syntax than the standard join, still produces the same output as a standard join:

```
select city_name, report_date, report_temperature
from cities c inner join
```

```
weather_reports w on c.city_id = w.city_id
```

```
city_name              report_date       report_temperature
-------------------    --------------    ------------------
Geneva                 Jan 30 1997       16
Geneva                 Jan 31 1997       19
Geneva                 Feb 1 1997        22
Phoenix                Jan 30 1997       45
Phoenix                Jan 31 1997       51
Sao Paolo              Jan 30 1997       75
Sao Paolo              Jan 31 1997       77
```

Left outer join

When you request a left outer join, you're asking the engine to list all rows in the left table, even if there isn't a corresponding row in the right table. SQL Server loops through all of the left table's rows, looking for a match in the right table. If it finds a match, it prints the right table's data. If there is no match, it still prints the left row, but places a '(null)' tag instead of the right table's data:

```
select city_name, report_date, report_temperature
from cities c left join weather_reports w on
c.city_id = w.city_id
```

```
city_name              report_date       report_temperature
-------------------    --------------    ------------------
Geneva                 Jan 30 1997       16
Geneva                 Jan 31 1997       19
Geneva                 Feb 1 1997        22
Singapore              (null)            (null)
Phoenix                Jan 30 1997       45
Phoenix                Jan 31 1997       51
Sao Paolo              Jan 30 1997       75
Sao Paolo              Jan 31 1997       77
Tangier                (null)            (null)
```

In our sample data, Singapore and Tangier have no temperature reports. Since we asked for a left outer join, SQL Server still lists these rows, but with no corresponding temperature information. Left outer joins are very common when you want to produce a master-detail report that displays all master rows, even those without matching detail data.

Right outer join

This type of join is the exact opposite of a left outer join: SQL Server first looks at the right table's rows, looking for a match on the left. Using our sample tables, look at the following two queries to see how important table location is:

```
select city_name, report_date, report_temperature
from cities c right join weather_reports w on
c.city_id = w.city_id
```

city_name	report_date	report_temperature
Geneva	Jan 30 1997	16
Geneva	Jan 31 1997	19
Geneva	Feb 1 1997	22
Phoenix	Jan 30 1997	45
Phoenix	Jan 31 1997	51
Sao Paolo	Jan 30 1997	75
Sao Paolo	Jan 31 1997	77

Even though we asked for an outer join, the right table (weather_reports) doesn't have any nonmatched rows in the left table (cities), so the engine only returns matched rows. Look what happens when we simply switch the table order in the FROM clause:

```
select city_name, report_date, report_temperature
from weather_reports w right join cities c on
c.city_id = w.city_id
```

city_name	report_date	report_temperature
Geneva	Jan 30 1997	16
Geneva	Jan 31 1997	19
Geneva	Feb 1 1997	22
Singapore	(null)	(null)
Phoenix	Jan 30 1997	45
Phoenix	Jan 31 1997	51
Sao Paolo	Jan 30 1997	75
Sao Paolo	Jan 31 1997	77
Tangier	(null)	(null)

Now, 'weather_reports' is on the left, and 'cities' is on the right. Since we've asked for a right outer join, SQL Server first looks at all rows in the 'cities' table and then compares them with the 'weather_reports' table.

Full outer join

The full outer join was introduced in SQL Server 6.5. The engine first takes all rows from one of the tables and inserts them in a work table. Next, SQL Server moves on to join this work table with the other tables in the query that match on the join criteria. As a last step, the engine takes all rows from the other tables that didn't match on the join and adds them to the end of the result set. Using our sample tables, look at the query, query plan, and results for this request:

```
select city_name, report_date, report_temperature
from cities c full join weather_reports w on
c.city_id = w.city_id

STEP 1
The type of query is INSERT
The update mode is direct
Worktable created for REFORMATTING
FROM TABLE
cities
Nested iteration
Table Scan
TO TABLE
Worktable 1
STEP 2
The type of query is SELECT
FROM TABLE
weather_reports w
Nested iteration
Table Scan
FULL OUTER JOIN : nested iteration
   FROM TABLE
   Worktable 1
   Nested iteration
   Using Clustered Index
```

city_name	report_date	report_temperature
Geneva	Jan 30 1997	16
Geneva	Jan 31 1997	19
Geneva	Feb 1 1997	22
Phoenix	Jan 30 1997	45
Phoenix	Jan 31 1997	51
Sao Paolo	Jan 30 1997	75
Sao Paolo	Jan 31 1997	77
Singapore	(null)	(null)
Tangier	(null)	(null)

Numeric vs. non-numeric joins and searches

A surprising number of developers and DBAs assign the CHAR data type to columns that really only contain numeric information. This can decrease performance on filters and join conditions, as well as increase storage requirements. For example, assume that you have an application that tracks pieces of equipment that are stored at several different sites:

Table 5.3   Inventory_header

part_number	part_desc .....
78	Monochrome ASCII terminal
143	Monochrome 3270 terminal
.	.
.	.
11058	Filing cabinet

Table 5.4   Inventory_detail

location	part_number	part_count....
Phoenix	78	0
Detroit	78	25
New York	78	148
.	.	.
.	.	.
Tampa	11058	17
Boston	11058	62

During your design, you note that the 'part_number' is a number that is always between 1 and 12000. However, when you create the tables, you define the fields as a CHAR(20), and you place an index on these columns in each table.

A commonly used report in your application prints a listing of the count of inventory items at all locations:

```
select b.location,  a.part_number,
       a.part_desc, b.part_count
from   inventory_header a, inventory_detail b
where  a.part_number = b.part_number
order by b.location, a.part_number
```

If the 'part_number' columns in both tables is defined as CHAR(20), the join operation requires the engine to compare the values in each table byte-by-byte, up to 20 times per row.

Since you know from your research that the 'part_number' column is always numeric and always between 1 and 12000, you should redefine the column in both tables as SMALLINT. This aids your application in several ways:

- Since SMALLINTs are stored in only two bytes, you save a significant amount of CPU work during join operations or filter conditions, especially if there are many rows to process. Instead of comparing up to 20 bytes to see if two rows are logical join candidates, the engine can finish its work after two bytes.

- You save 18 bytes per row per table (assuming that it was previously defined as CHAR(20)).

- You save 18 bytes per row per table for all indexes that use this column. Your savings are even greater when you factor in index B-Tree depth.

Ideally, as part of your initial systems analysis, you determine which fields should be stored as TINYINT, SMALLINT, INTEGER, or BIT. DBAs can use SQL Server's user-defined data type feature to assign logical names to specific data types. This can simplify the task of table creation. We covered this subject in Part 1 on efficient database design. If you're running a production system and don't have the luxury of making database changes, you should still consider examining the data in CHAR columns to see if there are any candidates for data conversion. Perhaps you could make this type of change during the next application upgrade.

When designing your tables, pay special attention to join columns; many times you find a CHAR field being joined to an INTEGER or SMALLINT. SQL Server blocks this type of join, with the following error message:

```
Msg 260, Level 16, State 1
Disallowed implicit conversion from datatype 'char' to
datatype 'int'
   Table: 'tempdb.dbo.parent', Column: 'col1'
   Use the CONVERT function to run this query.
```

SQL batches

One helpful feature that SQL Server provides is its batch SQL capability. Batch operations let you submit a group of several SQL operations at once. You terminate a batch with an end-of-batch marker (the GO command). In many cases, administrators and developers find it useful to group these batches into scripts, which can be run via a number of tools. There are situations where this can help performance, but there are also occasions where batches can hinder throughput. First, let's look at some rules that you must follow when requesting an SQL batch.

- If you're using a version of SQL Server prior to 6.5, you won't be able to create a table with rules or defaults and then insert data into the same table within the batch. For example, the following code fails:

```
create table demo_batch
(col1 integer default 0, col2 integer default 4)
insert into demo_batch default values
go


Msg 233, Level 16, State 2
The column col1 in table demo_batch may not be null.
Msg 233, Level 16, State 2
The column col2 in table demo_batch may not be null.
```

In this case, you would need to break up the batch into two separate statements by adding a 'go' between the 'create' and 'insert' operations.

- You can't drop an object and then attempt to re-create it during the same batch:

```
drop table demo_batch
create table demo_batch
(col1 integer default 0, col2 integer default 4)
go


Msg 2714, Level 16, State 1
There is already an object named 'demo_batch' in
the database.
```

This type of error message is confusing, so it's important to make sure that you separate these operations with a 'go.'

- You are limited to a maximum of 128 kilobytes of inserted or updated data in a batch. If you exceed this amount of information, SQL Server returns an error. Realistically, it's not very likely that you would submit such an enormous batch, but it's a good idea to keep this limitation in mind when building your batches. Also, note that this restriction doesn't apply to data inserted or updated with the WRITE-TEXT or READTEXT functions.

- You can't submit any of the following statements within a batch:

```
CREATE DEFAULT
CREATE PROCEDURE
CREATE RULE
CREATE TRIGGER
CREATE VIEW
```

How should you decide when to create an SQL batch? There's no hard-and-fast rule, but you can follow some general guidelines.

- **Are the SQL statements related?**   If all of the SQL statements that make up your batch are related, then it makes sense to combine them into one operation. If they have no relation to each other, however, there still may be a good reason to treat them as part of the same batch operation if they don't interfere with each other.

- **Are you in a client/server environment?**   Minimizing communication between client and server is usually helpful in a client/server environment. If you are working in such a situation, batching SQL helps reduce the overall amount of communication, as well as the number of times that the client must await acknowledgment from the server.

- **Would the batch violate any of the earlier restrictions?**   If your batch would create rules or defaults or would contain greater than 128K of information, then there's no point in creating a batch only to have it fail.

CASE expression

SQL Server 6.0 introduced a new feature that adds new power to your SQL statements. In the past, if you wanted to perform conditional logic, you relied on your programming language, such as Transact-SQL, Visual Basic, or C. With the CASE expression, you can customize your queries to bring back more intelligent information. Let's use the weather report sample tables described in our join examples earlier to illustrate how you can use this expression to add new power to your queries.

Suppose that you want to write a simple query that reports on the conditions in a particular city, particularly with regard to required clothing for the current temperature. With traditional programming logic, your algorithm would look like this:

```
Get the weather report for the city.
Determine the reported temperature.
Compare the temperature with pre-set values
```

```
        to determine clothing requirements.
Report on the requirements.
Get the next row
```

There is an easier way to perform the same work. It involves using the CASE statement embedded inside the standard query:

```
select  c.city_id,
        c.city_name,
        w.report_date,
        w.report_temperature,
        "Clothing required" =
        case
            when w.report_temperature < 30
                then "Winter clothing"
            when w.report_temperature
                between 31 and 59
                then "Spring clothing"
            when w.report_temperature
                between 60 and 100
                then "Summer clothing"
        end
from cities c,
     weather_reports w
where c.city_id = w.city_id
```

This query produces the following output:

```
1    Geneva      Jan 30 1997    16          Winter clothing
1    Geneva      Jan 31 1997    19          Winter clothing
1    Geneva      Feb 1 1997     22          Winter clothing
3    Phoenix     Jan 30 1997    45          Spring clothing
3    Phoenix     Jan 31 1997    51          Spring clothing
4    Sao Paolo   Jan 30 1997    75          Summer clothing
4    Sao Paolo   Jan 31 1997    77          Summer clothing
```

This is far simpler than following the original algorithm. However, it's up to you as the programmer to make sure that your Boolean logic is correct; it wouldn't be good to have a row fit into more than one criterion. What happens when a row exists outside of your expected values? You can always use the ELSE keyword as a catch-all for those values that don't fit your expected model. For example, using the above query, suppose that a city reported a temperature of 200 degrees. How would you classify this? You could simply add another line to the 'case' statement to handle this condition:

```
case
    when w.report_temperature < 30
        then "Winter clothing"
    when w.report_temperature
        between 31 and 59
        then "Spring clothing"
    when w.report_temperature
        between 60 and 100
        then "Summer clothing"
    else
        then "Something very wrong"
end
```

COALESCE function

When you are using the CASE statement, there may be times when you want to return information based on whether a certain value is null or not. You can use the COALESCE function to simplify your code in these circumstances. For example, using the weather report example described earlier, suppose that we want to return either the temperature or a predetermined value of -99 if the temperature column is null. We could use one of the following two SQL commands:

```
select c.city_id,
       c.city_name,
       w.report_date,
       case
           when w.report_temperature is not null
               then w.report_temperature
           else
               -99
           end
from cities c,
     weather_reports w
where c.city_id = w.city_id
```

Using the COALESCE function slightly changes the SQL syntax:

```
select c.city_id,
       c.city_name,
       w.report_date,
       coalesce(w.report_temperature,-99)
from cities c,
     weather_reports w
where c.city_id = w.city_id
```

Another variation on the COALESCE function lets you return a value based on a list of possible values:

```
select c.city_id,
       c.city_name,
       w.report_date,
       coalesce(c.city_name, c.city_id)
from cities c,
     weather_reports w
where c.city_id = w.city_id
```

In this case, SQL Server returns either the 'city_name' or 'city_id' column. If 'city_name' is not null, then it is the first returned column. If 'city_name' is null, then SQL Server tests the 'city_id' column. If 'city_id' is not null, then it is returned instead. If both are null, then SQL Server returns null. You can place numerous values into this clause. Keep in mind that SQL Server returns the first non-null value, regardless of the length of the list.

NULLIF function

In contrast to the COALESCE function, which returns data if a value is not null, the NULLIF function tests for situations where two values are identical. If the two values are identical, NULLIF returns a null. If the two values are not equal, then NULLIF returns the first value:

```
create table demo_nullif
(
     col1 smallint,
     col2 smallint
)
insert into demo_nullif values (23,23)
insert into demo_nullif values (44,43)
insert into demo_nullif values (3,2)

select nullif(col1,col2) "Results"
from demo_nullif

Results
------
(null)
44
3
```

In this query, for each row in the table, NULLIF examined 'col1' and 'col2,' checking for equality. If the two values were equal (as in the first row), then SQL Server returned (null). In cases where the two values were not equal, SQL Server returned the data contained in 'col1.'

Substring searches

Searching through indexed character data is inherently easier when your search criteria start in the leftmost position and move to the right, than when your search criteria begin elsewhere in the data. For example, imagine that you were handed an enormous phone book and told to locate two types of information:

- All last names in the phone book that start with the letter "L."
- All entries in the phone book that have "L" as the third letter in the last name.

The first request would be far easier to produce, since the phone book is already "indexed" (by last name, first name). You would simply turn to the section of the book that starts with "L" and begin reading off the names until you found the first entry where the last name began with "M." This type of processing is analogous to running the following SQL statement:

```
select * from names
where last_name >= 'L%' and last_name < 'M%'
```

If there is an index on the 'last_name' column in the 'names' table, the optimizer uses it to help process the above query:

```
STEP 1
The type of query is SELECT
FROM TABLE
names
Nested iteration
Index : na_lastname_ix
```

The second request is harder to process, for both machines and humans. If you had the phone book in front of you, you would need to read the first three letters of every entry, from cover to cover. You would mark off all records where the third letter was "L." This type of processing is analogous to running the following SQL statement.

```
select * from names
where substring(last_name,3,1) = 'L'
```

```
STEP 1
The type of query is SELECT
FROM TABLE
names
Nested iteration
Table Scan
```

Even though there is an index on 'last_name,' the optimizer is unable to use it. To satisfy your request, the optimizer is forced to operate sequentially on what could be an enormous table. This definitely hurts performance.

If you find that there are cases where you need to sort on a noninitial substring, consider revising your database design. For example, assume that you are working with a table like this:

Table 5.5   Contracts

client_num	sign_date ....
E1203T	Dec 15 1996
S0054D	Nov 17 1996
C0078D	Apr 24 1996
W0003M	Feb 2 1996
E0144T	May 17 1996
C0012M	Sep 3 1996
.	.

This table tracks the status of contracts signed with clients, and has many thousands of rows. The 'client_num' field is indexed and is composed as follows:

1. The first byte indicates the customer's region.
2. The next four bytes are a sequential account number.
3. The last byte indicates where the lead came from (T: Telemarketing, D: Direct, M: Magazine).

At some point, a user requests a report that only retrieves information based on the account number, which is the middle four bytes of the 'client_num':

```
select * from contracts
where substring(client_num,2,5) between '0025'
and '0100'

STEP 1
The type of query is SELECT
```

```
FROM TABLE
contracts
Nested iteration
Table Scan
```

On a large table, this type of query results in very slow performance. It would be better to redesign the table and separate the account number into its own field. As an additional benefit, you could now change the 'account_num' data type to SMALLINT, which yields better performance on joins and conserves disk storage as well:

Table 5.6 Contracts

region_code	account_num	lead_source	sign_date ....
E	1203	T	Dec 15 1996
S	54	D	Nov 17 1996
C	78	D	Apr 24 1996
W	3	M	Feb 2 1996
E	144	T	May 17 1996
C	12	M	Sep 3 1996

```
select * from contracts
where account_num between 25 and 100

STEP 1
The type of query is SELECT
FROM TABLE
contracts
Nested iteration
Index : co_account_num_ix
```

There are also cases where you search for information by using the LIKE and MATCHES keywords. Again, watch for cases where you do not use initial strings. Run SHOWPLAN if you are not sure whether you are using indexes.

Temporary and work tables

Temporary and work tables are a double-edged sword: They can be very helpful when used properly; they can also greatly diminish your application's performance.

These tables are created in one of two ways:

- **Implicitly:**   by the SQL Server engine
- **Explicitly:**   by the application program or query

Temporary tables can be either local or global in scope. Let's explore temporary table scope, in conjunction with implicit and explicit temporary table types. We'll also look at situations where they can either help you or hurt your application's performance.

Local temporary tables

A local temporary table can be seen within your current connection; other users, and other connections, won't be able to see your local temporary table. This is useful when you don't need to share your temporary table's data with anyone else. When you close your connection and detach from the database, SQL Server automatically drops any of your local temporary tables. There are two ways to create a local temporary table:

```
CREATE TABLE #<TABLENAME> (...)
```

—or—

```
SELECT <COLUMN LIST> INTO #TABLENAME
```

The single pound sign in front of the table name is SQL Server's indicator that you want this temporary table to be local in scope.

Global temporary tables

Unlike local temporary tables, global temporary tables can be seen by anyone with an active connection. Global temporary tables can be helpful when you need to share data among a number of active connections but don't want to create a permanent table. SQL Server drops a global temporary table only after all connections that have used the temporary table have been closed. The syntax for a global temporary table is:

```
CREATE TABLE ##<TABLENAME> (...)
```

—or—

```
SELECT <COLUMN LIST> INTO ##TABLENAME
```

The double pound sign in front of the table name is SQL Server's indicator that you want this temporary table to be global in scope.

Implicit work tables

The SQL Server engine creates an implicit temporary table, also known as a work table, when you request any of the following:

- SELECT INTO
- SELECT DISTINCT/SELECT UNIQUE
- ORDER BY for nonindexed columns
- Other nonindexed operations

SQL Server may also choose to create an implicit temporary table as a means to speed up certain join or WHERE clause operations.

One of the worst types of implicit work tables is created when a user or application requests an enormous set of data, sorted by a nonindexed column(s). These types of implicit work tables hurt performance in at least four ways:

1. Their CPU usage slows down the application that creates them.
2. Their disk usage slows down the application that creates them.
3. They devour CPU time that could probably be spent on other applications.
4. They consume disk space that other applications may legitimately need. This disk space is found in the tempdb database, which is shared by all users and applications. If one process fills up tempdb, other applications may start failing due to lack of temporary table space, leading to aborted transactions and frustrated users.

See the "Sorting" section of this chapter for more details on how to construct efficient sorts.

Explicit temporary tables

You create explicit temporary tables voluntarily, through your application, by using one of the three following statements:

```
select  <column list>
into    #(#)<temporary table name>
from    <source table>
where   <where condition>
```

—or—

```
create table #(#)<temporary table name> <column list>
```

—or—

```
create table tempdb..<temporary table name>
    <column list>
```

There are certain types of situations where you can improve performance by creating and using a relatively small temporary table as a subset of a much larger table.

For example, assume that you have a transaction table that contains 40 million rows and spans four months. Suppose that you need to run a series of reports for only one day's data. By analyzing your query plan and application code, you realize that your program makes multiple passes of the transaction file to retrieve roughly only 1/120th (one day out of four months) of the data. This is a case where you would benefit from creating a temporary table and populating it with the (relatively) small subset of data. You could then create any necessary indexes on the temporary table and begin your multiple pass process.

Improving temporary table performance

If you create explicit temporary tables, there are several steps that you can take to improve their performance, including:

- **Index appropriate columns.**   Just because a table is temporary doesn't mean that it shouldn't be indexed. If you create an explicit temporary table and then plan to access its information, try creating indexes on your search columns, especially if the table will have more than a few data pages. You can use the same indexing guidelines for temporary tables as you use for permanent tables.

- **Temporary table placement.**   You can create temporary tables on different, faster devices. For example, suppose that you want to place a heavily accessed temporary table on your fastest disk drive, which has been assigned driver letter F. You could use the SQL Enterprise Manager, or you could follow these steps:

  1. Create a new database device that uses this new drive:

      ```
      disk init
      name = "temp_table_space",
      physname = "F:\data\tempspace.dat",
      vdevno = 99,
      size = 20480
      ```

The 'vdevno' value is the virtual device number that you want to assign to this device; it can be between 1 and 255. Virtual device number 0 is reserved for the MASTER database device.

The 'size' value is the number of 2-kilobyte blocks that you want assigned to the device. In this case, we've requested a total device size of 40 megabytes.

2. Alter your database to use this new device. Make sure that you run this command from the MASTER database:

```
alter database benchmark on
temp_table_space = 40
```

In this case, we've asked that the database use the full 40 megabytes that we just created.

3. Add a segment that uses this new device. Think of the segment name as a logical name for the device. Therefore, make the name meaningful:

```
sp_addsegment
temp_table_segment, temp_table_space
```

4. You can now place temporary tables on this new segment:

```
create table #current_payments (...)
on temp_table_segment
```

Since the disk drives are often the biggest bottleneck when retrieving data, placing the temporary table onto a separate drive lets SQL Server spread disk I/O among more than one device.

- **Store tempdb in RAM.** As an SQL Server administrator, you have the option of storing the tempdb within RAM. There may be situations where this is appropriate. However, placing this database in RAM may crowd out other memory-based objects, such as data and stored procedure pages. For more details on the costs and benefits of this option, see Part 3 on efficient engine management.

- **UPDATE STATISTICS.** If you explicitly create a temporary table and plan to repeatedly use it over a period of time, consider running UPDATE STATISTICS on the temporary table to give the optimizer more information about the new temporary table:

```
create table tempdb..xxx (col1 char(10)...)

insert into xxx select * from yyy

create index idx1 on xxx(col1)

update statistics for table xxx
```

You may even want to consider creating distributions for the columns within your temporary table. For more information about UPDATE STATISTICS and data distributions, see Chapter 4, "Understanding the SQL Server Optimizer."

In summary, temporary tables by themselves are not necessarily a bad thing. They only become a problem when the database engine is repeatedly forced to create dozens of them because there is no other way to process the data. If you have an existing application, try to find all places where the server creates temporary tables. Turn on SHOWPLAN for a day and monitor the output. You may be surprised at what you learn.

Subqueries

Subqueries let you pass search criteria into a filter condition. This greatly increases the power and flexibility of your queries. For example, the following query lets us retrieve all column names for a table, even though we only know the table name:

```
select name from syscolumns
where  id =
 (select id
  from sysobjects
  where name = "partners")
```

The output from this query is:

```
NAME
------------------------------
partner_code
partner_description
```

The subquery is processed first. In this case, it returns the 'id' for the 'partners' table. The outer query then uses this information to locate the column names from the 'syscolumns' table.

This type of subquery is known as an "uncorrelated" subquery, because the inner SELECT doesn't rely on the outer SELECT for information.

Correlated subqueries, on the other hand, need information from the outer SELECT to locate rows. This means that the engine runs the inner query after every row that the outer query returns. Here is an example of a correlated subquery:

```
select distinct account_number, last_name, first_name
from    customer_master
where "SFO" in
(select origin
 from    customer_flights
 where   customer_flights.account_number =
         customer_master.account_number)


STEP 1
The type of query is INSERT
The update mode is direct
Worktable created for REFORMATTING
FROM TABLE
customer_flights
Nested iteration
Table Scan
TO TABLE
Worktable 1
STEP 2
The type of query is SELECT
FROM TABLE
customer_master
Nested iteration
Table Scan
FROM TABLE
Worktable 1
EXISTS TABLE : nested iteration
Using Clustered Index
```

This type of subquery can greatly degrade performance, especially on a large table with a nonindexed selection criteria. Therefore, try to avoid correlated subqueries whenever possible. If you must use them, make sure that the selection criteria columns are indexed.

Costs of views

Views provide DBAs and developers with a number of important benefits, including:

- **Enhanced security.**   You can use views to restrict users from accessing certain rows or columns.

- **Simpler picture of the database.**   You can use a view to join a number of related tables and thereby present a less complex picture of the database to programmers or end users.

Sometimes, however, views have the potential to hurt performance. This is especially true when a programmer or user uses a view when they should work on the underlying tables instead. Let's look at an example to illustrate this potential problem.

Suppose that you have an application that tracks service calls. The database is made up of four tables and one view:

Table 5.7   Employees

employee_num	first_name	last_name ....
104	Carl	Lafong
1265	Ed	DeBevic
1926	Lee	Hanson

Table 5.8   Service_calls

service_num	customer_num	employee_num	service_date ....
73	496	1265	Jan 30 1997
74	92	104	Jan 31 1997

Table 5.9   Customers

customer_num	company_name	address1 ....
92	ABC Inc.	77 Sunset Strip
93	Bob's Flowers	155 E. 79th St.

Table 5.10   Responses

response_num	service_num	comments ....
11	73	Technician was great!
12	194	We're calling our lawyers

```
create view service_status as
   select s.service_num,
          s.service_date,
          r.comments,
          c.customer_num,
          c.company_name,
          e.first_name,
          e.last_name
   from   service_calls s,
          responses r,
          customers c,
          employees e
   where  s.employee_num = e.employee_num
   and    s.service_num  = r.service_num
   and    s.customer_num = c.customer_num
```

The view was created by the DBA for programmers. It masks the relationships among the tables. Generally, this is not a problem. However, if a programmer wants only one or two columns from the view, it would be better to simply retrieve those columns from the base tables instead of using the view and forcing the engine to join all the tables.

For example, assume that a user requests a simple report, showing the service number, date, and any comments. If the programmer retrieves this information from the view, the query plan looks like this:

```
select service_num, service_date, comments
from service_status

STEP 1
The type of query is SELECT
FROM TABLE
service_calls
Nested iteration
Table Scan
FROM TABLE
responses
Nested iteration
Table Scan
FROM TABLE
customers
Nested iteration
Table Scan
FROM TABLE
employees
Nested iteration
Table Scan
```

If, on the other hand, you run the query against only the two base tables that have the necessary columns, your query plan looks like this:

```
select  s.service_num, s.service_date, r.comments
from    service_calls s, responses r
where   s.service_num = r.service_num

STEP 1
The type of query is SELECT
FROM TABLE
service_calls s
Nested iteration
Table Scan
FROM TABLE
responses r
Nested iteration
Table Scan
```

Notice how the second query accesses two fewer tables: Retrieving data from the view forces the optimizer to read unnecessary tables. The savings in processing time that the latter query provides could be substantial on a large system. If you make extensive use of views, consider documenting their underlying structure. Place this documentation in a location where programmers have easy access to it.

Using math inside SQL

There are times where you want to perform mathematical operations on one or more columns stored in a table. For example, assume that you have the following table that tracks labor costs:

Table 5.11   Resources

resource_id	resource_desc	resource_cost ....
CL1	Clerk level I	12.55
CL2	Clerk level II	14.03
AA1	Admin level I	13.39
AA2	Admin level II	16.39

During the design of a labor scheduling system, you learn that one report allows management to specify an across-the-board raise on an input screen. Your program then uses this value to produce a "what-if" report, showing what the 'resource_cost' column would contain if the raise was applied. You could write your query this way (assuming that the raise is 20 percent):

```
select  resource_desc,
        resource_cost old,
        resource_cost * 1.2 new
from    resources
```

If you are operating against a small to midsize table (less than 10,000 rows, for example), this type of query is fine. On larger tables, however, you can get better performance by moving the math outside the SQL and into your application code.

In a client/server processing environment, making this kind of change might not be optimal, however, because moving the math processing from server to client can add extra cost, namely:

- **Extra network traffic.** If there are a large number of rows being sent between client and server, application performance might suffer.

- **Extra client load.** If your client machines are not powerful, this type of change could subject them to unnecessary, added processing load.

With this in mind, conduct some analysis before you move math calculations out of SQL, especially if you're using client/server processing.

Another instance where math expressions can hurt performance is when you are joining between two tables. Using the 'resource' table from above, suppose that you want to join this table to another table, using the 'resource_cost' column. In the first case, we're performing a simple join:

```
select * from resources, parts
where resources.resource_cost = parts.part_cost

STEP 1
The type of query is INSERT
The update mode is direct
Worktable created for REFORMATTING
FROM TABLE
parts
Row estimate:  141
Cost estimate: 32
Nested iteration
Table Scan
TO TABLE
Worktable 1
STEP 2
```

```
The type of query is SELECT
FROM TABLE
Worktable 1
Row estimate:   141
Cost estimate: 32
Nested iteration
Table Scan
FROM TABLE
resources
JOINS WITH
parts
Row estimate:   141
Cost estimate: 746
Nested iteration
Index : resource_cost_ix
```

Although SQL Server creates a work table to hold intermediate results, the engine is able to take advantage of an index on the 'parts' table to speed the join. Watch what happens when we perform math inside the join clause:

```
declare @inflator integer
select @inflator = 0
select resource_desc,
       part_desc
from   resource, parts
where  resource.resource_cost =
       parts.part_cost + @inflator


STEP 1
The type of query is DECLARE
STEP 1
The type of query is SELECT
STEP 1
The type of query is SELECT
FROM TABLE
parts
Row estimate:   141
Cost estimate: 16
Nested iteration
Table Scan
FROM TABLE
resources
Row estimate:   353205
Cost estimate: 4440
```

```
Nested iteration
Table Scan
```

Sometimes, this type of operation is unavoidable. In any case, you should always be aware of the potential hidden costs of embedded math in your SQL.

Unions

There are times when you can use unions to speed query retrieval. One instance is when you are retrieving two distinct sets of data (separated by an OR). Consider dividing the query into two different queries, and use a UNION to merge the results.

In this case, you have a table containing parts for outboard motors. There are indexes on the 'part_num' and 'part_cost' columns. You want to retrieve two sets of rows in one query:

- All rows that have a part number between 1 and 50 and cost more than $100.00

—or—

- All rows where the cost is greater than $55.00

Table 5.12 Parts

part_num	part_description	part_cost ....
22905	4-blade propeller	165.03
3467	engine cowling	205.44
910	interior gasket	.58
1093	drive shaft	443.00
.	.	.
22906	3-blade propeller	145.99
911	lower unit gasket	3.00
.	.	.

You can construct this query by using an OR statement, as follows:

```
select * from parts
where (part_num between 1 and 50
    and part_cost > 100.00)
or      part_cost > 55.00
```

Depending on a number of factors, the optimizer may:

- Sequentially scan the table once, looking for rows that fit both criteria, resulting in this type of query plan:

```
STEP 1
The type of query is SELECT
FROM TABLE
parts
Nested iteration
Table Scan
```

- Make two passes through the table, using the index on 'part_num' for one pass and the index on 'part_cost' for the other:

```
STEP 1
The type of query is SELECT
FROM TABLE
parts
Nested iteration
Index : pt_part_cost_ix
FROM TABLE
parts
Nested iteration
Using Clustered Index
FROM TABLE
parts
Nested iteration
Using Dynamic Index
```

For more information about multiple index query processing, see "Dynamic Index" in Chapter 4.

If you find that these types of queries are running poorly, try rewriting the query as follows:

```
select * from parts
where part_num between 1 and 50 and
     part_cost > 100.00

union

select * from parts
where part_cost > 55.00
```

In many (but not all) cases, the optimizer may now choose the correct indexes to speed up the query. Review your slow-running queries to see if they are candidates for this type of enhancement. Take care when running this type of query against a large table. It's possible that SQL Server, in an effort to satisfy the UNION request, might create an enormous temporary table to hold results from each pass of the query. This table might be so large that it fills up all available temporary storage space.

Sorting

No matter how much research and analysis you put into your database design, someone is going to want data sorted in an order you never imagined. This is not necessarily a bad thing; perhaps your existing indexes will be sufficient. More likely, however, a new sorting request means more work for you.

One of the most dangerous types of sorts occurs when a user or application requests an enormous set of data, sorted by a nonindexed column(s). For example, assume that you have a million-row transaction history table, defined as follows:

Table 5.13   pos_detail

sku_no	store_no	sale_date	amount ....
5409	636	Nov 1 1996	1.55
112	636	Nov 1 1996	32.00
.	.	.	
1154	709	Nov 2 1996	93.99
5903	709	Nov 3 1996	5.87
.	.	.	

This table has a composite index on 'sku_no,' 'store_no,' and 'sale_date.' After the system has been in use for several weeks, management requests a report showing all rows in the table, sorted by the 'amount' and 'sale_date' fields:

```
select *
from   pos_detail
order by amount, sale_date

STEP 1
The type of query is INSERT
The update mode is direct
Worktable created for ORDER BY
FROM TABLE
```

```
pos_detail
Nested iteration
Table Scan
TO TABLE
Worktable 1
STEP 2
The type of query is SELECT
This step involves sorting
FROM TABLE
Worktable 1
Using GETSORTED Table Scan
Msg 1105, Level 17, State 1
Can't allocate space for object '-321' in database
'tempdb' because the 'system' segment is full. If you
ran out of space in Syslogs, dump the transaction log.
Otherwise, use ALTER DATABASE or sp_extendsegment to
increase the size of the segment.
```

This is an especially dangerous situation. The query returns all rows in the table. What is worse is that the optimizer constructs a temporary table that is as big as the original table itself. It is entirely possible that you will run out of space to store the temporary table, and the query will "crash." In fact, this is exactly what happened during this query.

Fortunately, there are ways to prevent this situation:

- If you cannot afford a full-time index on the sort columns, consider creating a temporary index, running your report, and then dropping the index.

- Try to limit the use of SELECT * on large tables. Determine if you really need all those columns.

- Try to limit wildcard searches of tables without any filter conditions. Consider prompting users to be more selective, or at least warn them that their query may run slowly. For more information on this topic, see Chapter 7, "General Tips."

- For large table sorts, always try to have an index in place on the sort columns. Run SHOWPLAN to make sure that the index is being used for the sort. Keep in mind that this change won't always help. For example, if the index is already being used to resolve a filter or join condition, the optimizer may still need to create a temporary table. For example, look at this query and query plan:

```
select account_number,
        last_name,
```

```
        first_name,
        award_description
from    customer_master,
        awards
where   last_name = 'McIlwane'
and     customer_master.account_balance >=
        awards.mileage_level

STEP 1
The type of query is SELECT
FROM TABLE
customer_master
Nested iteration
Index : cm_lastname_ix
FROM TABLE
awards
Nested iteration
Table Scan
```

If we modify the query to sort by 'account_number,' the SQL Server engine still needs to create a work table, even though this field has an index:

```
select account_number,
       last_name,
       first_name,
       award_description
from   customer_master,
       awards
where  last_name = "McIlwane"
and    customer_master.account_balance >=
       awards.mileage_level
order by account_number

STEP 1
The type of query is INSERT
The update mode is direct
Worktable created for ORDER BY
FROM TABLE
customer_master
Nested iteration
Index : cm_lastname_ix
FROM TABLE
awards
```

```
Nested iteration
Table Scan
TO TABLE
Worktable 1
STEP 2
The type of query is SELECT
This step involves sorting
FROM TABLE
Worktable 1
Using GETSORTED Table Scan
```

Keep this in mind if you can't figure out why you still sometimes see temporary tables.

ROLLUP

SQL Server 6.5 introduces a new operator that you can use to enhance your application's data summation ability. This operator, called ROLLUP, is used in association with the GROUP BY clause of the SELECT statement. It's very useful when you want to display running totals and other interim information.

Let's look at some examples that illustrate how you can use this operator to enhance your reports. First, let's create and populate a sample table that we'll use to demonstrate both ROLLUP and CUBE:

Table 5.14   restaurant_reviews

restaurant_name	city	review_date	score	price....
Chez Nicole	Miami	Jul 4 1997	9.5	75
Chez Nicole	Miami	Jul 7 1997	8.6	82
China Clipper	Miami	Aug 3 1997	9.2	61
Cinderfellas	Los Angeles	Jun 28 1997	8.9	35
Damphouse	New York	May 31 1997	3.5	110
Eat	Los Angeles	Jun 3 1997	5.5	54
Eat	New York	Jun 5 1997	6.2	67
Griscom's on Fifth	New York	Jul 1 1997	2.5	125
Rosetti's	New York	Jun 17 1997	6.4	55
Sammelas	Los Angeles	May 22 1997	7.0	40
Todo Cuero	Miami	Jul 1 1997	8.2	67

Suppose that you want to get the average score for all of the restaurants in each city, further broken out by the individual restaurant. You would use this SQL:

```
select city, restaurant_name, avg(score)
from restaurant_reviews
group by city, restaurant_name

STEP 1
The type of query is SELECT (into a worktable)
GROUP BY
Vector Aggregate
FROM TABLE
restaurant_reviews
Nested iteration
Table Scan
TO TABLE
Worktable 1
STEP 2
The type of query is SELECT
FROM TABLE
Worktable 1
Nested iteration
Table Scan
```

city	restaurant_name	
Los Angeles	Cinderfellas	8.900000
Los Angeles	Eat	5.500000
Los Angeles	Sammelas	7.000000
Miami	Chez Nicole	9.050000
Miami	China Clipper	9.200000
Miami	Todo Cuero	8.200000
New York	Damphouse	3.500000
New York	Eat	6.200000
New York	Griscoms on Fifth	2.500000
New York	Rosettis	6.400000

The GROUP BY has combined the two separate reviews for 'Chez Nicole' into one line item, yet kept the two reviews for the 'Eat' restaurant separate. Why is this? The reason is that although there are indeed two reviews for 'Eat,' each review applies to a restaurant in a different city.

What if you wanted to know the average score for all of the restaurant reviews for a particular city? Adding the ROLLUP operator makes this possible:

```
select city, restaurant_name, avg(score)
from restaurant_reviews
group by city, restaurant_name
with rollup

STEP 1
The type of query is INSERT
The update mode is direct
FROM TABLE
restaurant_reviews
Nested iteration
Table Scan
TO TABLE
Worktable 1
STEP 2
The type of query is SELECT
FROM TABLE
Worktable 2
 GROUP BY WITH ROLLUP
 Vector Aggregate
 FROM TABLE
 Worktable 1
 Using GETSORTED Table Scan
 TO TABLE
 Worktable 2
```

city	restaurant_name	
Los Angeles	Cinderfellas	8.900000
Los Angeles	Eat	5.500000
Los Angeles	Sammelas	7.000000
Los Angeles	(null)	7.133333
Miami	Chez Nicole	9.050000
Miami	China Clipper	9.200000
Miami	Todo Cuero	8.200000
Miami	(null)	8.875000
New York	Damphouse	3.500000
New York	Eat	6.200000
New York	Griscoms on Fifth	2.500000
New York	Rosettis	6.400000
New York	(null)	4.650000
(null)	(null)	6.863636

Notice how the query plan changed: SQL Server now uses a second work table to process the intermediate query results. With regard to the output, notice how there now is a summation line for each city. You can tell that this is a summary line by the '(null)' value in the 'restaurant_name' column. In addition, there is a new summary line at the end of the query, showing the average score for all restaurants in all cities.

CUBE

When you request the CUBE option with GROUP BY, SQL Server takes two steps to satisfy your request. First, the engine creates a work table, where it holds qualifying information. Next, after the worktable has been generated, SQL Server sorts and groups the data and places it into a second worktable. Your actual data comes from the second table. This is very similar to the approach taken with GROUP BY WITH ROLLUP.

GROUP BY WITH CUBE is mainly used when creating cross-referenced reports. It provides a superset of the data that GROUP BY WITH ROLLUP provides. The added value for CUBE comes at the end of the report, when it creates a new set of aggregate information. This is best illustrated by rerunning the earlier query and replacing WITH ROLLUP with the CUBE operator:

```
select city, restaurant_name, avg(score)
from restaurant_reviews
group by city, restaurant_name
with cube

STEP 1
The type of query is INSERT
The update mode is direct
FROM TABLE
restaurant_reviews
Nested iteration
Table Scan
TO TABLE
Worktable 1
STEP 2
The type of query is SELECT
FROM TABLE
Worktable 2
  GROUP BY WITH CUBE
  Vector Aggregate
  FROM TABLE
  Worktable 1
```

```
Using GETSORTED Table Scan
TO TABLE
Worktable 2
```

city	restaurant_name	
Los Angeles	Cinderfellas	8.900000
Los Angeles	Eat	5.500000
Los Angeles	Sammelas	7.000000
Los Angeles	(null)	7.133333
Miami	Chez Nicole	9.050000
Miami	China Clipper	9.200000
Miami	Todo Cuero	8.200000
Miami	(null)	8.875000
New York	Damphouse	3.500000
New York	Eat	6.200000
New York	Griscoms on Fifth	2.500000
New York	Rosettis	6.400000
New York	(null)	4.650000
(null)	(null)	6.863636
(null)	Chez Nicole	9.050000
(null)	China Clipper	9.200000
(null)	Cinderfellas	8.900000
(null)	Damphouse	3.500000
(null)	Eat	5.850000
(null)	Griscoms on Fifth	2.500000
(null	Rosettis	6.400000
(null)	Sammelas	7.000000
(null)	Todo Cuero	8.200000

GROUP BY WITH CUBE produced nearly the same output as GROUP BY WITH ROLLUP did earlier. The major difference between the two operators occurs after the highlighted summary line showing the average score for all restaurants in all cities. After this point, SQL Server now averages the scores for each individual restaurant, regardless of city. This added information is very helpful in learning what the average score is for the 'Eat' restaurant, since there is a location in both Los Angeles and New York. The only way to get this line item is by using GROUP BY WITH CUBE.

If you don't need this level of detail, however, it's best to use GROUP BY WITH ROLLUP. If you don't need even that level of detail, then continue to use standard GROUP BY, since it uses one less work table to provide its results.

INSERT from stored procedures

A new SQL Server 6.5 capability lets you capture data from local or remote stored procedures and then insert these results into the local database. This is simpler and more efficient than writing a special program to perform the same work. Let's look at an example of how to use this new feature.

Suppose that you want to retrieve information from a remote server and place it into a table on your machine. You would first create the procedure on the remote server:

```
create procedure locate_detail (@search_criteria)
as
select transaction_date, transaction_amount
from sales_detail
where sales_id = @search_criteria
```

Once you've created the procedure, you can insert its returned information into a local table by running a simple INSERT statement:

```
insert into local_transaction_detail
execute kerouac.sales.dbo.locate_detail 3093
```

We've asked SQL Server to run the 'locate_detail' procedure, owned by 'dbo,' in the 'sales' database, on the 'kerouac' server. In addition, we're trying to locate records with a 'sales_id' value of 3093. There's no reason that you can't run this type of operation locally. You could omit the server name, and if you are operating in the same database, there is no need to specify a database or owner name, either.

INSERT and default values

During table creation, SQL Server lets you define default values for your columns. If you plan on inserting an empty row containing default values on all columns, you can simply request default values, rather than providing a column list. For example, suppose that you've used the following syntax to create a table:

```
create table sample_defaults
(
     col1 integer identity primary key,
     col2 char(10) default current_user,
```

```
        col3 datetime default current_timestamp,
        col4 smallint default 5
)
```

You can then insert a new row into the table with the following simple syntax:

```
insert into sample_defaults default values
```

This produces this row:

```
col1          col2        col3                        col4
-----------   ----------  --------------------------  ------
1             dbo         Mar 29 1997   9:50PM         5
```

You must ensure that all of the columns in the table either have a default assigned or can accept null values. If not, you'll get the following error message:

```
Msg 233, Level 16, State 2
The column col5 in table sample_defaults1 may not
be null.
```

Update extension

Transact-SQL provides an extension that lets you update data in one table by retrieving data from other tables. This can simplify your application code, since you may be able to avoid intermediate storage for these values. For example, look at the following syntax:

```
update combination
set last_name =
(select last_name
 from   customer_master
 where  customer_master.account_number =
        combination.account_number)
```

Instead of first selecting the 'last_name' value into a variable and then updating the 'combination' table, this extension lets you perform the update in one operation. Keep in mind that feature is an extension to SQL; if your goal is to develop a database-independent application, you may not find this same capability in other databases.

Multiple table deletes

Traditional SQL limits your delete operations to one table at a time. Transact-SQL has a multiple table delete capability that you can use to reduce the number of individual engine calls. For example, suppose that you want to delete rows in both the 'resources' and 'parts' tables described earlier. You could issue two SQL statements:

```
delete from resources where resource_cost > 5000
delete from parts where part_cost > 5000
```

As an alternative, you can use Transact-SQL's multiple table DELETE extension:

```
delete from resources
delete from parts
where resources.resource_cost = parts.part_cost
and resources.resource_cost > 5000
```

There is one shortcoming to this technique: If you are planning to have your application run against a variety of different databases, this approach is not portable. However, if you anticipate that you need only work with Microsoft SQL Server, multiple table delete provides a convenient shortcut.

Large delete operations

Sometimes, developers want to delete all rows from a particular table. There are several ways of doing this:

- **DELETE.** You could use the DELETE statement without a qualifying WHERE clause. This would essentially delete all rows from the table in one pass. However, this approach can take a long time to complete, since SQL Server must note, in the transaction log, information about every row that you're deleting. This information would be necessary to restore the table's data should you decide to abort the delete operation before it completes. In addition to taking a great deal of time, using DELETE to remove all rows from a table consumes vast amounts of transaction log space, especially if the table contains many rows. As we'll see in Part 3 on efficient engine practices, a full transaction log hurts all users by bringing many database operations to a halt. Consequently, it's a good idea to avoid excess transaction log usage whenever possible, which is another argument against the DELETE statement for this kind of operation.

- **DROP TABLE.**   By definition, dropping the table removes all of its data and schema. However, users need appropriate permission to drop a table. Unless you never planned to use the table again, someone would also need to re-create the table after it has been dropped. This also requires adequate permission, which you may be reluctant to assign to all users.

- **TRUNCATE TABLE.**   The third option for performing table cleaning is to truncate the table. Using this command causes SQL Server to free up entire data pages at one time. This eliminates all data from the table, yet preserves the table's schema, constraints, index, rules, and column defaults. SQL Server also resets any identity values, so that when you repopulate the table, your identity values will start from the beginning. Perhaps the biggest benefit of this command is that SQL Server doesn't make as many log entries as it does with the delete operation. This greatly improves speed, as well as conserving transaction log space. However, once you've launched this command, there's no way to reestablish the table to its original state without restoring from a backup. For this reason, use TRUNCATE TABLE wisely: If you don't care about the table's contents and are satisfied with the possibility of reissuing the command if necessary, feel free to use this performance-enhancing request.

Some additional comments about TRUNCATE TABLE. First, you can't use this command if the table has a foreign key in place:

```
truncate table pos_transactions

Msg 4712, Level 16, State 1
Cannot truncate table 'pos_transactions' because
it is being referenced by a foreign key constraint.
```

Another TRUNCATE TABLE limitation deals with triggers. Even if there is a trigger in place on a table, a TRUNCATE TABLE operation doesn't cause the trigger to fire. We'll discuss more about triggers in Chapter 6.

Finally, if you use this command to clear a table, remember to rerun UPDATE STATISTICS after you've repopulated the table. This is necessary because truncating a table clears its index distribution pages. For more detail about the benefits and usage of UPDATE STATISTICS, see the chapters in Part 1.

Chapter 6
Stored Procedures and Triggers

Stored Procedures

In a nutshell, stored procedures are functions composed of procedural language and SQL statements. The procedural language is known as Transact-SQL. You use Transact-SQL and SQL to create functions that are stored in the database engine, instead of in application code or libraries.

Creating and maintaining stored procedures

You create stored procedures following these steps:

1. Connect to the database. You need to have sufficient privilege to create stored procedures.

2. Using Transact-SQL, write a script that contains the stored procedure logic.

3. Run the script.

The SQL Enterprise Manager provides you with a simple, straightforward way to build and maintain stored procedures:

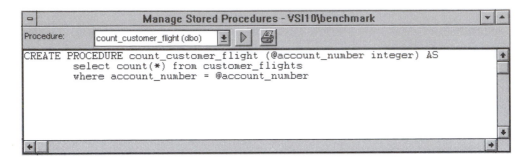

Figure 6.1

The database server performs these tasks when you create a stored procedure:

1. Checks the syntax of the procedure.

2. Parses the procedure.

3. Creates entries in the 'sysprocedures,' 'sysobjects,' 'syscomments,' 'sysdepends,' and 'syscolumns' tables. These tables have the following layouts:

Table 6.1   sysprocedures

column name	type	purpose
type	smallint	Type of object: 1 = Entry describes a plan 2 = Entry describes a tree
id	integer	Object ID
sequence	smallint	Sequence number for this entry
status	smallint	System's internal status
number	smallint	Subprocedure entry (if applicable)

Table 6.2   sysobjects

column name	type	purpose
name	varchar	Name of the object
id	integer	Object ID
uid	smallint	User ID of the owner object

Table 6.2 sysobjects (Continued)

type	char	Type of object: C = Check constraint D = Default constraint F = Foreign key constraint K = Primary key/Unique constraint L = Log P = Stored procedure R = Rule RF = Replication stored procedure S = System table TR = Trigger U = User table X = Extended stored procedure
userstat	smallint	Type information—dependent on application
sysstat	smallint	Type information—from system
indexdel	smallint	Index delete counter
schema	smallint	Schema modification counter
refdate	datetime	Reserved for future use
crdate	datetime	Timestamp of object creation
version	datetime	Reserved for future use
deltrig	integer	Delete trigger's stored procedure ID
instrig	integer	Insert trigger's stored procedure ID
updtrig	integer	Update trigger's stored procedure ID
seltrig	integer	Reserved for future use
category	integer	Reserved for publications, constraints, and identity
cache	smallint	Reserved for future use

Table 6.3 syscomments

column name	type	purpose
id	integer	Object ID
number	smallint	Order within the stored procedure
colid	tinyint	Row sequence number (if procedure is longer than 255 characters)

Table 6.3   syscomments (Continued)

texttype	smallint	Comment type: 0 = User-supplied comment 1 = System-supplied comment 4 = Encrypted comment
language	smallint	Reserved
text	varchar	Actual text for the stored procedure

Table 6.4   sysdepends

column name	type	purpose
id	integer	Object ID
Number	smallint	Stored procedure number
depid	int	Dependent object's ID number
depnumber	smallint	Dependent stored procedure number
depdbid	smallint	Reserved
depsiteid	smallint	Reserved
status	smallint	SQL Server's internal status indicator
selall	bit	Enabled if the object is a SELECT * statement
resultobj	bit	Enabled if the object gets updated
readobj	bit	Enabled if the object is read

Table 6.5   syscolumns

column name	type	purpose
id	integer	ID of the table or stored procedure
Number	smallint	Subprocedure number
colid	tinyint	Column ID number
status	tinyint	Bitmap to describe one or more properties of the column
type	tinyint	Physical storage description
length	tinyint	Length of the data
offset	smallint	Indicates location in the row of this column
usertype	smallint	User-defined type ID

Table 6.5   syscolumns (Continued)

cdefault	integer	Identifier of the particular stored procedure that generates a default value for this column (if applicable)
Domain	integer	Identifier of the particular stored procedure that sets the rule for this column (if applicable)
Name	varchar	Name of the column
printfmt	varchar	Reserved for future use
prec	tinyint	Column's precision
scale	tinyint	Column's scale

You can learn about stored procedures by using the SQL Enterprise Manager or by running the 'sp_stored_procedures' stored procedure:

Table 6.6   sp_stored_procedures output

column name	type	purpose
procedure_qualifier	varchar	Name of the procedure qualifier
procedure_owner	varchar	Name of the procedure owner
procedure_name	varchar	Name of the stored procedure
num_input_params	smallint	Reserved for future use
num_output_params	smallint	Reserved for future use
num_result_sets	smallint	Reserved for future use
remarks	varchar	Description of the stored procedure
procedure_type	smallint	Type of the procedure: 0 = SQL_PT_UNKNOWN 1 = SQL_PT_PROCEDURE 2 = SQL_PT_FUNCTION

Before you modify an existing procedure via Transact-SQL, you must remove it from the database server by dropping it. Then, you can modify the script and re-create the procedure. The SQL Enterprise Manager makes this operation more automatic.

Why use stored procedures?

Now that we've seen how you create stored procedures, let's examine why you would make them part of your applications.

Some of the major benefits of stored procedures are:

- **Elimination of runtime parsing.** Since stored procedures are already parsed at creation time, the database engine can skip this time-consuming step at runtime.

- **DBA privileges for regular users.** You can designate certain stored procedures to run with DBA privileges, even if the user running them does not have this level of security. This lets you combine a high level of data access with tight security.

- **Centralization of commonly used operations.** You can easily create libraries of functions, thereby reducing the amount of original code that your programmers must write.

- **Simplified software distribution.** Today's graphical applications are constantly changing. Distributing new versions of these applications to each client within an organization can be very complex. By using stored procedures to move application logic onto the server, you can greatly reduce the amount of work necessary to perform an upgrade.

- **Memory caching.** SQL Server uses memory buffering to help reduce the overall amount of costly disk I/O operations. In addition to buffering data and index pages, SQL Server also caches stored procedures. This means that the engine might be able to avoid reading stored procedures from the disk, since they may already be present in the stored procedure cache. The overall savings from this bypass can be substantial and are yet another argument for making use of stored procedures. We'll cover this structure in more detail in Chapter 12.

- **Reduction of traffic between server and client.** In a distributed environment, stored procedures let you cut down the amount of information traveling between the front end (client) and the back end (server). This can add up, especially if client and server are separated by a long distance.

Let's explore situations where you can use stored procedures specifically to improve system performance.

Frequently used routines

In many applications, different programs often perform the same set of operations. Typically, these include several SQL statements, along with procedural language flow control. You can convert some of these heavily used operations into stored procedures, thereby simplifying and speeding up your application.

For example, suppose that you are developing a manufacturing application. One of your most important tables tracks the historical tolerances of various parts. Another table tracks the actual tolerances of these parts during particular manufacturing runs:

Table 6.7   parts

part_num	part_desc	part_tolerance
1	Drive shaft	0.01500
2	Manifold cover	0.12000
3	Main gasket	0.00200
.	.	.
.	.	.

Table 6.8   manuf_status

part_num	run_id	run_date	run_tolerance
2	17	Mar 2 1997 4:45PM	0.01600
3	18	Mar 2 1997 4:48PM	0.00700
1	19	Mar 2 1997 5:15PM	0.00100
1	20	Mar 2 1997 7:03PM	0.19000
.	.	.	.
.	.	.	.
.	.	.	.

You are asked to produce a report, displaying which manufacturing runs produced parts that met or failed to meet historical part tolerances. This entails joining the 'parts' and 'manuf_status' tables on the 'part_num' key, and then comparing the 'part_tolerance' (historical value) and the 'run_tolerance' (actual batch value). Traditionally, you would tackle this problem by writing a program to do the joins and compare the values.

An alternate approach would be to let a stored procedure do the comparison for you. Your program could then call the stored procedure, rather than issuing the SQL itself.

You benefit from converting common functions into stored procedures in at least five ways:

- **Performance.**   The stored procedure should yield better performance, especially in a distributed environment (see Chapter 8, "Client/Server Considerations").

- **Development time.**   Programmers no longer need to write their own versions of these routines, since they can now access the shared stored procedures.

- **Error reduction.**   Since programmers no longer need to write, test, and support their own versions of the shared functions, you minimize the number of potential application errors.

- **Change control.**   If you need to change the operation, you change it in only one place.

- **Simplicity.**   New programmers do not need to learn the internal intricacies of these functions; they only need to know the name, parameters, return values, and purposes of your stored procedures.

How can you tell whether an operation is a good candidate for conversion to a stored procedure? Use these guidelines:

1. **Does the operation contain several related SQL statements?**
   It doesn't necessarily make sense to write a separate stored procedure for each SQL statement. Ideally, your stored procedures should contain several closely tied database operations.
   For example, if you're writing a banking operation, you could write one stored procedure to handle the transfer of funds between accounts. The procedure would incorporate SQL statements to handle these operations:

   - Check existing balance in source account.

   - Update the target account by adding the transferred amount.

   - Update the source account by subtracting the transferred amount.

2. **Is the operation used by more than one program?**   If only one program performs the task, it may not make sense to convert it into a stored procedure.

3. **Does Transact-SQL have the features that you need to replicate the logic of your existing routines?**   Only you can determine the answer to this question; try to learn as much as you can about the features of Transact-SQL before you start converting existing routines into stored procedures.

4. **Will moving the operation into a stored procedure simplify your application?**   In many cases, the answer to this question is a definite yes. If the answer is no, it may not pay to make the conversion.

5. **Will moving the operation into a stored procedure reduce network traffic?** If excess network traffic is hurting performance, stored procedures may be the answer.

6. **Does the operation require higher-level security?** Stored procedures let you grant users temporary DBA authority.

Auto startup stored procedures

As an administrator, you can request that SQL Server automatically run one or more stored procedures during the startup operation. SQL Server then runs these procedures each time you start the engine, unless you've set trace flag 4022, which disables this capability. Let's look at how you make these types of requests, along with situations that warrant further attention from a performance standpoint.

For example, suppose that you want to create a work table each time the system starts. All users on the system have access to this table as long as SQL Server is running. This is a good reason to use a startup stored procedure. How would you create this procedure? Follow these steps:

1. Log in to SQL Server as the "sa" user. You can use either the SQL Enterprise Manager or any other tool that lets you enter Transact-SQL.

2. Connect to the 'master' database.

3. Create the stored procedure:

```
create procedure build_work_table as

if exists (select * from
largo.dbo.sysobjects where id =
object_id('largo.dbo.work_table') and
sysstat & 0xf = 3)
drop table largo.dbo.work_table

create table largo.dbo.work_table
(
work_id integer identity primary key,
text_value text
)
```

4. If you don't log in as "sa" but you still try to create the startup stored procedure, SQL Server returns an error:

```
Msg 229, Level 14, State 1
EXECUTE permission denied on object
sp_makestartup, database master, owner dbo
```

5. Once you've created the stored procedure, you can tell SQL Server to treat it as a startup procedure by running the 'sp_makestartup' stored procedure:

```
sp_makestartup build_work_table

Procedure has been marked as 'startup.'
```

6. To remove a stored procedure from the startup process, run the 'sp_unmakestartup' stored procedure:

```
sp_unmakestartup build_work_table

Procedure is no longer marked as 'startup.'
```

7. To get a list of startup stored procedures, you can run the 'sp_helpstartup' stored procedure:

```
sp_helpstartup

Startup stored procedures:
-----------------------------
build_work_table
sp_sqlregister
```

Startup stored procedures are a useful tool, but there are potential performance liabilities that you should be aware of. SQL Server has no way of knowing if your startup procedure is well-written or if it consumes enormous amounts of resources. For example, there is nothing stopping you from writing a startup stored procedure that drops and then rebuilds all indexes. This could take a tremendous amount of time to finish and would serve to delay the entire startup procedure. How can you combat this potential problem? First, the SQL Server administrator should maintain control over what stored procedures are executed during startup. Next, it's a good idea to review periodically all stored procedures that are part of the startup operation. You might be surprised to learn that an out-of-date, resource-intensive, or other unnecessary procedure was being started.

Extended stored procedures

SQL Server gives administrators and developers the ability to run external tasks from within SQL Server itself. These are known as extended stored procedures, and we'll spend some time examining how you can use this feature. While it's beyond the scope of this book to furnish a thorough explanation of how to build and maintain extended stored procedures, we will provide a high-level description of this helpful utility. We'll also itemize some helpful extended stored procedures that are built in to SQL Server. Let's begin by discovering how extended stored procedures work.

You can build an extended stored procedure from anything that can be placed inside a dynamic link library (DLL). For example, suppose that you want to write a C or C++ program that performs a data communications operation. By using the Open Data Services API when constructing your program and creating a DLL instead of a standalone executable, you can request that SQL Server initiate your external functions as external. This DLL architecture helps speed performance as opposed to a process-based technique. It's much faster to call a function contained in a DLL than to start up a separate program containing the extended stored procedure. In fact, SQL Server takes advantage of the existing user thread to start and run the extended stored procedure, thereby greatly reducing potential overhead.

Once you've written your external stored procedure, you must make SQL Server aware that the procedure exists. You can do this in one of two ways. First, you can run the 'sp_addextendedproc' stored procedure:

```
sp_addextendedproc xp_download_data, myfile
```

where 'myfile' is the name of the DLL that contains the 'xp_download_data' function. Keep in mind that you should only add extended stored procedures to the "master" database.

If you want to drop an extended stored procedure, you can run the 'sp_dropextendedproc' stored procedure:

```
sp_dropextendedproc xp_download_data
```

Another way to maintain external stored procedures is to use the SQL Enterprise Manager's new graphical interface. To use this new interface, connect to your "master" database and then examine the 'object' folder. You'll now see a subfolder for extended stored procedures:

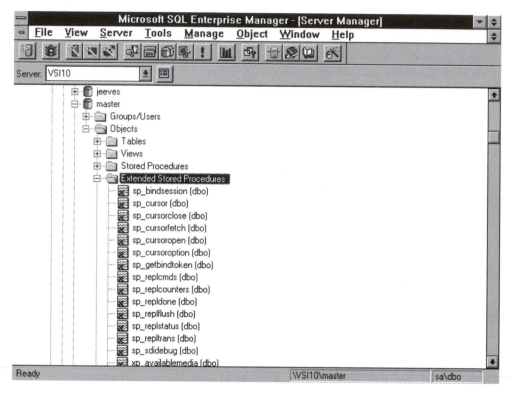

Figure 6.2

You can add or delete extended stored procedures through SQL Enterprise Manager:

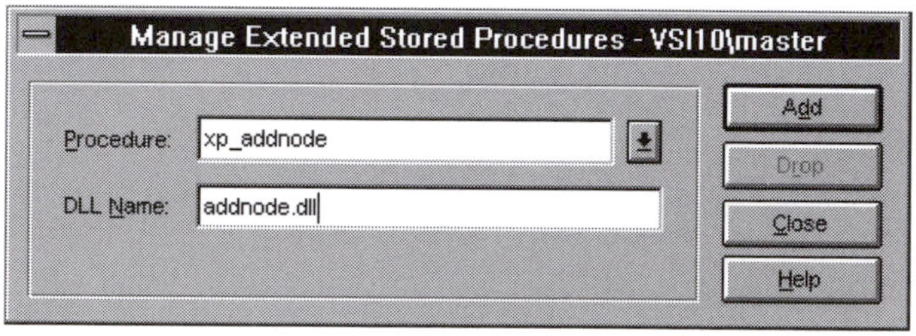

Figure 6.3

You can also use a stored procedure to get a list of all extended stored procedures, along with their associated DLLs, by running 'sp_helpextendedproc':

```
sp_helpextendedproc
```

```
name                      dll
-------------------- ----------------------------
sp_bindsession            (server internal)
sp_cursor                 (server internal)
sp_cursorclose            (server internal)
sp_cursorfetch            (server internal)
sp_cursoropen             (server internal)
sp_cursoroption           (server internal)
sp_getbindtoken           (server internal)
sp_replcmds               replcmds extended procedure
. . .                     . . .
. . .                     . . .
. . .                     . . .
xp_stopmail               sqlmap60.dll
xp_subdirs                xpstar.dll
xp_unc_to_drive           xpsql60.dll
```

The above list represents a small portion of the extended stored procedures that Microsoft provides with SQL Server 6.5. These extended stored procedures provide a rich source of administration, maintenance, and monitoring information that you can use. Let's look at a few situations where you can take advantage of this library of procedures.

Suppose that you want to issue an operating system-level command from inside SQL Server and then track the command's results. How would you make this happen? You could write a specialized, extended stored procedure that performed the command and then stored the command's output in a table. A simpler, cleaner way would be to use the 'xp_cmdshell' extended stored procedure. In this case, we want to get a file listing of the SQL Server directory:

```
xp_cmdshell "dir c:\sql60"

output
------------------------------------------------------

Volume in drive C is MS-DOS_6
Volume Serial Number is 1E3A-13E1
(null)
Directory of c:\sql60
(null)
```

```
11/13/95        12:12p        <DIR>            .
11/13/95        12:12p        <DIR>            . .
11/13/95        12:12p        <DIR>            BINN
11/13/95        12:12p        <DIR>            SQLOLE
01/25/96        10:41a        <DIR>            DATA
01/25/96        10:41a        <DIR>            BIN
01/25/96        10:41a        <DIR>            INSTALL
01/25/96        10:41a        <DIR>            SYMBOLS
01/25/96        10:41a        <DIR>            CHARSETS
01/25/96        10:41a        <DIR>            LOG
01/25/96        10:41a        <DIR>            REPLDATA
03/04/96        04:37p        <DIR>            SNMP
03/04/96        04:37p        <DIR>            BACKUP
               13 File(s)    0bytes
                     234,838,720 bytes free
```

You could even create a work table to hold results from operating system commands:

```
create table #os_work_table (value_1 text)
go

insert into #os_work_table
execute xp_cmdshell "dir c:\sql60"
```

In another example, you can use the 'xp_logevent' extended stored procedure to write a message into the Windows NT message log. Assume that you have just loaded data into a particular table and would like to record this event in the Windows NT application log. You could use the following SQL to make this happen:

```
declare @message varchar(255)
select @message = 'Polling process has finished
loading data'

exec xp_logevent 99999, @message, informational
```

You can now view this event by examining the application log's contents:

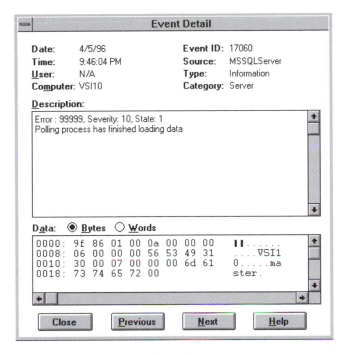

Figure 6.4

Finally, if you want to learn about your system's current login security profile, you can run the 'xp_loginconfig' stored procedure:

```
xp_loginconfig

name                    config_value
--------------------    --------------------
login mode              standard
default login           guest
default domain          VSI10
audit level             none
set hostname            false
map _                   domain separator
map $                   space
map #                   -
```

These three examples are only a few of the numerous built-in extended stored procedures that SQL Server provides. For more detail on the other extended stored procedures, see the Transact-SQL reference.

SQL Server provides built-in mechanisms to prevent an external stored procedure from "crashing" the database engine. Despite this safeguard, it's wise for database administrators to understand what a particular extended stored procedure does before making it available for general use. For example, there is little you can do to stop an external stored procedure from consuming vast amounts of CPU, disk, or memory. This could dramatically degrade performance, and it would be very difficult to determine the exact cause of the delay. SQL Server requires that the creator of a stored procedure have "sa" permission, which can help prevent unauthorized users from defining and registering their own extended stored procedures. This is another reason why you should limit the number of people who have access to the "sa" account.

Client/Server

One area that typically bogs down in a client/server configuration is data communication over the network. Clients often request enormous amounts of data from servers, only to process the data locally and reduce it to a fraction of its original size. As we've seen, you can move much of this reduction process onto the server by using stored procedures.

For example, assume that you have an order-tracking application where PC-based Windows™ clients request line item detail information from an NT server. This information serves as raw data for a calculation routine that the client runs. After running the calculation, the client displays the results. The user on the client never needs to see the line item details.

By analyzing the situation, you realize that you are using up a tremendous amount of network bandwidth just in sending the data from the server to the client. After you determine that by rewriting the calculation routine in Transact-SQL, you can move the entire processing operation onto the server. After the change, the client passes search criteria to the server's stored procedure and waits for the server to return the calculated results. Once the client receives the results, it displays the information. To the user, there is no change in functionality.

The benefit of this change is chiefly the elimination of the transfer of thousands of lines of detail data over the network. This conserves valuable network bandwidth. When you multiply this by all of the concurrent clients that perform this operation, you should see a noticeable network improvement.

The downside to this change is that the server now has more work to do. Therefore, you should only move logic from the client to the server if it is apparent that the savings from the network's speed improvement outweighs the cost of extra server processing.

Security

Stored procedures provide you with more options for data security. You can place very restrictive security on a table but still allow users to access its information via stored procedures.

For example, suppose that you are developing a sales prospecting system. One of the tables in the system contains sensitive data, such as your prospect's contact names, telephone numbers, and expected revenue potential.

Table 6.9 prospects

contact_first	contact_last	company	phone	class....
Larry	Lashow	Valet 2U	415-555-3333	C
Nicole	Taylor	Baby Togs	510-966-0918	A
Buddy	Cheugaie	Labrador Post	201-543-7765	A
.	.	.	.	.
.	.	.	.	.

Your user community has numerous tools available for reading information directly from tables. You are concerned that certain users may use SQL to bypass the security that you set up on your database and provide your competitors with proprietary data.

To restrict access to this table, you could GRANT and REVOKE the SELECT, UPDATE, INSERT, or DELETE privileges for each user or for PUBLIC. The problem is that sometimes, users really do have legitimate reasons for seeing this data. For example, you might allow junior employees to see only prospects with a class of C (not as much revenue potential as classes A or B). Another set of users may need to insert data into the table (via your application), but not actually see the other data in the table. You could, via a home-grown security application, dynamically GRANT and REVOKE privileges as needed. Instead, let's explore a stored procedure-based alternative for the INSERT privilege:

1. First, REVOKE all privileges on the table:

   ```
   revoke all on prospects from public
   ```

2. Next, create a DBA-level procedure that allows the user to insert rows into the table:

   ```
   create procedure prospects_insert
   @contact_first varchar(30),
   @contact_last varchar(40),
   ```

```
@company varchar(40),
.  .  .  .
as
insert into prospects values
(@contact_first, @contact_last, @company...)
```

3.   Finally, allow only certain users to execute the procedure you just created:

```
grant execute on prospects_insert to user
```

You can also use the SQL Enterprise Manager. This figure shows that you've revoked all privileges on the table from 'public':

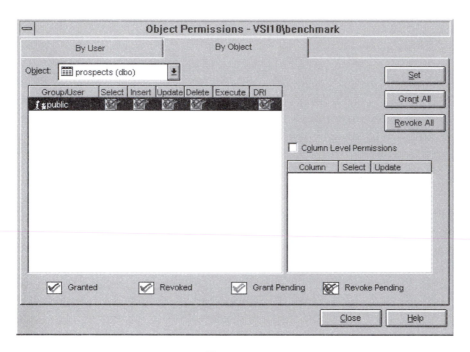

Figure 6.5

Next, you've created the procedure.

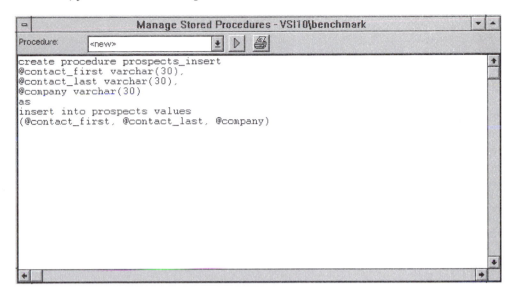

Figure 6.6

Finally, you've granted execute permission to all users.

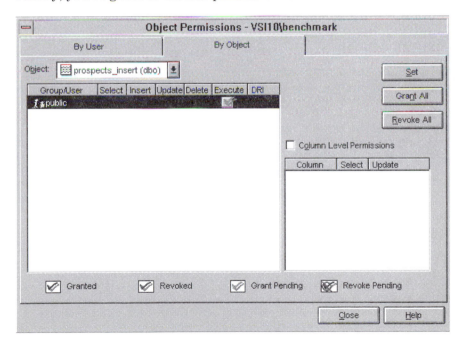

Figure 6.7

At this point, your programmers can replace the direct SQL entries in their programs with calls to this stored procedure. Other users, via their direct access tools, will not be able to directly retrieve information from this table.

Improving stored procedure performance

Getting the most speed from your stored procedures is generally no different from getting good query and application program performance: An efficient database design and SQL strategy are essential. It's also wise to check your Transact-SQL procedural code to make sure it's efficient, too. Despite these general suggestions, there is one stored procedure-specific technique that you can follow to improve response: It's a good idea to recompile stored procedures when appropriate.

Recompiling stored procedures

When you define a stored procedure, the SQL Server optimizer compiles the procedure. If, after creating the procedure, you alter the table or change the index structure, it's a good idea to consider recompiling the stored procedure. SQL Server does this automatically after you restart the engine or when the table structure changes. However, if you add or modify an index used by the procedure but don't restart the engine right away, SQL Server continues to use the original compiled stored procedure. Therefore, if you change your index strategy but don't want to shut down and restart the database engine, consider running the 'sp_recompile' system stored procedure. This procedure accepts the name of a table as a parameter. This means that the next time any stored procedure that uses the table is run, SQL Server recompiles the procedure.

Triggers

Triggers are statements that are invoked, or "triggered," when certain operations are performed on a table. Triggers can, in turn, invoke SQL or stored procedures. You create triggers by following these steps:

1. Connect to the database via the SQL Enterprise Manager or other tool. You must have sufficient privilege to create a trigger.

2. Write a script that contains the trigger creation statements.

3. Run the script.

4. You can also create triggers by using an application program or one of many other database tools.

When you create a trigger, the database engine makes entries in the 'sysobjects' and 'syscomments' tables. You can see the layout of these tables in the section "Creating and Maintaining Stored Procedures."

If you want to learn about the actual text of a trigger (or a stored procedure, rule, view, or default), you can use the 'sp_helptext' stored procedure. The only exception is when the object that you want to research was created with the ENCRYPTED option.

Let's look at a few examples of how triggers can simplify and speed your applications.

Audit trails

There are many times when you want to track modifications to a table. You could code audit trail logging directly into your applications, but this approach has several drawbacks:

- Users could potentially modify the data by using an unsecured end-user tool. You would have no way of knowing what changes were made and who made them.

- Programmers could omit audit trail logging from new applications, either accidentally or intentionally. Again, this allows unaudited access to your data.

- Even if programmers included audit trail logging in their programs, they could do so in a terribly inefficient way.

Instead of embedding audit trail logic into your applications, consider using a combination of triggers and Transact-SQL:

1. First, create a table to store audit trail records:

```
create table audit_trail
(
    source_table        char(32),
    user_id             char(8),
    action_code         char(1),
    action_timestamp    datetime,
    old_value           varchar(80),
    new_value           varchar(80)
)
```

The table above was designed to be a general-purpose repository, instead of being specifically tailored to hold information about only one database table.

2. Next, create triggers on any tables that you want to audit. The trigger listed below is for an INSERT on a table where we want to track one column's value:

```
create trigger employee_ins
on employee
for insert
as
declare @salary integer

select @salary = salary
from   inserted

insert into audit_trail
values ("employee", user_name(), "i",
        getdate(),  "",
        convert(varchar(30),@salary))
```

If you want to track more than one column's value, you can simply create a header/detail relationship in your audit tables. You would also modify your triggers accordingly.

When triggers are placed on your sensitive tables, there is no possible way for users to modify data without generating an audit trail record.

If you are interested in more detailed audit trail information, consider using the SQL Server trace utility. This utility, introduced with SQL Server 6.5, provides even more statistics about database access. We cover this new tool in Chapter 9.

Data replication

In earlier versions of SQL Server, you could implement a data replication strategy by using triggers. Beginning with SQL Server version 6.0, data replication is now built in to the database engine. This means that you no longer need to create and maintain triggers to achieve data replication.

Cascading deletes

One goal of referential integrity is to eliminate the possibility of "orphaned" child records. This means that you generally need to delete the child records first, then delete the appropriate parent record. You can use triggers to build cascading deletes, which provide an easier and more flexible approach to deleting parent and child records.

If you've defined a cascading delete relationship between a parent and child table and then delete a record from the parent table, the database engine automatically deletes any corresponding child records. Let's look at some sample SQL that creates a parent and two child tables that have a cascading delete relationship:

```
create table parent
(
    parent_id integer primary key
)

create table child1
(
   child_id integer primary key,
   parent_id integer
)

create table child2
(
   child_id integer primary key,
   parent_id integer,
        .    .    .
)
```

The code to create the cascading delete trigger looks like this:

```
create trigger parent_cascade
on parent for delete
as
begin
     declare @id integer
     select @id = d.parent_id
     from deleted d

     delete from child1
     where child1.parent_id = @id
     delete from child2
     where child2.parent_id = @id
end
```

By setting up this trigger, you can now delete a row from the parent table and have corresponding rows in the two child tables deleted as well. Keep in mind, however, that you may have difficulty with cascading deletes when there are foreign key relationships among these tables. In these cases, SQL Server may return an error message stating that an attempt was made to delete a parent record before all child records were deleted. In situations like this, you might have better luck with a stored procedure that first deletes child records and then moves on to delete the parent record.

In addition to simplifying your applications, cascading deletes also help reduce traffic between the engine and application processes, since you only need one SQL statement to handle two delete operations. This can be especially important in a client/server system.

Another way to delete data from multiple tables at one time is to use Transact-SQL's DELETE extension, as discussed in Chapter 5.

Chapter 7

General Tips

In this chapter, we continue our discussion about general application coding techniques that can help improve the performance of your programs. These suggestions can help improve your application's performance regardless of your choice of front-end tool.

We first cover the important topic of transactions, which are crucial for any application that depends on database integrity. We discuss how to make the best use of transactions, the value of adding transactions to existing applications, along with some traps that you should avoid in the process. Since error checking is such an important part of transactions, we also use this section to explore how to place comprehensive error checking inside your programs. Next, because cursors are such an important tool in developing robust database applications, we describe ways to improve cursor performance.

In a multiuser environment, it's important that your application maximize concurrency. In the ensuing section, we discuss several methods you can use to increase the level of concurrency in your applications. We explain what concurrency is, how locking affects concurrency, and the importance of isolation levels.

Finally, in "Miscellaneous tips," we suggest ways to improve bulk data transfer, as well as some ideas regarding object transfer.

Transactions

If your goal is to develop robust applications that guarantee the integrity of your data as well as provide predictably good service to your user community, you should use transactions in your programs and stored procedures.

Regardless of the role you play in your organization's data-processing environment, transactions are a key aid in performing your job. As an administrator, you should insist that any application or stored procedure that modifies data in the database use transactions. As a programmer, you should insist that your underlying database environment be supportive of transactions.

No discussion on transactions would be complete without exploring error checking issues. For more information about error checking, see the "Error checking" section of this chapter.

Let's begin by looking at a situation where an application program that doesn't use transactions damages the referential integrity of a database. In this example, you're maintaining a truck rental system. Customers call in to reserve a certain type of vehicle for a certain day. Two of the key tables in the system are the 'reservations' table, which contains entries for all reservations, and the 'vehicle_status' table, which stores the status for each vehicle for each day:

Table 7.1   reservations

res_num	vehicle_id	res_date
11095	15	Nov 12 1997
11096	16	Nov 12 1997
11097	17	Nov 13 1997
.	.	.

Table 7.2   vehicle_status

vehicle_id	vehicle_type	vehicle_date	vehicle_status
15	Pickup truck	Nov 11 1997	Available
15	Pickup truck	Nov 12 1997	Booked
16	Pickup truck	Nov 12 1997	Booked
17	12000 pound truck	Nov 12 1997	Available
17	12000 pound truck	Nov 13 1997	Booked
.	.	.	.

When a customer calls in to request a truck for a certain date, your program first checks the 'vehicle_status' table to see if there are any available trucks of the desired type for that date. If it finds any, you make an entry into the 'reservations' table and also update the status for the selected vehicle in the 'vehicle_status' table.

Suppose that one day, during the middle of a reservation, you lose power and your system goes down. What happens if the power loss happens after the entry into the 'reservations' table but before the update of the 'vehicle_status' table? Since you're not using transactions, you've damaged the referential integrity of your database. In real-world terms, your customer is going to arrive on the designated day and expect the designated type of vehicle. Since you didn't get the chance to update the 'vehicle_status' table for this customer's reservations, chances are there won't be a truck there for her when she arrives.

It's very easy to prevent these types of problems from occurring: Use transaction logging for multitable operations. For the case described above, your pseudocode would look like this:

```
check for vehicle availability
begin transaction
insert into reservations table
check error status
if no error
    update vehicle_status table
    check error status
    if no error
        commit transaction
    else
        rollback transaction
else
    rollback transaction
end if
```

Next, we'll look at some important issues to consider when you use transactions in your applications.

Transactions and DDL

Until SQL Server version 6.5, you could not place data definition language (DDL) inside a transaction. However, version 6.5 now supports this capability, meaning that you can commit or roll back transactions that make DDL calls. For example, suppose that you want to create a table if and only if a record exists in another table. In earlier versions of SQL Server, you could provide conditional logic to get a count of rows from the table in question and then create the new table if the row count exceeded a certain value. On the other hand, SQL Server 6.5 lets you perform all of this work within one transaction:

```
declare @record_count integer
select @record_count = 0
begin transaction
begin
    create table demo_ddl (col1 char(10))
```

```
      select @record_count = count(*)
      from source_table where pk_number = 909943
      if (@record_count > 0)
          commit transaction
      else
          rollback transaction
end
```

You can place any of these SQL statements inside a transaction:

- ALTER TABLE
- CREATE DEFAULT
- CREATE INDEX
- CREATE PROCEDURE
- CREATE RULE
- CREATE TABLE
- CREATE TRIGGER
- CREATE VIEW
- DROP DEFAULT
- DROP INDEX
- DROP PROCEDURE
- DROP RULE
- DROP TABLE
- DROP TRIGGER
- DROP VIEW
- GRANT
- REVOKE
- SELECT INTO
- TRUNCATE TABLE

You need to exercise caution when creating tables that might be accessed by other users. This is especially true if another user might make decisions based on a table that was created but not yet committed. Other users might find later that the table in question never really existed, since its creator eventually rolled it back. You can help prevent this undesirable situation by setting your transaction isolation levels correctly. We'll discuss this important topic in more detail later in this chapter.

Nested transactions

SQL Server lets you embed BEGIN TRANSACTION and COMMIT/ROLL-BACK TRANSACTION statements inside other transactions. This feature is known as nested transactions, and it can add a great deal of flexibility to your applications. Why would you use nested transactions? The primary reason would be because you have one or more SQL statements or stored procedures that in turn call other stored procedures. The following pseudocode may help illustrate this concept:

```
stored procedure 1
    begin a transaction
        perform a database operation
        call stored procedure 2
    commit the transaction
end stored procedure 1

stored procedure 2
    begin a transaction
        perform a database operation
        perform a database operation
    commit the transaction
end stored procedure 2
```

If the called stored procedures began and committed (or rolled back) their own transactions, and SQL Server didn't allow nested transactions, you would never be able to link these procedures. Keep in mind, however, that only the outer BEGIN TRANSACTION and COMMIT/ROLLBACK TRANSACTION statements control the actual work; subsequent transaction declarations merely increment the TRANCOUNT global variable. In the above example, only the COMMIT TRANSACTION statement in stored procedure 1 commits the work performed by both stored procedure 1 and 2. The COMMIT TRANSACTION statement in stored procedure 2 has no effect on the transaction.

SQL Server lets you name transactions, which helps improve program readability. However, if you attempt to roll back by name to a nested transaction, you'll receive an error:

```
    .   .   .   .   .
    .   .   .   .   .
begin transaction payment_update
begin
    update payments set payment_date = current_timestamp
    where payment_id = 1
    if (@@error = 0)
```

```
      begin
          begin transaction customer_update
          update customers set last_payment_date =
          current_timestamp
          where customer_id = @update_customer
          rollback transaction customer_update
          commit transaction payment_update
      end
end
```

```
Msg 6401, Level 16, State 1
Cannot rollback customer_update - no transaction or
savepoint of that name found.
```

One way that you could achieve your desired functionality would be to use a savepoint instead of the second transaction:

```
 .    .    .    .    .
 .    .    .    .    .
begin transaction payment_update
begin
      update payments set payment_date = current_timestamp
      where payment_id = 1
      if (@@error = 0)
      begin
          update customers set last_payment_date =
              current_timestamp
          where customer_id = @update_customer
          save transaction customer_updated
          rollback transaction customer_updated
          commit transaction payment_update
      end
end
```

In general, if you want to mark a commit point within a transaction or group of transactions, it's best to use SQL Server's savepoint feature. We'll cover this topic next.

Savepoints

In most cases, you can view transactions as "all or nothing" events. Either you want to save all of the work performed in a transaction or you want to remove all traces of your changes. To do otherwise essentially means that your data could be in an unknown and potentially unstable state. However, there are also times when an administrator or application developer may want to save part of a transaction, while discarding the rest. To make this possible, SQL Server provides an added statement not found in most other relational database management systems. This statement is called SAVE TRANSACTION, and you can use it to mark a savepoint within your transaction. If you set a savepoint and then decide to rollback your transaction, SQL Server saves all work performed up until the savepoint, while discarding all work after the savepoint. Let's look at an example to help clarify this concept.

Suppose that you want to update rows in a parent table and then update other rows in child tables. While you would like all of this work to complete successfully, you are prepared to resubmit the request for the child table updates should a problem arise. On the other hand, you want to update the parent table only once. You could do this by breaking your operation into two separate transactions:

```
begin transaction parent_update
    update parent set col2 = 'abc'
    if (@@error = 0)
        commit transaction parent_update
    else
        rollback transaction parent_update

begin transaction child_update
begin
    update child set col2 = 'cde'
    if (@@error = 0)
        commit transaction child_update
    else
        rollback transaction child_update
end
```

The SAVE TRANSACTION statement lets you combine these two transactions into one, while retaining control over the total operation:

```
begin transaction parent_and_child_update
    update parent set col2 = 'abc'
    if (@@error <> 0)
        rollback transaction parent_update
    else
        save transaction parent_completed_ok

    update child set col2 = 'cde'
    if (@@error <> 0)
        rollback transaction parent_completed_ok

commit transaction parent_and_child_update
```

Regardless of what happens with the child table update, the parent table has its work committed (as long as there were no problems with that part of the operation). Savepoints are the best technique to use when you need this kind of flexibility, as opposed to nested transactions. Nested transactions don't really help in this case and can actually lead to a false sense of security when you are designing your application.

Preventing long transactions

One particularly crucial transaction issue is the length of time that your transactions take. It is extremely important to keep your transactions as brief as possible.

Let's look at an illustration of the dangers of long, open transactions. Suppose you develop a client support application for a large insurance company. Customers call in, requesting information about their policies. This information includes benefits, payments, and refunds. One day, an operator is working with a customer, using your payment record screen to modify the customer's record. The customer states that she paid her bill two days earlier than your company said that they received her check. After researching the case, the operator agrees and offers to correct the record. The customer thanks your operator and hangs up. Since it is so close to the end of the day, your operator decides to leave the customer's record on the screen and make the change the next morning. If your application looks like the following pseudocode example, can you spot the potential problem?

```
get the customer's name and account number
begin transaction
build up a query
retrieve the record
display the record
prompt the user for changes
update the record
check for errors
if no errors
     commit transaction
else
     rollback transaction
```

If the operator goes home (or to lunch, or on break) after pulling up the record but before changing it, you have a long transaction. The transaction log cannot be freed until this transaction completes. The transaction log is an integral part of SQL Server's operations. If it can't be freed, there is a very good possibility that all data modification operations will come to a grinding halt until the log can restore its empty space. Consequently, it's imperative that all of your programs and database operations avoid long transactions whenever possible.

Modifying the above example to avoid the long transaction problem produces the following pseudocode:

```
get the customer's name and account number
build up a query
retrieve the record
display the record
prompt the user for changes
begin transaction
update the record
check for errors
if no errors
    commit transaction
else
    rollback transaction
```

By making this simple change, you eliminate the potential for a long transaction. You might want to add some logic to this code to make sure that the contents of the record haven't been changed by someone else between the time you select it and the time you update it.

When not to use transactions

There are some situations for which you should not use transactions. In fact, using transactions may actually hurt your performance in these instances:

1. **Queries.**   Remember that you only need to use transactions if your program modifies the database. If you're running a query and it doesn't have any INSERT/UPDATE/DELETE statements, you can omit transactions. There's no need to incur the overhead of a transaction if you don't make any data changes.

2. **Reports.**   Many programmers make the mistake of issuing BEGIN TRANSACTION statements at the start of reports. Running a report inside a transaction does nothing to help the report (unless you are also updating the table(s) as you proceed through the report). In fact, an open transaction during a report may even hurt your system's performance. See "Preventing long transactions" in this chapter for more information.

3. **Work tables.**   There are occasions when you need to create and employ temporary work tables. However, the traditional concepts of database integrity and transactional control may not apply in cases where you're using work tables. Thus, you may be able to avoid using transactions when populating or modifying information affecting your work tables.

4. **Bulk operations.**   We can define bulk operations as those procedures that make substantial changes to database tables. In many cases, there is no need to record these events in the transaction log. You have two options to disable transactions for bulk operations. First, SQL Server lets you set a database configuration flag that bypasses transactions during bulk inserts and SELECT INTO statements. We'll discuss this option later in the chapter. The second technique that you can use is to omit transactions within your application code itself when performing a bulk operation.

With all of this said, be aware that you may have no choice but to use transactions if you want to reduce the chances of data modifications during an operation. For example, during the running of a long query or report, you may want "freeze" the underlying data until the report has finished. To make this happen, you may need to issue a request that the optimizer lock all rows until the operation has finished, which requires that you begin a transaction. For more details on concurrency, see our discussion of this topic later in the chapter.

Location of BEGIN TRANSACTION and COMMIT TRANSACTION

You can greatly improve the clarity and maintainability of your programs by making it easy to locate the beginning and end of any transactions that you use. It's hard enough to debug programs; having to search for the start and end of a transaction adds unnecessary difficulty to the process. Consequently, always try to have your BEGIN and COMMIT/ROLLBACK TRANSACTION commands in the same block. For example, see how hard it would be to debug the following section of a stored procedure:

```
.  .  .  .  .  .
.  .  .  .  .  .
declare @all_ok smallint
.  .  .  .  .  .
.  .  .  .  .  .
begin transaction
insert into partners values (@partner, @partner_desc)
if (@@error = 0)
     select @all_ok = 1
else
     select @all_ok = 0

.  .  .  .  .  .
.  .  .  .  .  .
```

```
    goto decision_point
    .  .  .  .  .  .
    .  .  .  .  .  .

    decision_point:
        if (@all_ok = 1)
            commit transaction
        else
                rollback transaction
```

The difficulty would be compounded for each nested label that you call. Imagine what it would look like if the calls went four or five levels down.

A much cleaner way of achieving the same goal would look like this:

```
    declare @return_value smallint
    .  .  .  .  .  .
    .  .  .  .  .  .
    begin transaction
    execute @return_value = insert_handler @partner,
@partner_desc
    .  .  .  .  .  .
    .  .  .  .  .  .
    if (@return_value = 0)
        commit transaction
    else
        rollback transaction


    create procedure insert_handler (@partner char(4),
@partner_desc varchar(40))
    as
        insert into partners values (@partner,
@partner_desc)
        return @@error
```

By providing a single point of control for your transactions, you make the job of maintaining your code much easier.

Adding transactions to existing applications

If you're maintaining an existing application that doesn't use transactions, you should consider adding this powerful feature to your programs. While retrofitting existing code is usually an unenviable chore, adding transactions is one enhancement that aids you in the long run. Transactions (and error checking) benefit you and your users by increasing the reliability, data integrity, and ease of maintenance of your applications.

Transaction logging and text/image

Using the TEXT and IMAGE data types can place an extra burden on the transaction log. The transaction log has a finite size and is crucial to the smooth operation of your database engine. Text and image data can range in size from one byte all the way up to over two gigabytes, which could potentially fill up the transaction log. One of your most important tasks as an administrator is to keep your transaction log from filling, since all database-modifying operations come to a halt whenever the log is at capacity. How can you prevent text and image columns from filling the transaction log? There are a variety of ways, including using large datatype management features found in common application development tools and languages, as well as the UPDATETEXT and WRITETEXT functions. Let's focus on these two Transact-SQL statements.

UPDATETEXT and WRITETEXT let you circumvent the transaction log when inserting, updating, or deleting text and image data. For example, if you are inserting a row that contains a number of different fields, including a text or image column, you can insert the standard data by using traditional SQL. For the text or image data, you can then use WRITETEXT or UPDATETEXT to complete the insert operation. Since you used standard SQL for the regular columns, SQL Server logs their contents. On the other hand, the text or image column information never gets entered in the log, thereby saving space. The implied downside to this capability would be realized if your system crashed after you had completed the transaction but before SQL Server wrote the change out to disk during a checkpoint. Another, less likely problem could arise if the following sequence of events occurs:

1. You issue an SQL statement inserting the standard data.

2. You utilize the WRITETEXT statement to insert the text or image data.

3. The WRITETEXT operation fails due to a lack of available disk space.

4. You commit the transaction (having not checked the result of the WRITETEXT operation). This, by the way, is one of many good reasons for error checking.

At this point, you have a data integrity problem, since you've committed the standard columns in your row, yet the text or image information never made it onto disk. Realistically, both of the above potential problems are fairly unlikely. However, only you can determine whether the risks of not logging text or image data outweigh the transaction log space preservation that these two functions provide.

Implicit transactions

SQL Server 6.5 introduces a new way to begin transactions automatically. You can now inform the engine that you want it to start a transaction after any of these commands:

- ALTER TABLE
- CREATE
- DELETE
- DROP
- FETCH
- GRANT
- INSERT
- OPEN
- SELECT
- TRUNCATE TABLE
- UPDATE

You control this behavior by setting the IMPLICIT_TRANSACTIONS variable with the SET command. Let's look at how this feature works.

To begin, let's create a small sample table:

```
create table demo_implicit
(
    record_id integer identity primary key,
    sample_value char(10)
)
```

Next, let's insert a row, then retrieve it:

```
insert into demo_implicit (sample_value)
values ('hello')
select * from demo_implicit

record_id    sample_value
-----------  ------------
1            hello
```

What happens if we next try to roll back the operation?

```
rollback transaction

Msg 3903, Level 16, State 1
The rollback transaction request has no
corresponding BEGIN TRANSACTION.
```

SQL Server has returned an error, since we never issued a BEGIN TRANS-ACTION request. Observe what happens when we drop and re-create the table, then set the IMPLICIT_TRANSACTIONS variable:

```
set implicit_transactions on

insert into demo_implicit (sample_value)
values ('hello')

select * from demo_implicit

record_id    sample_value
-----------  ------------
1            hello

(1 row(s) affected)

rollback transaction

select * from demo_implicit

record_id    sample_value
-----------  ------------

(0 row(s) affected)
```

With the implicit transactions variable enabled, SQL Server began a trans-action when it encountered the INSERT statement. This meant that we could then roll back the transaction later.

Should you set this variable? Generally, it's better for you to control the transaction flow within your own application logic. Setting this variable takes away that control and gives it to SQL Server instead. This can lead to poten-tially undesirable results. For example, what happens if a user has set this variable, inserts a row, and then leaves for the day with his application still ac-tive? His transaction is still considered open and won't be committed or rolled back until the user explicitly makes that request or logs off. SQL Server won't let you truncate the transaction log for any uncommitted transactions. If this user's transaction started late in the log, it's possible that a truncate log operation may have little or no effect on the amount of free space. The end result may be a hung system, since SQL Server blocks users from making any data changes if there isn't sufficient space in the transaction log.

Transaction abort control

SQL Server 6.5 introduces a new option that controls engine behavior upon encountering an error. The XACT_ABORT setting tells the engine whether or not to abort the entire transaction should an error arise. When you set this parameter to ON, SQL Server aborts the entire transaction and rolls back all statements if an error occurs during any SQL statement. Setting the parameter to OFF apprises SQL Server that you want the engine to keep working, even if it encounters an error on a particular statement.

Which technique should you incorporate into your applications? Database integrity should always be your guiding principle when making these decisions. If you are writing a particular group of SQL statements and then bundling them together in a transaction, there usually is no benefit in having some of the statements succeed while others fail. This defeats the whole purpose of transactions. For the sake of transactional integrity, unless you can think of a compelling reason, it's a good idea to leave the XACT_ABORT enabled. This helps to safeguard the quality and integrity of your data.

Distributed transactions

What are distributed transactions?

Beginning with release 6.5, SQL Server incorporates enhanced technology that improves the reliability of transactions that span more than one machine. These types of transactions are known as "distributed transactions." When a transaction is said to be distributed, it means that more than one system participates in the steps necessary to complete the work.

For example, suppose that you've written a human resources application that you've rolled out to your entire organization. When your company hires a new employee, your application inserts a record into the central payroll database, as well as at the employee's new work location. How can you ensure data integrity? If both tables were in the same database on the same, local system, the SQL Server engine is responsible for making sure that no errors occurred during the insert operation. However, this task is made more complicated when the tables are in different databases and are separated by hundreds of kilometers and a shaky network. This more complex environment has many more chances for failure. What happens if your program successfully inserts the record into the central payroll database, along with the remote database, but the remote database server fails before the transaction is committed? From the central database's perspective, the transaction completed normally and the employee was added correctly. However, the remote server never finished its work, and the new employee is unknown from its perspective. In another situation, the circumstances are reversed: The remote server stays active and therefore thinks that the transaction was good, whereas the local server crashed, leaving this transaction forever uncommitted. Handling these situations programmatically places a large burden on application developers. The amount of code necessary to coordinate among disparate servers is complex to design, difficult to maintain, and nearly impossible to guarantee.

In cases like this, you need more reliable, robust engine features that can handle complex, distributed requests, rather than relying on programmer-developed code. Developers on mainframes and UNIX® systems have had this type of technology for many years. "Transaction monitors" is the name that has been assigned to most of these utilities. Among other functions, a transaction monitor ensures that all parties to a transaction are ready to commit before actually issuing the commit order. If any of the components in a transaction are unable to proceed, the transaction monitor safely rolls back the work on the rest of the systems, thereby guaranteeing data integrity. What do we mean by data integrity? Generally, for a transaction monitor to maintain data integrity, its transactions must pass the "ACID" test. The ACID test stands for:

- **Atomicity.** Atomicity refers to the fact that all participants in a transaction work together, thereby guaranteeing that the underlying databases are not left in an inconsistent state. If one database commits its part of the distributed transaction, you can be confident that all the other databases committed their fragment as well. On the other hand, if one database fails to complete the transaction and rolls back, then all other databases roll back as well.

- **Consistency.** This means that all the steps in the transaction lead to a consistent result. For example, if during the middle of the new employee add operation, you decide to roll back the transaction, the consistency features of the transaction monitor warrant that all participating databases will roll back their portions of the transaction.

- **Isolation.** This concept is identical to the concept of transaction isolation on a single machine: Other users or processes are not allowed access to our transaction's data until the data has been committed. This also means that transactions can't interfere with each other: It wouldn't be helpful if distributed transaction A wrote data into distributed transaction B.

- **Durability.** When a transaction is durable, it means that once it has been committed, it can't be undone, even if any of the computers or network components that participated in the original work go on to fail at a later time. For example, let's use our human resources application that we described earlier. If the field computer fails two days after adding the new employee, the durability of the transaction means that the new employee's record on the central system is safe.

It's beyond the scope of this book to describe distributed transactions to their fullest. However, it's worthwhile for us to consider how we can make most efficient use of this new feature.

Distributed transaction coordinator

At the heart of SQL Server's distributed transaction capabilities is a new tool known as the distributed transaction coordinator (DTC). Microsoft provides this tool with all copies of SQL Server 6.5. You can start the DTC as a Windows NT service, or you can use the SQL Enterprise Manager. DTC also can work within the framework of other popular transaction managers, such as Top End™, Tuxedo™, and Encina™.

You can set a variety of DTC options from within SQL Enterprise Manager:

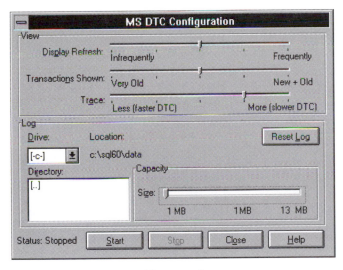

Figure 7.1

What do these options mean? Let's examine each one, especially as it relates to performance:

1. **Display refresh.** You can set how often SQL Server updates the DTC display. Values for this option can range between 20 seconds all the way down to 1 second. The lower the value, the more frequently SQL Server updates the screen showing the status of all transactions. However, this regularity costs more overhead.

2. **Transactions shown.**   You can configure how old a transaction must be before SQL Server displays its information. Values can range between 5-minute-length transactions down to 1-second transactions. The longer settings may suffice if you only want to monitor potential long transactions. If, on the other hand, you want to watch all transactions, use a shorter interval.

3. **Trace.**   You can request five different degrees of tracing, from no tracing all the way through traces that show error, warning, and informational details. Using the more descriptive trace settings can generate copious amounts of data, so choose this option with care.

4. **Log capacity.**   The DTC relies on a file called MSDTC.LOG. You can select how large this file should be.

Once DTC is running, you can use it to monitor the state of all current distributed transactions.

You can also request statistics that describe the overall state of your system's distributed transactions:

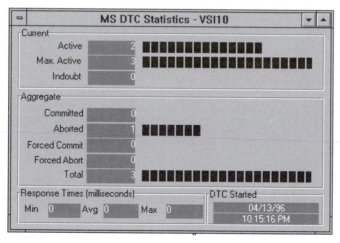

Figure 7.2

BEGIN DISTRIBUTED TRANSACTION

To launch a distributed transaction, you issue the BEGIN DISTRIBUTED TRANSACTION statement. This statement lets the DTC know that you want it to assign the resources necessary to support a multiple-machine operation. The DTC on each machine that participates in the transaction must be running, or you receive an error message:

```
Msg 8501, Level 16, State 1
DTC on server 'MRP' is unavailable
Msg 8524, Level 16, State 1
The current transaction couldn't be exported to
remote site. It has been rolled back.
```

If you haven't started the DTC on the coordinating machine, you receive a slightly different message when starting a distributed transaction:

```
Msg 8501, Level 16, State 1
DTC on server 'STATISTICS' is unavailable
```

When you issue this statement, you are responsible for providing the corresponding COMMIT TRANSACTION or ROLLBACK transaction command. No other user, process, or database instance can make this request. What happens when you issue a COMMIT TRANSACTION request? SQL Server performs these steps:

1. The DTC checks with all other DTCs on the other machines that are part of the transaction.

2. For each machine that is participating in the transaction, the DTC issues a prepare-to-commit message. After preparing, these remote DTCs are said to be in an "in-doubt" state.

3. If all transaction managers in the transaction are ready to commit, the coordinating DTC issues a commit request.

4. If one or more of the remote transaction managers is unable to prepare to commit, the coordinating DTC issues an abort command to everyone in the transaction.

After a successful commit, the distributed transaction is finished. On the other hand, if any of the participating DTCs never leave the in-doubt state, the coordinating DTC can abort the entire transaction.

Savepoints

Earlier in this chapter, we saw how you can use savepoints to mark acceptable rollback points within a transaction. However, if you're using a distributed transaction, SQL Server ignores any savepoints when performing a rollback. This means that even if you defined a savepoint and then later explicitly rolled the transaction back to the savepoint, SQL Server will roll all the way back to the BEGIN DISTRIBUTED TRANSACTION statement.

Implicit distributed transactions and stored procedures

SQL Server 6.5 introduces a new option that lets you determine the default behavior when running a remote stored procedure. This option is called 'remote_proc_transactions.' When you enable this option, SQL Server automatically begins a distributed transaction whenever you execute a remote stored procedure. With this option disabled, SQL Server performs no special distributed transaction steps when you execute a remote stored procedure.

What happens if you have this option enabled and you've already begun a local transaction prior to executing the remote stored procedure? As part of the distributed transaction operation, SQL Server places the already-running local transaction under DTC control. This means that when you commit or roll back the distributed transaction, the local transaction is controlled by the results of the distributed transaction.

Distributed transactions and performance

Given all that we've learned about distributed transactions, what are some guidelines that you can follow to amplify their performance? Although a detailed exploration of efficient distributed transaction processing could fill an entire book, here are a few steps you can take to reduce bottlenecks:

- **Network quality and speed.**   One of the biggest obstacles to a well-running distributed transaction system is the speed or quality of the network. It's hard to get transactions committed quickly when the network is forced to resend packets because of line noise. If you don't have a high-quality, high-speed network, distributed transactions may not be for you.

- **Remote system management.**   Make sure that all remote systems that are participating in distributed transactions are well-tuned. In addition, don't forget to check other response-related issues, such as indexing, UPDATE STATISTICS, and disk layout.

- **Replication.**   Not all transactions need to be distributed. Before you go to the trouble and expense of issuing a distributed transaction, double-check that these updates need to happen in real time. SQL Server has a very sophisticated replication feature (which we'll discuss in Chapter 16). In many cases, there is no need to make multiple updates via a transaction; replication often delivers information long before it's needed at the remote site.

Error checking

While it is a known fact that programmers never make mistakes, it is still a good idea to humor the users by checking for errors at critical points in your programs. If you aren't checking for errors, your programs may still fail, and you then have the added burden of trying to figure out what went wrong without the benefit of the information that error checking provides you.

Let's demonstrate what we mean with a simple pseudocode example. Suppose you are maintaining a program that listens to a communication line, collects data, and then inserts rows into a table. The segment of logic of interest looks like this:

```
connect to the database
while (still receiving data)
     insert a row of information
end while
```

This logic is fine if you never encounter an error, but, realistically, you can expect that your program will run into problems from time to time. What happens in the above example if, while attempting to insert a new row into the table, the database returns an error indicating a duplicate value in a unique index? Since the program has no error checking, the data contained in the buffer is lost, potentially forever. It's especially dangerous not to check for errors when the data that you are working with is transitory in nature, since if you lose it you may not be able to replicate it. Adding error checking to the above sample is a simple task, but it greatly improves your program's ability to recover from a communication or database error:

```
connect to the database
while (still receiving data)
     insert a row of information
     if an error occurred
         copy the record to a log file
         report on the error
     end if
end while
```

Incomplete error checking

Just adding error checking to your programs is not enough. You also must make sure that you're checking for errors in all places where they might occur. It's all too common to take over the maintenance of an existing application, notice that the application has error checking in place and then, later, realize that the error checking logic is incomplete.

Let's look at an example of this. In this illustration, your stored procedure inserts records into a shipment request table, then logs this information into a table that tracks user access to the data. You use transaction logging and also check for errors.

```
declare @status_message varchar(80)
   .            .            .
   .            .            .
```

```
begin transaction

insert into shipment_requests values (....)
   .              .              .
   .              .              .
insert into transaction_audits values (....)

if (@@error = 0)
begin
   commit transaction
   print "records updated"
end
else
begin
   rollback transaction
   select @status_message = 'record update failed' +
                              convert(char(5), @@error)
   print @status_message
end
end if
   .              .              .
   .              .              .
```

While this example does check for errors, it only checks for errors just prior
to issuing a COMMIT TRANSACTION or ROLLBACK TRANSACTION command. If any errors occur earlier on in the program, they might pass unnoticed
if the last SQL statement executes correctly. When using transactions, always
make sure to check for errors along the way, as well as immediately before finishing the transaction:

```
declare @status_message varchar(80)
   .              .              .
   .              .              .
begin transaction

insert into shipment_requests values (....)
if (@@error <> 0)
begin
   rollback transaction
   select @status_message = 'record update failed' +
                              convert(char(5), @@error)
   print @status_message
   return
end
   .              .              .
```

```
         .                .                 .
insert into transaction_audits values (....)

if (@@error = 0)
begin
    commit transaction
    print "records updated"
end
else
begin
    rollback transaction
    select @status_message = 'record update failed' +
                              convert(char(5), @@error)
    print @status_message
end
end if
         .                .                 .
```

Remember to check for errors after any of the following statements:

- INSERT
- UPDATE
- DELETE
- SELECT
- EXECUTE
- DECLARE CURSOR
- OPEN CURSOR
- CLOSE CURSOR
- BEGIN TRANSACTION
- COMMIT TRANSACTION
- ROLLBACK TRANSACTION

Timing of error checking

So far, we've learned that your programs should check for errors and that you should check for errors after all appropriate statements. There's one more thing to consider: the timing of your error checking.

Generally, if you're writing SQL or Transact-SQL, you check the value of the @@ERROR global variable to learn if your program encountered an error. This variable is maintained for you by SQL Server; you only need to examine its contents. Be aware, however, that you may run into problems if you delay checking @@ERROR. This is because many operations reset @@ERROR, and by the time you check it, it may have been changed. @@ERROR gets reset by more operations than you may realize.

For example, let's look at a section of code to see how you might run into this type of problem. In this example, you are deleting a row from a table, based on the value contained in a variable:

```
declare @id_to_delete integer
    .           .           .
    .           .           .

select @id_to_delete = 123456
begin transaction
delete from students
where student_number = @id_to_delete
    .           .           .
    .           .           .
delete from student_classes
where student_number = @id_to_delete

if (@@error = 0)
    commit transaction
else
    rollback transaction
```

Can you see what is wrong with this example? The problem is that you check the @@ERROR value too late. You execute the SQL DELETE statement, delete another record, and only then check the @@ERROR value. Many operations reset the @@ERROR value. This means that even if there is a problem with the first DELETE statement and the @@ERROR variable is set to an error status, you lose the error status by executing the next DELETE statement, because that statement also resets the value.

Therefore, it's crucial that you don't wait too long to check the value of @@ERROR. You can do this by checking it after each operation, or you can save it into your own variable:

```
declare @id_to_delete integer
declare @stored_error_status smallint
    .           .           .
    .           .           .

select @id_to_delete = 123456
begin transaction
delete from students
where student_number = @id_to_delete
```

```
select @stored_error_status = @@error
    .           .           .
    .           .           .
delete from student_classes
where student_number = @id_to_delete

if (@@error = 0) and (@stored_error_status = 0)
    commit transaction
else
    rollback transaction
```

By saving the value of @@ERROR into a variable that you maintain, you preserve the state of your program during the operation in question. You can then check the contents of your variable when appropriate.

Cursors

Cursors are an integral part of most database applications. SQL Server provides developers with a choice of many different cursor options. In this section, we explore each of these cursor options, with particular attention to their effects on performance.

Server cursors

One of the key technical concepts of relational databases is that data is oriented in "sets." When you issue an SQL statement, the database engine normally returns all results to you in one group, or set. However, there are occasions when you may want to operate on the individual rows within a set. Server cursors let users and programmers perform these kinds of tasks. This helps reduce the amount of data sent over the network and can accelerate response time.

Let's look at some server cursor examples. In the first example, SQL Server uses a server cursor to retrieve a single row from a query, update or delete the row, and then fetch the next row:

```
declare @lookup_number integer

select @lookup_number = 5588656

declare C_balance_update cursor for
select * from customer_master
where account_number = @lookup_number
open C_balance_update
```

```
fetch C_balance_update

if (@@fetch_status = 0)
    update customer_master
    set account_balance = account_balance * 1.1
    where current of C_balance_update

close C_balance_update

deallocate C_balance_update
```

In another example, you can construct a query that identifies a set of data. Using a server cursor, you can then move anywhere in that data set and perform a positioned update or delete:

```
declare @start_number integer
declare @stop_number integer

select @start_number = 100000
select @stop_number  = 200000

declare C_range_update scroll cursor for
select * from customer_master
where account_number between @start_number and
@stop_number

open C_range_update

fetch last from C_range_update

if (@@fetch_status = 0)
    update customer_master
    set account_balance = account_balance * 1.1
    where current of C_range_update

close C_range_update

deallocate C_range_update
```

Bear in mind that you can perform positioned updates and deletes on only those tables that have a unique index. If there is no unique index and you attempt to update or delete based on cursor position, you'll get an error message:

```
Msg 16929, Level 16, State 1
Cursor is read only
```

This type of cursor behavior is similar to what happens when you set the IN-SENSITIVE option. We'll discuss this option in more detail in the next section.

SQL Server does not use a server cursor when you perform any of these types of operations:

- **Simple fetches from the database engine.** In this type of operation, your program wants to retrieve the entire result set from the engine, so there is no need to keep any data on the server.

- **READ-ONLY concurrency.** If your application only reads data and doesn't plan to make any updates, SQL Server can pass all data from the server down to the client.

- **FORWARD-ONLY cursor types.** If your program moves through your data in only the forward direction, there is no need for the engine to hold any data on the server.

- **Rowset size of 1.** With only one row to fetch, it doesn't make much sense for SQL Server to hold data back on the server.

INSENSITIVE cursor option

Normally, when you create a cursor, you retrieve data from the actual data tables. However, there may be times where you want to create your own copy of the data. You can do this by using the INSENSITIVE option when you declare the cursor. Using this option tells SQL Server that you want the engine to create a temporary table and then copy the result set into this new temporary table:

```
declare C_awards insensitive cursor for
select * from awards
open C_awards
while (@@fetch_status <> -1)
begin
      fetch C_awards
end
```

Remember that if you declare a cursor with the INSENSITIVE option, you have these limitations:

1. You won't be able to see any changes to the base table data. If another user modifies the data that you're currently examining, you won't be able to tell, regardless of the transaction isolation that you've specified, since you are looking at a copy of the data.

2. You won't be able to make changes to the resulting data set. Since you're working with a copy of the data, SQL Server returns an error if you try to modify:

```
declare C_awards insensitive cursor for
select * from awards
open C_awards
while (@@fetch_status <> -1)
begin
      fetch C_awards
      update awards set mileage_level =
            mileage_level * 1.25
      where current of C_awards
end

Msg 16929, Level 16, State 1
Cursor is read only
```

Don't forget that creating temporary tables comes at a price. If your IN-SENSITIVE cursor retrieves all rows from a large table, for example, you could inadvertently fill up all tempdb space. Make sure that these types of cursors retrieve limited sets of information.

One final note regarding INSENSITIVE cursors: If you declare a standard cursor (e.g., a cursor that doesn't use the INSENSITIVE option) and each of the underlying tables does not have a unique index, SQL Server automatically treats your cursor as if it was declared with the INSENSITIVE option. This means that you won't be able to perform a positioned update or delete on the cursor.

Scrollable cursors

For many applications that use cursors, your goal as a developer is to move for-ward through the result set, returning information to the user as needed. There may be times, however, when you also want to move backward within a result set, as well as position anywhere within the result set. For these circumstanc-es, a scroll cursor is the best solution. In addition, scroll cursors also let you see any committed updates or deletes that any other users make to your base table. Let's look at some examples of how you can use scroll cursors.

Imagine that you are writing an application that lets users navigate within a results set. Once users have queried for the data, they can then move forward and backward within the result set. They can even request a particular record number:

```
declare C_calls scroll cursor for
     select * from sales_calls
open C_calls
fetch C_calls
fetch C_calls
```

```
fetch prior from C_calls
fetch absolute 3 from C_calls
```

In this example, the user fetches two rows from the 'C_calls' cursor and then moves back one row. Finally, the user fetches the third row in the result set. You can even combine a scroll cursor with an update cursor (we'll discuss update cursors later in this section):

```
declare C_calls scroll cursor for
     select * from sales_calls for update
open C_calls
fetch absolute 3 from C_calls
fetch relative 1 from C_calls
update sales_calls set
     call_length = 32.55 where current of C_calls
```

We used FETCH RELATIVE to move the cursor forward one row from the third row in the result set. SQL Server 6.5 now lets you assign variables to the FETCH RELATIVE and FETCH ABSOLUTE statements:

```
declare @cursor_pos smallint
select @cursor_pos = 45
. . .
. . .
open C_calls
fetch relative @cursor_pos from C_calls
```

Should you use scroll cursors? The answer depends on whether you think that your application will need to use the advanced cursor navigation features provided by scroll cursors. If so, then make use of scroll cursors. If not, then standard forward-only cursors should suffice. Prior to SQL Server 6.5, another reason to use scroll cursors was to have the engine notify you when underlying rows changed. However, SQL Server 6.5 now incorporates this feature into standard, forward-only cursors. We'll discuss this a little later in this section, during our analysis of dynamic cursors.

Keep in mind that if you decide that you want to use the advanced fetching mechanisms furnished by scroll cursors, you'll need to declare your cursor as a scroll cursor. Otherwise, you'll receive these types of messages:

```
Msg 16911, Level 16, State 1
fetch: The fetch type FETCH_PRIOR cannot be used
with forward only cursors

Msg 16911, Level 16, State 1
fetch: The fetch type FETCH_ABSOLUTE cannot be
```

```
used with forward only cursors

Msg 16911, Level 16, State 1
fetch: The fetch type FETCH_RELATIVE cannot be
used with forward only cursors
```

Read-only cursors

You can direct SQL Server to prevent updates on your cursor by setting the READ ONLY option. Setting this option alters the default cursor behavior, which normally allows updates. Consider using this option if you are sure that you don't need to update any information.

Detecting data changes with cursors

One common concern of database application programmers is how to tell if the underlying data has changed during the running of their program. Below, we examine a number of cursor types, each of which has its own strengths and weaknesses for handling data alterations.

Static cursors

When you retrieve data from a static cursor, you don't see any changes made to underlying data after you opened the cursor. If you want to see these changes, you'll need to close and then reopen the cursor. A static cursor corresponds to a cursor created with the INSENSITIVE option. If you're programming with ODBC, SQL Server automatically creates a static cursor (even if you've requested a dynamic cursor) when any of the following are in effect:

- DISTINCT
- GROUP BY
- Outer join
- UNION
- UNION ALL

Dynamic cursors

A dynamic cursor detects all changes to underlying data before you fetch each row of the result set. This means that if a row was part of the result set but is deleted before you fetch it, the cursor won't return this removed row. This can be very helpful when writing applications in environments where there is a high degree of data turnover. In these types of situations, it's very possible that one user may change or delete a row while another user is getting ready to query for the same row. Let's look at how dynamic cursors can help improve the timeliness of your data.

For the purposes of this illustration, let's create and populate a small table:

```
create table demo_cursor
(
      demo_id integer identity primary key,
      demo_text char(20)
)
insert into demo_cursor (demo_text)
      values ("This is the first row")
insert into demo_cursor (demo_text)
      values ("This is the second row")
insert into demo_cursor (demo_text)
      values ("This is the third row")
insert into demo_cursor (demo_text)
      values ("This is the fourth row")
insert into demo_cursor (demo_text)
      values ("This is the fifth row")
```

Next, let's imagine two users working on the system at the same time. We can summarize their actions by using the following sequence of events:

Table 7.3   activity

time	Bud	Lou
13:45.57	declare C cursor for select * from demo_cursor	
13:46.01	open C	
13:46.02	fetch C	
13:46.02	demo_id demo_text ------- --------- 1 This is the first row	
13:46.03		delete from demo_cursor where demo_id = 2
13:46.05	fetch C	
	demo_id demo_text ------- --------- 3 This is the third row	

Table 7.3   activity (Continued)

13:46.09		update demo_cursor set demo_text = "An updated fourth row" where demo_id = 4
13:46.22	`fetch C`	
13:46.23	demo_id demo_text ------- --------- 4 An updated fourth row	

In this case, the dynamic cursor has kept the user well-informed about the exact state of the data. Bud's cursor was continually refreshed, discovering the delete and update operation while they happened. In fact, if Lou or anyone else had added one or more rows to the 'demo_cursor' table during the fetch operation, Bud's cursor would have detected the newly inserted rows.

SQL Server 6.5 introduces two new features that have a major effect on dynamic cursors. First, you no longer need to have a unique index in place on the underlying table when you want to update data using a dynamic cursor.

Next, SQL Server 6.5 now opens forward-only cursors as dynamic cursors, which helps improve performance, as well as letting users know when underlying data has changed. This new default behavior explains the example we just saw, since we needed no extra code to inform SQL Server that we wanted a dynamic cursor. The only exception to this rule occurs when the query that defines the cursor makes use of aggregate functions or outer joins.

If you're programming with ODBC and you've requested a forward-only dynamic cursor, SQL Server may still choose to use a static cursor if certain conditions exist. See the discussion on static cursors for more detail about these conditions.

FOR UPDATE

When you declare your cursor, you can instruct SQL Server that you plan to update the underlying data, based on the cursor's current position. For example, the following SQL statements demonstrate how you can use a cursor to locate and then update a row:

```
declare C cursor for select * from employees
for update
open C
```

```
fetch C
update employees set location = 'Maidenhead'
where current of C
```

This update statement affects the first row retrieved from the cursor. In a more typical situation, you would use an update cursor to find a series of rows and then apply a change to some or all of the located rows:

```
declare C cursor for select * from employees where
     location in ("Reading", "London", "Maidenhead")
for update
open C
fetch C
update employees set location = "Maidenhead"
where current of C
```

This time, we're updating only those employees that work in one of the three specified locations.

If you attempt to update on a cursor that was created as INSENSITIVE, SQL Server returns an error:

```
Msg 16929, Level 16, State 1
Cursor is read only
```

Cursor deallocation

Once you've finished using a cursor and don't plan on employing it again during the running of your program, it's a good idea to deallocate the cursor. You can do this by issuing the DEALLOCATE statement. Calling this statement frees up all internal data structures used by the cursor:

```
declare C_partners cursor for
select * from partners
open C_partners
fetch C_partners
. . .
. . .
close C_partners
deallocate C_partners
```

Unlike the CLOSE statement, once you've deallocated a cursor, you won't be able to reopen it later.

Concurrency

Concurrency can be thought of as the ability of your programs to peacefully co-exist with other programs running at the same time. In this section, we discuss how to maximize concurrency in your application environment.

When you design a single-user application, you generally don't give concurrency much thought. This is only natural: The one user is king and has exclusive control over all system resources. Problems can arise, however, when you port this application to, or develop a new application for, a multiuser environment. Before we discuss how to improve concurrency, however, let's look at a typical problem situation that illustrates how concurrency can become an issue.

Suppose that you have a ticket reservation application. Customers call in and request seats for a particular event. Two of the more heavily accessed tables in the application are:

Table 7.4   events

event_id	event_title	event_date	seats_left
1105	A Night with Sammy Spear	Dec 7 1997	405
1106	Air Supply: The Reunion	Dec 19 1997	25034
1107	Featuring Nikki Sierra	Dec 30 1997	18
.	.	.	.
.	.	.	.

Table 7.5   purchases

purchase_id	event_id	amount_paid	payment_type....
23098	1107	25.99	V
23099	1144	203.99	C
23100	1104	63.99	A

Your application processes ticket requests as follows:

1. You determine what event the customer would like to see. This entails locating the correct row in the 'events' table.

2. If 'seats_left' is greater than zero, you add a row into the 'purchases' table.

3. You update the 'events' table to lower the number of 'seats_left.' Your UPDATE statement uses the 'event_id' to find the correct row to change.

During development, everything seemed fine with this approach. Once the system rolls out, however, you begin hearing complaints from your users. Periodically, they receive "record locked" error messages from the applications. When this happens, they must reenter the data into the system. Some customers have even lost out on fast-selling events. What is happening, and how can you correct it?

When you update the 'events' table, you briefly hold a lock on the updated row's page. If other users are trying to update the same row or other rows on the same page, their application will receive an error message from the engine. This error message tells the front-end process that the engine is unable to make the modification because the page containing the row is locked.

If your programs aren't specifically coded to gracefully handle locked records, they may fail at this point. Let's move on and learn more about locks, and how to code your programs to work with them.

Locking issues

Locking scenarios

How does SQL Server choose which type of lock to use? A great deal depends on what type of operation you're performing. First, we must differentiate between actual and intent locks. The main difference between these two types of locks is that an intent lock blocks other processes from acquiring their own actual or intent lock on an object, whereas an actual lock goes ahead and locks the object itself. The object can be a table, data page, or an extent, which is composed of eight 2K data or index pages. Each lock type has the following profile:

- **Shared locks.** When you run a standard SELECT statement that reads but does not write data, SQL Server places shared locks on the objects that you are reviewing. Other users or processes are free to read, or even place locks on, the same objects that your process has locked. In fact, several users can have active shared locks on the same objects at one time. Shared locks are the least restrictive lock type. However, don't forget that your transaction isolation level can affect whether even a shared lock is requested. We'll discuss transaction isolation levels later in this chapter.

   Shared locks are helpful in read-only operations but are not strong enough in situations where you want to modify data. For these scenarios, SQL Server chooses a stronger locking mechanism.

- **Update locks.** An update lock is the next most restrictive lock mechanism. When you alter data within a table, SQL Server places an update lock on any affected pages. Right before the actual change, the engine raises, or promotes, update locks to exclusive locks.

- **Exclusive locks.**   When SQL Server places an exclusive lock on an object, no other processes can make any changes to the locked object. This helps protect your data integrity, since it would be dangerous for multiple processes to be modifying the same objects at the same point in time. Once your transaction finishes, the engine releases exclusive locks so that others can access the just-modified data.

SQL Server introduces two new types of locks that let your applications perform row-level locking:

- **Insert page locks.**   This lock signifies that a process is inserting data into a table that has been permitted to use the Insert Row-Level locking (IRL) feature.
- **Link page locks.**   As pages fill with data, SQL Server needs to assign additional pages to be part of the table. This is known as linking the new pages to the existing table and is represented by a link page lock. The link page lock is actually a promoted insert page lock and belongs to the first transaction that caused added pages to be linked to the table. The lock is held until the transaction either commits or is rolled back.

You have a choice of two ways to determine what kinds of locks are being held and who is holding them. You can use the **SQL Enterprise Manager** to get this information:

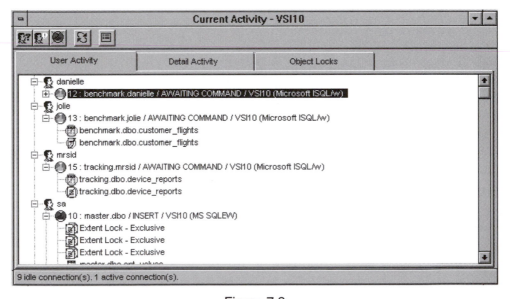

Figure 7.3

SQL Enterprise Manager also reports on locks at the object level:

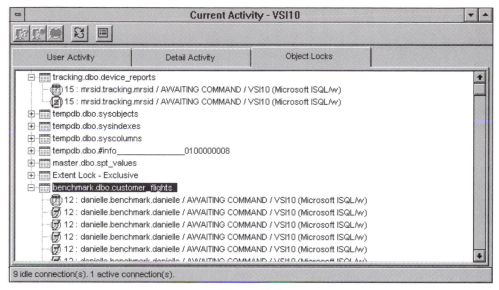

Figure 7.4

If you're more inclined to use character-based reports, you can also get locking information by running the 'sp_lock' stored procedure:

spid	locktype	table_id	page	dbname
10	Sh_intent	640005311	0	master
11	Ex_table	16003088	0	benchmark
17	Insert_page	48003404	362	tracking
17	Link_page	48003404	362	tracking
.	.	.	.	.
56	Ex_page	48003202	320	tempdb

Once you've learned the 'spid' of a particular user, you can then learn the user's identity, by running 'sp_who':

spid	status	loginame	hostname	blk	dbname	cmd
1	sleeping	sa		0	master	MIRROR HANDLER
2	sleeping	sa		0	master	LAZY WRITER
3	sleeping	sa		0	master	CHECKPOINT SLEEP
4	sleeping	sa		0	master	RA MANAGER
10	runnable	sa	VSI10	0	master	SELECT

```
11    sleeping mrsid VSI10    0    benchmarkAWAITING COMMAND
17    sleeping danny SAMMY    0    trackingAWAITING COMMAND
56    sleeping james VSI10    0    tempdb   AWAITING COMMAND
```

Avoiding running out of locks

The default (and minimum) number of locks for SQL Server is 5000; in many cases, this is sufficient. If you need more, you can have up to two billion locks. Regardless of how many locks you have configured, it is always possible to run out of this important resource. If this happens, you'll see a message like this:

```
SQL Server has run out of LOCKS. Rerun your command
when there are fewer active users, or ask your System
Administrator to reconfigure SQL Server with more LOCKS.
(Msg 1204, Level 19, State 2).
```

How can you prevent this from happening? Let's look at a number of situations where you can run out of locks, along with some possible solutions:

- **Bulk data loading.**   It's possible that a particularly large, bulk-data load operation could demand more locks than you have. If this happens, you have several options, including these:

    1. Reduce the size of the transaction. See "Bulk Data Loading" later in this section for more information.
    2. Increase the number of locks.

- **Long transactions.**   If one or more other users have a long transaction open, it's possible that additional users may have their processes fail due to a shortage of locks. Fortunately, you can reduce the possibility of long transactions by following the suggestions in "Preventing long transactions."

- **Large number of users.**   In spite of your best efforts, you may still encounter situations where you run out of locks. Luckily, SQL Server lets you set up to two billion locks, so chances are you can raise the number of locks to a sufficient level. Keep in mind that these additional locks have a price: 32 bytes of memory per lock. Therefore, try to come up with a realistic number of configured locks. For more information about setting the number of locks for your server, see the "Locking" section of Chapter 12.

Transaction isolation levels

A common area for concern when developing multiuser applications is "trusting" the data that your program sees. For example, what if two users, user A and user B, are working on the same record? How can you ensure that each user is seeing "real" data? Furthermore, what happens if user A changes a row while user B is searching for it? The number of potential data access and reliability problems is virtually unlimited. Fortunately, if you develop applications that run using the SQL Server database engine, you can use transaction isolation levels to help mitigate these types of situations.

Determining current isolation level

You can determine your current isolation level by running the DBCC command with the USEROPTIONS parameter:

```
dbcc useroptions

Set Option                     Value
------------------------       -------------------------
textsize                       64512
language                       us_english
dateformat                     mdy
datefirst                      7
arithignore                    SET
isolation level                serializable
```

In this example, the user has set his transaction isolation level to SERIALIZABLE. Let's turn our attention to understanding more about each of SQL Server's transaction isolation options.

READ UNCOMMITTED

This is the lowest level of isolation. Your program holds no locks on data rows. For example, in the following instance, a user is running a query against the 'customer_flights' table:

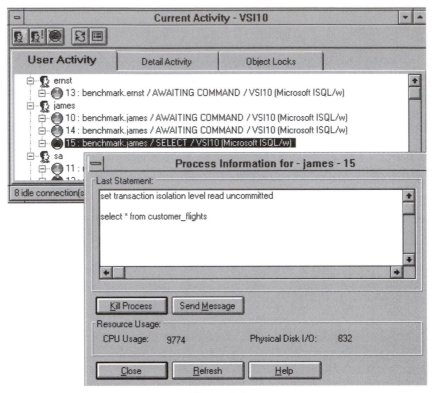

Figure 7.5

If the query encounters a lock being held by another process, it disregards that lock and retrieves the row anyway. While this is the fastest and most efficient way to retrieve data, it also means that you may occasionally see a row that was never truly in the database. For example, assume that there are two users on your system, A and B. B is inserting rows into a table via a transaction. A has a transaction isolation level of READ UNCOMMITTED and is looking at some of the same rows that B is inserting. If B later rolls back his transaction, A saw rows that were never really there. These types of data are known as "phantom rows" and can confuse your users and complicate your job responsibilities. We can represent this phenomenon with a simple graphic:

Table 7.6   activity

time	User A	User B
8:01.32	set transaction isolation level read uncommitted	begin transaction insert into customer_master values (44004,"McMahon","Ric" ...

Table 7.6 activity (Continued)

8:02.23	select * from customer_master where last_name = "McMahon"	
8:02.24	account_number last_name -------------- --------- 44004 McMahon	
8:03.48		rollback transaction
8:05.12	update customer_master set account_balance = 55000 where account_number = 44004	
8:05.13	(0 row(s) affected)	

User A made a decision and issued an UPDATE statement, all based on a row that was never truly established in the database. These phantom rows can cause many problems for your users, who may arrive at incorrect conclusions based on query results. Be very careful when using this transaction isolation level. However, even with these warnings in mind, there are still certain circumstances where a transaction isolation level of READ UNCOMMITTED is appropriate:

- **Single user batch jobs.** If you're running a job that you know will be the only process working with a table(s), you can safely set your transaction isolation level to READ UNCOMMITTED.

- **Unchanging tables.** If you're running a process that reads static, unchanging tables, there's no need to use any higher isolation level than READ UNCOMMITTED.

- **Summary reports.** If you're running a report that can tolerate the slim possibilities of finding a phantom row, such as a large scale summary report, you can improve performance by setting your transaction isolation level to READ UNCOMMITTED for the duration of the report.

Another way to set this transaction isolation level is by using the NOLOCK option from within your SQL statement. We'll cover all SQL statement locking alternatives later in this chapter.

READ COMMITTED

This is the next higher level of isolation. In this case, before returning a row, the engine tests it to see if there are any locks on it. If there aren't, the engine returns the row. This level of isolation is almost as efficient as READ UNCOMMITTED; it is also the default isolation level for a database that is not ANSI-

compliant. If your application must never receive a phantom row, use this iso-
lation level. If we modify the earlier example demonstrating READ UNCOM-
MITTED to use this transaction isolation level instead, SQL Enterprise
Manager reports:

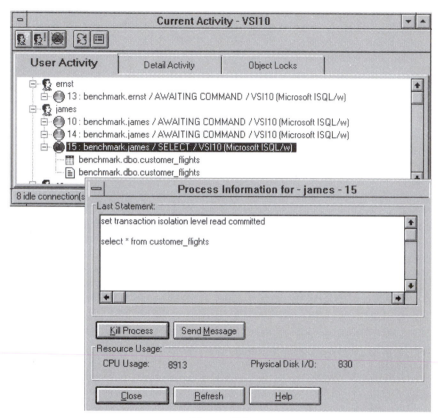

Figure 7.6

Let's look at a more interesting example of the READ COMMITTED transaction isolation level. Suppose that there are two users on the system, Ernst
and James. Ernst is adding a row to the 'customer_flights' table. However,
Ernst has not completed his transaction:

```
begin transaction
insert into customer_flights
      values (999, 4004, "12/26/96", "SFO", "LHR","")
```

The transaction is still open and remains so until Ernst issues either a COMMIT TRANSACTION or ROLLBACK TRANSACTION statement. SQL Enterprise Manager shows the current lock status:

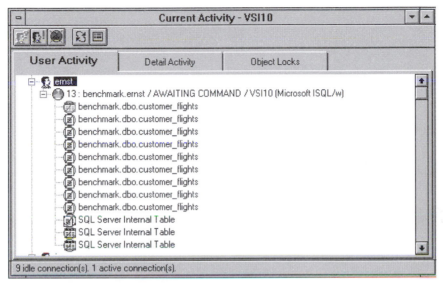

Figure 7.7

Now, James logs in and wants to locate information about this customer's flight:

```
set transaction isolation level read committed

select * from customer_flights
      where account_number = 999
```

However, James's process "hangs," since his program is blocked on the data page lock held by Ernst's transaction.

The SQL Enterprise Manager illustrates the predicament:

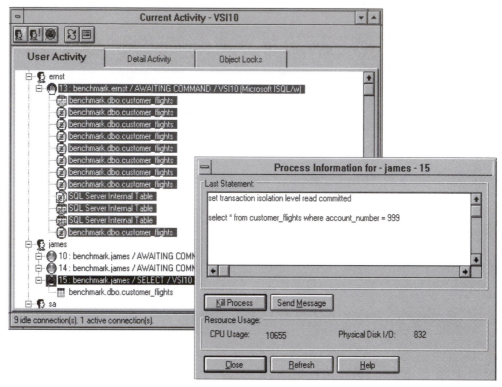

Figure 7.8

Once Ernst commits or rolls back his transaction, James is able to proceed with any operation that affects data on the pages formerly held by Ernst.

Keep in mind that this isolation level (along with the more stringent ones) might cause your application to wait unnecessarily. How can this happen? Since SQL Server locks at the page level instead of at the row level, your application will wait to access a row on a page that is locked by another process. This delay happens even if the desired row is on the side of the data page opposite from the row being modified by the other user. For this reason, use the more restrictive isolation levels with care. If you are accessing the database for decision support queries, informal reports, and other non-critical operations, you may be able to use a less restrictive isolation level. On the other hand, if you're building an OLTP system, where there is a potential for incorrect phantom rows to cause data havoc, it's wise to tighten your isolation levels.

Earlier in this chapter, we discussed how important it is to keep your transactions as brief as possible. Combining a long transaction with a fairly restrictive isolation level can cause significant concurrency problems. Let's look at how a seemingly innocuous statement can cause unexpected delays and difficulties for other statements.

Using the 'customer_master' table example described earlier, suppose one user is running the following SQL statements:

```
begin transaction
update customer_master
set account_balance = account_balance * 1.1
where account_number in (40000,50000)
```

Since the 'customer_master' table's primary key is 'account_number,' the table's pages are physically ordered by the primary key. This means that as long as this transaction remains open, any number of other, seemingly unrelated queries may hang (as long as their transaction isolation levels are set to READ COMMITTED or higher):

```
select * from customer_master
    where account_number between 38000 and 43000
-- or --
select * from customer_master
    where account_number >= 40003
-- or --
select * from customer_master
    where account_number >= 50000
-- or --
select * from customer_master
    where account_number < 50000
```

Basically, the UPDATE statement listed earlier locks the data pages containing account numbers 40000 and 50000. This means that any other query operations that need to access data on these pages may fail, even if they don't need to access the rows with account number 40000 or 50000. This illustrates how you might undergo strange, inexplicable program delays during normal database operations.

REPEATABLE READ

Certain applications are so sensitive about data integrity that programmers must restrict access to data for all other processes until the application has finished its work. There are a number of ways to ensure this degree of integrity. One of the more popular approaches is to use the REPEATABLE READ transaction isolation level. Let's spend some time learning more about situations where you would use this processing alternative.

Imagine that you are developing an account balancing program. Your program opens a cursor to read all rows in a transaction detail table. For each detail row, you then read the appropriate master record, searching for an important piece of information. At the end of the operation, you perform a summation routine. As part of the summation routine, you reread some of the rows from the master table. Your application can potentially return incorrect information if other users are allowed to alter data in this master table while the balancing program is running:

Table 7.7   activity

time	Balancing program	Account maintenance program
...	...	...
10:17.03	`fetch next from trans_cursor`	
10:17.06	`select * from account_master where account_number = 3002`	
...	...	...
10:19.55	`fetch next from trans_cursor`	
10:33.12		`begin transaction update account_master set credit_limit = 4000 where account_number = 3002 commit transaction`
...	...	...
11:55.28	`select * from account_master where credit_limit < 3500`	
...	...	...

What has happened here? It appears that in the middle of the account balancing operation, someone updated the 'credit_limit' column in the 'account_master' table for a particular row. Unfortunately, your balancing program read that row earlier and may be making a decision based on the original value. For this reason, in these types of programs, it's important to safeguard the values in rows that your program accesses, even if your programs merely read information. You could lock the entire table, but that would drastically reduce concurrency for all other programs. This isn't desirable: Why block other programs that may have nothing to do with the data your original program uses? This can cause substantial delays and program failures. Instead, you can simply set a more restrictive isolation level within the update program itself:

Table 7.8 activity

time	Balancing program	Account maintenance program

9:44.55	`set transaction`
	`isolation level`
	`repeatable read`	

...	...	...
10:17.03	`fetch next from` `trans_cursor`	

10:17.06	`select * from`
	`account_master where`
	`account_number = 3002`	

...	...	...
10:19.55	`fetch next from` `trans_cursor`	

10:33.12		`begin transaction`
		`update account_master`
		`set credit_limit = 4000`
		`where`
		`account_number = 3002`
		`(operation halts until`
		`other program finishes)`

...	...	...

11:55.28	`select * from`
	`account_master where`
	`credit_limit < 3500`	

...	...	...

SERIALIZABLE

In Microsoft SQL Server, an isolation level of SERIALIZABLE is identical to the REPEATABLE READ isolation level.

Changing isolation level

Finally, remember that you can change the isolation level within the same program. For example, this means that you could set your isolation to READ UNCOMMITTED for a lookup and then change it to REPEATABLE READ when you actually modify heavily accessed data.

SQL statements and isolation levels

Each of the transaction isolation levels that we have just discussed can be simulated by issuing a locking request when you build your SQL. Let's look at a few examples of how you can use this option to achieve your desired concurrency. Note that setting any of these options temporarily overrides any existing isolation levels specified by the SET TRANSACTION ISOLATION LEVEL statement.

NOLOCK

You can simulate an isolation level of READ UNCOMMITTED by using the NOLOCK option within your SELECT statement:

```
select * from customer_flights (nolock)
```

Setting this parameter means that your SELECT statement won't request any shared locks on data pages. In addition, if the query encounters an exclusive lock, it disregards the lock and returns information. Remember that this may have implications on data integrity, since your program may return phantom information. For more detail about the READ UNCOMMITTED transaction isolation level, see the discussion earlier in this chapter.

HOLDLOCK

If you want your application to hold its locks until it completes all operations within a transaction, you can provide the HOLDLOCK parameter. This is similar to the REPEATABLE READ or SERIALIZABLE transaction isolation level. For example, the following sequence guarantees that all rows that you read in the 'customer_master' table won't change for the duration of the transaction:

```
begin transaction
select * from customer_flights (holdlock)
where flight_date = "05/01/97"
```

Use this option (or transaction isolation level) with care: You may end up causing other applications to wait unnecessarily while your query completes.

UPDLOCK

Recall from our earlier discussions about update locks that SQL Server uses an update lock to reserve a page that you intend to alter. In this context, "alter" means to insert, update, or delete information. If you are writing a SELECT statement that you intend as the first step in an update operation, you can request that SQL Server use update locks instead of the more traditional shared locks. Using update locks in a query lets you know that any data that you see will not be changed by other users or processes. Once you're ready to update, the update locks have preserved the original state of the data. Functionally, this is similar to a transaction isolation level of REPEATABLE READ or SE-RIALIZABLE:

```
begin transaction
select * from awards (updlock)
where mileage_level between 20000 and 40000
. . .
. . .
```

All rows from the 'awards' table that match the 'award_code' criteria are now effectively locked until the transaction completes. One caveat is worth mentioning at this juncture: Remember that SQL Server 6.5 can lock at the physical row level only during insert operations and only if Insert Row-Level Locking (IRL) has been enabled for the table. For other operations, the engine locks the entire page that contains the data rows in question. This can lead to concurrency problems, especially in situations where you are accessing heavily used transaction tables. However, this can be very helpful if you plan to update these rows later in the transaction:

```
. . .
. . .
update awards set mileage_level = mileage_level - 500
where mileage_level between 20000 and 40000
```

TABLOCK

This optimizer hint enforces a more restrictive concurrency capability. When you request TABLOCK, SQL Server places a shared lock on the table until the end of the operation:

```
begin transaction
select * from customer_flights (tablock)
where flight_date between "01/01/97" and "01/31/97"
```

This query places a shared lock on the 'customer_flights' table until all qualified rows have been fetched. This means that no other users or processes can make any modifications to any data within the 'customer_flights' table until the query has finished. If you want even more restrictive locking, you could add the HOLDLOCK option to the same query:

```
begin transaction
select * from customer_flights (tablock holdlock)
where flight_date between "01/01/97" and "01/31/97"
```

In this case, SQL Server now keeps the shared lock active on the 'customer_flights' until the end of the entire transaction. This means that the lock remains, even if you work on other tables. This is very restrictive and could cause major concurrency obstacles if used incorrectly.

PAGLOCK

This optimizer locking hint tells the engine to use shared page locks on all affected (modified) pages. This is the default behavior (so you don't need to explicitly request it) and provides a fair balance between data integrity and concurrency.

TABLOCKX

If you feel that you need to lock a particular table for the duration of an operation and you don't want anyone else to even see the table, you can request that SQL Server place an exclusive lock. You would ask for this behavior by using an optimizer locking hint of TABLOCKX:

```
begin transaction
declare C cursor for
select * from awards (tablockx)
     for update of mileage_level
open C
fetch C
update awards (tablockx)
     set mileage_level = mileage_level * 1.1
where current of C
```

The 'awards' table is now locked exclusively by your process. No one else on the system can access this table; it doesn't matter even if they only want simply to read rows. This is the most restrictive isolation level of all; there is no way via the SET TRANSACTION ISOLATION to achieve this degree of access limitation.

When would you impose this kind of concurrency? Generally, exclusive table locks are useful when you are performing large insert, update, or delete procedures and you don't want anyone to obtain partial, transient, or potentially incorrect results. This level of locking also helps reduce the overall number of locks required to finish a particular process. For example, if you are updating 100,000 rows that reside on 20,000 pages, you'll use far fewer locks if you ask the engine to lock the entire table rather than each updated page. However, don't forget that SQL Server itself may decide to promote numerous page locks into a single table lock. We'll cover this topic in more detail in Chapter 12 on efficient engine maintenance.

In summary, use exclusive table locks when you are modifying information on vast numbers of pages and you are sure that no one else will need immediate access to the locked table.

Using optimizer hints vs. isolation levels

Given that you have two alternatives when requesting concurrency features, how should you choose between optimizer hints versus isolation levels? The answer largely depends on your application profile:

- **Do you need very restrictive locking?** If you need to enforce the most stringent locking characteristics to make your application work correctly, you may have no choice but to request the TABLOCKX option within your SELECT statement. There is no corresponding transaction isolation level for this degree of concurrency restriction.

- **Do you have a mixture of concurrency needs?** One of the beauties of embedding locking instructions within SQL versus setting a transaction isolation level is that SQL locking instructions work at the table level, whereas the transaction isolation level works for all tables within the transaction. For example, suppose that you're building a query that retrieves information from three tables. You want to place the most restrictive access on one table, a somewhat lower degree of locking on another, and no restrictions on the third. Embedding your concurrency wishes within SQL makes this possible:

```
select a.payment_date, a.payment_amount,
       b.last_name, c.account_class
from transactions a (tablockx),
customers b (tablock),
accounts c
where ....
```

  This degree of granularity wouldn't be possible with the SET TRANSACTION ISOLATION statement.

- **Does your concurrency profile change during the time your process is active?** If you need to raise and lower your transaction isolation profile, you can use either of the following methods:

  1. You can issue the SET TRANSACTION ISOLATION statement as often as you need.

  2. You can choose the optimizer locking hints within your SELECT statements based on your desired concurrency.

- **Is your application inserting, updating, or deleting data?** If you perform any of these operations, consider using the SET TRANSACTION ISOLATION statement. Remember that you can only provide optimizer locking hints within SELECT statements. This means that to set the appropriate concurrency for nonquery statements, you'll have no choice but to set an isolation level.

Miscellaneous tips

Bulk data loading

Regardless of the type of application that you're developing or maintaining, there's a good chance that you periodically need to load large amounts of data into your database. There are a number of ways to perform this task. In this section, we discuss the benefits and drawbacks of each method.

First, no matter what method you choose to load your data, you can improve throughput by performing the following steps:

1. Try to schedule the bulk data loading during off-hours. Dropping indexes or changing SQL Server shared memory parameters during peak hours will not make you very popular with your user community.

2. If the table size after the INSERT operation will be at least 10 percent larger than before the operation, drop any indexes on the table—if there are indexes in place, the engine must update these indexes after each new row is added. In addition, SQL Server logs bulk data operations if there are indexes in place on the table. Both of these operations can be highly inefficient; it is much better to simply re-create the indexes after you finish loading the data.

3. Consider allocating more memory to SQL Server. This can help speed up the operation by reducing the frequency of disk I/O during the operation. Don't forget, however, that the engine must eventually write the new information onto the disk drive.

4. Using whichever method you choose, load the data.

5. Re-create the indexes (if you first dropped them).

6. Run UPDATE STATISTICS for the table. Many administrators forget this important step after loading data. Unfortunately, this can lead to drastically degraded performance. See Chapter 4, "Understanding the SQL Server optimizer," for more detail about UPDATE STATISTICS.

bcp

The 'bcp' utility is a handy way of moving large amounts of data in and out of your database. Aside from the general bulk data loading suggestions listed earlier, how can you improve the throughput of this utility? There are several possibilities:

- **Packet size.** You can tune the size of the network packets sent between client and server. Normally, the administrator sets this value for the entire system. However, you can overrule this value for your session by using the /a parameter, along with the number of bytes that you want to be placed into the packet. The range of possible values for this parameter is between 512 and 65535. The default is 4096. If you believe that this parameter might help performance, try experimenting with a variety of values. If you request a value that SQL Server can't satisfy, the engine uses a value of 512.

- **Batch size.** The /b parameter tells SQL Server to break up the bulk data load operation into smaller transactions containing a number of rows, as opposed to the default single, large transaction. For example, if you provide a value of 200 for batch size and you have 2000 rows to load, SQL Server divides up the data load into 10 transactions. Since each transaction has overhead, your goal should be to have SQL Server finish the load with a minimum of transactions. However, using fewer and larger transactions could conceivably fill your transaction log. Consequently, if you feel that you need transaction logging for your bulk data load operations, your goal should be to come up with the biggest batch size that lets you successfully finish your task.

- **Avoid transaction logging.** If you want to speed up bulk data loading, one of the best ways is for SQL Server not to log this type of operation. However, to avoid logging, you must first remove all of the table's indexes, then instruct SQL Server not to log this type of operation. To do this, use the SQL Enterprise Manager and check the SELECT INTO/BULK COPY option.

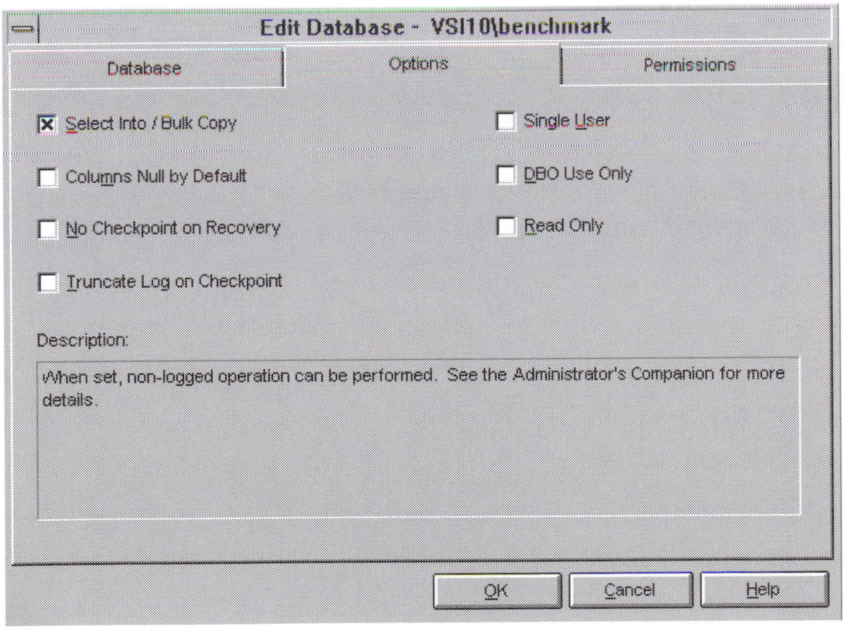

Figure 7.9

You can also use the 'sp_dboption' stored procedure to set this alternative. Keep in mind that if you forget to check this option, SQL Server returns an error to the user and proceeds with a logged bulk data load. In addition, if you have any indexes in place, SQL Server logs the bulk load as well. Finally, remember that turning off transaction logging has a price: If the load process encounters a serious error, you may be hard-pressed to restore the table to its original state. To protect your data, consider backing up the entire database before as well as after the load.

Object transfer and script generation

SQL Server provides administrators with easy-to-use, graphical tools for transferring objects among databases, as well as generating SQL scripts. These tools can help speed up the often mundane process of moving data or creating database schema. However, if you decide to take advantage of these powerful tools, don't forget to inform the engine that you want to preserve indexes, keys, dependencies, and other important database and table definition information when generating new scripts or transferring objects. For example, the following graphic shows the numerous options available when generating an SQL script:

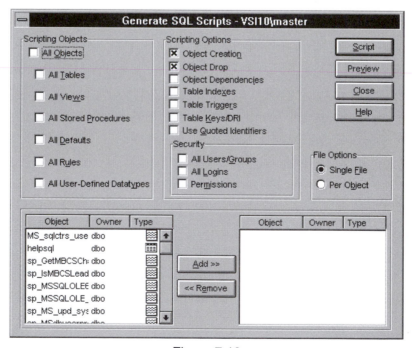

Figure 7.10

You can easily preview the automatically generated script:

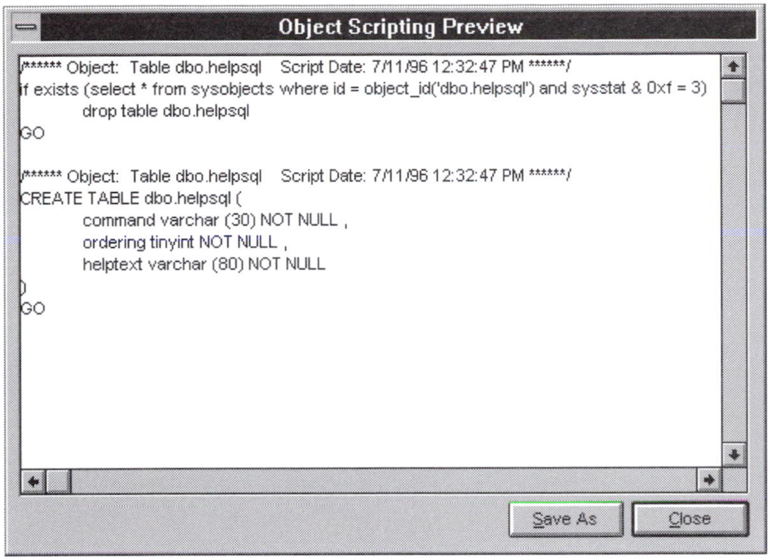

Figure 7.11

If you somehow overlook this vital step, your new database or table may have mysterious performance problems, since important indexes or other information may never have been transferred. If you forget to transfer stored procedures or triggers, you may also encounter data integrity problems.

Chapter 8

Client/Server Considerations

Distributed systems are becoming more commonplace each day. Organizations are incorporating both client/server and peer-to-peer technology into their most vital processing operations. Along with this new power and technology, however, comes increased complexity. Unfortunately, many organizations have learned the hard way that developing distributed applications requires much more analysis than traditional single-computer systems. This is especially true with regard to performance.

In this chapter, we explore a number of strategies that you can apply to your distributed systems environments. We begin by discussing how you can assess your network's capabilities, because without a reliable and rapid network, you'll have a hard time creating a distributed application that performs well.

Regardless of what kind of network you have, it's always a good idea to reduce the amount of data you send between your machines, so we evaluate a number of techniques that you can incorporate into your applications to minimize this communication. We conclude by citing several strategies that you can implement to diminish the possibility of delay.

Assessing your network's capabilities

A big factor in your distributed processing plan is your network's capabilities. You can think of capabilities as being composed of a number of features, including:

- **Network speed.** If you're connecting your systems at a relatively slow speed (9600 baud or lower), you may encounter built-in performance delays, especially if you move large quantities of data over the network. This can be very frustrating, since you might waste an enormous amount of time trying to optimize the application code, only to learn that the application was never part of the problem.

- **Network reliability.** If you're not confident about your network's data transmission reliability, you should seriously consider how much data you want to send between systems, as well as what kind of response you can expect. Most modern networks and communications devices have built-in error detection and correction. While this does reduce the chances of data corruption, it also delays the overall performance of the network.

- **Network complexity.** Networks that consist of leased lines are generally much easier to maintain than networks that rely on dial-up connections. If you write programs that must repeatedly dial remote systems as part of normal operations, you can expect them to fail more frequently than if the remote systems were directly connected. This has the potential to introduce significant delays into your application, especially if your users are running transactions that rely on real-time response from these remote systems.

Even if you have a low-speed, low-quality network, you can still take advantage of distributed processing. You may, however, need to write your programs to perform their remote updates asynchronously rather than synchronously. You can also use SQL Server's replication feature to move data among various systems.

Minimizing network traffic

Even if you have a lightning-fast network with unlimited bandwidth, you should still try to reduce the amount of traffic that you ask your network to handle. You can use any or all of these strategies to lower network traffic.

Improve distributed queries

If you're running a high-volume, transaction-intensive application and you're experiencing slow queries, check to see if your queries are joining widely separated tables. Remember that even if you're using server-based stored procedures to reduce network traffic between client and server, you might discover that these procedures are making inefficient network requests. This would lead to excessive server-to-server network traffic, which can be just as damaging as inordinate amounts of client/server traffic.

Take advantage of replication

SQL Server's replication provides a simple, reliable way to distribute information among many machines. Given this infrastructure, you might be able to use replication to create local copies of data. You could then satisfy your queries without ever needing to search for information on another machine. This is especially true if the underlying data is relatively static. We discuss replication in more detail in Chapter 16.

Retrieve only necessary columns

Just as you should strive to reduce the number of rows that your users request, you should also attempt to minimize the number of columns that are transported between the server and client. This isn't always that easy, because when you develop applications that use SQL to retrieve information, it's tempting to request all columns from a table, whether or not you need them in your program. After all, SELECT * requires far less typing than specifying each column that you need.

Unfortunately, SELECT * "costs" more than requesting individual columns, since returning all columns in a table results in higher traffic between the front-end and engine processes.

While SELECTing only those columns that you need does add some extra typing to your development effort, it also pays off in reduced traffic between the front-end and back-end processes. This is especially true in a networked environment, where hundreds of miles may separate the client from the server.

Use joins instead of sequential SELECTs

Many programmers, especially those with backgrounds in mainframe COBOL, dBASE®, or ISAM files, avoid joining between tables and instead process database records sequentially. While this approach may be comfortable and easier to visualize, you're not using the full power of the database and the SQL programming language. We can illustrate this with an example.

For the purposes of this example, assume that you are developing a system to track sales calls by your company's representatives. To write the report, you work with two tables, 'personnel' and 'sales_calls.' The 'personnel' table contains information about each representative, and the 'sales_calls' table tracks individual sales call statistics:

Table 8.1 personnel

personnel_id	first_name	last_name	date_of_hire.....
805	Sylvia	Migdal	Aug 2 1984
.	.	.	.
1108	Earl	O'Snyder	Nov 1 1992
1109	Robert	Gordon	Nov 8 1992

Table 8.2 sales_calls

call_id	personnel_id	date_of_call	company_name....
1309	805	Jan 30 1997	Hasenffefer Corp.
.	.	.	.
.	.	.	.
2709	1509	Aug 15 1997	Freedom Rider, Inc.

Your task as the programmer is to produce a report that shows all sales calls that an employee has made between January 1 and December 31 1997. Your output from the report must look like this:

```
   .                 .                  .
   .                 .                  .

Employee number:   nnnnn
Employee name  :   last, first

Sales call date          Company name......
-----------------------------------------
mm/dd/yyyy               xxxxxxxxxxxxxxxxxx
mm/dd/yyyy               xxxxxxxxxxxxxxxxxx
```

If you processed the report without joins, your pseudocode looks something like this:

```
declare cursor to get records from 'personnel' table
open cursor
foreach cursor into host variable structure (personnel)
    print employee name and number and header info
    declare cursor to get records from 'sales_calls'
```

```
          table
     open cursor using the contents of personnel
        host variable as key into sales_calls table
     foreach cursor into host variable structure
        (sales_calls)
           print sales call information
     end foreach
     close cursor
  end foreach
  close cursor
```

Can you see all the extra engine work that this process contains? For every employee found in the 'personnel' table, you declare, open, and close a cursor to get data from the 'sales_call' table. If you have only a few employees, this extra engine work may not be much of a problem. On the other hand, what happens if you have many thousands of employees that you need to report on?

In this case, a better approach would be to let the database engine handle the joining of records between the 'personnel' and 'sales_calls' tables. You can do this by using the 'personnel_id' column as a foreign key. Your new pseudocode now looks like this:

```
declare a cursor to get records from 'personnel' and
'sales_calls' tables
open cursor
foreach cursor into host variable structure
     (personnel + sales_calls)
        print employee name, number and header info
        (only once)
        print sales call information
end foreach
close cursor
```

You could also accomplish this by using a server-based stored procedure and returning only appropriate rows to the client.

What happens if a particular employee made no sales calls during this period but you still want him to appear on the report? It's true that the sequential processing approach makes handling this situation easy, but it's also fairly simple to process it using an SQL, join-based method. Instead of performing a normal join between the tables, use an OUTER join, with the 'personnel' table as primary and the 'sales_calls' table as outer:

```
select *
from    personnel, outer sales_calls
where   personnel.personnel_id =
        sales_calls.personnel_id
```

By joining between tables, you take better advantage of database engine performance features.

Take advantage of stored procedures

One way to reduce overall traffic between the client and server process is to use stored procedures. You can write stored procedures to perform a number of important tasks, including:

- Summation
- Aggregation
- Data collection
- Auditing
- Remote operations

In fact, you can use stored procedures for just about any database operation. For more information about these powerful tools, see Chapter 6, "Stored Procedures and Triggers."

Select only necessary rows

Even if your database and program designs are optimal, your system can still get bogged down if your users always ask to look at all rows from all tables. Requesting such enormous data sets results in tremendous traffic, as the server dutifully sends huge amounts of data to the client. From your users' perspective, the system's response is horrible, since it may take several minutes to get the information they requested. How can you, as an administrator or programmer, prevent this problem? There are several ways:

- **Monitor user-entered selection criteria.**   When you develop applications that allow users to enter free-form queries, let the users know (either through a message at runtime or in the documentation) that they should always specify search criteria, rather than asking for all rows.

- **Let the engine do the filtering, rather than your program.**
  Some programmers request all rows from a table, and filter these rows through their conditional clauses inside their programs instead of using the WHERE clause to reduce the number of rows that the engine returns. This definitely impairs system performance, as the server sends large volumes of data to the client, which then performs the CPU-intensive task of filtering out unneeded data. In a distributed processing environment, this may cause a drastic degradation of re-

sponse time. It's much better to build up a WHERE clause in your program and let the engine do the filtering for you, or use a stored procedure to summarize information. Let's look at an example that demonstrates what we mean:

In this case, you're developing a sales tracking system for a clothing manufacturer. One report tracks outerwear sales. Your program reads through the very large 'sales_history' table and prints only outerwear records. The pseudocode looks like this:

```
declare a cursor to select all records
     from the sales_history table
open the cursor
while not end of data
     retrieve row
     if the sales_history record's garment type
          is "O" (for outerwear)
     then
          print the record
     end if
end while
close the cursor
```

This design is inherently inefficient, because the engine returns all rows from the 'sales_history' table, and then your report has to apply the filter on the 'sales_history.garment_type' element. It's better to let the server do the work of data filtering:

```
declare a cursor to select all records from
the sales_history table where garment type
is "O"
open the cursor
while not end of data
   print the record
end while
close the cursor
```

Update only columns that have changed

Just as it's "easier" to SELECT * from a table rather than itemize the columns that you need, it's also "easier" to UPDATE all columns in a table, whether or not more than one of them has changed. Just as using a wildcard in your SELECT statement increases traffic between the front-end and engine processes, so does a wildcard UPDATE statement.

For example, suppose that you are writing a program to track the status of shipments. You maintain a table that stores the current location of each package. As the package moves between different sites, you update this table with the package's current location, along with the date and time the package arrived. The table that tracks these packages is large, having both many rows and many columns. It's your task as the programmer to make the update process as rapid as possible.

One of the easiest ways to do this is to UPDATE only those columns that need to be changed. In this example, since the only modified data is the package's current location and timestamp, you should only change those columns. This means that instead of issuing a wildcard UPDATE statement, you only update those columns that have changed. While this approach results in somewhat longer SQL statements, it's still worth the effort. Fortunately, many of today's client-based application development languages and tools automatically take care of this for you.

Another reason to avoid wildcard UPDATE statements is that they may fail if you've set up referential integrity relationships for the table. For example, suppose that you have another table that has a referential integrity relationship with the 'package_status' table, and you attempt to run the above wildcard UPDATE statement. The database server detects that the relationship is about to be violated, and returns an error.

Tuning your network

Today's networks are highly powerful and sophisticated. However, with this power and capability comes great complexity. As we've seen, your network can contain many potential bottlenecks that can act as unseen drags on performance. Consequently, as an administrator maintaining or programmer developing a distributed system, you may always wonder if program delays are the responsibility of the network or of the underlying code or database design. To remove this potential confusion, it's always a good idea to have a networking professional examine and tune your network. Unfortunately, many organizations ignore the network's impact on performance, and never analyze network throughput. This is a mistake, because sometimes a simple network tuning change leads to astounding performance improvements.

If you're running a distributed application, and you think that you have a performance problem, consider letting a network specialist analyze your environment. One easy way to tell if you have a network problem versus a program or database design problem is as follows:

1.   Construct a test case that you can run on the client, as well as directly on the server. This may mean cutting the SQL components out from the programs, and running them alone, via a tool like "isql" or a third-party query program.

2. Run the test case on the client, and then run it on the server. Make sure that you're looking at the same data on both the client and server. In addition, try to ensure that the number of users and processes on the server is approximately the same between test runs. See the "Setting up an optimization test environment" section for more details on good optimizing practices. When you've finished your tests, carefully record your results.

3. Compare the performance figures from the client test versus the performance figures from the server. If there's a substantial difference, you probably need to either rethink your application architecture or tune your network. Before you go to the trouble of redesigning your system, try tuning your network; you might be pleasantly surprised.

Duration of client/server connection

When you're creating a client/server application, it's a good idea to evaluate how long clients and servers should stay connected. One of your jobs as a developer or administrator is to decide whether your client applications should either remain connected to the database server when idle, or should disconnect instead. When making your decision, remember that the act of connecting to a remote server can be costly. Your networking software may need to perform a complex lookup to determine the IP address that corresponds to the name of the requested client. This can be a potential bottleneck, especially if your network has hundreds or even thousands of IP address and machine name entries. It can also take a long time to connect to the engine itself, especially if there are large database jobs running at the time of connection. Once you have connected, however, there is very little overhead from an inactive connection.

On the other hand, leaving an idle connection active can pose several risks. First, there is the possibility of a security breach should the user leave her workstation connected to the database. An unauthorized user could gain access to sensitive information by simply running the already-connected application. Another potential problem relates to the number of licensed connections. If you have licensed SQL Server by connection, it makes no sense to "waste" connections by maintaining idle sessions. Finally, there is the potential for a degree of extra engine overhead when there are a high number of relatively idle client connections.

In summary, if you expect that your users will need to get information from the database on a frequent basis, it's a good idea to keep their connections alive, even when the user is idle. If you plan for long periods of database inactivity, however, it's smart to drop the database connection and login later.

Part 3

Optimizing the SQL Server Engine

Optimal database systems and applications rely on well-tuned database engines. Your database design can be carefully planned, your SQL and procedural code can be perfect, yet your system can still be lethargic. This is very frustrating, especially in large organizations, where the application developers, database administrators, and system administrators may not communicate frequently (or may not be on speaking terms). In many cases, database administrators blame sluggish system response on poor application code; system administrators ascribe the problem to inefficient database design or engine tuning, and the application developers conclude that the performance issue is directly related to the operating system.

In Part 3 we devote our attention to ensuring that your database engine is as well-tuned as possible. In Chapter 9, we discuss some of the many SQL Server administration and monitoring tools that you have at your disposal. SQL Server is very tightly integrated with the Windows NT operating system. Our next chapter, therefore, covers how to make the most of this connection. We continue in Chapters 11 and 12 by examining efficient disk and engine management. Next, in Chapters 13 through 15, we look at how to use a variety of powerful tools to track current user activity. Finally, we close Part 3 by probing how you can make the most of SQL Server's potent replication technology.

Chapter 9

Monitoring Tools

Before we discuss how to best configure and maintain your SQL Server engine, let's briefly examine some of the more commonly used monitoring tools that help you learn about the state of your database. We'll continually refer to these monitoring tools throughout the chapter.

SQL Server administrators have an array of configuration and monitoring tools at their disposal. Some tools date back to earlier versions of the engine and provide a character interface. Other, more recent tools are graphical in nature. As an administrator, on which type of tool should you focus? Generally, it's a good idea for SQL Server administrators to know how to use both types of tools. Each tool has its own strengths and weaknesses, and you may have no choice but to use a mix of these tools to perform your administration responsibilities. Consequently, we'll cite character and graphic examples throughout this chapter.

Using the performance monitor

The SQL Performance Monitor is one of the most effective tools that you can use to track the current state of your system. By using this monitor, you can observe present conditions, set flags to alert you if certain criteria are met, log activity, etc. In this section, we research how to use this powerful tool, as well as discuss the statistics that the monitor provides. Before we begin our discussion, it's a good idea to point out that the act of monitoring your system can have a slight performance cost. For this reason, it's a good idea to be sensitive to your users' needs: Running the monitor during peak activity out of curiosity may not be the best idea. However, don't hesitate to use the monitor on a regular basis or whenever you suspect that system throughput may not be up to par.

To further our awareness of the performance monitor, we begin by examining the various monitor objects that relate to SQL Server. Next, we turn our attention to how you can also use the performance monitor to set alerts, create log files, and generate reports.

Objects

The SQL Server Performance Monitor divides its statistics into a number of different objects. In this section, we outline each of the SQL Server performance objects. We then discuss each of these objects in more detail later in the chapter.

SQL Server object: This object covers a number of general performance metrics, including data caching, I/O operation, network traffic, and read-ahead status.

SQL Server licensing object: Beginning with SQL Server 6.5, you can now use the licensing object in conjunction with the performance monitor to determine the current state of your system's license profile.

SQL Server locks object: This object covers over a dozen different locking indicators.

SQL Server log object: This log object tracks, by database, information about the overall size of the transaction log and its current available space.

SQL Server procedure cache object: This object, introduced in version 6.5, lets administrators oversee the state of their stored procedure cache.

SQL Server replication-published DB object: This object reports on your server's replication publication activity.

SQL Server replication-subscriber object: This object reports on your server's replication subscription activity.

SQL Server user-defined counters object: This object, new in SQL Server 6.5, lets you assign stored procedures or SQL statements of your own choosing to statistics that you can watch through the performance monitor.

SQL Server users object: This object provides a variety of information about each user and process's resource consumption.

Setting alerts

One of the most useful features of the performance monitor is its alert capability; you can instruct the monitor to notify you if a particular counter exceeds or falls below a specified number. When these conditions are met, the monitor notes the date, time, host name, and condition in the alert window. The monitor stores up to 1,000 events. Once your alerts exceed 1,000, the monitor simply overwrites the oldest alerts. Let's look at a few examples to illustrate how to use the alerts feature. We'll cover what these statistics mean in more detail later in Part 3.

In our first sample, we've asked SQL Server to alert us if any one of the following three conditions exists:

1. The transaction log usage for database 'jeeves' exceeds 85%.

2. The Windows NT page file reaches 60% of capacity.

3. SQL Server's cache hit ratio falls below 50%.

When alerts start happening, we can view them through the performance monitor:

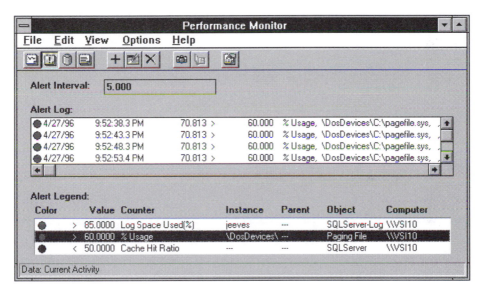

Figure 9.1

Next, we're interested in following a variety of caching, I/O, and user connection statistics, including:

-   When the number of free cache buffers falls below 5000

-   When the count of I/O lazywrites per second is less than five

-   When read-ahead pages fetched fail to reach 65 or more

-   When there are more than 15 user connections

-   When the outstanding reads counter exceeds 200

The performance monitor records these events as they occur:

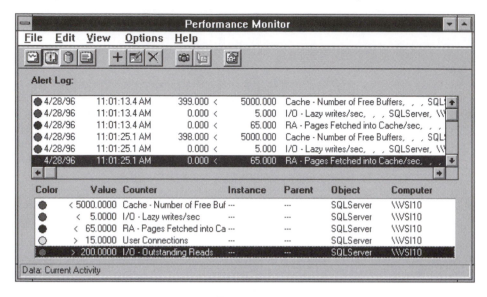

Figure 9.2

In our final example, we're examining statistics from other computers on our network. Administrators can use this feature to centralize coordination and control of all SQL Server systems on their network.

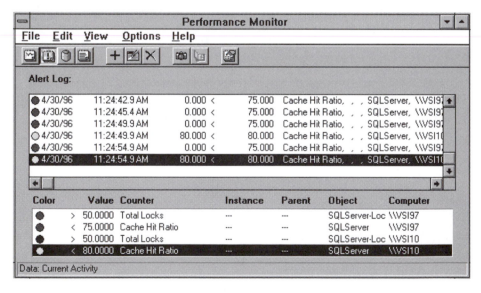

Figure 9.3

Logging

You can use the performance monitor to log statistics from all of Windows NT and SQL Server's objects. For example, in this case, we've asked SQL Server to log information from the log object:

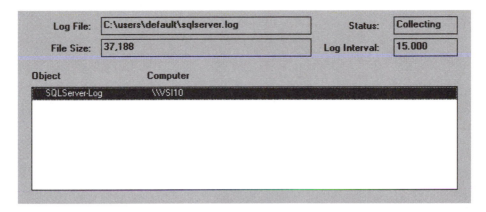

Figure 9.4

Next, we're asking to log information from a number of objects on more than one machine:

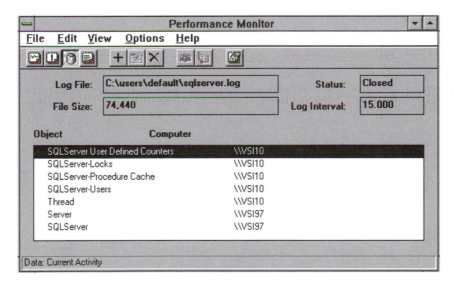

Figure 9.5

Once you have finished collecting your log information, you can export this data into a tab-delimited or comma-delimited file. You can then use a spreadsheet, graphical, or other program to analyze your data.

Reports

You can use the performance monitor to create and maintain reports that track any of the available statistics. The monitor then continually updates these reports. Let's create some sample reports to illustrate this concept. We'll describe these statistics in much more detail later; at this point they merely serve to show how SQL Server structures these reports.

In the first example, we're monitoring the state of the transaction log for a particular database:

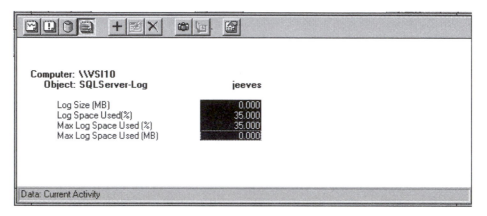

Figure 9.6

Next, we're reporting on information from a variety of sources:

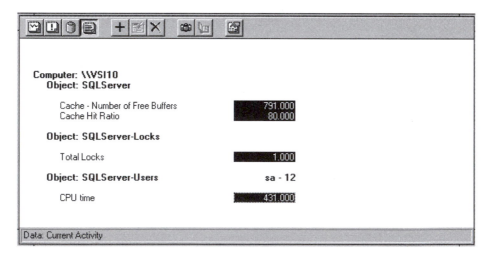

Figure 9.7

Finally, we're incorporating Windows NT operating system data with our SQL Server metrics:

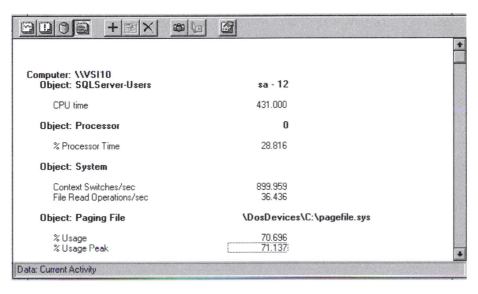

Figure 9.8

sp_monitor

You can use the 'sp_monitor' system stored procedure to get information about a variety of system throughput statistics, many of which are also available through the performance monitor. Let's look at some sample output:

```
1> sp_monitor
2> go
 last_run                current_run             seconds
 -------------------     -------------------     -----------
  Apr 18 1996 12:17AM     Apr 18 1996 12:17AM               1

cpu_busy                io_busy                 idle
----------------        ------------------      ---------
5(0)-0%                 9(0)-0%                 610(0)-0%

packets_received        packets_sent            packet_errors
------------------      ------------------      -------------
23(0)                   19(0)                   0(0)
```

total_read	total_write	total_errors	connections
4072(0)	610(0)	0(0)	2(0)

We'll cover each of these statistics in detail later in Part 3.

The DBCC utility

SQL Server affords administrators a useful utility for examining disk usage and validity, along with a variety of other performance and status information. This utility is called DBCC, which stands for Database Consistency Checker. While you can obtain many of the same statistics from the graphical SQL Enterprise Manager and Performance Monitor services, it's still a good idea to know how to use DBCC. We'll discuss this program throughout Part 3. For example, in Chapter 11 on efficient disk use, we'll look at how you can scrutinize the soundness of your tables. During our discussions on memory, we'll survey some important DBCC memory options.

Trace flags

There may be times when you want to monitor a specific SQL Server attribute that the standard engine objects don't normally cover. There may be other times when you want to enable or disable a certain behavior, yet there is no way to make this happen by using the SQL Enterprise Manager or system stored procedures. Trace flags are one configuration and diagnostic tool that you can use, with extreme caution.

You can set trace flags in a variety of ways:

- When starting the engine from the command line. Use the -T parameter, along with the trace number:

  ```
  C:\sql65\binn>sqlservr -T 1200 -T 3643
  ```

- Through the SQL Enterprise Manager server configuration options parameter screen. This is the nearly the same as issuing the request from the command line. The difference is that SQL Server will continue to use the specified trace flag at startup unless you remove it from this screen later.

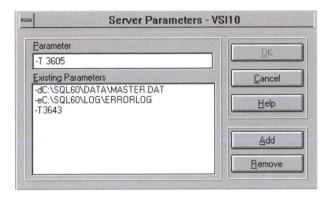

Figure 9.9

Note that you can also get to this screen from the SQL Server setup utility.

- Through the DBCC TRACEON and DBCC TRACEOFF command. You can issue this command from any SQL query tool:

```
1> dbcc traceon (1200)
2> go
DBCC execution completed. If DBCC printed error
messages, see your System Administrator.
```

In the above example, we've asked SQL Server to provide detailed information about any locks that our process creates. To disable this feature, just run DBCC TRACEOFF:

```
1> dbcc traceoff (1200)
2> go
DBCC execution completed. If DBCC printed error
messages, see your System Administrator.
```

After a flag is set, it generally remains in effect until you disable it and then restart the server. The only exception is when you have set the flag using DBCC: In this case, you can disable the flag's trace behavior by running DBCC TRACEOFF and providing the appropriate flag number.

Using trace flags

There is a wide variety of trace flags; let's focus on some specific performance-related options. Again, keep in mind that you probably don't want to use these in production unless you are sure that they will help you achieve your through-put goals. You can use these flags to do the following:

- **Set the trace flag globally, for all client sessions.** When you set a trace flag through the command line or through the SQL Server setup utility, the engine automatically applies the flag to all sessions. However, when you set a trace flag through DBCC, the setting normally only holds true for your session. By using a trace flag of -1, you're telling SQL Server that you want your trace flag to affect all other connections as well. Be very careful using this option: You might erroneously have negative effects throughout your entire organization.

- **Block the SELECT statement from using ANSI join capabilities.** We reviewed the differences between ANSI joins and SQL Server joins in Part 2 on improving database access. With SQL Server 6.5, you can request that the optimizer not use the ANSI join syntax, by setting trace flag 110 to TRUE.

- **Disable the CUBE and ROLLUP Transact-SQL aggregate operators.** Recall that SQL Server 6.5 introduced two new SQL clauses: CUBE and ROLLUP. We discussed these operators in Chapter 3; if you want to disable these operators, set trace flag 204 to TRUE.

- **Disallow interim constraint violations.** Remember that SQL Server uses constraints to enforce referential integrity and other administrator-defined rules. There are times, however, where constraints might be briefly violated, as in the middle of a transaction. In normal operation, SQL Server identifies and then allows these momentary violations, which are called interim constraint violations. This approach requires SQL Server to create some work tables and perform additional labor. Setting a trace flag of 244 tells the engine not to allow these interim violations. Instead of silently handling the violation, the engine now displays a standard integrity violation message.

- **Provide detailed information about joins.** With SQL Server 6.5, you can ask the query optimizer to furnish you with all aspects about join operations when you are using SHOWPLAN. To get this information, set trace flag 330 to TRUE.

- **Disable read-ahead for the entire server.** Later, we review SQL Server's sophisticated read-ahead capabilities. To disable this feature for all connections, set trace flag 652.

- **Disable read-ahead for this connection.** To disable the read-ahead feature for this connection only, set trace flag 653.

- **Provide deadlock lock information.**   If your system encounters a deadlock, you can use trace flag 1204. This flag shows the command that is affected by the deadlock, as well as the locks that are causing the deadlock.

- **Provide deadlock command detail.**   Trace flag 1205 returns detailed information about what's happening when a deadlock occurs.

- **Provide checkpoint detail.**   You can instruct SQL Server to write details about checkpoints into the error log. Setting a trace flag of 3502 informs the engine to log the beginning and end of each checkpoint.

- **Send trace output to the client.**   If you want to monitor trace information from a client connection, you can set trace flag 3604. Note that this only takes effect if you enable tracing with the DBCC TRACEON and DBCC TRACEOFF commands.

- **Send trace output to the error log.**   Normally, when you request tracing and start SQL Server from the command line, all trace information is displayed on the screen. However, you may want to log this output. Setting trace flag 3605 tells SQL Server to write all trace information into the error log. Remember that there is a finite amount of room in the error log; detailed trace information may quickly fill up available space.

- **Avoid automatic recovery for all databases.**   We'll examine SQL Server's automatic recovery feature later. If you want SQL Server to disregard this step for all databases on your server, set trace flag 3607.

- **Avoid automatic recovery for all databases except 'master.'**   Setting trace flag 3608 is almost identical to setting trace flag 3607. The only difference is that this trace flag tells SQL Server to perform automatic recovery for the 'master' database only.

- **Prevent creation of a 'tempdb' database.**   You can inform SQL Server that you don't want the engine to automatically create the 'tempdb' database. The only reason that you would request this behavior is if the device where you normally store 'tempdb' is unavailable. To ask for this adaptation, set trace flag 3609.

- **Prevent running of automatically started stored procedures.**   SQL Server lets you specify certain stored procedures to be run when the database starts. With the 6.5 release, you can instruct the engine not to start these procedures, by setting trace flag 4022.

- **Follow 6.0 dynamic cursor behavior.**   With SQL Server 6.5, forward cursors are automatically assigned as dynamic. Version 6.5 also removes the requirement that underlying tables all have unique indexes before a dynamic index can work. If you want to retain the older behavior, set trace flag 7501 to TRUE.

sp_configure

The 'sp_configure' system stored procedure lets you inquire about one or more configuration values. You can also use this stored procedure to set particular parameters. Let's look at some sample output.

In the first example, we're asking for details about the 'memory' configuration parameter:

```
sp_configure 'memory'

name        minimum     maximum     config_value run_value
--------    --------    --------    ------------ -----------
memory      1000        1048576     4096         4096
```

How can you interpret this output? The columns have these meanings:

Name.   This is the configuration parameter name.

Minimum.   This is the minimum value that you could provide for this parameter.

Maximum.   This is the maximum value that you could provide for this parameter.

Config value.   This is the current configuration value.

Run value.   This is the value that the engine used when it most recently started. It is possible for this number to differ from the 'config value' column. For example, you may have just changed the 'config value,' but not yet restarted the engine.

Next, we're asking for all configuration values:

```
sp_configure

name                    minimum maximum    config_value  run_value
----------------        ------- -------    ------------  ----------
allow updates           0       1          0             0
backup buffer size      1       0          1             1
backup threads          0       32         5             5
```

database size	2	10000	2	2
default language	0	9999	0	0
default sortorder id	0	255	52	52
fill factor	0	100	0	0
language in cache	3	100	3	3
LE threshold maximum	2	500000	200	200
LE threshold percent	1	100	0	0
locks	5000	2147483647	5000	5000
logwrite sleep (ms)	-1	500	0	0
max async IO	1	255	8	8
max text repl size	0	2147483647	65536	65536
max worker threads	10	1024	255	255
media retention	0	365	0	0
memory	1000	1048576	4096	4096
nested triggers	0	1	1	1
network packet size	512	32767	4096	4096
open databases	5	32767	20	20
open objects	100	2147483647	500	500
procedure cache	1	99	30	30
RA worker threads	0	255	3	3
recovery flags	0	1	0	0
recovery interval	1	32767	5	5
remote access	0	1	1	1
remote conn timeout	-1	32767	10	10
remote proc trans	0	1	0	0
show advanced option	0	1	0	0
tempdb in ram (MB)	0	2044	0	0
user connections	5	32767	20	20
user options	0	4095	0	0

Finally, we're using this stored procedure to set a parameter value:

```
sp_configure 'open objects', 550
```

The SQL Trace utility

Beginning with SQL Server 6.5, Microsoft has added a powerful new tool to help database administrators and developers learn about what is happening on the database server. This new tool is called SQL Trace, and it provides copious amounts of useful monitoring information. As an added benefit, you can narrow your tracing operations down to the user, application, or server level. Let's look at how you can use this utility.

You start SQL Trace by double-clicking on its icon. If you haven't defined any filters, SQL Trace prompts you to create one when you first start the utility:

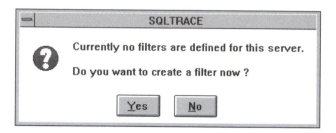

Figure 9.10

Let's define a filter to monitor access to one of our tables:

Figure 9.11

Let's define the events to trace:

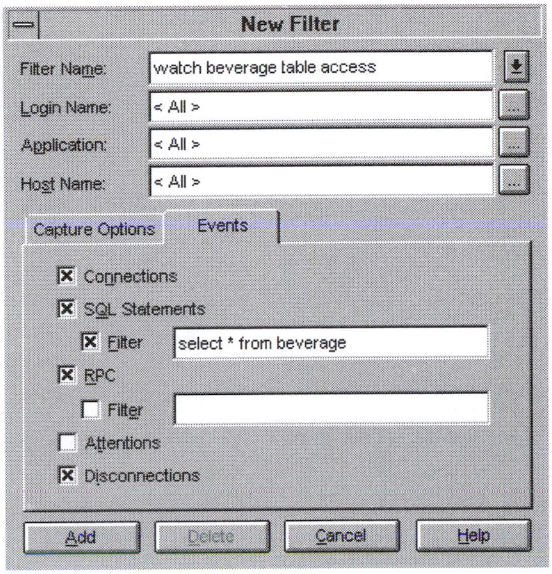

Figure 9.12

This filter criterion means that we want to know whenever someone executes a 'SELECT * FROM BEVERAGE' query. The trace utility displays this information on a screen, as well as in a log file or SQL script, if you request these options.

You can also use the trace utility to watch for other, non-SQL events, including access from:

- Application
- Login name
- Host name

SQL Server provides dialog boxes for each of the options.

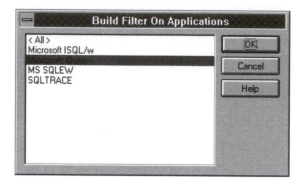

Figure 9.13

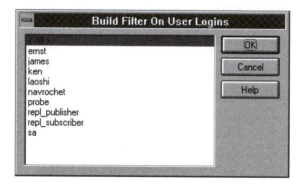

Figure 9.14

Figure 9.15

For example, suppose that we want to be notified when user 'sidney' logs in by using the Microsoft Query application. We would fill in the trace utility dialog box like this:

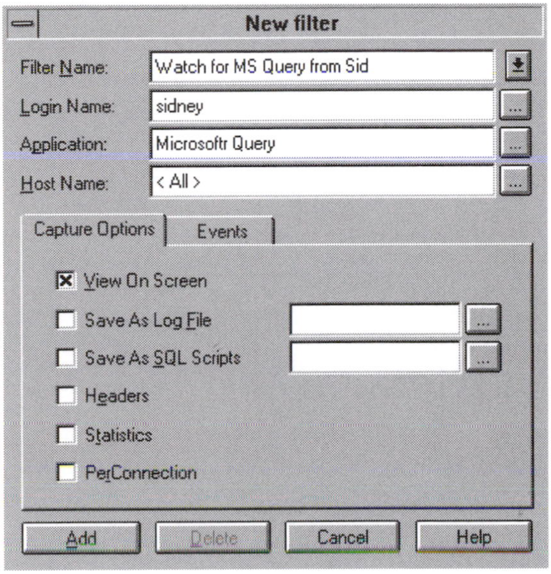

Figure 9.16

Once Sidney connects through this application, we can observe numerous details about his work:

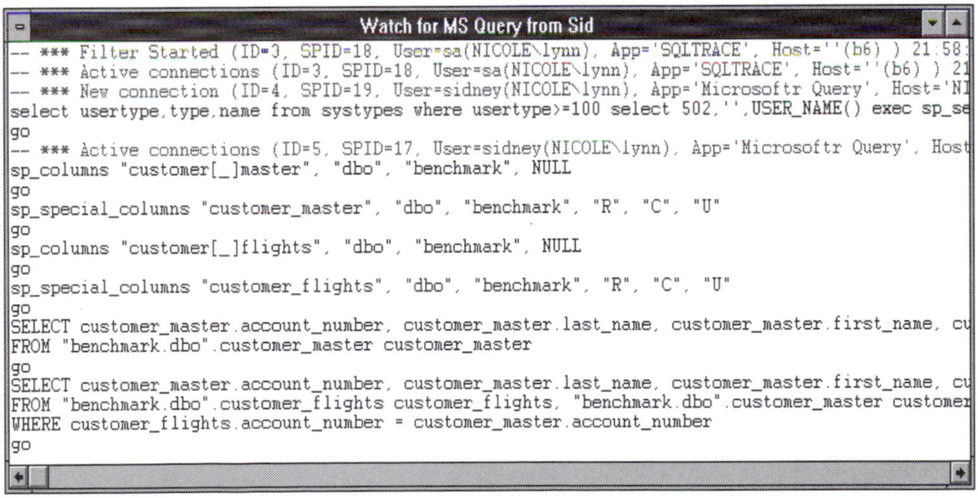

Figure 9.17

We requested that the trace utility also log this information, as well as create an SQL file for later review. Here's an excerpt of the log file, followed by a portion of the SQL script:

Log file

```
Start   sa  NICOLE  lynn    SQLTRACE                    5/8/96   21:58:43.900
        5/8/96  21:58:43.900   18   b6   3    0    20   0  0
Active  sa  NICOLE  lynn    SQLTRACE                    5/8/96   21:58:43.016
        5/8/96  21:58:43.900   18   b6   3    0    20   0  0
Connect sidney NICOLE lynn  Microsoftr Query  NICOLE           5/8/96
        21:59:01.933   5/8/96   21:59:02.293       19   af   4  0      0
        0   0
SQL sidney  NICOLE lynn    Microsoftr Query NICOLE     select
usertype,type,name from systypes where usertype>=100 select 502,'',USER_NAME()
exec sp_server_info 500 select 501,'',1 where 'a'='A' set textsize 2147483647
set ansi_defaults on set cursor_close_on_commit off dbcc traceon(208) set
implicit_transactions off    5/8/96       21:59:03.006  5/8/96
        21:59:05.110   19   af   4     2103   30   0     0
Active  sidney  NICOLE  lynn Microsoftr Query    NICOLE        5/8/96
        21:57:31.243   5/8/96   21:59:37.776       17    af 5   126    1823
        0   0
RPC sidney  NICOLE  lynn    Microsoftr Query    NICOLE    sp_columns
"customer[_]master", "dbo", "benchmark", NULL 1/1/00    00:00:00.000
        5/8/96  21:59:37.303     17    af    5    79177303  711   0    0
RPC sidney NICOLE lynn       Microsoftr Query    NICOLE    sp_special_columns
"customer_master", "dbo","benchmark", "R", "C", "U" 5/8/96 21:59:37.846
        5/8/96  21:59:38.046   17    af    5    200     40  0  0


        .      .       .      .       .        .
        .      .       .      .       .        .
        .      .       .      .       .        .
```

SQL script

```
-- *** Filter Started (ID=2, SPID=19, User=sa(NICOLE\lynn),
App='SQLTRACE', Host=''(b6) ) 21:58:08.566 ***
-- *** Active connections (ID=2, SPID=19, User=sa(NICOLE\lynn),
App='SQLTRACE', Host=''(b6) ) 21:58:08.656 ***
-- *** Filter Started (ID=3, SPID=18, User=sa(NICOLE\lynn),
App='SQLTRACE', Host=''(b6) ) 21:58:43.900 ***
-- *** Active connections (ID=3, SPID=18, User=sa(NICOLE\lynn),
App='SQLTRACE', Host=''(b6) ) 21:58:43.900 ***
-- *** New connection (ID=4, SPID=19, User=sidney(NICOLE\lynn),
App='Microsoftr Query', Host='NICOLE'(af) ) 21:59:02.293 ***
select usertype,type,name from systypes where usertype>=100 select
502,'',USER_NAME() exec sp_server_info 500 select 501,'',1 where 'a'='A'
set textsize 2147483647 set ansi_defaults on set cursor_close_on_commit
off dbcc traceon(208) set implicit_transactions off
go
-- *** Active connections (ID=5, SPID=17, User=sidney(NICOLE\lynn),
App='Microsoftr Query', Host='NICOLE'(af) ) 21:59:37.776 ***
sp_columns "customer[_]master", "dbo", "benchmark", NULL
```

```
go
sp_special_columns "customer_master", "dbo", "benchmark", "R",  "C", "U"
go
sp_columns "customer[_]flights", "dbo", "benchmark", NULL
go
sp_special_columns "customer_flights", "dbo", "benchmark", "R", C"," U"
go
SELECT customer_master.account_number, customer_master.last_name,
customer_master.first_name, customer_master.street,
customer_master.city, customer_master.account_balance,
customer_master.account_number

FROM "benchmark.dbo".customer_master customer_master
go
```

You can also enable auditing, which provides many of the same benefits of tracing, without the graphical front end. For example, suppose that we want to create an audit record whenever Sylvia logs in. We can request this behavior through the server auditing dialog box:

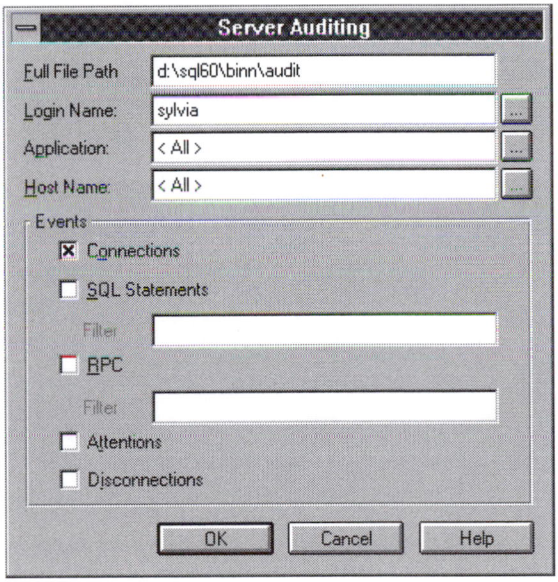

Figure 9.18

The next time that Sylvia logs on, we'll get messages similar to the following in the designated audit file:

```
Connect sylvia  NICOLE  lynn Microsoft ISQL/w        5/8/96
    22:28:58.476    5/8/96    22:28:59.960    18   ae  6       0
    0   6   0
```

```
Connect sylvia  NICOLE  lynn Microsoft ISQL/w NICOLE  5/8/96
    22:29:08.733     5/8/96     22:29:08.873    18  ae  7      0
    0    0    0
```

Describing all of the uses and benefits of the SQL Trace utility and server auditing could fill an entire book; it's wise for an administrator to spend some time examining how to use these powerful tools. As with most of the SQL Server utilities, the best approach is simply to begin practicing. To increase your knowledge, try experimenting with different trace options at different times.

Global variables

SQL Server provides a number of helpful, built-in global variables. The engine automatically maintains the contents of these variables; you don't need to worry about "stale data." To use these variables, you need only issue a SELECT statement against them. There are other ways to get this information, such as running the 'sp_monitor' stored procedure or using the SQL Enterprise Manager.

At this point, let's spend a few moments examining each of the available global variables, along with how you can use them. Note that some of these variables are primarily for application developers, while others are meant for database administrators. Regardless of your role, it's always a good idea to know what global variables are available for your use.

@@CONNECTIONS

This global variable shows the number of connections since the SQL Server engine was most recently started. These connections can be from 'isql,', isql/w,' or end-user applications and tools. Remember that this number is cumulative; it keeps growing until you restart the engine.

@@CPU_BUSY

This global variable measures the amount of logical I/O work spent since SQL Server was last started. The unit of measure for this global variable is "ticks." See the @@TIMETICKS section later in this chapter for more detail.

@@CURSOR_ROWS

SQL Server provides sophisticated cursor capabilities. You can use the @@CURSOR_ROWS global variable to learn more about the status of the most recently opened cursor. The values in this variable can include:

> 0 : You haven't yet opened any cursors, or the most recently opened cursor was closed and deallocated.

n : The number of rows found in a fully populated cursor.

-m : SQL Server supports asynchronous cursors. If the engine is populating this cursor by using asynchronous features, this value shows the number of rows in the active keyset.

For more detail on the important topic of cursors, see Chapter 7.

@@DATEFIRST

Recall that SQL Server assigns a number to each day of the week. Monday is 1, Tuesday is 2, etc. You can configure the first day of the week to be whatever number is appropriate for your area, by using the SET DATEFIRST command. You can then monitor the current setting by examining the contents of this global variable.

```
select @@datefirst

7
```

This means that Sunday is the first day of the week for your location.

@@DBTS

This global variable records the current timestamp value for the database.

```
select @@dbts

------------------
0x010000005fa00000
```

Keep in mind that this value varies by database; each database will have its own value for this global variable.

@@ERROR

SQL Server uses this global variable to store the status of the last database operation. Application programmers should always carefully monitor the contents of this variable, as it changes between operations. When set to 0, it indicates that the last operation was successful:

```
select @@error
go
select count(*) from non_existent_table
go
```

```
select @@error
go


-----------
18

(1 row(s) affected)


-----------
0

(1 row(s) affected)

Msg 208, Level 16, State 1
Invalid object name 'non_existent_table'.

-----------
208

(1 row(s) affected)
```

Notice how the last interrogation of @@ERROR yielded 208, which corresponds to SQL Server's previous error message number.

@@FETCH_STATUS

When you fetch information from a cursor, SQL Server reports on the cursor's status by using this global variable. It can have the following values:

   0 : The fetch was successful.

   -1 : The fetch failed, or the returned row was out of bounds for the query.

   -2 : The row fetched is no longer present in the database.

@@IDENTITY

As we saw in Part 1 on relational database design, SQL Server lets you define one column per table as having the identity property. When you define a column with this attribute, the database engine automatically assigns a unique numeric value to each inserted row. You can use the @@IDENTITY global variable to learn the value of the most recently inserted identity column for your connection:

```
create table demo_identity
    (col1 integer identity primary key)
insert into demo_identity default values
insert into demo_identity default values
insert into demo_identity default values

select @@identity

------
3
```

@@IDLE

In addition to tracking the amount of CPU activity, SQL Server also monitors how much idle CPU time has elapsed since the database engine was started. Like other CPU measurements, @@IDLE is gauged in ticks (one three-hundredths of a second):

```
select @@idle

-----------
6038
```

@@IO_BUSY

This global variable keeps track of how much time (in ticks) the CPU has spent performing physical input/output (I/O) operations for SQL Server since the engine was most recently started:

```
select @@io_busy

-----------
100292
```

@@LANGID

When you configure SQL Server, you have a choice of languages. This global variable holds a numeric identifier that identifies SQL Server's current configured language.

@@LANGUAGE

SQL Server lets you specify the language to be used by the database engine. You can learn what your language setting is by examining the contents of this global variable:

```
select @@language

us_english
```

@@MAX_CONNECTIONS

You can set the maximum number of user and process connections to your SQL Server engine. This global variable tells you the current value of this parameter:

```
select @@max_connections

-----------
32767
```

@@MAX_PRECISION

SQL Server normally starts with a precision of 28, meaning that any number defined in the database can be up to 28 digits long. However, you can start the engine with a /p flag, thereby overriding this value. You can monitor the maximum current precision setting by checking this global variable:

```
select @@max_precision

---
28
```

@@MICROSOFTVERSION

Microsoft assigns a version number to each release of SQL Server. This global variable tracks Microsoft's internal number:

```
select @@microsoftversion

    393337
```

This number isn't very meaningful to an application or user. If you want to access a more significant version number, use the @@VERSION global variable.

@@NESTLEVEL

SQL Server stored procedures can call other stored procedures. This is known as nesting; this global variable tells you the current nested level. For example, if you write a stored procedure called 'a' and check the contents of @@NESTLEVEL, the result will be 0. If 'a' calls another stored procedure 'b,' the contents of this variable will be 1.

@@OPTIONS

In earlier versions of SQL Server, you would use the SET command to configure a variety of different user options. With SQL Server 6.5, you can also use the 'sp_configure' stored procedure, with a parameter of 'user_options,' to set these options. These options include behavior such as closing a cursor on commit, whether implicit transactions should be enabled, whether data should be padded, etc. To learn what options have been set, you can examine the contents of this new global variable, which has a unique value for each user. Let's look at an example that illustrates what we mean.

Suppose that you want to see if the database will treat a user's SQL statements as being part of an implicit transaction, as well as whether the engine will close cursors on commit. Here's a sample script that sets and then tests for these options:

```
select @@options
go

if (@@options & 2) > 0
     raiserror ('Implicit transactions enabled',1,1)
else
     raiserror ('Implicit transactions disabled',1,1)
go

if (@@options & 4) > 0
     raiserror ('Cursor close on commit enabled',1,1)
else
     raiserror ('Cursor close on commit disabled',1,1)

SET IMPLICIT_TRANSACTIONS ON
```

```
select @@options
go

if (@@options & 2) > 0
    raiserror ('Implicit transactions enabled',1,1)
else
    raiserror ('Implicit transactions disabled',1,1)
go

if (@@options & 4) > 0
    raiserror ('Cursor close on commit enabled',1,1)
else
    raiserror ('Cursor close on commit disabled',1,1)

SET CURSOR_CLOSE_ON_COMMIT ON

select @@options
go

if (@@options & 2) > 0
    raiserror ('Implicit transactions enabled',1,1)
else
    raiserror ('Implicit transactions disabled',1,1)
go

if (@@options & 4) > 0
    raiserror ('Cursor close on commit enabled',1,1)
else
    raiserror ('Cursor close on commit disabled',1,1)
```

Output:

```
-----------
0

(1 row(s) affected)

Implicit transactions disabled
Cursor close on commit disabled

-----------
2

(1 row(s) affected)
```

```
Implicit transactions enabled
Cursor close on commit disabled

-----------
6

(1 row(s) affected)

Implicit transactions enabled
Cursor close on commit enabled
```

The unique numeric value for implicit transactions is 2; the value for close cursor on commit is 4. We can test for these values by using the logical AND (&) operator.

@@PACK_RECEIVED

SQL Server counts the number of packets received since the last engine startup and stores the result in the @@PACK_RECEIVED global variable:

```
select @@pack_received

-----------
6965
```

@@PACK_SENT

SQL Server counts the number of packets sent since the last engine startup and stores the result in the @@PACK_SENT global variable:

```
select @@pack_sent

-----------
4325
```

@@PACKET_ERRORS

There are occasions when SQL Server may encounter an error when communicating over a network. If the error occurs when sending or receiving packets of data, SQL Server increments this value. In many cases, such as on local networks or high-quality remote networks, this value can remain at 0 for long periods of time, since it's unlikely that SQL Server will encounter a network transport error.

@@PROCID

Each stored procedure has an associated identifier. You can examine the contents of the @@PROCID global variable to learn the identifier for the active stored procedure:

```
create procedure bbb as
select @@procid
go

execute bbb
go

create procedure ccc as
select @@procid
go

execute ccc
go

output:
-----------
80003316

(1 row(s) affected)


-----------
96003373

(1 row(s) affected)
```

@@REMSERVER

If you connect to a remote server, you can probe the contents of this global variable to learn the remote server's name. If you're on a local server and you query this variable, you'll get back a value of NULL.

@@ROWCOUNT

This global variable holds a count of the number of rows affected by the most recent database operation. SQL Server also populates this variable even if your operation merely retrieves data. If the operation doesn't affect any rows at all, SQL Server places a 0 into the variable:

```
update customer_flights
set destination = "VOID"
where destination is null
go

select @@rowcount

output:

(226 row(s) affected)

-----------
226
```

@@SERVERNAME

SQL Server requires the database administrator to provide a name for the server. You can learn what your server's name is by checking the contents of this global variable:

```
select @@servername

ARUGULA
```

@@SERVICENAME

This global variable reports the name of the database service currently running:

```
select @@servicename

MSSQLServer
```

@@SPID

SQL Server assigns a numeric process ID to each user and process that connect to the engine. You can learn the ID of your process by examining the contents of this variable:

```
select @@spid

10
```

@@TEXTSIZE

SQL Server supports enhanced data types, such as text and image. Columns of these types can hold large quantities of data. You can control the amount of information that the engine returns from these columns to your application by running the SET TEXTSIZE command. If you want to learn what the current setting is for this parameter, examine the contents of this global variable:

```
select @@textsize
set textsize 4096
select @@textsize

output:

-----------
64512

(1 row(s) affected)

-----------
4096

(1 row(s) affected)
```

@@TIMETICKS

Timeticks refers to the number of microseconds per "tick." Recall that a tick is a unit of measurement to help us understand the amount of time that the system spends performing a certain operation. When you request the contents of this global variable, SQL Server reports the number of microseconds per tick for this particular CPU:

```
select @@timeticks

------------------
31250
```

@@TOTAL_ERRORS

SQL Server keeps track of the total number of read or write errors it encounters. You can learn what this value is by examining the contents of this global variable. Note that SQL Server resets this number each time the engine starts.

@@TOTAL_READ

This global variable summarizes the number of physical (not buffered) reads that SQL Server has performed since the last time the engine was started. Once you shut down and then restart the engine, SQL Server erases the original value.

@@TOTAL_WRITE

This global variable reports on the number of physical disk writes performed by SQL Server since the last time it was started. Since this number is a cumulative counter, it rises over time and is reset only when you stop and then restart the server.

@@TRANCOUNT

SQL Server tracks the number of your active transactions in this global variable. For example, look at the following operation:

```
1> begin transaction
2> select @@trancount
3> go

    -----------
            1
begin transaction payment_update
            1
(1 row affected)
1> begin transaction
2> select @@trancount
3> go

    -----------
            2

(1 row affected)
```

Notice how SQL Server increments the contents of the @@TRANCOUNT variable after each transaction.

@@VERSION

You can use the @@VERSION global variable to learn about the exact release
of SQL Server that you're running:

```
Microsoft SQL Server 6.0 - 6.00.121 (Intel X86)
     Jun 13 1995 11:32:40
     Copyright (c) 1988-1995 Microsoft Corporation
```

Don't confuse this global variable with the @@MICROSOFTVERSION
variable. Only @@VERSION provides a meaningful version string.

Chapter 10

Windows NT Operating System Integration

One of SQL Server's most notable advantages over other Windows NT-based relational databases is its integration with the underlying operating system. In this chapter we describe how you can use this integration to further your performance goals. We begin by discussing some hardware issues, such as CPU, memory, and disk drives. We then turn our attention to the question of whether you should dedicate a machine to SQL Server. Next, we look at performance monitor integration between SQL Server and Windows NT. Finally, we examine a few configuration parameter issues.

Machine issues

Let's look at a few important areas of concern when purchasing or setting up your hardware environment. We'll cover each of these themes in more detail later in Part 3.

CPU

Microsoft recommends that you run SQL Server on at least a 486-class machine. This should suffice if you plan on running the database for no more than one or two users or for a simple decision support system. However, if you plan on using SQL Server to support more users or for a critical system, you should expect to need a Pentium™ or RISC processor. However, if you have no choice but to use an older 486 machine, don't skimp on memory: Enough memory may let you get away with using an underpowered machine.

Client machines generally don't require as much horsepower as the server. This is especially true if you make heavy use of server-based stored procedures and cursors, since this minimizes the amount of processing that takes place on the client.

Memory

When it comes to computer resources, there's no concept of too much of a good thing. This especially holds true for memory. Windows NT and SQL Server both perform better when there is ample memory. When you don't have enough memory, the operating system and database are forced to spend crucial CPU cycles using the disk drives to create virtual memory. The limit on virtual memory is bound only by the amount of disk space that you allocate, but your system will bog down long before you exhaust all of your available virtual memory.

How can you determine how much memory to allocate to SQL Server? You should never attempt to run SQL Server with less than 16 megabytes of memory on an Intel® platform. Non-Intel platforms require even higher minimums. You should also avoid dedicating all memory on the system to SQL Server, since you may force the operating system itself to start swap. If you're using SQL Server to support a large number of users, your memory requirements will grow, perhaps significantly. One simple rule of thumb that you can follow is to add 100K of memory for each active, concurrent user. For example, if your system has a base memory of 32 megabytes and you expect 100 active users at any given time, you would add an additional 10 megabytes (100 users * 100K/user) of memory. Your actual numbers may vary depending on the actual usage profile of your database. However, given the relatively low cost of memory, this added investment is much cheaper than the cost of a slow system and frustrated users. We'll explore more specific memory management and monitoring ideas later in Part 3.

Disk drive

Your disk drive choices will largely be dictated by the amount of data that you plan to store. It would be foolish to attempt to keep five gigabytes of data on a one-gigabyte machine: Data storage is limited by the amount of available disk space. Even if you allocate five gigabytes of disk drive, you still run the risk of running out of temporary or work space, as well as not being prepared for future data growth. In fact, the most common mistake administrators make when setting up their system is to underestimate future disk space requirements. For these reasons, don't be too stingy when allocating disk space: Remember that data tends to grow very rapidly in a short time. We'll delve more deeply into disk space allotment and management later.

Dedicated server vs. non-dedicated server

One common question that administrators ask is whether they should dedicate the computer running SQL Server to database-only tasks. This is an excellent idea in most cases. For example, suppose that you're installing SQL Server as the database engine for an inventory system. A department of fifteen users will use the inventory application, which connects to the SQL Server database. To keep costs down, your management has asked you to install the engine on one of the users' machines. You decide to place the engine on the fastest, most powerful user machine. The installation goes well, and the users appear to be happy with system reliability and response. However, after about a week, you begin to get sporadic reports of very slow response. You log on, run some sample queries and reports, and find no difficulties. You advise the users that you could not find any trace of the problem. Yet the reports of response obstacles persist, and users begin to grow frustrated. You spend more and more time trying to isolate the cause of the problem. In the end, you discover that the user who has SQL Server installed on her machine sometimes likes to play video games. Some days she's too busy to play at all, while other days she's bored and plays for large stretches of time. These video games gobble up huge amounts of CPU, causing other active users to perceive the delays as being related to the database and application.

This type of scenario is more common than you might think and highlights one of the benefits of dedicating a machine to SQL Server. If you dedicate a machine to be the database machine, then there can be no nonapplication and database factors slowing down system speed. Finding throughput barriers is hard enough without having to reconstruct every detail of every user's activity.

Performance monitor

As we saw earlier, SQL Server comes with a powerful monitoring tool. When you install the engine, SQL Server asks if you want to integrate the database reporting monitor with the operating system monitor. You should always select this option; doing so makes it much easier to understand how your SQL Server engine fits into the overall Windows NT environment.

Configuration options

Let's look at some Windows NT operating system configuration options that can have an effect on SQL Server performance.

Swap file

Modern operating systems use one or more files on the disk drive as alternate storage locations when RAM begins to run low. For example, if you have 16 megabytes of RAM, yet your system requires 20 megabytes of memory storage, the operating system uses 4 megabytes of disk space to satisfy the extra necessity. This is known as swapping. Windows NT uses PAGEFILE.SYS as its swapping location. You control the size of this swap file from the Windows NT control panel's system virtual memory dialog box:

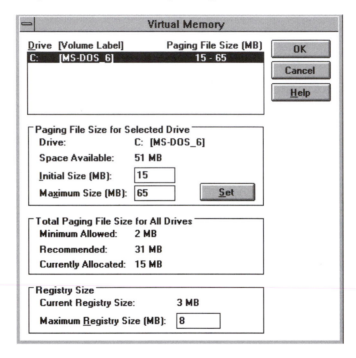

Figure 10.1

How many swap files should you create? How large should you make each swap file? One rule of thumb that you can follow is to create one swap file for each disk drive. Each swap file should then have three times as much space as is available in RAM. As an example, suppose that you have one disk drive, with 32 megabytes of RAM. Following the rule of thumb listed earlier, this would equate to one swap file of 96 megabytes. This may seem overly large, but it's likely that you would be surprised to learn how much swapping actually occurs on a typical system. You can learn more about the state of your swap file by using the Windows NT performance monitor's Paging File object.

In spite of this sizing suggestion, an argument can also be made that you can actually decrease the amount of space in your swap files as the overall amount of RAM on your system grows. For example, a system with only 16

megabytes of RAM may be swapping all the time, whereas one with 128 megabytes may have so much memory that it never needs to swap. Therefore, your
choice of swap file size largely depends on the activity profile of your system.
Raw memory alone is not enough of a predictor of swap file size; the number of
users and their work patterns also have an effect. Keep this in mind when sizing your swap file. Fortunately, you have the freedom to alter the swap file size
as often as your needs or experiences dictate.

Priority boost

You can tell SQL Server to run at a higher priority than the rest of other NT
processes by setting the priority boost flag to 1. This means that when the NT
operating system kernel allocates resources among various processes, this flag
tells it to give the SQL Server engine quicker response. The default value is 0,
which tells the NT operating system to treat SQL Server equally with other
processes. How should you set this value? Much depends on how you use your
NT system. If you plan on dedicating the machine to be a database server, it's
a good idea to set the parameter to 1 and thereby give SQL Server higher priority. On the other hand, if your machine performs many other tasks, giving
SQL Server priority might have a detrimental effect on other applications and
processes.

   If you decide to enable priority boost, make careful performance measurements before and after the change, since you might experience unexpected response results.

Server tasking

As part of its multitasking features, Windows NT lets you determine whether
you want the operating system to give preference to either foreground or background processes. You also have the option of equal treatment between these
process types. Which should you choose? Generally, if you plan on having a dedicated database server, you can give preference to background processes, since
the SQL Server engine falls into this category. On the other hand, if you'll be
running local applications on the database server, ask that the operating system take a balanced approach to foreground and background processes. This
will help your applications run at an acceptable speed, while preserving database engine response.

Chapter 11

Disk Management

Proper disk configuration and utilization are essential components of a well-running SQL Server system. In this chapter, we explore a variety of topics that relate to this important subject. Before beginning a serious discussion of this theme, we start off by explaining some commonly used terms relating to disk storage. With these terms now familiar to us, we then spend some time focusing on various disk storage options, including RAID devices, striping, mirroring, segments, and selecting a file system type.

At that point, we examine how to use the DBCC utility to gain more knowledge about your disk environment. Next, we move on to the theme of fragmentation and index fill factors. Once we've finished these subjects, we then cover a variety of I/O topics, including asynchronous I/O, SQL Server's lazywriter process, and read-ahead. SQL Server provides administrators with numerous statistics and configuration parameters that report on, and control, I/O performance. We discuss these options in detail, before closing out the chapter by examining the benefits and drawbacks of storing the tempdb in RAM.

Disk storage concepts

Before we begin our discussion on how to most efficiently set up and maintain your SQL Server disk, let's define a few important disk terms and concepts.

Page

A page is the smallest unit of measurement for SQL Server disk storage. Pages are 2 K in size and can hold data or indexes. You can't change the page size.

When SQL Server reads or writes data, it generally performs these tasks at the page level.

When you first create a database, SQL Server takes a few moments and initializes all bits on all pages on the device to 0. However, note that there are two exceptions to this rule:

1. **If you've set the 'create for load' option.**   When you choose this alternative, SQL Server skips the disk initialization portion of the database creation operation.

2. **If the device previously had information.**   If SQL Server detects older data on the device, it bypasses the clearing phase.

Extent

An extent is a grouping of eight pages. These pages are sequential:

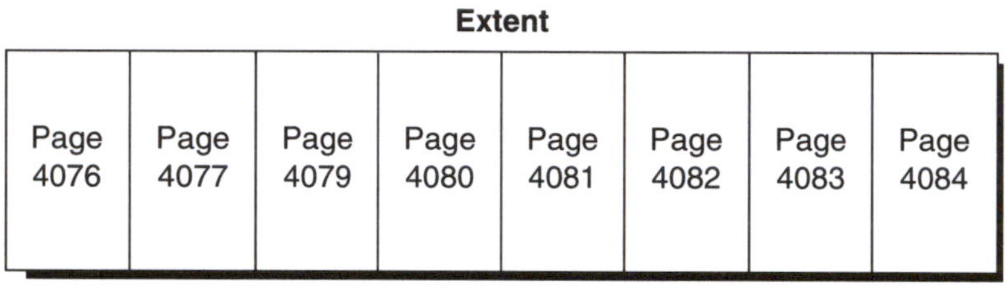

Extent

Page 4076	Page 4077	Page 4079	Page 4080	Page 4081	Page 4082	Page 4083	Page 4084

Figure 11.1

Allocation unit

An allocation unit is 32 extents, for a total of 256 pages. The first page in an allocation unit is called the allocation page. This is a "map" of the balance of the allocation unit, leaving 255 pages for data or indexes:

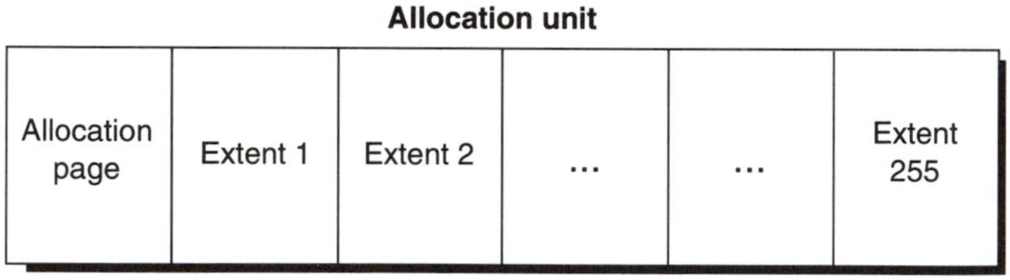

Allocation unit

Allocation page	Extent 1	Extent 2	...	...	Extent 255

Figure 11.2

Device

A device is a Windows NT operating system file or a tape drive. SQL Server uses two types of devices: database devices and dump devices.

Database device

A database device is an area of disk defined by an SQL Server administrator. A database device can support one or more full or partial databases. You can learn about your existing devices by using the SQL Enterprise Manager or by running the 'sp_helpdevice' stored procedure:

```
device_name    physical_name               description
status cntrltype device_number    low       high
 dbspace1       D:\SQL60\DATA\space1        special, physical disk, 80 MB
2       0            1            16777216   16818175
 diskdump       nul                         disk, dump device
16      2            0            0           20000
 diskettedumpa a:sqltable.dat               diskette, 1.2 MB, dump device
16      3            0            0           19
 diskettedumpb b:sqltable.dat               diskette, 1.2 MB, dump device
16      4            0            0           19
 master         D:\SQL60\DATA\MASTER.DAT  special, default disk, physical disk,
50 MB
3       0            0            0           25599
MSDBData        D:\SQL60\DATA\MSDB.DAT     special, physical disk, 2 MB
2       0            127          2130706432 2130707455
MSDBLog         D:\SQL60\DATA\MSDBLOG.DAT special, physical disk, 10 MB
2       0            126          2113929216 2113934335
```

The minimum size of a database device is one megabyte.

Dump device

A dump device is a location on disk, diskette, or tape that SQL Server uses to back up data or transaction logs. These are crucial components of your system administration responsibilities. You can create dump devices by using the Create Dump Device screen in the SQL Enterprise Manager:

Figure 11.3

SQL Server 6.5 made slight changes to this screen:

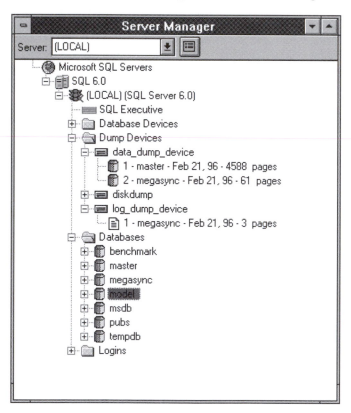

Figure 11.4

In this example, we're creating a tape device to be used for dumping data or transaction logs. You can get a list of available dump devices by using the SQL Enterprise Manager Server Manager screen. You can also learn what has been sent to the dump device by clicking on the device's '+' sign:

Figure 11.5

In this case, we've done a backup of the 'master' and 'megasync' databases to the 'data_dump_device' dump device. We also did a 'megasync' transaction log backup to the device called 'log_dump_device.'

If you prefer to use stored procedures for your dump device management, you can use the 'sp_adddumpdevice' procedure to create a new device, 'sp_dropdevice' to delete it, and 'sp_helpdevice' to retrieve information about existing dump devices.

Default devices

When you create a database device, you can add it to a pool of available devices that SQL Server can use for future databases. These devices are known as default devices. SQL Server chooses from this list in alphabetical order, moving on as each device fills. You can specify that a device be added to the default devices pool by checking the default device box when you create the device. For example, in the next case, we've asked SQL Server to add 'dbdevice5' to the default devices list:

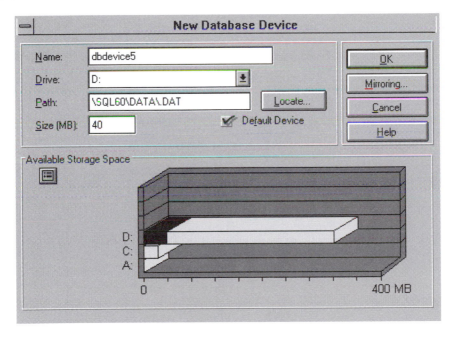

Figure 11.6

To remove a device from the default list, simply clear the default device checkbox. Another way to change a device's relationship with the default device list is to use the 'sp_diskdefault' stored procedure.

Finally, it's a good idea to back up the MASTER database whenever you add or remove a device from the default devices list. This protects you should the MASTER database become damaged during this operation.

Null device

SQL Server provides a dump device that you can use to dump databases quickly. This device is known as the 'null device' and is assigned a logical name of DISKDUMP. This is very similar to the concept of '/dev/null' on UNIX; sending data to DISKDUMP is very fast, but it also means that you won't be able to recover from that device later on.

Database

A database is a grouping of tables and objects, defined by an SQL Server administrator. Databases can reside entirely on one database device, or they can span multiple database devices:

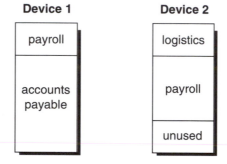

Figure 11.7

For example, in the above graphic, the 'payroll' database uses space on both 'device 1' and 'device 2.' On the other hand, both the 'logistics' and 'accounts payable' databases fit on one device.

Physical name

A physical name refers to the actual Windows NT operating system file name. The physical name includes the entire path. Some example physical names are:

```
C:\DATA\DBSPACE1.DAT
E:\DEVICES\SQLSERVER\MAINFILE.DAT
D:\DATABASE FILE1.DAT
```

Logical name

These are meaningful names that SQL Server system administrators assign to physical devices. Some sample logical names are:

```
PAYROLL_DATABASE
TRANSACTION_LOG_1
SUPPORT_INFORMATION
```

Disk storage options

RAID

RAID is an acronym that stands for Redundant Array of Inexpensive Disks. This is a concept common to a number of powerful operating systems, including Windows NT and UNIX. When speaking about RAID, be aware that there are various options, or levels, of RAID compliance. The following describes the six levels of RAID compliance:

- **Level 0.**   This is the lowest level of RAID functionality. When a RAID system is level 0, it means that your data is divided among all of the disks that make up the disk array. This improves performance, since read and write operations are now being serviced by more than one disk drive. This load-balancing helps eliminate response bottlenecks. Administrators may be familiar with another name for this type of RAID technology: disk striping. One drawback to this approach is that losing one disk drive can lead to a serious data loss, since this RAID level has no mechanism for fault tolerance.

- **Level 1.**   This level of RAID compliance provides built-in disk mirroring. Whenever SQL Server writes to the primary disk, it also writes to the secondary disk. This keeps both disk drives in synchronization. From a performance standpoint, it's possible that write operations may be slightly degraded, since the system now has to make two writes as opposed to one. However, read performance may improve, since the system now has two locations to find information, thereby potentially reducing disk latency. Given that typical applications spend much more time in reading data than in writing it, the potential write degradation is more than offset by the potential read betterment.

- **Level 2.**   This level introduces rudimentary error correcting logic. Data is divided among the disk drives, and error correcting code is added. The error correction code requires you to assign several disks. This reduces the chances of data loss, but the overall performance for this level is not as good as for other levels.

- **Level 3.** RAID 3 enhances level 2 by requiring only one disk for the error correcting code.

- **Level 4.** This level breaks data into larger blocks before spreading it among your disk drives. Error correction code is still stored on only one disk. However, tests have shown that this level provides disappointing throughput.

- **Level 5.** This level of RAID is similar to level 0, with the added benefit of more sophisticated error correction.

RAID implementation

Regardless of the level of RAID compliance that you choose, you must decide whether to implement this strategy via hardware or the operating system. Let's look at the benefits and drawbacks of each approach.

Hardware-based RAID

When you choose hardware-based RAID, the disk drive controller manages the actual RAID operations. These RAID disk controllers typically cost more than standard disk drive controllers. However, the extra cost is neutralized by the greater performance benefits, since the controller handles the supplemental RAID processing within hardware, instead of consuming valuable main system CPU time. This means that the operating system is completely unaware of the extra work carried out by the disk controller.

Operating system-based RAID

When you assign the task of managing RAID to Windows NT, the operating system has the responsibility of maintaining parity and reliability. Although this can place an extra burden on the CPU, you are relieved of having to spend the extra money on enhanced RAID disk controllers that a hardware approach would require. However, given that our goal is to enhance overall throughput, the extra hardware expenditures are usually not as significant as the potential for delay when you force the operating system and CPU to labor on maintaining RAID.

Operating system disk striping

Administrators can use Windows NT disk striping to advance I/O performance. When you set up disk striping, you're asking the operating system to spread data across more than one disk. This helps to balance the load among disk drives, which in turn can eliminate potential bottlenecks. Let's look at an example that illustrates how striping works.

Suppose that you have four disk drives, C through F. To enhance disk I/O speed, you've asked Windows NT to stripe across these drives. The following diagram shows how the operating system will write files to the striped set:

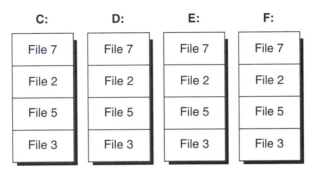

Figure 11.8

This diagram would be applicable even if you had chosen hardware-base RAID disk striping instead of software-based Windows NT striping. In fact, operating system striping actually implements RAID level 0.

How does striping lead to better response? The reason for these gains derives from the fact that I/O is up to 10 times slower than memory access. Consequently, anything that you can do to shorten the amount of I/O time has the potential to contribute directly to a faster system. Given that I/O is slow, I/O bottlenecks are even worse. Imagine that you have an I/O-intensive data loading program that continually waits for the operating system to finish its writes to a single disk drive. What would happen if you implemented striping? You would probably notice an immediate improvement, since the operating system could now issue more than one write request at a time. Read operations should also get better, since there is a good chance that different read requests will be serviced by different disk drives.

Disk striping's performance augmentation is even more dramatic in a multiprocessing, multithreading environment like Windows NT, where threads can service individual disk drives. The response picture gets even brighter if you are using multiple disk controllers or multiple CPUs. Adding controllers or CPUs increases the processing power brought to bear on the expensive and time-consuming tasks of disk I/O.

Aside from performance gains, are there any other benefits to disk striping? The answer is a qualified yes. Using parity with disk striping can help you safeguard your data. Let's learn more about parity, and the role it can play in your environment.

Parity vs. no parity

When you set up Windows NT disk striping, you have a choice of selecting parity or no parity. Choosing parity means that the operating system uses a small area on each disk drive to hold data redundancy details. Using our diagram from earlier, note the slight change that happens after we opted for parity:

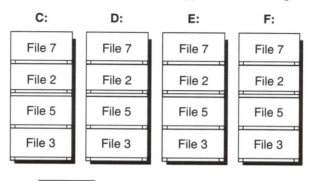

Figure 11.9

There is now a small stripe of parity data as part of each partition. Should one of these disks have a serious failure, you can re-create your information as if you had implemented disk mirroring. Operating system striping with parity is equivalent to RAID level 5. However, the overall amount of space necessary to fulfill striping is much less than mirroring. Mirroring requires that you reserve an amount of space exactly equal to the original storage, whereas striping with parity adds only slight overhead.

Remember that disk striping with parity can only be effective when you are dealing with separate disk drives. If you've created four logical disk drives from one physical drive, you won't be able to reap the data integrity benefits of striping, since all the data resides on a single device.

Mirroring

One of an administrator's most important responsibilities is to safeguard the data under his control. In this section, we explore how you can use mirroring to increase the chances of your data being able to survive a serious system failure. You have a choice between asking the operating system to mirror your data or requesting that the SQL Server engine itself mirror information. We examine both of these options, as well as the difference between mirroring and duplexing. Next, we focus on how you can determine what data to mirror. We close out the section by explaining the role of data backups in a mirrored environment.

Operating system disk mirroring

Of the many advanced features of the Windows NT operating system, disk mirroring is of particular interest to SQL Server database administrators. You can use the operating system disk administrator to create a mirror set. Creating a mirror set means that each time that you write to the primary disk, Windows NT also writes to the mirrored disk. If either the primary or mirrored device should suffer a serious failure, the operating system can continue to work by relying on the remaining disk drive. What are some common causes of serious disk failures? These unfortunate incidents can be caused by one or more of the following:

- Disk head crash
- Major data corruption
- Disk motor failure
- Disk controller card failure

Mirroring imposes a superficial extra cost during data write operations, since the operating system performs this task twice. However, on read operations, mirroring can actually further performance, since Windows NT now has two equally valid sources of information: the primary disk and the mirrored disk. The operating system is free to choose between either disk.

Note that if you want to use operating system mirroring, you must be running the server version of Windows NT; the client version doesn't have this capability.

Operating system duplexing

Duplexing is operating system mirroring taken one step further. When you employ duplexing as part of your mirroring strategy, you use separate disk controllers for the primary and mirrored disks. This augments your protection, since you've removed a potential common point of failure.

SQL Server device mirroring

When you create a device, you can instruct SQL Server to mirror the device. For example, in the next illustration, we're creating a device called images and have just selected the mirroring button:

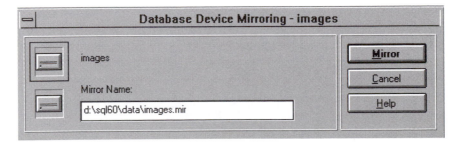

Figure 11.10

This dialog box has changed slightly with SQL Server 6.5:

Figure 11.11

If you want to use Transact-SQL instead, there are several commands at your disposal, including:

- DISK MIRROR
- DISK UNMIRROR
- DISK REMIRROR

When you use SQL Server to mirror a device, the database engine writes all changes to the database twice: once to the primary device and once to the mirror device. This has the effect of infinitesimally slowing write performance, while greatly reducing the chance of data loss should you suffer a catastrophic disk failure.

Keep in mind that mirroring only makes sense if you are working with distinct disk drives. If you've partitioned a single drive into several smaller drives, mirroring has no data integrity benefits; all the data still inhabits one drive, no matter how many partitions you've created.

Choosing between operating system mirroring and SQL Server mirroring

Given all that we've discussed about mirroring, how can you decide which method to follow? It's a good idea to examine each of the following criteria, then apply the results to your environment:

1. **Windows NT Advanced Server vs. Windows NT Workstation.** If you're running the workstation version of Windows NT, you have no choice but to implement SQL Server mirroring. This is necessary because your version of Windows NT doesn't support operating system mirroring.

2. **Easy access to Windows NT administrator.** If you work in an environment where it's easy to work with your operating system

administrator (or if you serve as both the system and database admin-istrator), then it should be simple to set up and maintain operating system mirroring. On the other hand, if your Windows NT adminis-trator is not the most pleasant person to deal with, you're probably better off using your own (i.e., SQL Server's) mirroring, since you won't need much assistance from your system administrator after the physical drives are in place.

3. **Availability of hardware RAID.** If you've purchased disk drives that incorporate RAID technology, it's probably best to use the oper-ating system mirroring capabilities rather than the SQL Server mir-roring architecture. RAID is faster, more effective, and consumes less disk space than pure database mirroring.

Selecting data to mirror

Now that we've researched the different mirroring options available to SQL Server administrators, let's turn our attention to determining which informa-tion to mirror. Generally, with disk prices so low, there's very little reason not to mirror all of your system's data. By doing this, you are greatly increasing the chances that you won't lose any of your information should a failure happen. In addition, mirroring lets you continue working during a situation that would previously have required a complete work halt. Contrast the minimal cost of extra disk drives with the expense of downtime, not to mention lost data.

If you don't have enough disk space to mirror everything and you're run-ning a system where you can afford any lost transactions, you should still mir-ror the transaction log. Let's discover why this is so.

Transaction log mirroring

The transaction log holds important information about data changes that have happened in your database. When you restart the SQL Server engine after a stoppage, it examines the contents of the log to determine what data alter-ations had been marked as permanent versus what changes were still in pro-cess when the engine halted. Using this knowledge, the engine is able to restore your database to its state prior to shutting down the system.

If you decide not to mirror the transaction log, you risk losing all transac-tions, both committed and in-process, should the transaction log device fail. This lost work could account for several days of efforts; replacing the informa-tion could be difficult, if not impossible. Mirroring the transaction log device means that even if the original log device fails, the contents of the transaction log are still available for backup or recovery.

Keep in mind that if you choose only to mirror the transaction log device and a data device then fails, you will lose table data itself. If you don't change your data very much (meaning that your transaction log doesn't hold very much information), you may therefore elect to mirror data devices, leaving the transaction log device unprotected. Once again, it's best not to have to make this unpleasant decision; you'll be better off if you simply mirror everything.

Mirroring and backups

Since mirroring is so powerful, do administrators even need to perform normal database backups? The answer is a definite yes. Although mirroring protects you from disk drive failures, it does nothing to address how you could recover from larger, more encompassing problems, such as a damaged, destroyed, lost, or stolen computer. Other disasters such a fire or an earthquake can also completely disable your system. In these predicaments, your disk drive status is not relevant, since there are larger issues at hand. What would you do if you had to rebuild your data on a new system?

A carefully-thought-out backup strategy lets you deal with any number of lost data situations, from erroneously deleted rows all the way through completely destroyed systems. While it's beyond the scope of this book to describe all backup scenarios, administrators should plan on devoting some time to developing an effective backup plan.

One final note on backing up data: Consider replication as part of your backup strategy. We depict replication in Chapter 16.

Segments

When it comes to enhancing I/O operation throughput, it's usually a good idea to take a "divide-and-conquer" approach. For example, following this approach would mean that instead of placing all information on one disk drive, you would divide it among several. When there are several drives working to process a request, information usually comes back more quickly, since there is less chance of encountering a bottleneck.

To divide your information among several disk drives, you can use segments. Segments are logical names that administrators assign to disk space. For example, suppose that you have three disk drives, named C, D, and E. Your goal is to divide your information among these drives. By creating segments and mapping them to these drives, you can ask SQL Server to store specific objects on each segment:

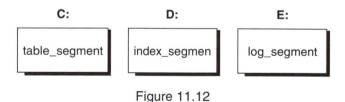

Figure 11.12

In this model, we've created three segments, one for each disk drive. The first segment, 'table_segment,' is to be used for holding tables. The second, 'index_segment,' will hold non-clustered indexes. The third, known as 'log_segment,' will be the home for SQL Server's transaction log.

We can specify which segments to use when we create new tables and indexes:

```
create table parts_detail
(
    id integer identity primary key,
    part_efficiency decimal(5,2),
    .    .    .    .
    .    .    .    .
)
on table_segment
create index pd_efficiency_ix on
parts_detail(part_efficiency)
on index_segment
```

Note that you can't place clustered indexes on different segments than their parent tables. While segments are very helpful and can indeed speed disk I/O throughput, it's usually easier to get the same enhanced results by using an automated strategy, such as disk striping or RAID. These automated techniques require far less administration than the more labor-intensive segment approach.

In summary, don't forget that disk layout and management are topics worthy of serious thought and analysis. Don't skimp on your research and investigation into this important subject. After contrasting the RAID approach versus a segmenting strategy, you may determine to choose the RAID system, which usually requires less administration than segmenting.

File system types

As an administrator, you have two choices regarding file system types: FAT and NTFS. You use the Windows NT Disk Administrator utility to choose between these file systems. Let's examine both choices in more detail.

FAT

The FAT file system stands for File Allocation Table. This is a legacy file system that dates back to the early days of MS-DOS. It doesn't offer much in the way of security or recovery features, although it does let you boot both MS-DOS and Windows NT. If you plan on using your database server to run the MS-DOS operating system, leave your file systems as FAT.

NTFS

NTFS stands for NT File System. It was introduced with the Windows NT operating system and provides a number of added features, such as enhanced security, recovery, and performance. In addition, you can take advantage of NTFS file compression to conserve space, although you might suffer some performance setbacks. If you plan on dedicating your NT machine to be a database server and plan never to boot MS-DOS, use this file system. If you're using a non-Intel platform, such as DEC® Alpha™ or MIPS®, then you will have no choice but to use NTFS, since these environments can't run MS-DOS.

The DBCC utility and disk information

As we discussed earlier, the DBCC utility provides valuable disk status information for database administrators.

Since it's hard to have a well-running system if you have serious data storage errors, it's worth your time to understand DBCC. Let's look at this important tool and how you can use it to better discern the state of your system's disk storage.

You can run DBCC with a number of different parameters. Let's look at those parameters that help us understand if your disks have any problems.

CHECKALLOC

Running DBCC with a parameter of CHECKALLOC tells SQL Server to check the validity of allocated space versus used space. Note that CHECKALLOC was provided for backwards compatibility with earlier versions of SQL Server. It's probably best to use the NEWALLOC option instead. NEWALLOC provides more details than CHECKALLOC and is also able to keep working if it encounters an error.

If you still settle on using CHECKALLOC, you can pass in a database name as a parameter. If you don't provide a database name, SQL Server examines the current database. Here's some sample output:

```
DBCC CHECKALLOC (LARGO)

Checking largo
Database 'largo' is not in single user mode - may find
spurious allocation problems due to transactions in progress.
Alloc page 0 (# of extent=32 used pages=42 ref pages=42)
Alloc page 256 (# of extent=31 used pages=178 ref pages=178)
Alloc page 512 (# of extent=32 used pages=243 ref pages=243)
Alloc page 768 (# of extent=25 used pages=191 ref pages=191)
Alloc page 1024 (# of extent=1 used pages=0 ref pages=0)
Alloc page 1280 (# of extent=1 used pages=0 ref pages=0)
```

```
.       .       .       .       .       .       .       .       .       .
.       .       .       .       .       .       .       .       .       .
Alloc page 2304 (# of extent=1 used pages=0 ref pages=0)
Alloc page 2560 (# of extent=1 used pages=0 ref pages=0)
Alloc page 2816 (# of extent=24 used pages=192 ref
pages=187)
Alloc page 3072 (# of extent=1 used pages=0 ref pages=0)
Alloc page 3328 (# of extent=1 used pages=0 ref pages=0)
Total (# of extent=153 used pages=846 ref pages=841) in this
database
```

How can you interpret this output? First, the reason that SQL Server displays the error message about single-user mode is that you should try to run this command during periods of reduced activity or, ideally, in single-user mode. This is because users may have transactions that are still open, which can throw off SQL Server's accuracy when analyzing disk usage. In addition, running many DBCC commands can have a deleterious effect on system performance. In the next part of the command's output, SQL Server examines each allocation unit. Recall that an allocation unit consists of 32 extents of 8 pages per extent, which totals 256 pages of data. Within each allocation unit, DBCC compares the number of actually used pages versus the number of referenced pages.

One common parameter that you can provide to those commands that check table and database structure and reliability is NOINDEX. Normally, SQL Server checks all indexes, including non-clustered and non-primary key indexes, when searching for damage. Setting this option tells the engine to skip any indexes (except for clustered indexes) when examining tables. This effectively speeds up these operations, since index inspection can be quite time consuming. Remember that this option applies only to user-defined tables: DBCC still checks all aspects of system tables, including non-clustered indexes.

Even though NOINDEX helps diminish the amount of time that it takes to run many DBCC operations, it's wise to run the full version of these commands from time to time. You may learn that there is a problem with a non-clustered index, which you would miss if you always ran with the NOINDEX option.

CHECKCATALOG

It's important to regularly check the validity of your database's system catalog. You can use the DBCC CHECKCATALOG command to instruct SQL Server to examine a number of important system components to make sure they are synchronized. You can pass in a database name, or SQL Server looks at the current database:

```
DBCC CHECKCATALOG

Checking current database
```

```
    The following segments have been defined for database 6
(database name largo).
    virtual start addr        size        segments
    ------------------        ------      --------------------
              16777216        2560
                                                  0
                                                  1
              33554432        1024
                                                  2
```

We've discussed database segments in our section on SQL Server's disk structures. DBCC examines the validity and quantity of these segments, along with these other important integrity checks:

- **Transaction log.**   DBCC makes sure that the transaction log (syslogs) has a valid checkpoint record.

- **Column names and data types.**   DBCC compares the entries in 'syscolumns' to make sure that each data type is represented in the 'systypes' table.

- **Table and column referential integrity.**   For each object in the database, DBCC checks the referential integrity between the object and its associated columns.

CHECKTABLE

Running DBCC CHECKTABLE instructs SQL Server to perform a detailed analysis of a table's internal structure, including:

- Data and index integrity
- Index sequencing
- Page linkage
- Internal structure validity

You can pass in a table name, along with a particular index name as well.

```
DBCC CHECKTABLE(equipos)

Checking equipos
The total number of data pages in this table is 305.
The number of data pages in Sysindexes for this table
was 310. It has been corrected to 305.
The number of rows in Sysindexes for this table was
```

```
9586. It has been corrected to 9439.
Table has 9439 data rows.
```

After the first run of the command, SQL Server has corrected its internal counts of pages and rows. If we rerun the command, we see these new, updated figures:

```
DBCC CHECKTABLE(equipos)

Checking equipos
The total number of data pages in this table is 305.
Table has 9439 data rows.
```

You can run this command against standard data tables, as well as against the 'syslogs' table, which checks transaction log consistency.

In earlier versions of SQL Server, DBCC CHECKTABLE was processed serially. However, beginning with version 6.0, the engine spawns multiple threads to help divide the overall amount of work necessary to finish the operation. This had a dramatic effect on performance, since many steps could be completed in parallel.

CHECKDB

To check table integrity, you can run DBCC CHECKTABLE for each table in your database. A simpler way to achieve the same results is to run DBCC CHECKDB. This command checks all tables, either in the current database or in a database of your choice. Let's look at some sample output:

```
DBCC CHECKDB

Checking largo
Checking 1
The total number of data pages in this table is 1.
Table has 23 data rows.
Checking 2
The total number of data pages in this table is 4.
Table has 35 data rows.
   .    .    .    .    .
   .    .    .    .    .
Checking 8
The total number of data pages in this table is 4.
The number of data pages in Sysindexes for this table
was 116. It has been corrected to 4.
The number of rows in Sysindexes for this table was
```

```
3209.  It has been corrected to 87.
*** NOTICE:  Space used on the log segment is 0.01
Mbytes, 0.39.
*** NOTICE:  Space free on the log segment is 2.04
Mbytes, 99.61.
Table has 87 data rows.
 .    .   .   .   .

 .    .   .   .   .
Checking 16003088
The total number of data pages in this table is 305.
Table has 9439 data rows.
Checking 80003316
The total number of data pages in this table is 37.
Table has 4051 data rows.
Checking 352004285
The total number of data pages in this table is 5.
Table has 377 data rows.
```

Observe how SQL Server first checks its internal system tables, which all have low object numbers. The next step is to move on to user-defined tables, which have much higher object numbers. For each table, the utility detects and corrects simple anomalies, while only reporting on more difficult problems. You may need to take additional steps to correct these other defects.

CHECKIDENT

Recollect from our discussions about efficient database design that SQL Server lets you assign the IDENTITY property to one numeric column per table. Identity columns can serve as built-in primary keys. If these primary keys become erroneously altered, however, you can have difficulty when accessing the table. Fortunately, you can use the DBCC CHECKIDENT command to ensure that your table's identity values are correct when compared against the maximum allowable identity value:

```
DBCC CHECKIDENT (reservations)

Checking identity information: current identity value
'4051', maximum column value '4051'.
```

If you try to run this command against a table that doesn't have a column assigned with an identity, SQL Server returns an error:

```
Msg 7997, Level 16, State 1
'particle' does not contain an identity column.
```

DBREINDEX

A new SQL Server 6.5 DBCC option lets administrators rebuild one or more indexes on a particular table. You use the REINDEX parameter to make this happen and can request this operation at the individual index level or on all indexes on the table. To rebuild all indexes, leave the index name blank:

```
DBCC REINDEX (customer_flights, ' ')

Clustered index 'PK__customer___accou__29F645A3'
is being rebuilt.
Non-clustered index 'cf_origin' is being rebuilt.
Non-clustered index 'cf_dest' is being rebuilt.
```

As part of this command, you can also stipulate what the index fill factor should be. We discussed this topic in more detail in Chapter 3. Finally, you can designate that SQL Server treat your data as already sorted, by using the SORTED_DATA or SORTED_DATA_REORG subparameters. Normally, when building a clustered index, SQL Server physically sorts the underlying data. By requesting either of these two alternatives, you're informing SQL Server that this step isn't necessary, since the data is already sorted. However, SORTED_DATA_REORG causes SQL Server to structure the data to satisfy the desired fill factor. Consequently, it is often used in conjunction with changing the fill factor value. This can help speed data access when a table has become fragmented. We discuss how to handle table fragmentation elsewhere in this chapter.

If you provide the SORTED_DATA or SORTED_DATA_REORG option, but the table is not ordered correctly, SQL Server aborts the re-index operation.

DBREPAIR

In most cases, if you want to drop a damaged database, you can use the DROP DATABASE SQL command. However, another way to drop a damaged database is to use the DBCC DBREPAIR command. SQL Server provides this command for backwards compatibility with older database versions. When you elect to use this command, SQL Server drops the damaged database. Note that no other users can be connected to the database for this statement to work. In addition, if SQL Server doesn't believe that the database is damaged, you won't be able to use this option, either:

```
DBCC DBREPAIR (packages, DROPDB, NOINIT)

Msg 2573, Level 16, State 1
Database 'packages' is not marked suspect. You cannot
drop it with DBCC.
```

The NOINIT option tells the engine not to modify the allocation pages that belonged to the database that was just dropped.

NEWALLOC

The DBCC NEWALLOC option is a more powerful replacement for the older CHECKALLOC parameter. It provides the same information as CHECKALLOC but adds a collection of new data, as well as more graceful error handling. You can provide a database name, or SQL Server will check the current database. Here's some sample output:

```
DBCC NEWALLOC (largo)

Checking largo
Database 'largo' is not in single user mode - may find
spurious allocation problems due to transactions in progress.
********************************************************
**
TABLE: sysobjects OBJID = 1
INDID=1 FIRST=1 ROOT=8 DPAGES=1 SORT=0
    Data level: 1.  1 Data  Pages in 1 extents.
    Indid   : 1.  1 Index Pages in 1 extents.
INDID=2 FIRST=40 ROOT=40 DPAGES=1 SORT=1
    Indid   : 2.  1 Index Pages in 1 extents.
TOTAL # of extents = 3
********************************************************
**

 .    .    .    .    .    .    .    .    .    .
 .    .    .    .    .    .    .    .    .    .
********************************************************
**
TABLE: sysreferences OBJID = 14
INDID=1 FIRST=16 ROOT=136 DPAGES=1 SORT=0
    Data level: 1.  1 Data  Pages in 1 extents.
    Indid   : 1.  1 Index Pages in 1 extents.
INDID=2 FIRST=208 ROOT=208 DPAGES=1 SORT=0
    Indid   : 2.  1 Index Pages in 1 extents.
INDID=3 FIRST=248 ROOT=248 DPAGES=1 SORT=0
    Indid   : 3.  1 Index Pages in 1 extents.
TOTAL # of extents = 4
********************************************************
**

 .    .    .    .    .    .    .    .    .    .
 .    .    .    .    .    .    .    .    .    .
```

```
* * * * * * * * * * * * * * * * * * * * * * * * * * * * * * * * * * * * * * * * * * * * * * * * * * * * * * * * * * * * *
* *
TABLE: equipos OBJID = 16003088
INDID=0 FIRST=320 ROOT=979 DPAGES=305 SORT=0
    Data level: 0.  305 Data  Pages in 39 extents.
INDID=2 FIRST=928 ROOT=858 DPAGES=216 SORT=1
    Indid   : 2.  244 Index Pages in 31 extents.
TOTAL # of extents = 70
* * * * * * * * * * * * * * * * * * * * * * * * * * * * * * * * * * * * * * * * * * * * * * * * * * * * * * * * * * * * *
* *
TABLE: reservations OBJID = 80003316
INDID=1 FIRST=608 ROOT=616 DPAGES=37 SORT=0
    Data level: 1.  37 Data  Pages in 5 extents.
    Indid   : 1.  1 Index Pages in 1 extents.
TOTAL # of extents = 6
* * * * * * * * * * * * * * * * * * * * * * * * * * * * * * * * * * * * * * * * * * * * * * * * * * * * * * * * * * * * *
* *
TABLE: equipos1 OBJID = 352004285
INDID=0 FIRST=688 ROOT=692 DPAGES=5 SORT=0
    Data level: 0.  5 Data  Pages in 1 extents.
INDID=2 FIRST=800 ROOT=801 DPAGES=1 SORT=0
    Indid   : 2.  7 Index Pages in 1 extents.
TOTAL # of extents = 2
* * * * * * * * * * * * * * * * * * * * * * * * * * * * * * * * * * * * * * * * * * * * * * * * * * * * * * * * * * * * *
* *
Processed 35 entries in the Sysindexes for dbid 6.
Alloc page 0 (# of extent=32 used pages=42 ref pages=42)
Alloc page 256 (# of extent=31 used pages=178 ref pages=178)
Alloc page 512 (# of extent=32 used pages=243 ref pages=243)
Alloc page 768 (# of extent=25 used pages=191 ref pages=191)
Alloc page 1024 (# of extent=1 used pages=1 ref pages=1)
   .       .       .       .       .       .       .       .       .       .       .
   .       .       .       .       .       .       .       .       .       .       .
Alloc page 2304 (# of extent=1 used pages=1 ref pages=1)
Alloc page 2560 (# of extent=32 used pages=256 ref pages=249)
Alloc page 2816 (# of extent=32 used pages=256 ref pages=256)
Alloc page 3072 (# of extent=32 used pages=256 ref pages=256)
Alloc page 3328 (# of extent=32 used pages=256 ref pages=256)
Total (# of extent=254 used pages=1684 ref pages=1677) in
this database
```

The warning message about the database not being in single-user mode refers to the possibility that DBCC may encounter an incomplete transaction or other operation. This could then cause the utility to report an inconsistency where none exists.

Let's examine how you can interpret the rest of DBCC's output. First, notice how SQL Server reports detailed information on each table in the database. For brevity's sake, we've eliminated most of the system tables from our sample output. For each table in the database, SQL Server reports the table's name and object ID. Next, for each index in the table, we learn the index ID number, along with the first and root page numbers. We also discover how many data pages make up the index, as well as the number of extents necessary to hold these pages. Finally, the sort flag tells us whether the table is sorted (clustered) on the index. After reporting on all of the table's indexes, SQL Server tells us how many extents (data and index pages combined) are used by the table.

Remember that like the older CHECKALLOC option, NEWALLOC runs more accurately if you keep database activity to a minimum while you run the command. In addition, this command can take a long time to finish. To cut down on the amount of time it takes to finish, you can pass in a parameter of NOINDEX. This option tells SQL Server to avoid examining non-clustered index pages. Even though this helps the procedure run faster, you should still periodically take the time to run the full command.

SHOW_STATISTICS

As we saw in Part 1 on efficient database design, the SQL Server query optimizer plays an essential role in constructing and executing efficient access to your data. The optimizer relies on up-to-date statistics that explain how your data is structured, factoring in this information when deciding on the right query plan. Consequently, it's important to keep these statistics as current as possible. You can use the DBCC SHOW_STATISTICS command to learn when you last updated the statistics for a particular index:

```
Updated                 Rows      Steps      Density
---------------         --------  --------   ------------
Feb 28 1997  6:55AM 4051          177        0.00122817

(1 row(s) affected)

All density                  Columns
----------------------       ----------------------------
0.00122817                   postal_code

(1 row(s) affected)

Steps
-----------
     35000
```

```
     .  .  .
     .  .  .
  95996
  95999
```

(177 row(s) affected)

For more detail about how to interpret this output, see Chapter 4, "Understanding the Microsoft SQL Server Optimizer."

SHOWCONTIG

The DBCC command, via the SHOWCONTIG option, lets you learn about the state of a table's disk space usage. We discuss the benefits of contiguous disk space elsewhere in this chapter. At this point, let's examine the output of the DBCC SHOWCONTIG command:

```
DBCC SHOWCONTIG (16003088)

[SHOW_CONTIG - SCAN ANALYSIS]
---------------------------------------------------------
Table: 'equipos' (16003088)  Indid: 0  dbid:6

TABLE level scan performed.
- Pages Scanned...............................: 305
- Extent Switches.............................: 38
- Avg. Pages per Extent.......................: 7.9
- Scan Density [Best Count:Actual Count].....: 100.00%
38:39]
- Avg. Bytes free per page...................: 33.4
- Avg. Page density (full)...................: 98.34%
- Overflow Pages.............................: 304
- Avg. Bytes free per Overflow page..........: 33.4
- Avg. Overflow Page density.................: 98.3%
- Disconnected Overflow Pages................: 0
```

To run this command, you need to provide the table's or index' object ID. You can get this by examining the 'sysobjects' table. Let's look at how we can understand this report:

- **Table name.**   This is the user-assigned name for the table.
- **Table ID.**   This is the internal SQL Server identifier for the table.
- **Database ID.**   This is the database identification number.
- **Pages scanned.**   This is the actual number of pages assigned to the table and includes index and data pages. This table has 305 pages.

- **Extent switches.**   Each time that SQL Server switched between extents when examining the table raises this value. In this case, SQL Server switched 38 times.

- **Average pages per extent.**   This indicator shows us the number of pages in the average extent for this table. Recall that SQL Server typically assigns eight pages per extent.

- **Scan density.**   The scan density is an indicator of potential table fragmentation. If the number is 100, it means that the pages in our table are all contiguous: There is no fragmentation. However, a number below 100 tells us that the table has become fragmented. The 'Best Count' and 'Actual Count' fields denote how many extent transitions would happen if the table was totally contiguous versus how many extent transitions actually happened. In this case, the ratio is nearly identical, which is in keeping with the scan density indicator of 100.

- **Average bytes free per page.**   When running this command, SQL Server averages how many bytes are free on each page. In this case, the average page only has 33 bytes of unused space. In general, higher numbers mean that our pages are less-than-ideally filled. However, if your row sizes are large, it's entirely possible that SQL Server has no way of filling in the extra space, since rows can't be split among pages.

- **Average overflow page density.**   This number shows, on average, a percentage of how full each page is. Since this statistic is aware of row size, you can use it with more confidence than the average bytes free per page marker. In this case, our average page is over 98 percent full: this bodes well for the table's efficiency.

- The remainder of this report's data (overflow page information) is for SQL Server's internal use only.

If you want to check space for an index only, provide the index ID as part of the command string.

SHRINKDB

You can use DBCC's SHRINKDB option to:

- Learn how small you can make a database
- Shrink a user's database
- Shrink the master database

If you don't furnish a new size, SQL Server simply reports how small you can shrink a database:

```
dbcc shrinkdb (teams)

Current size of database Size database can be shrunk to
------------------------ -----------------------------
2560                     2304

(1 row(s) affected)

Objects pvnt further shrink    Index
---------------------------    -----------------------
syslogs                        data
```

DBCC SHRINKDB shows the current size of the database, as well as how small it can be made. It also shows you what, if anything, is preventing you from shrinking the database more. In this case, the transaction log requires space that you could otherwise remove.

Supplying a new size instructs SQL Server to go ahead and attempt to shrink the database to the requested size:

```
dbcc shrinkdb (teams, 2304)
```

SQL Server doesn't report any additional details after you shrink the database.

You can also try to shrink the 'master' database, by setting the MASTER-OVERRIDE option. However, be extremely careful when doing this, since it's very possible that you could damage the master database and then have to rebuild your entire SQL Server instance.

If you try to run this command when the database is not set to single-user mode, SQL Server returns an error:

```
Msg 2595, Level 16, State 91
Database 'largo' must be set to single user mode before
executing this command.
Msg 7995, Level 16, State 1
```

A more user-friendly way to shrink a database is to use the Edit Database dialog box within the SQL Enterprise Manager:

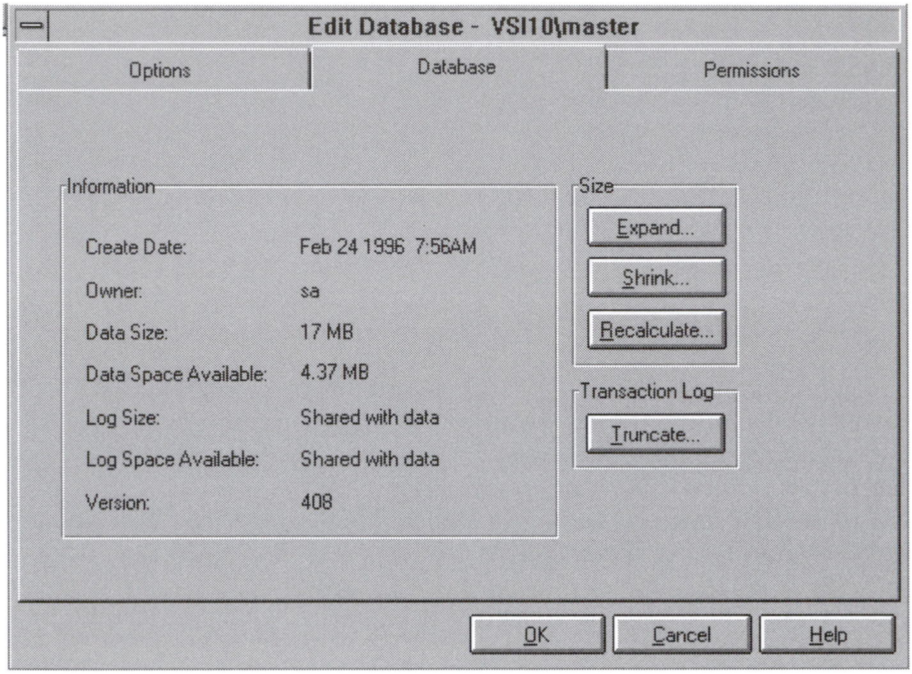

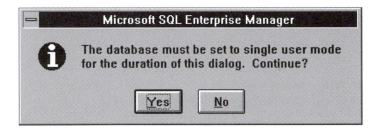

Figure 11.13

The SQL Enterprise Manager also protects you from shrinking a database when multiple users are connected:

Figure 11.14

TEXTALLOC

Recall from our discussions on text and image data types that SQL Server stores these columns in their own special structures of linked list pages. You can use DBCC's TEXTALLOC option to check the integrity of these linked lists:

```
dbcc textalloc (statements)

Checking credits
********************************************************
TABLE: statements                    OBJID = 1200007306
INDID=255 FIRST=528 ROOT=528 DPAGES=0 SORT=0
 Data level: 1.  8 Data  Pages in 0 extents.
 Indid  : 255.  540 Index Pages in 0 extents.
```

In default operation, DBCC generates a full allocation report, similar to the work done by the DBCC CHECKALLOC and DBCC NEWALLOC commands. If you want to speed up this command, you can pass a parameter of 'FAST,' which tells SQL Server to check the linked list pointers only.

TEXTALL

Running DBCC with the TEXTALL option instructs the engine to go through all tables in the database, looking for those that have at least one text or image column. For each of these tables, SQL Server then runs DBCC TEXTALLOC.

UPDATEUSAGE

As we have seen elsewhere in the book, the SQL Server query optimizer relies on a number of system tables. To get the best performance, it's crucial that these system tables contain correct information about the state of your database. One of the most important system tables is 'sysindexes.' The optimizer uses the statistical information found in this table to help make decisions on how to process queries. SQL Server 6.5 introduces a new DBCC command to help ensure that 'sysindex' data is as clean as possible. This new command is known as UPDATEUSAGE. When you run DBCC with this option, SQL Server examines 'sysindex' entries for all clustered indexes. In particular, DBCC is searching for inaccuracies in the following counts:

- Data page count
- Used page count
- Reserved page count
- Row count

Let's look at some sample output for this command.

```
DBCC UPDATEUSAGE (equipos)

DBCC UPDATEUSAGE: Sysindexes row for Table 'equipos1'
(IndexId=2) updated:
     DATA Pages: Changed from (1) to (6) pages
     USED Pages: Changed from (1) to (7) pages
     ROWS count: Changed from (0) to (377) rows
  DBCC UPDATEUSAGE: Sysindexes row for Table 'equipos'
(IndexId=2) updated:
     DATA Pages: Changed from (216) to (235) pages
     USED Pages: Changed from (224) to (244) pages
     RSVD Pages: Changed from (224) to (248) pages
     ROWS count: Changed from (9108) to (9439) rows
  DBCC UPDATEUSAGE: Sysindexes row for Table 'equipos'
(IndexId=0) updated:
     USED Pages: Changed from (559) to (549) pages
     RSVD Pages: Changed from (573) to (560) pages
```

.   .   .   .
.   .   .   .

DBCC found a number of issues with the indexes on these tables. Since 'sysindex' information is so central to a well-running system, it's a good idea to run this command on a regular basis.

Fragmentation

As we've seen so far, disk I/O operations are among the most expensive operations that you can solicit from SQL Server. In turn, fragmentation has the potential, in some cases, to damage this I/O performance. This impairment can then have an unduly large effect on overall system response. Accordingly, in this section, we examine how you can minimize fragmentation effects on your system's performance. We've divided our discussion into two sections: disk fragmentation and database fragmentation. There are different causes and solutions for both of these conditions.

Disk fragmentation

Disk level fragmentation occurs when the operating system has broken the underlying disk files into a number of pieces. This is a common occurrence. Suppose that you've purchased a new 500-megabyte disk drive, and allocated a

100-megabyte file to hold the data for one of your tables. At first, this space is contiguous, since the drive is new and there is no other data present. However, as time passes, your use of the drive increases, and the disk drive itself becomes fragmented. Your original 100-megabyte file is still contiguous, however, since SQL Server occupied that space when the drive was new. At this point, you realize that you need an extra 50 megabytes of space. The drive still has 75 megabytes free, so SQL Server complies with your request and adds the extra room to the database device, which you then in turn add to the database. From SQL Server's perspective, this space is contiguous, since there are no other databases using the database device. If this is true, how can we say that there is fragmentation? Basically, the file that contains the database device is itself scattered across the disk, since it's unlikely that Windows NT could find 50 contiguous megabytes to satisfy your request.

How can you detect and then correct this situation? First, to detect the anomaly, you should use a commercially available disk fragmentation reporting utility. These utilities can tell you if your disk is fragmented and, if so, the degree of fragmentation. You may learn that the fragmentation is not serious: Modern disk drives are extremely fast, and a small amount of fragmentation probably doesn't merit additional work. If you feel that the fragmentation is unacceptable, you can usually use the same utility that found the problem to correct it.

Database fragmentation

Database fragmentation can happen when data from a number of databases all reside on the same database device. For example, assume that you purchase a new 1-gigabyte disk drive, which you then entirely allocate to a database device named 'datadevice1.' Next, you create a database named 'sales' and select 100 megabytes of 'datadevice1' for its storage. At this point, your disk looks like this:

datadevice1

Figure 11.15

As time passes, you create another database called 'project_tracking' on this device. You estimate that this database needs 300 megabytes of space, which you secure from the remaining 700 megabytes on the 'datadevice1' database device:

datadevice1

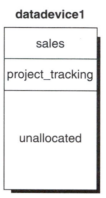

Figure 11.16

Up until this point, there is no database fragmentation: All data for each database lies in one continuous block. However, you now realize that due to additional data capture, you need to augment the amount of space for your 'sales' database by 50 megabytes. Your instincts tell you that it's likely that data usage will probably increase faster than management's expectation, but you still opt to add only 50 more megabytes, based on your reluctance to waste space. You now have this configuration:

datadevice1

Figure 11.17

This pattern repeats itself a number of times: You continue adding space to each database and quickly end up with data fragmentation:

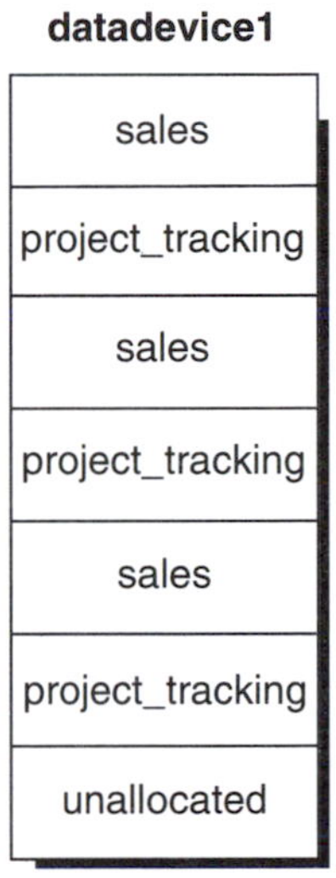

datadevice1

sales
project_tracking
sales
project_tracking
sales
project_tracking
unallocated

Figure 11.18

Is this a bad situation? In some cases, especially on machines that use older, slower disk drives, the answer is yes: Data fragmentation means that the disk heads will spend more time seeking data and less time reading and writing data. However, on newer, faster disk drives, this extra time is barely measurable. If you still judge that you want to eliminate the fragmentation, follow these steps:

1. Back up your entire system. This is in case of a serious problem during the upcoming steps.

2. Export the data from all of the tables on the fragmented device, using 'bcp' or other unloading utility.

3. Save the schema necessary to re-create the tables.

4. Drop all of the tables on the database device.

5. Drop the device.

6. Re-create the device.

7. Assign the device to the appropriate databases. This time, assign each database's portion in one block.

8. Re-create the tables.

9. Reload the data.

At this point, your data should all be contiguous. Clearly, it's best not to have to take these steps in the first place. You can prevent data fragmentation by allocating realistic amounts of space to your databases in advance. Given the low cost of disk drives in today's market, it's probably better to "waste" some space than have to go through the above steps on a regular basis.

'sp_spaceused' stored procedure

SQL Server provides administrators with the 'sp_spaceused' system stored procedure. You can use this procedure to get details about an entire database's storage requirements, or you can focus on a particular table.

For example, if we run this procedure without any parameters while connected to the 'master' database, we receive:

```
sp_spaceused

database_name   database_size      unallocated space
---------------   ---------------    ---------------
master            17.00 MB           6.96 MB
```

In the next example, we're passing in the name of a table in the 'largo' database:

```
sp_spaceused equipos

name        rows      reserved    data      index_size  unused
--------    ----      --------    ------    ------      ------
equipos     9586      1146 KB     620 KB    498 KB      28 KB
```

One additional parameter that you can pass to this statement is a flag that tells SQL Server whether or not to run the DBCC UPDATEUSAGE command. When you run DBCC UPDATEUSAGE, SQL Server examines the specified object and updates the following columns in the 'sysindexes' table, for any clustered indexes:

- rows
- used
- reserved
- dpages

If your tables are large, setting this flag to true can make the command take a long time to finish running. However, it's important to keep 'sysindexes' entries as accurate as possible, so don't forget to enable this flag periodically.

Index fill factor

As we saw in Chapter 3, "Indexing Strategies," you can use the index fill factor to customize the way that SQL Server fills in its index pages. Setting a low index fill factor means that SQL Server reserves extra space on each index page. Then, when you add additional rows, the engine is able to fit these added key values into the unused space.

From a disk storage perspective, how should you set the index fill factor to provide maximum I/O efficiency? The answer largely depends on the type of table supported by the index. For lookup tables that don't change very often, setting a high fill factor means that the tables' indexes will be tightly packed onto their pages. This can reduce the amount of space necessary for the index, as well as diminish the amount of I/O operations performed by the engine to retrieve data. On the other hand, if your underlying table experiences many changes, setting a high index fill factor can cause the engine to carry out superfluous alterations to the index pages as it searches for new space to handle the added rows. This extra work during write operations often offsets the I/O savings on read operations.

For more details on index fill factor and performance, see Chapter 3.

I/O topics

I/O, or input/output, refers to all operations where SQL Server moves data between the disk drive and memory. In this section, we examine various I/O topics, including several SQL Server advanced architectural features, such as asynchronous I/O, the lazywriter, and read-ahead. We then probe the configuration parameters you can set that affect I/O, as well as how to interpret the I/O related output from SQL Server's monitoring utilities. As part of our explorations, we cite several examples of how you can use the SQL Performance Monitor to gain a better understanding of I/O execution.

Asynchronous I/O

When an application or database system is said to perform asynchronous I/O, what it means is that I/O requests may actually be executed at different times than when originally requested. For example, SQL Server performs asynchronous I/O when writing data to the disk drive. You may add a record to a table at 3:01 p.m., yet SQL Server may not write the record to the database until 3:04 p.m.

SQL Server can also use asynchronous I/O when retrieving information from the database into your program's cursors. For instance, assume that you've declared a cursor that, when opened, pulls 10,000 rows into your application. Depending on a number of factors, the engine may decide to fetch all of these rows at once or may, instead, bring rows back asynchronously.

You can configure your system's asynchronous I/O behavior by setting the 'max async io' parameter. We discuss this parameter in more detail later. You can determine whether SQL Server uses asynchronous cursor operations by setting the 'cursor threshold' parameter. We reviewed this concept in the "Cursors" section of Chapter 7.

Lazywriter

The lazywriter is an important SQL Server process that merits some explanation. As part of normal processing, SQL Server continually needs to locate free buffer pages to store the latest data modifications. In addition, SQL Server also needs to synchronize updated memory pages with the data stored on disk. For both these reasons, the lazywriter process constantly scans the buffer pool and writes the oldest buffers to disk. This frees up new space for future data modifications.

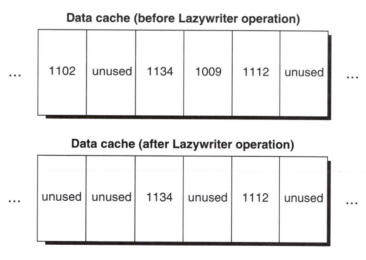

Data cache (before Lazywriter operation)

| ... | 1102 | unused | 1134 | 1009 | 1112 | unused | ... |

Data cache (after Lazywriter operation)

| ... | unused | unused | 1134 | unused | 1112 | unused | ... |

Figure 11.19

In this example, we're looking at a portion of SQL Server's data cache. The diagram shows the data cache's state before and after the lazywriter's work. The numbers represent relative page timestamps for modified pages. The lower numbers represent older, staler pages; the higher numbers represent more recently changed pages, while some pages are unused. When the lazywriter process examines these buffers, it flushes the oldest modified pages to disk, thereby freeing them for other uses.

Read-ahead

One new SQL Server feature that can dramatically improve query performance is read-ahead, also known as parallel data scan. When SQL Server detects certain query operations, such as table scans and other searches that return large quantities of data sequentially, it allocates a background thread to read ahead in the table. This means that by the time your program requests this information, SQL Server may have already fetched the data into the buffer pool.

To illustrate this concept, suppose that you're running a long report that pulls information from a large customer table. If you're reading large blocks of data sequentially, SQL Server may anticipate the next series of information that you want and read these rows into memory while you're still processing the first batch of data. This can lead to substantial performance gains, since your program may now be able to find what it needs in memory rather than on disk.

Statistics

Let's look at some read-ahead statistics, followed by the configuration parameters that you can set that can affect how efficiently SQL Server makes its read-ahead decisions.

RA pages fetched into cache per second

When the read-ahead manager is active, this statistic counts the number of pages fetched into the cache each second.

RA pages found in cache per second

This counter is incremented when the SQL Server read-ahead manager attempts to place a read-ahead page into the buffer pool, but the page is already present.

RA physical reads per second

This statistic keeps track of how many physical disk reads the read-ahead manager is performing each second. Remember that each physical read consists of eight 2 K pages (for a total of 16 K).

RA slots used

This statistic tracks the actual number of read-ahead slots that are currently being used. What are read-ahead slots? You can think of an individual read-ahead slot as a parallel data scan task that a thread managed by the read-ahead manager must perform. Consequently, the number of parallel data scan operations occurring at any given time is the number of read-ahead slots multiplied by the number of threads. As an example, suppose that your system currently has five parallel data scan threads working, with seven active read-ahead slots. Multiplying these two numbers yields 35, which is the total number of parallel data scan operations running at the moment.

Configuration parameters

In this section, we examine a number of configuration parameters that can affect read-ahead performance.

RA cache hit limit

There are occasions where the read-ahead manager attempts to locate data from the disk, yet still finds it in the buffer pool. This means that read-ahead is not very effective. You can set this parameter to limit the number of buffer pool hits that a read-ahead query encounters before abandoning the read-ahead strategy. The valid range of values is between 1 and 255 hits, with a default value of 4. Try not to set the value too high; if the read-ahead manager is finding pages already resident in the buffer pool, there's no reason to continue reading ahead.

RA cache miss limit

SQL Server uses this parameter to determine when to start reading ahead. For example, if you've set it to five, SQL Server starts reading ahead after not finding five pages in the buffer pool. The valid range of values is between 1 and 255, with a default of 3.

How can you determine what setting to choose for this value? Setting it too low means that SQL Server tries to read ahead on most queries; setting it too high causes SQL Server to avoid a potentially well-performing strategy. With this in mind, if your system is primarily used for reporting and other operations that usually fetch large batches of information, set the value very low. This tells SQL Server that you want to start read-ahead operations as quickly as possible in most cases. Conversely, if your system will work as an OLTP environment, with very few batch, sequential operations, raise this value high, since you want SQL Server to avoid read-ahead in all but the most obvious situations.

RA delay

SQL Server uses this parameter to determine how long to wait before starting to read-ahead. This is a necessary value, since some time always elapses between the start of the read ahead manager and the start of when it can service requests. The valid range of values is between 0 and 500 milliseconds, with a default value of 15. The default should suffice for most environments. Setting this parameter too high means that SQL Server may delay too long before embarking on a read-ahead.

RA prefetches

You can use this measure to tell SQL Server how many extents you want it to prefetch during read-ahead operations. The valid range of values is between 1 and 1000, with a default value of 3. If you expect that your applications will be performing primarily large sequential operations, you might consider setting this value to a bigger number. This means that SQL Server will bring larger amounts of data in to the buffer pool during each read-ahead operation. The risk of setting this number too high is that you may displace other users' buffer pool pages with your data. Consequently, be careful when experimenting with this number: It's better to gradually increase the value rather than set it to the maximum.

As an example, when changing this value, try raising it by five percent each time. Make sure to keep a record of overall system response between changes. It's important to determine if performance gains for one application are offset by performance degradation for others.

RA slots per thread

Read-ahead operations are handled by threads. You can configure the number of read-ahead requests that each thread is managing by setting this parameter. The valid range is between 1 and 255, with a default of 5. This means that each read-ahead thread processes up to five operations concurrently. Setting this value too high means that your read-ahead threads may become overloaded; the thread may spend more time switching between different read-ahead requests than servicing the requests themselves. An overly low value could lead to underworked threads, since the thread may be idle while waiting to service read-ahead requests. How should you choose a setting? Chances are that the default of 5 should be fine. If you do decide to experiment, keep a detailed watch on overall system performance. Documentation is very important when altering SQL Server engine parameters. Altering only one parameter at a time is also very significant, since you might misinterpret the results if you change multiple parameters.

RA worker threads

You can control the number of threads that SQL Server allocates to service read-ahead requests. Each configured thread then supports a number of individual read-ahead requests. This number is defined by the RA slots per thread parameter. The RA worker thread setting can range between 0 and 255. The default value is 3. It's a good idea to set this option to match the maximum number of concurrent users that you expect to access SQL Server. If you set this parameter too low, you run the risk of not having enough threads to service the volume of read-ahead requests. If you set it too high, you'll end up starting too many read-ahead threads. Note that if this parameter exceeds the RA slots per thread parameter, SQL Server generates an error message, since by definition you can't define more threads than the slots per thread.

Statistics

Now, let's move on to consider the other, non-read-ahead I/O statistics that SQL Server provides for administrators.

I/O batch average size

This statistic keeps track of the average number of 2 K pages that SQL Server was able to write to the disk during each batch operation. Checkpoints are the most common batch operations. If you're running a long, data-modification procedure that spans several checkpoints, you should see this number rise over time, as SQL Server is able to fit more work into each batch operation.

I/O batch maximum size

This statistic is the maximum number of 2 K pages that SQL Server was able to write to the disk during a batch operation. The normal value for this statistic is eight pages, but it can be controlled by setting the 'max async io' configuration parameter. We discuss this option in more detail later.

I/O batch writes per second

This statistic tracks the actual number of batch writes that SQL Server is performing per second. During typical periods, you can expect this number to vary widely, since most database modification operations are sporadic in nature. This means that while watching this statistic over the course of twenty checkpoints, you may see "spikes" in its value. These spikes are normal as SQL Server oscillates between periods of servicing heavy data changes that require significant batch writes, and periods of query-intensive operations that make little use of the transaction log.

I/O lazywrites per second

As we saw earlier, the lazywriter process performs essential synchronization between the buffer pool and disk. This statistic keeps track of the number of 2 K pages per second that the lazywriter has been flushing to disk. Note that you'll normally only see values for this indicator when you are performing data modifications, since, by definition, data modifications require synchronization between the memory buffer pool and disk. During periods of read-only access, this statistic may stay near zero, since there's no need for the lazywriter process to synchronize between memory and disk.

I/O log writes per second

This statistic counts the number of transaction log pages that SQL Server is able to write to the disk each second. Remember that the transaction log is fairly quiet during periods of read-only access. If you're monitoring this statistic, you may be curious why it seems to stay near zero even when there are dozens of users on the system. The reason is that while the transaction log is at the heart of insert, update, delete, and other data alteration activities, it doesn't have much to do when users are running queries. However, if the users' query activities are causing SQL Server to create and fill work tables, it's possible that you may still see this statistic rise. This comes about because SQL Server is using the transaction log to keep track of the changes to the work tables, even though the users aren't making any changes.

What can you do to speed up (i.e., raise) this statistic? Try implementing one or more of these suggestions:

1. Make sure that the device where you store your transaction log is as rapid as possible. Don't make the mistake of keeping your transaction log on an older, slower disk drive. This can quickly become a bottleneck, as SQL Server continually waits for the disk drive to finish its work before the engine can consider a transaction committed or rolled back.

2. If necessary, store the transaction log on its own device. Sometimes, drive speed is not enough; you may need to dedicate a disk to the transaction log. Suppose that you've just purchased the fastest disk drive on the market and have decided to keep the transaction log on this new disk. This is very good, but contention problems can arise if you also resolve to accumulate spreadsheets, word processing files, and other non-database related information on the same drive.

See the discussion in Chapter 12 on efficient transaction logging for more performance tips.

I/O outstanding reads

SQL Server tracks the number of reads that it has requested but not yet received from the disk. How can you interpret this statistic? As we'll see in much greater detail later, when you want to retrieve information from the database, SQL Server first looks in the memory (data and stored procedure) cache to see if the page that you asked for is already present. In situations where your cache percentage is high (e.g., relatively small databases or on popular, commonly used tables), chances are that many of the desired pages are waiting for you in memory. This greatly speeds data access, since the disk drive is often the slowest component on a modern database platform. Conversely, if SQL Server can't find the page it needs in memory, it looks for the necessary information on disk. In most cases, the disk rapidly returns the requested data and index pages. However, if the engine is forced to wait for the I/O subsystem to return these values, this can be thought of as an outstanding read.

When are you likely to encounter significant outstanding read instances? Generally, one or more of the following conditions must exist for this statistic to rise:

- **Heavy database use.**   If your system is attempting to acquire huge volumes of data for multiple users at one time while also trying to write out high numbers of transactions, you may encounter an I/O bottleneck.

- **Low commonality among programs' data sets.**   In situations where all users are working on the same relatively small set of data or where a large amount of RAM is assigned to the cache, it's conceivable that most data may already be present in memory. In these cases, it's very difficult to experience I/O bottlenecks, since the engine spends little time communicating with the disk drive (aside from the original data fetch operations). However, if users don't share much information, SQL Server may have no choice but to access the disk drives continually to satisfy all of the user data solicitations. In these cases, you can undergo I/O read delays.

- **Slow CPUs.**   If you are trying to retrieve millions of rows at one time on an ancient, sluggish CPU, it's possible that the computer itself may be unable to issue requests quickly enough to the I/O subsystem. This situation may disguise itself as an I/O subsystem problem, when, in fact, the obstacle lies in the CPU itself.

- **Slow I/O subsystems.**   This is often the biggest factor when encountering substantial outstanding read obstacles. If the disk drives are simply unable to spin fast enough to read all the requisite information, you may have to take other steps. These steps can include:

  1. Purchasing new, faster disk drives. Each year brings bigger and faster disk drives. You might benefit by upgrading your older, slower drives.

  2. Spreading data across existing drives. We discuss this option elsewhere in this section. In a nutshell, you may be able to coax added performance from your present drives by taking a "divide-and-conquer" approach to data storage.

  3. Enhancing your disk controllers. Compare the features and throughput rate of your current disk controller with some of the

newer disk controllers. Having speedy disk drives means nothing if the disk controller is a bottleneck.

I/O outstanding writes

SQL Server uses this statistic to keep track of the number of write requests that have issued but have not yet been executed. When does it mean when SQL Server increments this counter? Just as the 'outstanding reads' statistic chronicles the current backlog of pages that SQL Server needs to read, this indicator reveals how many write requests are currently queued.

You can use this information to help determine if your disk subsystem is performing optimally. Nevertheless, in most data processing situations, you'll be hard-pressed to get a significant reading for this number. Unless you are inserting, updating, or deleting thousands of rows in brief bursts, the disk subsystem is usually able to keep up with most modification requests without having to resort to queuing.

I/O page reads per second

This statistic follows the number of physical disk page reads that SQL Server is performing each second. Each time your application requests information from the database, SQL Server first looks in the data cache to see if the desired page is already present. If it is, the engine returns the memory-based page. If not, SQL Server dispatches a disk read request and increments this counter. Note that this counter tracks these requests across all databases, so you may see it rise during times of apparent minimal database activity.

Ideally, this indicator should be relatively low. Low numbers mean that the engine is able to find the data it needs within the shared data cache, rather than having to issue costly disk I/O demands. You can heighten cache performance by assigning enough space to memory, controlling the amount of memory assigned to the stored procedure cache, as well as creating useful indexes. These indexes can reduce the overall number of pages that SQL Server must read before finding the pertinent information. This effectively limits the number of physical page reads, which in turn boosts performance.

I/O single page writes per second

Most SQL Server disk write operations are performed in batch. This statistic, however, monitors the number of individual page writes that SQL Server is carrying out each second. When does SQL Server ask for single page writes? Generally, these writes occur during periods where the engine has run out of space in the free buffer pool. The only way to get this space is for SQL Server to select some candidate pages to write to disk. This extra processing is very costly; it's much more efficient for these write operations to occur in large batches, such as by the lazywriter or checkpoint process.

The best way to minimize the number of single page writes per second is to allocate enough memory for the buffer pool. If there is enough memory, chances are that the engine won't run out of space and be forced to issue special single write requests. This is why you should take care not to waste any memory, such as unnecessarily storing tempdb in memory or creating an overly large stored procedure cache.

I/O transactions per log record

SQL Server uses this statistic to track the number of transactions that the engine is able to include in each log record. SQL Server performs most efficiently when it is able to gather as many transactions as possible onto each log record. When log records are full, the engine can afford to issue proportionally fewer write requests. Since writing and other disk I/O operations are among the most expensive tasks that the engine must undertake, any reduction in these procedures can be very helpful.

The only way to influence SQL Server's transactions per log record usage is to adjust the logwrite sleep parameter. This configuration setting lets you control how long SQL Server waits between issuing log write requests. The longer the delay, the more transactions per log record. However, this may come at a price of lost data should the system crash before the engine gets around to requesting a log write. For example, suppose that you've asked SQL Server to wait 500 milliseconds before writing the transaction log buffer to disk if the buffer isn't yet full. During this delay, all committed transactions in the log buffer could be lost if the system crashed, since SQL Server never finished the write operation.

I/O transactions per second

This counter follows the number of batch operations that SQL Server is performing each second. This is somewhat misleading; the name of the statistic leads you to believe that this indicator charts the number of BEGIN TRANS-ACTION/COMMIT TRANSACTION pairs per second. This is not true; SQL Server is actually counting Transact-SQL batches. You can think of batches as single SQL statements or as a number of statements grouped together and terminated with a 'go' command.

When this number remains relatively high during periods of peak activity, you can be confident that your system is running fairly quickly. When the number stays low or you notice a deterioration, it usually means that some event is causing SQL Server to run at less-than-full efficiency. In cases such as these, you would be wise to investigate the current state of your system to learn what could be the culprit.

Max tempdb space used

You'll find a new statistic in SQL Server 6.5. This statistic tracks the maximum amount of space used within the 'tempdb' database. Keep in mind that the unit of scale for this statistic is megabytes; you may find it useful to alter the scale when monitoring its value. Finally, note that this statistic shows only what has been used. If you haven't yet performed any work that requires tempdb storage, this statistic will show zero. Once you start using tempdb storage, however, you will be able to track its usage with this indicator. Don't forget that this statistic displays the maximum amount of tempdb space that has been used so far; even if you delete all data from tempdb, this number remains at the high point.

Examples

Let's look at some examples of how you can use the performance monitor to learn more about how to track SQL Server's I/O standing.

In the next few examples, we're running a variety of queries to demonstrate how the SQL Server read-ahead cache works. In the first case, we've started a report that fetches large sequential blocks of data:

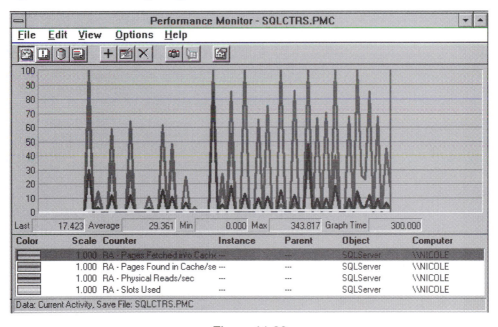

Figure 11.20

Notice how erratic the read-ahead statistics and graph appear to be. This is to be expected, since SQL Server detects that we're bringing back large, contiguous sections of data. As active as this chart is, notice how quiet the same query's I/O graph appears to be:

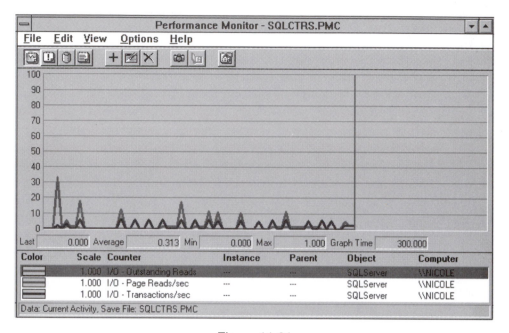

Figure 11.21

This is not surprising: Since our query is causing SQL Server to perform large read-ahead operations, there isn't much outstanding I/O activity.

In the next sample, we're evaluating the same statistics with one major difference. This time we're running a series of queries that locate data based on a random key:

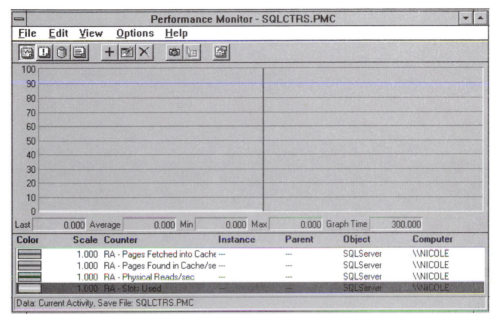

Figure 11.22

There's not much to see on this chart: SQL Server can't detect any pattern to our query, so the engine makes no attempt to perform any read-ahead operations. This makes sense: How can the engine read ahead when the requesting query is "jumping" from page to page? However, look at the I/O graphics for the same query:

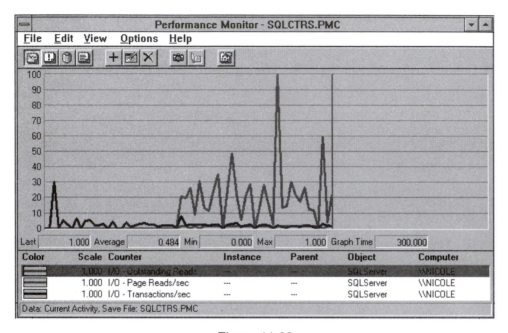

Figure 11.23

This chart shows quite a bit of activity. This is reasonable to expect, since SQL Server has no way of pulling in large blocks of data pages at one time, since the query is bringing back "unpredictable" data and index pages. This means that SQL Server must continually read from the disk drive or memory to satisfy your query's request for data.

In the next case, a number of users are running queries and updates. We're monitoring various I/O statistics:

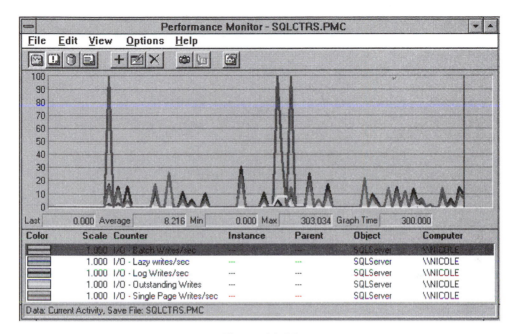

Figure 11.24

Since there's no fixed pattern to the users' updates, SQL Server isn't able to take much advantage of batch writes. Occasionally, the engine is able to batch enough information together to perform a batch write operation. This explains the periodic "spiking" of this indicator. For the most part, however, these operations cause the engine to process numerous single page write operations.

Let's turn our attention to watching the state of our transaction log. In the first case, we're running a large report process, which consists of searching for and then updating information:

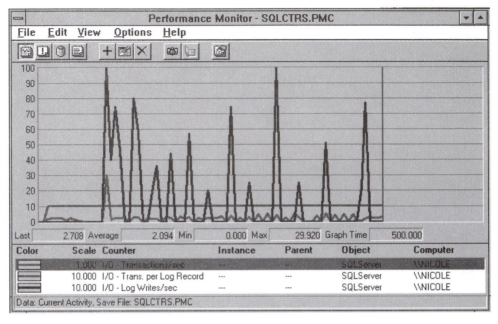

Figure 11.25

To make the number of transactions per log record and log writes per second indicators more meaningful, we've raised their scale to 10.0. You can see that the log writes per second number is fluctuating. This is largely dependent on the state of the process: The transactions themselves are happening sporadically. Keep this in mind when you review your system's statistics; sometimes statistical changes are due solely to user activity, rather than engine or configuration problems.

Configuration parameters

Maximum asynchronous I/O

This parameter controls the number of asynchronous I/O threads running at one time. It can range between 1 and 255, with a default value of 8. Unless you plan on using disk striping or storing your data on multiple disk drives, it's best to leave the parameter at the default. Setting this configuration parameter too low can lead to long queues, as operations that would normally be processed asynchronously would need to wait for an asynchronous I/O thread to become available. Conversely, setting the number of asynchronous I/O threads unnecessarily high means that SQL Server must perform extra thread management and maintenance, which comes at a response price.

Maximum lazywriter I/O

Just as the maximum asynchronous I/O parameter controls regular asynchronous I/O requests, this parameter controls asynchronous I/O requests specific to the lazywriter. This parameter can also range between 1 and 255, with a default of 8. The same caveats apply to this parameter as to the maximum asynchronous I/O parameter. Chances are that the default value of 8 should be sufficient for most environments. The major exceptions to this rule would be in cases where you have stored your data among a large number of disk drives. In this situation, the extra lazywriter I/O threads could be put to work servicing these added drives.

Storing tempdb in RAM

One technique that you can use in certain circumstances to improve system throughput is to store the 'tempdb' database in RAM. Remember that this database is the site where SQL Server builds temporary tables and performs much of its internal sorting. When is this a good idea?

- **When you have ample memory to spare.** If your system doesn't have enough memory to begin with, taking more for the tempdb database can actually decrease overall performance.

- **When your tempdb operations will fit into the space that you've allocated.** For example, suppose that you've allocated two megabytes for tempdb RAM. If each instance of your application routinely creates 10-megabyte work tables, having tempdb in RAM won't make much of a difference, since there won't be enough space to satisfy all user demands.

- **When your users and applications make heavy use of the tempdb database.** If you don't access the tempdb database often, placing it into RAM won't help performance and may hurt it instead, since tempdb now occupies valuable RAM storage. You can tell how heavily you're using tempdb by running the SHOWPLAN command against your queries. If you see frequent implicit work tables, chances are you're hitting the tempdb database quite often. On the other hand, if most of your queries don't require the engine to create work tables, it's probably not necessary to store tempdb in RAM.

- **When your applications don't access cached data frequently.** This means that your programs are continually accessing the disk drive to locate data, rather than finding it in memory.

This can happen in applications where individual users are looking at vastly different data records, thereby reducing the chance of one user finding data already cached by another user.

Given all of these limitations, chances are you don't need to store tempdb in RAM. Instead, it's probably better to use that memory for caching of data and index pages. However, if after reviewing these suggestions, you still decide to place tempdb in RAM, you can use the SQL Enterprise Manager utility:

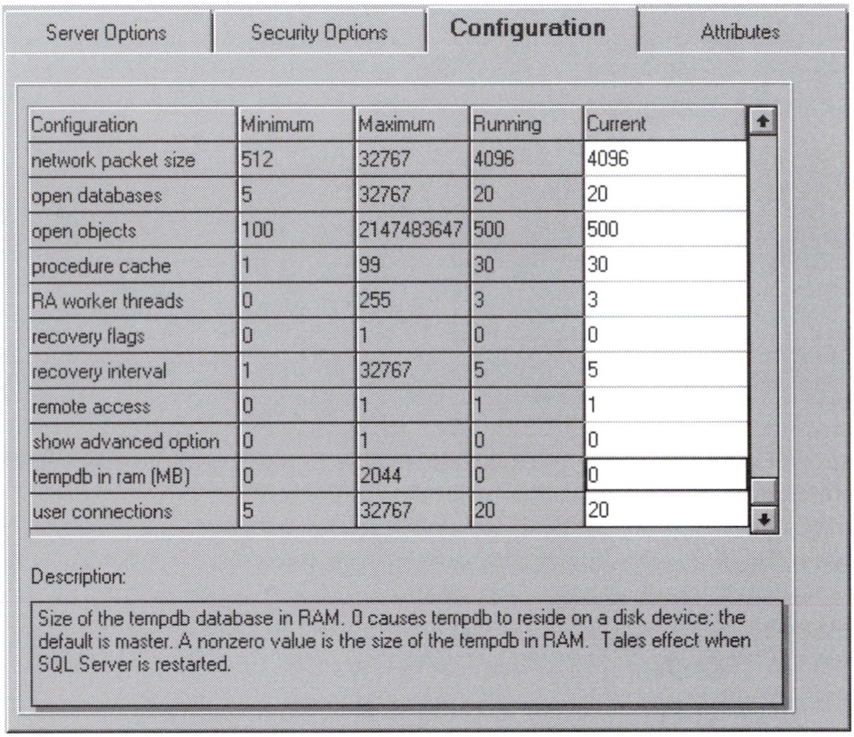

Server Options	Security Options	**Configuration**	Attributes

Configuration	Minimum	Maximum	Running	Current
network packet size	512	32767	4096	4096
open databases	5	32767	20	20
open objects	100	2147483647	500	500
procedure cache	1	99	30	30
RA worker threads	0	255	3	3
recovery flags	0	1	0	0
recovery interval	1	32767	5	5
remote access	0	1	1	1
show advanced option	0	1	0	0
tempdb in ram (MB)	0	2044	0	0
user connections	5	32767	20	20

Description:

Size of the tempdb database in RAM. 0 causes tempdb to reside on a disk device; the default is master. A nonzero value is the size of the tempdb in RAM. Tales effect when SQL Server is restarted.

Figure 11.26

As in all other cases where you're changing important parameters, use this feature with care. It's a good idea to vigilantly record your performance prior to making this change. If, after making the change, you don't experience significantly better throughput, keep your tempdb on disk.

Keep in mind that to get the best performance effect from storing tempdb in RAM, consider stopping and restarting the engine after making your change—because SQL Server may use noncontiguous memory to satisfy your request if you make the change while the engine is running. When you restart the engine, tempdb's memory will be coterminous.

Note that SQL Server 6.5 now lets you track the maximum amount of used storage in your tempdb via the performance monitor.

Engine Parameters

SQL Server administrators can control the engine's behavior in a variety of ways. In this chapter, we study a number of important engine architectural concepts. We combine this research with information on how you can monitor and control these features. We launch our discussion by focusing on SQL Server's usage of memory. Next, we explore how locking works, as well as its effect on system response. We then turn our attention to the powerful Windows NT threading and multiple processing features. Transaction logging is a key component in building reliable, robust database applications, so we spend some time examining logging. We also review the DBCC utility, especially as it relates to engine information. In Chapter 13, we examine parameters that affect database and network performance.

Memory

SQL Server relies on a variety of memory parameters and settings to achieve optimal performance. In this section, we delve into these parameters, examining both how to monitor and set them. We begin with an overview of how SQL Server allocates memory at installation time. Next, we examine how SQL Server caches data to perfect performance. We then focus on how to make sense of the plentiful number of memory statistics that SQL Server provides to administrators.

Stored procedure caching is another way that SQL Server enriches performance. We close out this section by discussing the new SQL Server 6.5 statistics that help administrators learn about stored procedure caching.

Installation memory parameters

When you install and start SQL Server for the first time, the installation process automatically allocates 2800 2 K pages of memory if your system has 16 megabytes of memory or less. If you have more memory, SQL Server chooses a larger value. Keep in mind that you are always free to adjust this value as needed.

Data caching

Each modern relational database management system has its own distinct architecture and methodology. However, one feature that all sophisticated database engines have in common is data caching. When a database engine caches data, it takes advantage of system memory to store data that is likely to be needed by other users or processes. Remember that disk I/O is the most time-consuming component of most applications. Some have estimated that to perform a disk operation is up to ten times slower than performing the same operation within memory. Consequently, database engine architects have created sophisticated algorithms to eliminate disk access wherever possible. Since SQL Server accesses data on the disk drive in units of pages, the engine creates corresponding areas of memory in the same units as the disk. These memory-based pages, taken together, are called the buffer pool. We now turn our attention to SQL Server's statistics that report on data caching. We illustrate these concepts by providing several examples of how to use these statistics. At the end of this section, we explore how to set a number of parameters to control SQL Server's memory performance.

Statistics

Cache—average free page scan: When searching for a free page for the free buffer pool, the lazywriter examines buffers in the free page cache. This statistic reports on the average number of buffers that were inspected by the lazywriter before it found an available buffer. Ideally, lower numbers are better for this statistic, since this means that the average search did not take too long. Long searches conducted over many pages means slower response, since the user's process is unable to proceed until this important internal resource is available.

Cache—maximum free page scan: This statistic reports on the maximum number of buffers that SQL Server's lazywriter process examined while searching for a free page. This number remains at the high value, no matter what happens to the average free page scan later.

Cache—number of free buffers: SQL Server uses this statistic to report on the current number of cache buffers available in the free buffer pool. Ideally, this number should remain relatively high. If it falls too low, SQL Server may be forced to initiate single page writes. These writes are necessary when this statistic is low because the engine needs to free up dirty pages to handle new data modifications. We'll devote more time to this subject later in this section.

Cache hit ratio: As we saw earlier, for best performance, SQL Server attempts to locate the data that you need from memory, rather than from the disk drive. This statistic tracks the percentage of time that SQL Server was able to achieve this result.

What kind of results indicate a good caching ratio? The answer depends on the mix of applications running at the time. No matter how much memory you have, certain operations simply don't lend themselves to high cache hit ratios. For example, suppose that many users run your application at one time but that most of them are searching for different data and index pages. This is very common in transaction-oriented systems, where there it's likely that users don't share much information, with the exception of lookup tables. Another instance where there typically isn't a high cache hit ratio occurs when you're running large sequential operations. By definition, these operations process large amounts of data. Pages don't have much time to remain in memory, since they're constantly being replaced by new pages from later in the sequential process. For both of these situations, a good caching ratio is 70 percent or higher.

For other types of operations where data is more likely to be shared among users, such as in decision support applications, your goal should be to obtain a cache hit ratio of 80 percent or higher. How can you raise this number? Since you can't easily change your applications' requirements or database schema, the easiest way is to raise SQL Server's memory parameter. Adding memory increases the number of available memory pages, which in turn helps to improve the cache hit ratio. Adding memory doesn't always equal better performance, however. We discuss the ramifications of providing too much memory to SQL Server in our discussion on the memory configuration parameter, later in this section.

Examples

Now, let's look at a few examples of how you can observe your system's memory cache statistics, using the performance monitor.

In the first simple example, we're running a read-only program that performs random reads from a table. We're observing the data hit ratio:

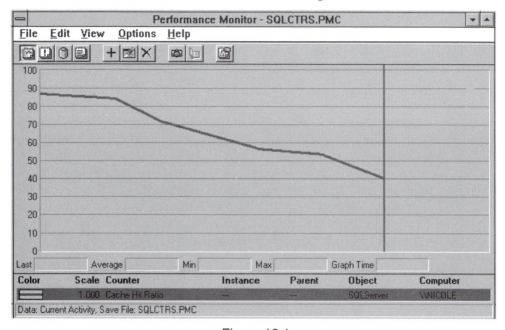

Figure 12.1

As we would expect, the overall data cache rate is slipping. Random page reads mean that it's unlikely that SQL Server will already have these pages present in memory. This reduces the cache hit ratio.

The next sample profiles an OLTP system. Users read large amounts of data and make changes to some of this information:

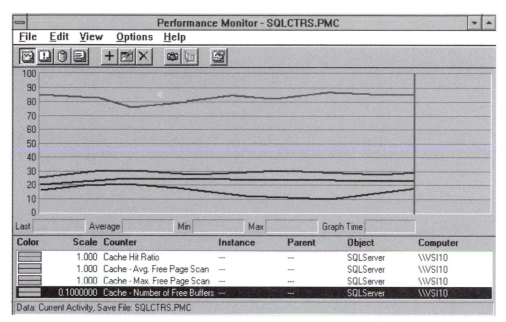

Figure 12.2

Based on the graph, this system appears to be running normally. Contrast this graph with the following graph, taken from a system that has an insufficient number of free buffers:

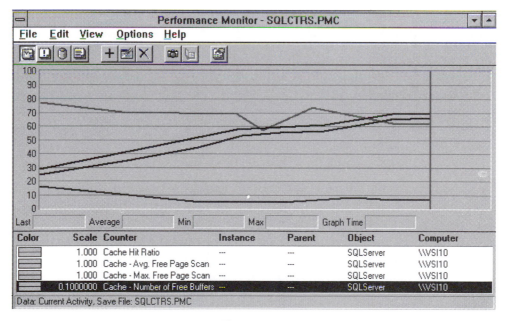

Figure 12.3

This is not a well-performing system. The cache hit ratio starts out well but gradually drops to overly low levels. Likewise, the number of free buffers is dropping, while the average and maximum free page scan numbers rise. How would you correct this situation? You could take any of these five steps:

1. **Increase SQL Server's memory parameter.**   This profile indicates that there is a memory shortage. Therefore, if possible, you should furnish more memory to SQL Server. However, if there isn't enough free RAM for this purpose, you might inadvertently degrade system performance, since this may force the operating system to perform extra swaps between memory and disk:

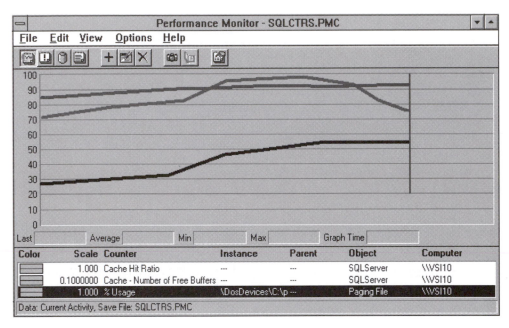

Figure 12.4

This graphic shows a seemingly well-performing SQL Server instance; the cache hit ratio and free buffer indicators all appear to be fine. The swap file usage statistic, however, shows a Windows NT machine that is making heavy use of the swap file. This testifies to the cost of the extra allocated memory.

2. **Lower the value of the 'procedure cache' configuration parameter.**   This parameter controls SQL Server's allocation of available memory to the procedure cache. If you don't use stored procedures frequently, there's no need to save space in RAM for proce-

dure buffering. Instead, this space could be put to better use for data and index caching.

3. **Raise the number of free buffers.** We discuss this option later in this section.

4. **Increasing the maximum asynchronous I/O parameter.** We reviewed this concept in the I/O parameters segment of Chapter 11.

5. **Increasing the maximum lazywriter I/O parameter.** We reviewed this concept in the I/O parameters segment of Chapter 11.

Finally, we're running a number of processes, some of which are simply reading data, while others are performing large bulk inserts:

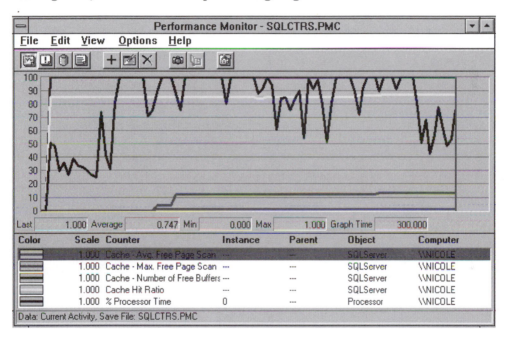

Figure 12.5

We've added in a CPU indicator; our system is fairly active, although there are breaks in CPU usage. Data caching is fairly steady at around 85 percent. The maximum free page scan parameter is slowly moving upward, which is what we'd expect as the query processes and bulk loading process began competing for available free pages. At the top of the page is the number of free buffers indicator. This graphic doesn't appear to be very impressive: The number stays right at the top of the page. This is because we've chosen the standard scale. If we were to use a scale of 0.1, the indicator would stay in the middle of the graph, and we could watch for meaningful trends.

Configuration parameters

Memory

This important parameter controls the amount of RAM that SQL Server requests from the Windows NT operating system when the engine starts. This memory is then partitioned into the data cache, the stored procedure cache, and other internal structures. Regardless of its final destination, the engine then divides this memory into a number of 2 K pages. This corresponds to the size of SQL Server's disk pages, which makes it easy for the engine to move data between memory and the physical disk drive.

To learn your current memory setting, you can use the SQL Enterprise Manager or run the 'sp_configure' stored procedure:

```
sp_configure 'memory'

name        minimum      maximum      config_value run_value
------------------- ----------- ------------ ---------
memory   1000         1048576      4096         4096
```

Armed with all of this information, we can now turn our attention to determining the right value for this important parameter. Microsoft provides a rule-of-thumb list in the SQL Server documentation, which we can summarize in this table:

Table 12.1   Comparison between System and SQL Server memory

Available memory	Amount allocated for SQL Server
16	4
24	8
32	16
48	28
64	40
128	100
256	216
512	464

Notice how the proportional gap between the machine's available memory and the amount of memory that you dedicate to SQL Server drops as the amount of available memory increases. This makes sense; on machines with higher memory, the Windows NT overhead requirements shrink as a proportion of available memory. This lets you assign larger and larger portions of memory to the database engine.

What happens if you set this value too high and allocate excess memory to SQL Server? Oversupplying memory to SQL Server merely increases the burden on the Windows NT operating system. This can result in swapping, which can quickly negate any performance gains you might have gotten by increasing the cache hit ratio. In fact, too high a memory value can even make booting SQL Server difficult, if not impossible.

The most logical approach to follow with memory is to raise the value gradually, with careful monitoring in between each change. If you don't see caching rates improve after an increase, then you know that you have reached the optimal value for memory. Remember to keep track of the swap rate as well, since raising the memory parameter can inadvertently increase swapping.

Set working set size

Windows NT uses very sophisticated memory management algorithms. From a high-level perspective, these algorithms make it appear that there is much more memory present than is actually there. This apparent extra memory, known as virtual memory, is found on most modern, multitasking operating systems. When a program makes use of memory on a Windows NT platform, any allocated memory is known as the program's working set. Given that the total size of all programs' working sets may exceed the amount of available virtual memory, the operating system may need to juggle the memory requirements of each program. In the case of SQL Server, the engine asks the operating system to reserve its working set in memory. This means that SQL Server's working set memory can't even be "borrowed" by any other processes, even if the operating system is desperate for space. This can accelerate database engine performance, since the act of juggling working set space can be very expensive.

Despite this ostensible performance benefit, there may be times when you don't want to reserve this space. For example, SQL Server may be only one of several important applications, all of which need to share memory equitably. To disarm this default behavior, you can use the 'set working set size' configuration parameter.

Procedure cache

SQL Server divides its memory among data and stored procedures, as well as other internal structures. As an administrator, you have a say in the ratio between data and stored procedures. You can use the 'procedure cache' configuration parameter to determine what percentage of available RAM is allocated to the stored procedure buffering area. The remainder is then assigned for data and index pages.

SQL Server measures the procedure cache parameter in percentage. For example, setting a value of 30 means that the engine reserves 30 percent of memory (assigned with the 'memory' parameter) for the stored procedure cache. The remainder of 70 percent is then available for data and index pages.

How should you set this value? If you anticipate heavy stored procedure usage, you may want to raise this setting above its default value of 30 percent. However, this would not be a good strategy in an environment where you barely make use of stored procedures. In fact, these kinds of situations merit a significant reduction in the procedure cache value, since you wouldn't be taking advantage of this space.

Free buffers

This parameter controls the minimum number of free buffers that SQL Server maintains at one time. The default setting is determined by the overall amount of memory available to SQL Server on your system. After you change the memory configuration setting, SQL Server reviews the accessible memory count, then assigns this parameter to be 5 percent of the newly altered memory value.

You can manually set the value to be between 20 and one-half of the maximum number of buffers on your system. Regardless of the setting, SQL Server uses the lazywriter to clean buffers until the number of free buffers reaches the amount you requested.

Is it ever necessary to change this parameter? Recall from our discussions on SQL Server's internal memory structures that performance can suffer if the engine is frequently forced to make single page writes. Single page writes happen when there is no more space in the free buffer pool. The engine needs free pages, so it flushes single pages to disk. Therefore, to reduce costly single page I/O operations, your goal should be to increase the number of free buffers. You can make this happen by taking one or more of these steps:

- Increase the maximum asynchronous I/O parameter.
- Increase the maximum lazywriter I/O parameter.
- Increase the number of free buffers.

We discussed options 1 and 2 in Chapter 11 in our review of I/O parameters. Option 3 should help diminish single page writes. Nevertheless, be prudent when raising this value. If you decide to increase the number of free buffers, try taking relatively small steps followed by scientific observations.

Hash buckets

SQL Server uses hash buckets as a quick way to link pages to buffers in memory. This parameter lets you set the number of hash buckets for your system. This value must be a prime number. This means that when you change this value, SQL Server may choose a slightly different number, which will be a prime number.

The scope of possible values for this parameter is partially dependent on the overall amount of memory available on your system. Assuming that you have less than 160 megabytes of RAM, valid settings can range between 4999 and 26500, with a default of 7993.

When should you alter this value? In most cases, there is no need to make any change; SQL Server's hashing algorithms work quite well with default values. However, if you add significant amounts of extra RAM, you might want to experiment with raising this value above the default.

Sort pages

While application and optimizer requirements drive the vast majority of sorting operations, administrators can still have some effect on these procedures. The 'sort pages' parameter lets you configure how many 2 K memory pages SQL Server sets aside for sorting maneuvers. If you anticipate that there will be a large number of concurrent sorts on your system, consider raising the value assigned to this parameter, which can range between 64 and 511 2 K pages. The default is 64.

If you opt to boost this value, consider that this extra memory comes at a price. It may be possible, for example, for you to augment sort operation speed while damaging overall database engine response. Accordingly, if you raise these values to high numbers, it's possible that you may need to add memory to your computer to make up for the extra sort space.

Backup buffer size

SQL Server lets administrators determine how large the backup buffer should be. The backup buffer is an area of memory storage used to speed up the backup process. You can set this value between 1 and 10, with a default value of 1. Each incremental unit provides 32 additional pages of memory to the backup buffer. For example, the default value of 1 means that SQL Server allocates 32 pages of memory to the backup buffer. If you set the value to 3, SQL Server allocates 96 pages to the backup buffer (3 * 32). Changes to this parameter take effect after the engine is restarted.

If you want to boost backup performance, consider setting this value higher than the default. However, as in all other memory settings, any additional memory that you assign to the backup buffer comes out of main SQL Server memory. In trying to boost backup throughput, you might erroneously damage overall system responsiveness.

Time slice

In a multiprocessing environment such as Windows NT, the operating system is responsible for switching processes in and out of the CPU. The time slice parameter controls how many times a process can avoid yielding control to another process. When raised above the default value of 100, SQL Server lets processes spend more time in the CPU without yielding. This can reduce concurrency, since longer periods of time elapse between these switches. Lowering this parameter means that processes are more prone to switching out of the CPU when confronted with another process' request for the CPU. However, this extra context switching can waste time; Windows NT spends more time on SQL Server process administration than on performing database requests.

Commonly, administrators have no need to make any changes to this configuration parameter. If you decide to experiment, do so cautiously; it's always better to take small steps than to make huge adjustments.

Stored procedure caching

As we saw earlier, internal memory caching is a key component of SQL Server's architecture. The internal memory cache is divided between storage for data and storage for stored procedures. The stored procedure storage area is known as the stored procedure buffer. Just as the data cache helps reduce the amount of disk I/O necessary to retrieve data, SQL Server uses the stored procedure buffer to locate procedures in memory, rather than having to read them from disk. Let's spend a moment understanding how this works.

When you try to execute a previously built stored procedure, SQL Server first looks in the procedure cache to see if the procedure is already resident in memory. If it is, then the engine uses the memory-based version of the stored procedure. If not, the engine reads the procedure from disk and places it into the stored procedure buffer, consuming as many 2 K memory pages as necessary. When you create or compile a stored procedure, SQL Server also uses the stored procedure buffer to cache this information for later users. However, the engine doesn't support multiple users working with the same query plan at the same time. This means that stored procedures are reusable, not reentrant. We discuss this concept in our next section.

Procedures found in the stored procedure buffer can be thought of as active or used. A procedure is considered to be active when some user or process is running the procedure at this moment. A used procedure is considered to be a procedure that is resident in the stored procedure buffer, was recently active, but is no longer running. By definition, an active procedure is also considered to be used.

SQL Server 6.5 introduces a new object, known as the procedure cache object, that provides additional stored procedure buffer statistics for administrators. After discussing the concept of reusable versus reentrant stored procedures, we then examine these new statistics, as well as portray several examples that show how to use this new object.

Reusable versus reentrant stored procedures

While SQL Server is able to take advantage of memory caching to reuse stored procedures, the engine must still produce a new query plan if another user is already using the existing query plan. This means that stored procedures are not reentrant. For example, suppose that Andy is the first user of the day to work with stored procedure 'add_new_customer.' The engine reads this procedure into the stored procedure cache, signifying that other users can retrieve the stored procedure from memory. Next, assume that Danielle wants to run the same stored procedure at the same time Andy is running his copy. She is able to retrieve the stored procedure itself from the cache, saving some potentially costly disk I/O. However, SQL Server must generate a new query plan for her, since Andy is still using his copy of the query plan. Once Danielle finishes running the stored procedure, the engine makes her query plan available for others to use, assuming that only one user at a time uses the plan.

Interestingly, it's possible that the optimizer may create two different query plans for the same stored procedure, even if the calls to the stored procedure are separated by only a few moments. This can happen for any number of reasons, including:

- **Different data profiles.** It's possible that someone may add, delete, or modify enough data to those tables referenced by the stored procedure to warrant an altered query plan.

- **Different parameters.** If you pass in vastly different parameter values to a stored procedure, SQL Server may need to generate a modified query plan.

- **New, different, or removed indexes.** Changing the index structure for your tables can require an adjusted query plan.

- **UPDATE STATISTICS execution.** If you run this command, the optimizer may make a different decision when it generates the next query plan.

Statistics

Maximum procedure buffers active percentage: SQL Server labels buffers that contain running stored procedure code as 'active.' This statistic shows the maximum number of active stored procedure buffers that have existed while you are running your monitoring operation.

Maximum procedure buffers used percentage: This statistic tells administrators the highest percentage of procedure buffers that were marked as 'used' during this monitoring session.

Maximum procedure cache active percentage: This number depicts the largest percentage of the stored procedure cache that were in the active state in this monitoring session.

Maximum procedure cache used percentage: This indicator describes the highest percentage of the procedure cache that were used during the current monitoring session.

Procedure buffers active percentage: This statistic shows the current percentage of stored procedure buffers that contain a stored procedure in the active state.

Procedure buffers used percentage: This number describes the current percentage of stored procedure buffers that can be said to be in the 'used' state.

Procedure cache active percentage: This value stands for the current percentage of the stored procedure cache that can be said to be active. For a procedure to be considered active, it must be currently running.

Procedure cache size: This number indicates the current number of 2-K pages that make up SQL Server's stored procedure cache. This number can waver during a monitoring session, since the engine may be carrying out other tasks that affect internal memory structures.

Procedure cache used percentage: This figure cites the percentage of the stored procedure cache that is currently occupied with stored procedure code.

Total procedure buffers: This number denotes the total number of buffers allocated to the stored procedure cache. Consequently, it does not change during a session, although the procedure cache size metric may experience slight oscillation.

Examples

Let's look at some examples that demonstrate what's provided by the SQL Server procedure cache object.

In the first case, we're monitoring all possible procedure cache object statistics during a period of relatively light activity:

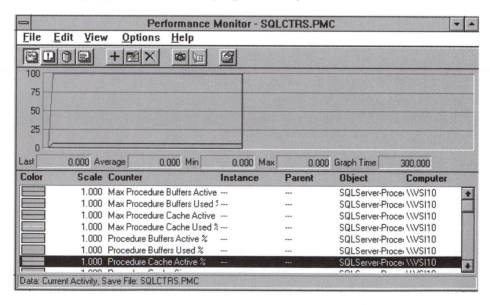

Figure 12.6

This is another example where too much information is not very helpful. Let's reduce the number of indicators that we're monitoring, while increasing the amount of system activity:

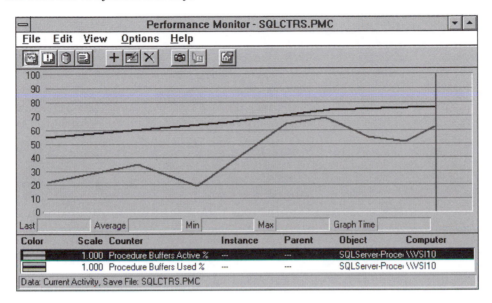

Figure 12.7

Notice how the stored procedure used percentage always is higher than the stored procedure active percentage. This makes sense: By definition, the number of used buffers will always be equal to or greater than the number of active buffers. The active percentage may approach or even equal the used percentage, but it can never exceed the user percentage.

In the final example, we're tracking both the current and maximum percentage used figures for the procedure cache:

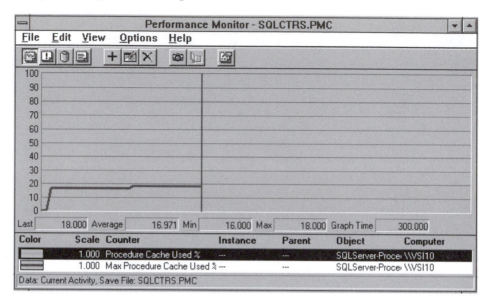

Figure 12.8

Even though there are two indicators, why is there only one line in the graph? Answer: Because the current and maximum percentage used figures are identical. Over time, however, we would expect the maximum number to continue to climb, since it records the top value for this statistic. On the other hand, it's likely that the current percentage value would fluctuate, based on a number of other criteria.

Locking

On single-user, single-process database management systems, your programs are assured of the database's complete attention at all times. However, sophisticated RDBMS engines like SQL Server need to support multiple users and processes at all times. The way these engines achieve this goal is through various data locking mechanisms. In this section, we examine how you can monitor and tune SQL Server to provide the best overall locking strategy. We begin by reviewing some general locking concepts, such as the different types of locks and their importance to SQL Server. Next, we move on to a detailed description of the SQL Server locks object, including how you can monitor this object to learn more about the current locking profile of your system. To better illustrate this concept, we review a few examples of locking situations. Armed with information on how to monitor locks, we then focus on how to configure your system to make most efficient use of locks. Finally, we close out the section by discussing other locking topics, such as deadlocks and lock starvation.

Lock concepts

In Chapter 7, we discussed how SQL Server uses locks. However, some of this information bears repeating here, since we'll be looking at a variety of statistics for each different type of lock. SQL Server can place locks at the page, table, extent, and database level. Each lock can be one of the following types:

- **Shared.** SQL Server typically places shared locks when performing operations that don't change data, such as SELECT statements. A shared lock means that other processes can read data from, and even place locks on, the object. However, until your process frees the lock, no other process can actually make any changes to the object. For example, if your process holds a shared lock on page 1235 of the 'items' table in the 'equipment' database, other processes can acquire a shared or update lock, but none of these processes can actually get an exclusive lock, which is necessary to insert, update, or delete data.

- **Update.** SQL Server uses update locks when making changes to data within tables. The engine "promotes" the lock to an exclusive lock just before actually changing the data.

- **Exclusive.** Exclusive locks are the mechanism that SQL Server uses to ensure data integrity during data modification. No data gets inserted, updated, or deleted without an exclusive lock.

- **Intent shared.** This type of lock signals that your process is getting ready to acquire a shared lock on a page.

- **Intent exclusive.** An intent exclusive lock means that your process is about to request an exclusive lock on a page.

- **Blocking lock.** A blocking lock occurs when one process holds a lock that another process needs to finish its work. For example, if process A holds a page lock that process B needs to obtain, process A's lock is known as a blocking lock.

SQL Server 6.5 now provides administrators with the ability to enable row-level locking for insert operations on individual tables. This feature is known as Insert Row-Level locking (IRL). Two additional lock types are now available:

- **Insert_page lock.** When processes are inserting rows into a table that has been IRL-enabled, they can request this type of lock for pages that are receiving data. Multiple processes can have this type of lock on the same page at the same time.

- **Link_page lock.**   As pages fill during an INSERT operation, SQL Server takes unused pages from the pool of free pages and makes them available to the original table. This is known as a link operation. The first transaction that fills up the original page receives a link page lock as the engine allocates additional pages. The link page lock is then held until the transaction completes.

There are times when SQL Server decides that your transaction is holding too many page locks and chooses to lock the table instead. This is known as lock escalation; we'll cover this in more detail in the lock configuration section.

SQL Server—Locks object

The SQL Server locks object provides a variety of informative statistics regarding your system's lock usage:

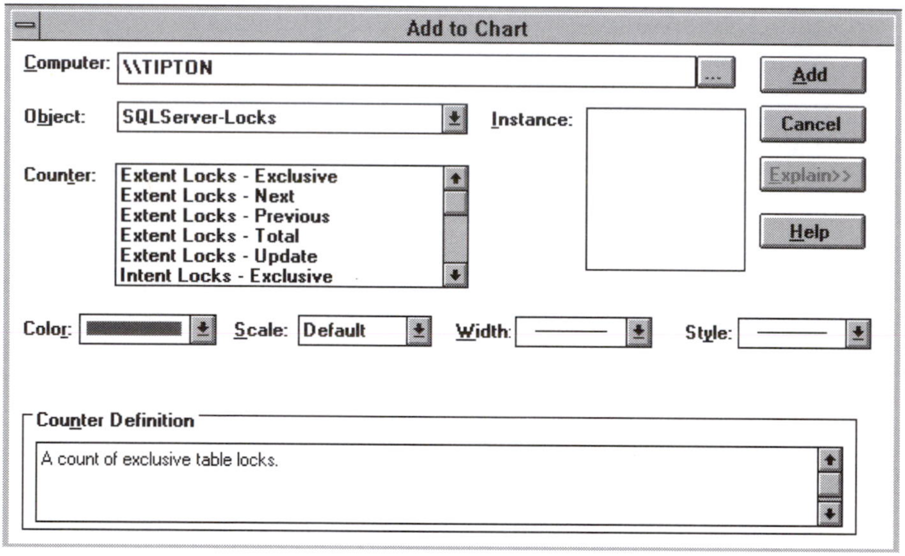

Figure 12.9

Statistics

Let's itemize the copious statistics provided by the locks object. We'll group these locks by their purpose.

Extent locks: As we saw earlier, an extent is a grouping of eight pages. SQL Server acquires an extent lock when a process that is inserting data into a table requires additional pages. The engine also requests an extent lock during CREATE and DROP operations. Available statistics on extent locks include:

- Extent locks – Exclusive
- Extent locks – Next
- Extent locks – Previous
- Extent locks – Update
- Extent locks – Total

Intent locks: SQL Server creates an intent lock when it plans to request an exclusive or shared lock on a page. The intent lock signals other processes that they won't be able to place their own exclusive locks on the resource in question. Intent lock statistics include:

- Intent locks – Exclusive
- Intent locks – Shared
- Intent locks – Total

Page locks: SQL Server requests page-level locks in a variety of situations, from simple SELECT statements through large-scale data modification. You can use these statistics to learn about the current state of page locks:

- Page locks – Exclusive
- Page locks – Shared
- Page locks – Update
- Page locks – Total

Table locks: SQL Server may choose to convert a group of page locks into a single table lock when the number of page locks becomes excessive or reaches an administrator-determined threshold. We discuss this threshold in this section, in our review of lock escalation parameters. You can use the performance monitor to get information about these table lock statistics:

- Table locks – Exclusive
- Table locks – Shared
- Table locks – Total

Blocking locks: One of the main purposes of locks is to help ensure data integrity by controlling access to data. This means that certain users or processes may be forced to wait while another user or process holds a lock on a resource. In these cases, the waiting users or processes can be said to be blocked. You can monitor a variety of statistics about blocking locks, including:

- Maximum users blocked
- Users blocked
- Total blocking locks

Total locks: These indicators show various lock totals, including:

- Total exclusive locks
- Total locks
- Total shared locks

Examples

Let's look at some SQL Server locks object performance monitor output for a variety of locking situations. To gain a better understanding of how to interpret these statistics, try experimenting with your own database operations, especially those that perform large insert, update, or delete procedures.

In the first case, we're looking at a graph showing the total number of locks, total number of shared locks, and total number of exclusive locks:

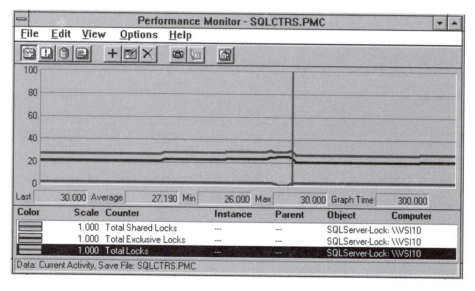

Figure 12.10

Next, we're looking at a chart of page locks versus table locks. Our output shows us what we'd expect: a much higher number of page locks in ratio to table locks.

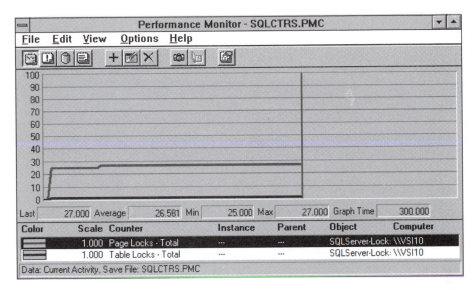

Figure 12.11

In the next case, we've set an alert to notify us if the total number of blocking locks exceeds ten at any given time:

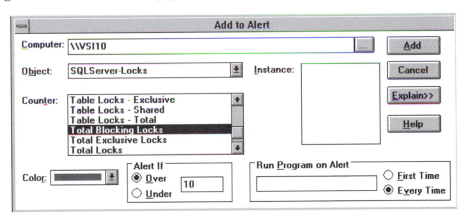

Figure 12.12

In the next example, we're watching all of the total lock statistics, including extent, intent, page, table, as well as the grand total count of locks. Realistically, there are simply too many indicators on this chart to make it easy to decipher:

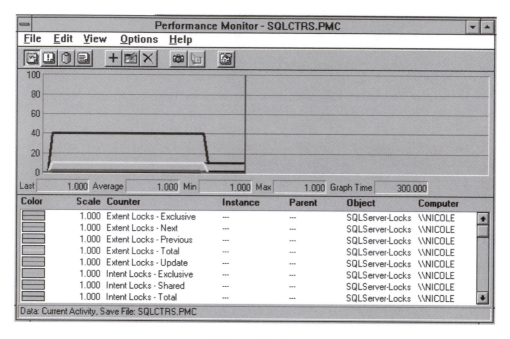

Figure 12.13

Try to avoid the temptation to chart all possible statistics. Crowded charts don't lend themselves to easy interpretation.

SQL Enterprise Manager and locks

You can use the SQL Enterprise Manager to get a snapshot of your system's current locking state:

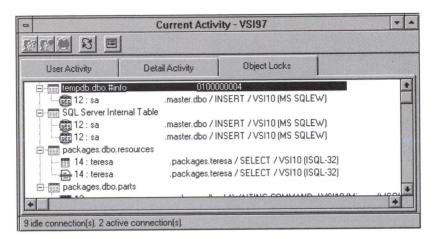

Figure 12.14

By highlighting an individual lock entry, you can learn about the underlying SQL statement:

Figure 12.15

SQL Enterprise Manager also reports on the new insert page locks and link page locks found in SQL Server 6.5:

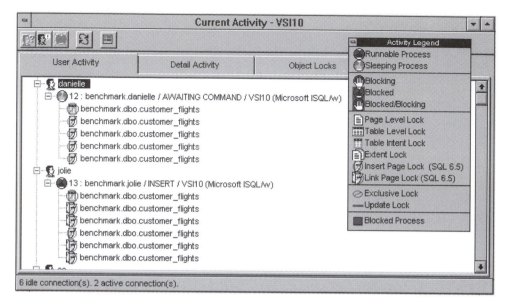

Figure 12.16

You can also look at individual process locks by using the detail activity portion of the same dialog:

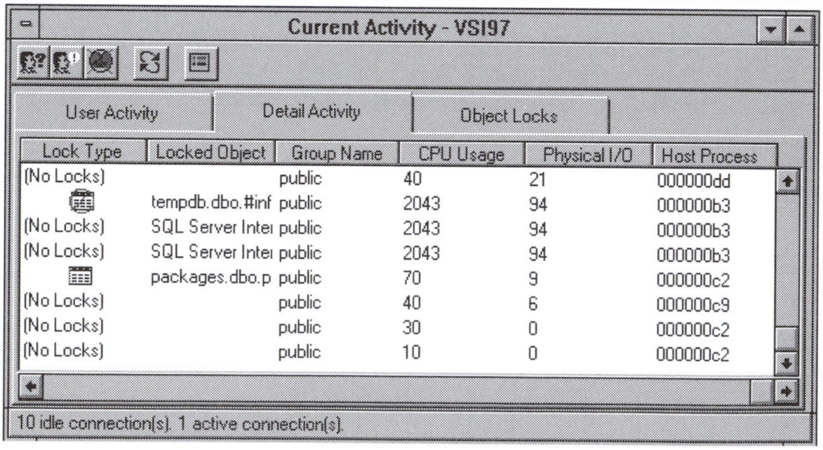

Figure 12.17

sp_lock stored procedure

Another way to get information about the state of your system's locks is to use the 'sp_lock' stored procedure. You can run the procedure without parameters, or you can pass up to process IDs to narrow the output. Let's look at some examples of 'sp_lock' output.

```
1> sp_lock
2> go
 spid  locktype           table_id      page      dbname
 ----- ------------------ ----------- --------- -------
    11 Sh_intent           640005311         0 master
    11 Ex_extent                   0       384 tempdb
    12 Ex_intent            16003088         0 largo
    12 Ex_page              16003088       663 largo
    12 Ex_table             16003088         0 largo

1> sp_lock
2> go
 spid  locktype           table_id      page      dbname
 ----- ------------------ ----------- --------- -------
    11 Sh_intent           640005311         0 master
    11 Ex_extent                   0       384 tempdb
    12 Ex_intent-blk        16003088         0 largo
    12 Ex_page              16003088       686 largo
    12 Ex_table-blk .       16003088         0 largo
```

In the next example, we're running two reports. Each report selects and updates data in different tables.

```
 spid  locktype           table_id      page      dbname
 ----- ------------------ ----------- --------- -------
    12 Ex_extent           0           768       largo
    12 Ex_extent           0           840       largo
    12 Ex_extent           0           912       largo
    12 Prev_extent         0           688       largo
    12 Prev_extent         0           800       largo
    12 Ex_intent           352004285   0         largo
    12 Ex_page             352004285   688       largo
    12 Ex_page             352004285   689       largo
     .    .                  .           .         .
     .    .                  .           .         .
    12 Ex_page             352004285   912       largo
```

```
12      Ex_table          352004285    0          largo
15      Ex_extent         0            384        tempdb
16      Ex_intent         16003088     0          largo
16      Ex_page           16003088     687        largo
16      Ex_page           16003088     921        largo
16      Ex_table          16003088     0          largo
```

The output shows us that each process (12 and 16) is holding a number of different exclusive page locks. This is to be expected on any process that makes numerous inserts, updates, or deletes.

You can determine the actual name of the table by using the 'object_name' function:

```
select object_name(16003088)


------------------------------
equipos


select object_name(352004285)


------------------------------
sistemas
```

Before running this function, make sure that you're currently connected to the database in question. If you are in another database, this function may return an unrecognizable name or null value.

Configuration parameters

At this point, let's focus on how you can use configuration parameters to control SQL Server's locking behavior.

Locks

The locks parameter controls the number of available locks for all SQL Server users. This value can range between 5000 and 2 billion. The default value is 5000. This may be too low for servers that have applications that perform large volumes of concurrent data modification. You'll know that you've exceeded your available locks when you receive an error message in the log.

Use care when increasing your lock parameter, since each additional lock comes at a cost of 32 bytes. For example, if you add 100,000 locks, you increase your system's memory requirements by more than three megabytes. For more information on developing an effective locking strategy, see the "Locking" section in Chapter 7 on efficient application practices.

Lock escalation

SQL Server provides a sophisticated lock escalation mechanism that can detect when a process holds more than a predefined number of page locks on a table. Once this number has been reached, SQL Server converts, or escalates, all of the page locks into a single table lock. This helps conserve the overall number of required locks, as well as improve performance.

In this section, we examine three important parameters that help control lock escalation behavior.

Lock escalation percent

Setting this parameter lets you specify, in terms of percentage, when SQL Server should escalate the page locks to a table lock. This value can range between 0 and 100 percent. For example, if you set the lock escalation percent to 50, SQL Server escalates page locks to table locks when the number of page locks exceeds 50 percent of possible locks. You can always override this value on an individual query basis by providing an optimizer hint.

Note that when you set this value to 0 percent, SQL Server disregards this parameter and instead looks to the lock escalation maximum to determine when to escalate.

The following two graphics illustrate what happens when SQL Server decides to escalate from page locks to a table lock. In the first example, we're updating a relatively small number of rows:

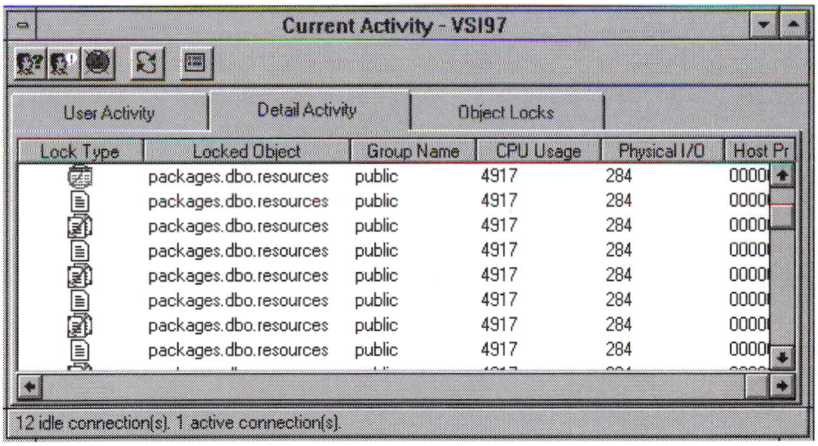

Figure 12.18

Based on our existing escalation parameters, SQL Server didn't judge it necessary to escalate the lock. Instead, there are numerous page and extent locks in place. However, if we either change the parameters or increase the number of updated rows, we get a different picture:

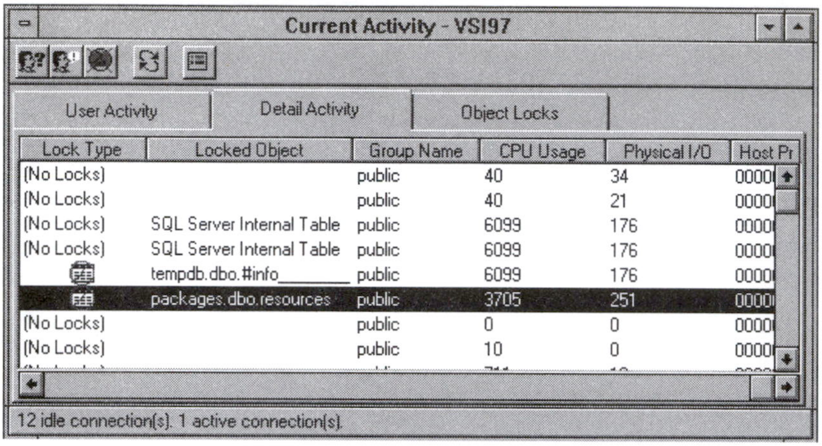
Current Activity - VSI97
User Activity
Detail Activity
Object Locks
Lock Type
Locked Object
Group Name
CPU Usage
Physical I/O
Host Pr
(No Locks) public 40 34 0000
(No Locks) public 40 21 0000
(No Locks) SQL Server Internal Table public 6099 176 0000
(No Locks) SQL Server Internal Table public 6099 176 0000
tempdb.dbo.#info_ public 6099 176 0000
packages.dbo.resources public 3705 251 0000
(No Locks) public 0 0 0000
(No Locks) public 10 0 0000
12 idle connection(s). 1 active connection(s).

Figure 12.19

By locking at the table level, SQL Server reduces the overall number of locks necessary to complete the operation.

Lock escalation maximum

Setting this parameter tells SQL Server to escalate from page locks to a table lock whenever a particular operation exceeds this value. This escalation occurs regardless of the lock escalation percentage status. The default for this parameter is 200, with a range of values between 2 and 500,000.

Lock escalation minimum

The lock escalation minimum parameter is often used in conjunction with the lock escalation percentage. This setting tells SQL Server to escalate page locks to a table lock when the following two criteria have been met:

1. The number of page locks meets or exceeds the lock escalation minimum parameter.
2. The percentage of locked pages exceeds the lock escalation percentage.

Let's look at an example of how these two parameters interact. Suppose that you've set the lock escalation minimum to 500 and the lock escalation percentage to 30. This means that whenever the raw number of page locks for a given table in a given process exceeds 500 and the percentage of pages locked exceeds 30 percent, SQL Server escalates the page locks to a table lock. This parameter ranges between 2 and 500,000, with a default value of 20.

Other locking concepts

Deadlocks

Deadlocks happen occasionally in multiuser database systems. The most common cause of deadlocks is two users or processes that each need to lock a resource the other holds. The two processes are said to be deadlocked, since neither user can proceed. Without database engine intervention, this deadlock can continue forever. Fortunately, SQL Server automatically detects deadlocks and takes steps to extricate the users from the situation.

For example, suppose that Zoe has a lock on a page in the 'properties' table but also wants to lock a page in the 'personnel' table. At the same time, Chloe has a lock on Zoe's desired page in the 'personnel' table but also wants to lock a page in the 'properties' table. If Zoe already has that page locked, then these two users are in a deadlock:

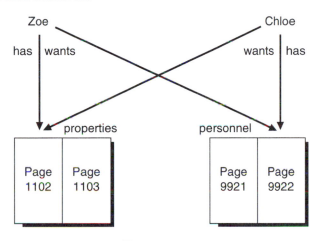

Figure 12.20

The engine picks one of these users and aborts her process. The user receives this message:

```
Msg 1205, Level 13, State 2
Your server command (process id 12) was deadlocked with
another process and has been chosen as deadlock victim.
Rerun your command.
```

How can you reduce the overall incidences of deadlocks? Follow these recommendations:

- **Keep transactions as short as possible.** If a transaction holds hundreds of locks for a long period of time, chances are it may become involved in a deadlock. As we've discussed elsewhere, it's always a good idea to keep your transactions as brief as possible.

• **Use the correct amount of transaction isolation.**   We discussed transaction isolation levels and their impact on performance in Chapter 7. Transaction isolation levels can also influence deadlocks, since these settings directly affect the overall number of locks that your processes can hold. In general, you'll be able to avoid deadlocks if you can keep the total number of locks to a minimum. Choosing the right transaction isolation level can go a long way toward keeping locking requirements down.

• **Have your applications follow the same steps in accessing resources.**   If you have a variety of different programs, written by different programmers, all performing similar tasks, try to ensure that the programmers all access tables and objects in the same order. For example, suppose that you have two different programs (program 1 and program 2) that access data in two different tables (table 1 and table 2). If you write the programs so that they both get data from table 1 and then move on to table 2, it's unlikely that you'll end up in a deadlock. Instead, one program may have to wait momentarily while the other does its work. On the other hand, if program 1 first updates table 1 and program 2 first updates table 2, you may encounter a deadlock, since both programs are proceeding in opposite directions. You can liken this to one-way streets versus two-way streets: Things generally proceed more smoothly when traffic flows in one direction.

• **Check for error code 1205.**   SQL Server returns an error code of 1205 when it experiences a deadlock. As a developer, it's always wise to check for errors in general. Error 1205 has a special significance: Your process probably would have completed if the deadlock hadn't happened. This means that you should presumably restart the transaction, since the other process has probably completed already. If you're developing ODBC applications, you can check for the generic ODBC error code that indicates a deadlock. We cover this topic in more detail in Chapter 7.

DEADLOCKPRIORITY

As we've just seen, when two processes are deadlocked, only one can proceed. SQL Server returns an error message to the other process, informing it that it has been the victim of a deadlock. As a developer, you can set an option that tells the engine that you want your process to receive "special treatment" in the event of a deadlock. This option, known as DEADLOCKPRIORITY, can be set to either LOW or NORMAL. When set to LOW, the engine treats this process as expendable during a deadlock. This means that the other process is allowed to proceed while this process halts. When set to NORMAL, the engine makes no bias when determining which process to interrupt.

Lock starvation

Lock starvation occurs when one reading process dominates the locking status of a table. This can cause writing processes to halt until the reading process completes. SQL Server automatically prevents this situation from arising by serving these requests in the order in which they are received. For example, if process A is in a 'while' loop, reading all rows in a table, and process B makes a write request, SQL Server works on process A's first read request, then switches to process B's write request. This forestalls lock starvation.

Threading

One advanced feature of the Windows NT operating system is its integration of multithreading within the basic operating system architecture. This is known as native multithreading, since the threading feature is built in to the operating system. SQL Server takes this architecture one level further, using multithreading as an integral part of its engine technology. In this section, we research multithreading in more detail and explain how you can configure SQL Server parameters to make the most optimal use of multithreading.

When an application is multithreading, it means that there can be multiple logic paths, or threads, existent at one time within the same process. For example, a single multithreaded application could monitor user input on one thread while concurrently sending a data stream across the network on another thread. Only one copy of the program is running, yet the program is performing a variety of tasks in parallel.

Windows NT threads object

While it's beyond the scope of this book to describe all of the Windows NT monitoring objects, it is worthwhile for us to review the Windows NT threads object, since that helps shed light on several multithreading concepts. You can get a variety of interesting multithreading statistics from this object:

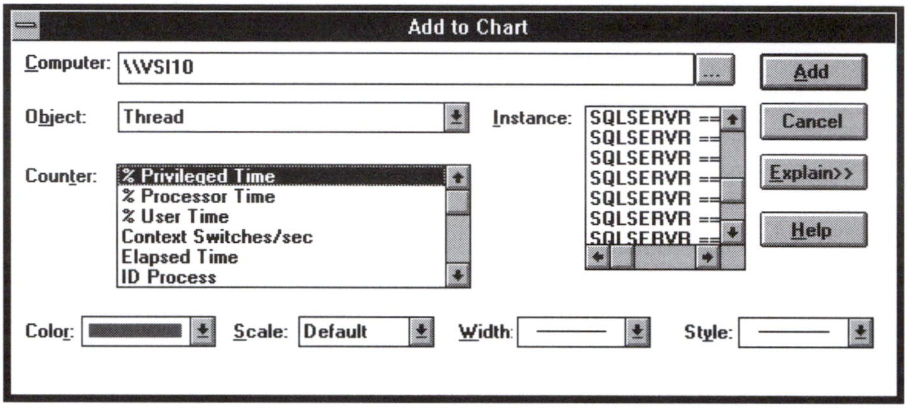

Figure 12.21

Let's look at how you can interpret these statistics.

Statistics

Percent privileged time: Windows NT is a multiprocessing, multi-threading environment. At any given point in time, all processes and threads are in one and only one mode. This indicator shows the percentage of elapsed time that a particular thread has spent in the Windows NT privileged mode.

Percent processor time: This number shows how what percentage of elapsed time a given thread has spent working on the processor.

Percent user time: This statistic measures how much elapsed time the thread has spent in the Windows NT user mode. User mode is the most common state for typical user applications and processes.

Context switches per second: A context switch happens when a thread switches in and out of the CPU. This indicator counts how many times per second this event occurs. One of the main benefits of multithreading is that it reduces context switching, which can be very expensive.

Elapsed time: This statistic displays the total amount of time, measured in seconds, that this thread has been running.

ID process: Windows NT uses this number as a distinct identification for a particular process. Note that the operating system may recycle this number for future use with another process once this process has finished.

ID thread: As we just saw, the process ID represents a Windows NT-assigned unique identifier for a particular process. This statistic performs the same function, only at the thread level. Consequently, this also means that the operating system can reuse a thread ID once the original thread finishes.

Priority base: Windows NT assigns a priority to threads. This priority helps determine how much CPU time gets allocated to the thread. This indicator shows the original base priority for the thread. The operating system may raise or lower the actual thread priority, depending on the kind of procedure currently performed by thread.

Priority current: As we saw in the previous statistic, Windows NT uses internal algorithms to set the priority for a thread. However, based on processing activity, the operating system may alter the thread's priority at any time. This statistic shows us the current priority for the thread.

Thread state: There are a finite number of conditions, or states, that can apply to a thread at any given time. This statistic reports on the thread's state. Numeric values can be:

0. **Initialized.**

1. **Ready.**   When a thread is in the ready state, it is prepared to work but is unable to do so until a processor becomes available.

2. **Running.**   Threads that are in a running state are being serviced by a processor.

3. **Standby.**   A thread in standby state is about to run on a processor.

4. **Terminated.**   Windows NT terminates a thread once it has finished working.

5. **Wait.**   When a thread is said to be waiting, it means that the thread has submitted a non-CPU operation, such as an I/O request. Until the system satisfies this request, there is no work for the thread to undertake until the original requisition has been completed.

6. **Transition.**   Threads in a transition state are almost ready to work, except that they are awaiting system resources.

7. **Unknown.**

Thread wait reason: In situations where a thread is in a wait state, Windows NT lets you see the reason for the wait:

Table 12.2   wait reasons

value	purpose
0, 7	Executive
1, 8	Free page
2, 9	Page in
3, 10	Pool allocation
4, 11	Execution delay
5, 12	Suspended condition
6, 13	User request
14	Event pair high
15	Event pair low
16	LPC receive
17	LPC reply
18	Virtual memory
19	Page out

Configuration parameters

Maximum worker threads

One reason that SQL Server works so well in the Windows NT environment is that the database engine takes advantage of native operating system threads to perform its work. These threads are known as worker threads and service three main areas:

- User requests
- Network connections
- Checkpoints

In situations where there are fewer users than worker threads, SQL Server assigns one thread per user. However, should the number of user connections grow beyond the number of worker threads, the engine groups, or pools, these threads so that a thread can service more than one user at a time.

As an administrator, you can use the 'maximum worker threads' parameter to determine how many native operating system threads should be created to participate in the user thread pool. The default value is 255, which means that 255 threads will be available to service user connections. If there are less than 255 connections, then some of these threads will be idle. On the other hand, if there are more than 255 user connections, these threads will then work to divide the user load.

Backup threads

You can use this parameter to set the number of threads that SQL Server starts up for operations that load data from, or dump data to, a striped device. This value can be set between 0 and 32. Setting this to 0 means that SQL Server won't perform striped dumps at all.

Remember that when you change this parameter, you need to restart the engine for the alteration to take effect.

Affinity mask

This parameter, new in SQL Server 6.5, lets you assign a thread to a particular processor. This is significant only on a symmetric multiprocessor (SMP) machine; on other machines this parameter has no effect. The affinity mask corresponds to a bit mask. This bit mask, which you enter in hexadecimal format, tells the engine which processors you want to mark as available for servicing threads.

When should you set this parameter? As we've seen earlier, Windows NT is a multithreading operating system that has multiprocessor capabilities built in. This means that there are already sophisticated algorithms in place to handle situations where several processors are available to work on a task. For this reason, your setting of an affinity mask may actually degrade performance, since you are instructing the engine to bypass the operating system's internal algorithms. Accordingly, use affinity masks with care. As in any other parameter change, make sure to alter only one variable at a time. Keep detailed performance records to ensure that you can determine whether your alteration had any positive effect.

Multiple processor considerations

While the vast majority of current Windows NT operating system instances run on single processor machines, more and more sites are installing and employing multiprocessor platforms. Multiprocessor environments, Windows NT, and SQL Server work very well together. By design, Windows NT and SQL Server are optimized to take advantage of features found on multiprocessor systems. In this section, we investigate how you can configure SQL Server's engine parameters to make the most of your multiprocessor machine.

SMP concurrency

On multiprocessor machines, SQL Server spawns threads to take advantage of the extra processors. These extra processors help speed response by dividing the work load. As an administrator, you have a choice about how many processors are available to the database engine. You control this behavior by setting the SMP Concurrency parameter.

Values for this parameter can range between -1 and 64, with a default of 0. On uniprocessor machines, SQL Server automatically chooses a setting of 1, since there is only one processor. On the other hand, when you install the engine on a multiprocessor platform, SQL Server selects a value of 0 for this parameter. This means that SQL Server performs its own processor detection routines and then sets the value to be the number of processors minus one. In most cases, this is the best approach. If you want to set your own value, you can choose between providing a number or simply using -1. Setting SMP concurrency to -1 signifies that you want SQL Server to use as many processor resources as possible. While this leads to faster database performance, it also has the potential to hurt response of nondatabase applications, since they will be forced to endure long waits for processor time. However, if you have assigned the multiprocessor computer to be a dedicated database server, there's probably no harm in requesting that SQL Server take control of all processors.

Spin counter

On uniprocessor machines, SQL Server uses a "test-and-set" algorithm to determine if a resource is available. If the resource is available, the process acquires the resource. If it is not available, the requesting process sleeps and periodically awakens to retry the test-and-set operation.

For single-processor machines, this is the most efficient way to handle shared resource requests. On multiprocessors, however, a requesting process could be resident in a different CPU. Instead of context switching, sleeping, and then retrying, it is more efficient for the process to remain resident in the CPU. The requesting process could then keep retrying: Chances are that the requested resource will be available momentarily.

Windows NT supports this concept; it is called "spinning." When a process "spins," it does not switch out of the CPU. Instead, it continually loops and retries its request. The number of times that it loops can be controlled by the 'spin counter' parameter.

If you are on a uniprocessor machine, SQL Server sets this value to 10. For multiprocessor machines, the default value is 10000. Potential values for this parameter range from 1 to over 2 billion. What setting should you use? Ordinarily, you can use the default value set by the engine. However, if you are on a multiprocessor machine and you expect a high degree of the type of user activity that can cause momentary resource locks, consider raising this parameter. After making this change, watch for significant differences in performance. If system responsiveness doesn't increase, go back to the original setting.

Affinity mask

We discussed this new SQL Server 6.5 parameter in this chapter's section on multithreading.

Logging

In this section, we probe a number of important transaction logging subjects. We begin by understanding what purposes a transaction log serves, in addition to a brief discussion of automatic recovery. Next, we look at what SQL Server stores in the log, along with how dumping the log affects performance. We then turn our attention to checkpoints. Finally, we examine the SQL Server logs object, including its statistics, as well as some monitoring samples.

Describing the transaction log

Most relational database applications store their information in a number of tables. This decentralization requires that any data alterations be consistent: If you make a change to table A and table B, it's crucial that both changes either happen or not happen. If table A gets updated successfully but table B's change fails, you have an integrity problem. Likewise, if you abort the operation on table A, yet table B somehow receives the change, you also have an integrity issue. Note that you can have integrity problems on single table updates as well. For instance, what happens if you add several rows to table A, but then change your mind? If you are unable to cancel these modifications, then your table contains incorrect information.

Fortunately, one of the best features of today's powerful relational databases is their ability to maintain a high degree of data integrity. Transactions are the heart of this capability. When you use transactions in your applications, you can safely perform multitable updates. If your program encounters an error, you can restore the underlying tables to their original state. How does SQL Server provide this safety system? The answer is that the engine uses an object known as the transaction log to control database alterations, as well as to provide for an orderly recovery after a crash or shutdown.

The transaction log is the repository where SQL Server stores all of its pertinent transaction information. If problems occur or if you decide to abort an operation, the engine uses this log to determine which changes to keep and which to discard. Let's look at how this is possible.

Where is transaction log information kept?

SQL Server stores transaction logging information in the 'syslogs' table. This table has the following layout:

Table 12.3   syslogs

column name	type	purpose
xactid	binary	Transaction ID
op	tinyint	Update-operation number

Under no circumstances should you attempt to add or modify data in this table. In fact, it's probably a good idea not even to retrieve any data from it. We show it here for informational purposes only.

There is one transaction log per database.

Automatic recovery

When SQL Server starts, it performs a number of important steps to guarantee the soundness of your data. Taken together, these operations constitute automatic recovery:

1. SQL Server examines each database's transaction log. This process begins with the 'master' database and then moves on to the 'model,' 'pubs,' and all other user databases. SQL Server also rebuilds the tempdb database as part of this operation. If you've elected to have your server replicate information, automatic recovery also works on the 'distribution' database.

2. If SQL Server finds a committed transaction in the log that was executed after the last checkpoint but not written to disk, it reruns the transaction.

3. If SQL Server finds an unfinished transaction, it rolls the transaction back.

4. Once the system databases have been inspected, SQL Server is ready for user login. Keep in mind that user databases won't be accessible until they also have been checked and cleaned.

You can also perform a manual recovery by restoring a previously saved version of the data and transaction log. SQL Server performs the above tasks regardless of whether recovery is automatic or user initiated.

As an example, suppose that the system goes down with these transactions and checkpoints in the transaction log:

Table 12.4   transaction log

time	action
10:17.03	begin transaction smith
10:17.06	update account set balance = 1000 where account_id = 112003
10:17.07	commit transaction smith
10:19.55	checkpoint
10:22.00	begin transaction jones
10:22.01	update accounts set balance = 2012.22 where account_id = 509944
10:22.02	commit transaction jones
10:23.16	begin transaction walsh
10:23.55	update accounts set balance = 670 where account_id = 990022

During fast recovery, SQL Server doesn't need to redo the first transaction, since the checkpoint at 10:19.55 wrote it to disk. However, the second transaction needs to be rerun, since the system crashed after the transaction was committed but before the disk was synchronized with memory during a checkpoint. On the other hand, SQL Server doesn't rerun the third transaction, since there was no commit transaction entry in the log.

What information does SQL Server log?

SQL Server logs a number of important database operations, including, but not limited to:

- INSERT
- UPDATE
- DELETE
- Table alteration
- Index alteration

To help illustrate what the engine logs, let's look at some hypothetical cases. In the first example, suppose that you add a new row into a particular table. The table has the following schema:

```
create table log_demo
(
        log_demo_id integer identity primary key,
        log_demo_numeric smallint,
        log_demo_text varchar(80)
)
create index ld_numeric_ix on log_demo(log_demo_numeric)
create index ld_text_ix on log_demo(log_demo_text)
```

What SQL Server logs largely depends on the underlying table. In this example, new rows require the ensuing information in the transaction log:

1. A record citing newly inserted data, including the actual information

2. A record citing a newly updated index for the primary key (ld_demo_id)

3. A record citing a newly updated index for the ld_numeric_ix index

4. A record citing a newly updated index for the ld_text_ix index

5. If this insert operation requires any new data or index page definitions, a record of these new pages

Items 2, 3, and 4 illustrate why it's wise to be careful when creating new indexes. Consider what would happen if this table had many more columns and indexes. Each insert operation would require the engine to update all of those indexes, as well as place records of these updates in the transaction log. We discussed this concept in much greater detail in Chapter 3.

Next, what happens if you update an existing row in the same table? SQL Server adds this into the transaction log:

1. A record citing newly updated data, including the original and updated information

2. A record citing a newly updated index for the primary key (ld_demo_id) if you changed this value

3. A record citing a newly updated index for the ld_numeric_ix index if you changed this value

4. A record citing a newly updated index for the ld_text_ix index if you changed this value

5. If this update operation requires any new data or index page definitions, a record of these new pages

Excess indexing can hurt even if you're only updating data, since the engine is forced to update any affected indexes, as well as make a record of these updates in the transaction log.

Finally, if you delete a row from this table, here's what gets logged:

1. A record citing deleted data, including the original information
2. A record citing a newly updated index for the primary key (ld_demo_id)
3. A record citing a newly updated index for the ld_numeric_ix index
4. A record citing a newly updated index for the ld_text_ix index
5. If this update operation frees any data or index pages, a record of these freed pages

When does SQL Server make transaction log entries?

When you initiate a transaction with a BEGIN TRANSACTION command, SQL Server makes a record of this in the log. The transaction is assigned an identifier, which is then associated with the balance of operations for the transaction.

Most transactions are logged; there is no way to disable transaction logging. The only exceptions are for specific types of operations, including bulk copies, SELECT INTO, and the UPDATETEXT and WRITETEXT statements (in certain situations).

SQL Server writes information about transactions into the transaction log in advance of modifying the actual data in the tables. During a checkpoint, SQL Server synchronizes the contents of the transaction log with the underlying data. After the checkpoint is finished, the data tables reflect all transactions committed prior to the beginning of the checkpoint. We discuss checkpoints elsewhere in this chapter; it's a good idea to familiarize yourself with the relationship between transaction logging and checkpoints.

Sizing the transaction log

It's important to correctly size your system's transaction log. You can start by allocating approximately 15 to 25 percent of your total database disk storage to the transaction log. For example, if your database is 100 megabytes, you can start out by assigning 15 to 25 megabytes to the transaction log. A number of factors affect the transaction log's overall usage, including:

- **The amount of data affected by INSERT, UPDATE, and DELETE statements.** An application that performs primarily read-only data access is not likely to require a large transaction log, since the log is used only when information is modified. Conversely, if your application performs millions of these operations each day, you can count on needing a larger transaction log.

- **The overall volume of data affected by these operations.** If your application performs frequent data modifications but the average size of these alterations isn't large, you may not need an enormous transaction log.

- **The amount of time specified in the recovery interval parameter.** Recall that the recovery interval parameter helps control how often checkpoints occur. The longer it takes between checkpoints, the larger the transaction log needs to be.

- **Your transaction log storage strategy.** If you're saving the transaction log to media infrequently, as opposed to automatically truncating the log, you'll need to add more size to your transaction log. You always have the option of frequently saving the log to media, however, which you can use as a tactic to avoid creating an overly large transaction log. Also, remember that automatically truncating the transaction log means that you're willing to "lose" transactions between data backups if your system should experience a serious failure, since there's no way to restore transactions once your truncate the log.

You specify initial transaction log size when you create your database. If you use the CREATE DATABASE statement, you can specify log size with the following syntax:

```
[LOG ON database_device [= size]
     [, database_device [= size]]...]
```

If you're using the SQL Enterprise Manager, you set the transaction log size by using this screen:

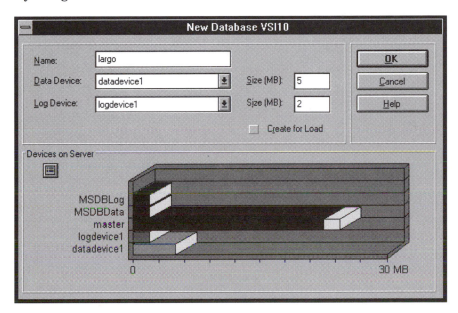

Figure 12.22

This dialog box is slightly different in SQL Server 6.5:

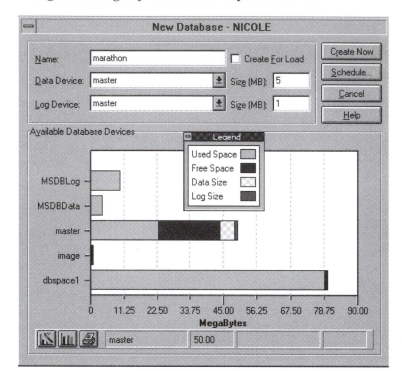

Figure 12.23

If you plan on having the data and transaction log on the same database device, you have the option of leaving the transaction log size value empty. This means that the data and transaction log will share the device and that the transaction log will consume only as much space as necessary. For the balance of this section, however, let's assume that you're using different database devices to hold your data and transaction log.

Generally, while you're experimenting with log size, it's better to size your transaction log smaller than larger. If you find that you've made the transaction log too small, it's easy to add space. However, if you've made the log too large, it's not easy to reduce its size without a significant amount of work. If you need to make the transaction log bigger, you can increase the size in one of two ways:

1. By using the ALTER DATABASE command and 'sp_logdevice' stored procedure. For example, suppose that you want to add 50 megabytes to the 'acquisition' database. The syntax for adding log space would be:

```
alter database acquisition on logdevice5 = 50
sp_logdevice acquisition, logdevice5
```

2. By using the SQL Enterprise Manager expand database screen. This screen lets you pick a preallocated device and then extra assign storage to the transaction log:

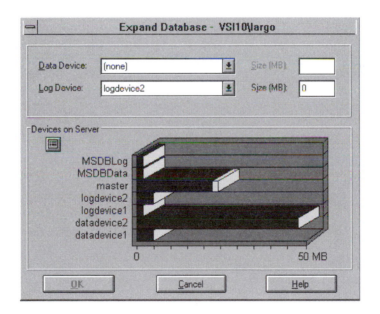

Figure 12.24

The updated version of this screen looks like this:

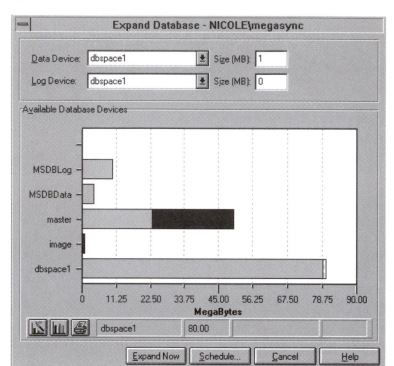

Figure 12.25

Once you've resolved to increase the transaction log size, it's a good idea to back up the master database before and after the alteration. This protects you if your system encounters difficulty once the change has been made.

Examples

Let's look at a few examples of different system profiles, along with corresponding transaction log sizing decisions.

In the first case, suppose that you're administering a database that will be used as an executive information system. The system tracks sales data from all of your organization's stores. Data is loaded nightly from a variety of other systems. The data arrives in text files, and you plan to use the bcp utility to load it into your tables. As part of this loading operation, you plan to drop and then re-create indexes. No other users are on the system at this time. During the day, users only read data; there are no write operations. You anticipate total database size to be about five gigabytes at any one time, although management (and your experience) have both told you that this number will probably grow.

How should you size the transaction log? In this scenario, there are at least two factors pointing to a smaller transaction log:

1. **You can reduce transaction log usage by "turning off" bcp's transaction logging.** We discussed this in Chapter 7, but it bears repeating here: You can configure your database to let the bcp utility skip transaction logging. This has the effect of speeding up large data loads, while minimizing transaction log usage. Since you're loading from text files, you can always reload if bcp encounters an error. This diminishes the importance of transaction logging.

2. **Your users won't be updating data.** Since this system is strictly read-only, you can expect that your transaction log won't be seeing heavy use.

Given these facts, you can probably assign a transaction log of 10 percent of the overall data size, which yields 500 megabytes in this case. Realistically, even this number is probably too high, but since you know that your database will grow over time, the proportion of log space to database space will only diminish.

The next case is radically different from the previous situation. In this circumstance, you're going to administer a banking teller system. You expect a total of one gigabyte of data on your system at any one time. Your management has told you that there will be large numbers of individual transactions happening each second throughout the day. They've also made it clear that all transactions must be saved; losing a transaction due to a system outage isn't acceptable. Both of these factors point to an increased reliance on your transaction log. This means at least two things:

1. **You must size the transaction log to be big enough.** If you make the log too small, you run the very real risk of running out of space. Having your applications come to a complete halt won't be good for your reputation.

2. **You must back up the log frequently.** One strategy for dealing with a full transaction log is to truncate the log on checkpoints. This won't work in your environment, however, since you need to restore all transactions in the event of a system failure. This means that you should perform frequent transaction log backups to permanent media, such as tape. It's also a good idea to mirror the transaction log to another disk drive, thereby reducing the risk of a catastrophic disk failure. Remember that only mirroring the transaction log doesn't protect your table data should you have a disk failure. See our discussion on mirroring in Chapter 11.

In this type of environment, it's better to oversize the transaction log. Since you have an overall data space of 1 gigabyte, you decide to allocate 25 percent of this space to the transaction log. This translates to a transaction log of 250 megabytes.

For the last case, you're administering a mixed-use human resources database. Users add, update, and delete data throughout the day, but they also run reports and queries. Your data amounts to a fairly steady 500 megabytes. During your design meetings, your users told you that response time is very important. They've also remarked that if the system goes down during the day, they'll be able to reenter transactions. In a typical mixed-use environment, it's a good idea to choose the middle ground when sizing the transaction log. In this case, you figure on a total transaction log of 15 percent of the total space. Since you have 500 megabytes, this amounts to a 75 megabyte transaction log. Since your users have told you that they can re-create any of the day's transactions if necessary, you probably don't need to perform frequent transaction log backups. You might even be able to truncate the log on a checkpoint. Remember that if you truncate your transaction log, you won't be able to reapply those transactions should you restore a data backup.

Placing the transaction log

SQL Server gives you a variety of options regarding where you store the transaction log. For most read/write applications, the transaction log is one of the most heavily accessed disk structures. Since I/O is often the bottleneck on today's fast systems, it's a good idea to spread the I/O load among as many devices as possible. To quicken I/O performance, consider placing the transaction log on a different physical device than the database. Another reason to place the transaction log on a different device is that this strategy lets you perform periodic transaction log dumps, which helps increase database recoverability.

Examples

Let's look at a few examples of how you can determine if you should place your transaction log on another device.

In the first case, suppose that you're administering an executive information system that tracks enrollment in your company's extended warranty program. You update the database each night, when there are no other users on the system. Is it necessary to move the transaction log to another device? In this instance, probably not. Given that you don't expect a high volume of transaction log activity during normal system operating hours, you probably won't see much of an additional performance gain by separating the transaction log from the data itself. One caveat about this recommendation is this: If your application makes heavy use of temporary or work tables, it still may be a good idea to separate the log from the data. This may be necessary because SQL Server logs temporary table write operations just as it logs regular table write operations. Therefore, you might make heavier use of the transaction log than you expect.

Next, assume that you're the database administrator on a distributed, high-volume reservations system. Users add and modify data around-the-clock. What should you do about your transaction log in this situation? In cases such as this, where you expect frequent, continual access to the transaction log, it's wise to place the log on another device. How can you select which device to use as the transaction log's new home? In general, try picking a device with the fastest controller. Another way is select a device that is serviced by a different controller than the device that holds your most active tables. Try to achieve a balance among your disk controllers: Overloading one controller while leaving another nearly inactive is not a good idea. Remember that it's often not enough to store the transaction log on a separate device; you must also make sure that this device is not overly used by nondatabase applications. Otherwise, it's possible that transaction log access might be unduly delayed by these other processes.

Finally, what should you do if you're maintaining a number of small (less than 10 megabyte) databases? Is it worth your time to keep the transaction logs on different devices than their data? For small databases, especially those that don't see high volumes of daily changes, you don't need to take the trouble to off-load the transaction logs.

sp_logdevice

The 'sp_logdevice' system stored procedure lets you place all future log pages on a different device. This can be useful when you want to transfer your transaction logging to another device for performance reasons. However, this stored procedure only affects future transaction log pages, so your initial log pages still remain on the original device. Therefore, it's a good idea to place your transaction log on a separate device when you first create your database.

Monitoring log usage

There are diverse ways that you can track your database's transaction log status. One way is by using the SQL Enterprise Manager's Edit Database screen:

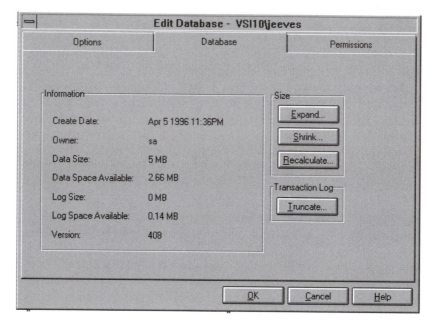

Figure 12.26

Another method is to run the DBCC command:

```
1> dbcc checktable(syslogs)
2> go
Checking syslogs
The total number of data pages in this table is 5.
*** NOTICE:  Space used on the log segment is 0.01 Mbytes, 0.12.
*** NOTICE:  Space free on the log segment is 8.18 Mbytes, 99.88.
Table has 148 data rows.
```

Finally, you can get log space information for all databases on your system by running:

```
1> dbcc sqlperf (logspace)
2> go
 Database Name  Log Size (MB)   Log Space Used (%)   Status
 ------------   ------------    ------------------   ------
 megasync       2.000000        0.097656             0
```

```
benchmark    8.000000    0.097656    0
msdb         2.000000    0.683594    0
pubs         0.000000    0.000000    1
tempdb       0.000000    0.000000    1
model        0.000000    0.000000    1
master       0.000000    0.000000    1

(7 rows affected)
```

Dumping the transaction log

SQL Server lets you dump databases and transaction logs to disk or tape. This is a crucial part of any database administration strategy, since it lets you restore data if you suffer a serious disk failure. To dump a database, you need to create a dump device, which can be done via the 'sp_adddumpdevice' stored procedure or via the SQL Enterprise Manager:

Figure 12.27

This dialog box has been updated in SQL Server 6.5:

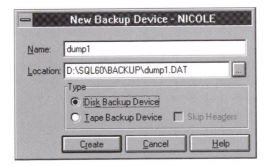

Figure 12.28

Once you've added a dump device, you can use the DUMP statement or
SQL Enterprise Manager to initiate a dump:

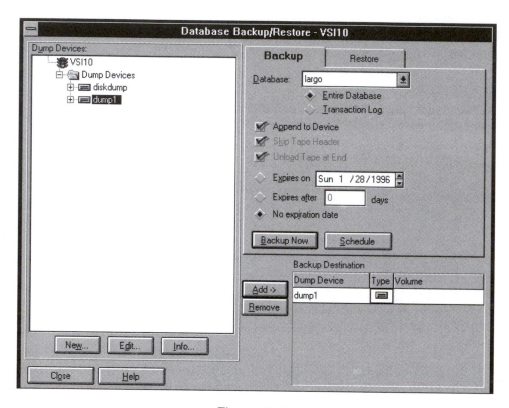

Figure 12.29

SQL Server 6.5 makes substantial changes to the backup initiation screen:

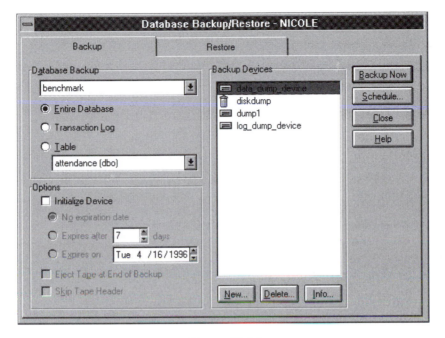

Figure 12.30

Remember that to dump the transaction log by itself to a dump device, you must have stored the log on a different segment than the database itself. See the "Transaction Log Placement" section of this chapter for more details on how to relocate the transaction log.

If you use the SHOWPLAN command, you'll see that this type of operation has a query type of DUMPXACT.

If you try to dump the transaction log to the same device that you dump your database and you've already set the 'truncate log on checkpoint' option, you'll get an error message back from SQL Server:

```
DUMP TRANsaction is not allowed while the trunc. log on
chkpt. option is enabled: use DUMP DATABASE, or disable
the option with sp_dboption.
```

Dumping the log to another device is not affected by the 'truncate log on checkpoint' option.

Once you've chosen which information you want to back up, SQL Server lets you schedule the backup at a set date and time:

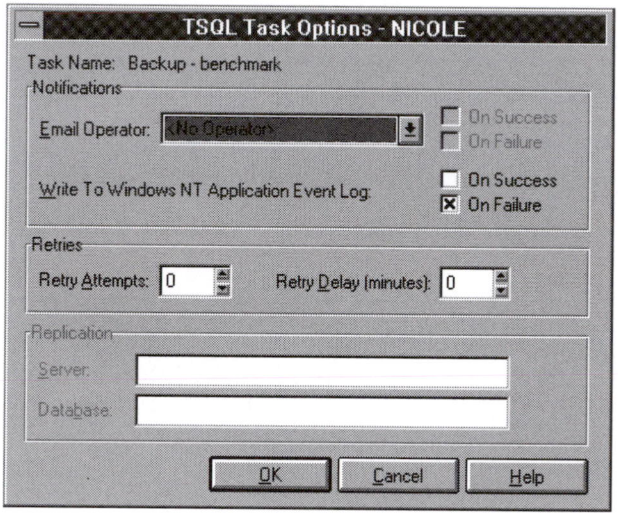

Figure 12.31

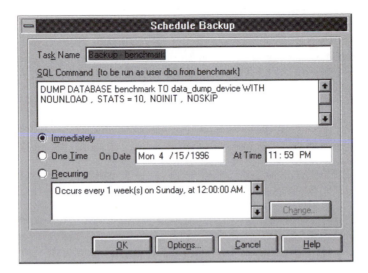

Figure 12.32

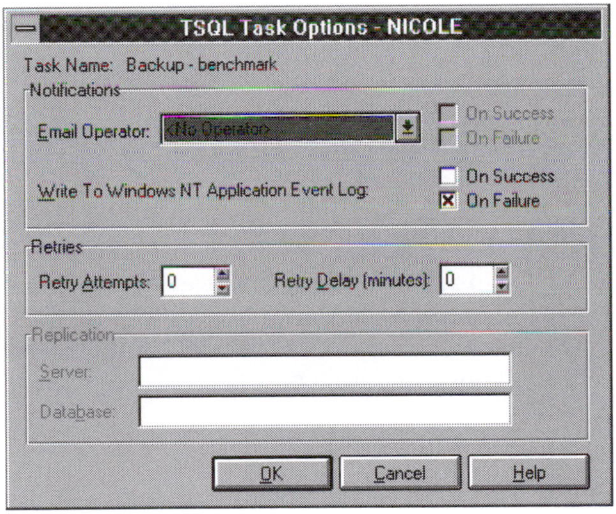

Figure 12.33

Truncating the transaction log

The transaction log is an integral part of SQL Server's operations. For production environments, it's a good idea to back up the transaction log periodically, since you'll need it if you have to manually restore a database and its transactions. Once you've backed up the transaction log, you can free its space. However, if you don't free up the transaction log's space frequently enough, and you run out of room in the log, all logged database operations will cease and you'll get the following message:

```
Msg 1105, Level 17, State 2
Can't allocate space for object 'Syslogs' in database
'jerome' because the 'logsegment' segment is full. If
you ran out of space in Syslogs, dump the transaction
log. Otherwise, use ALTER DATABASE or sp_extendsegment
to increase the size of the segment.
```

For this reason, there may be occasions when you want SQL Server to recycle the transaction log's space as quickly as possible. You can do this by instructing the engine to truncate the transaction log whenever it performs a checkpoint. The 'truncate log on checkpoint' option causes this behavior. When SQL Server truncates the log, it frees up all space up to the page that holds information about the most recent open (not committed or rolled back) transaction. Note that this only happens if the checkpoint was automatic; if you requested it through the CHECKPOINT statement, the log is not truncated, regardless of configuration options.

If you do elect to truncate the log after every checkpoint, be aware that if you suffer a catastrophic disk failure, you'll only be able to restore from your last data backup. Any transactions that took place after the backup will be lost, since you won't have the necessary transaction logs to recover. This may not be a problem in environments where the data doesn't change very often, but for systems that are heavily modified, this may be unacceptable.

Using checkpoints

Checkpoints are important events for SQL Server. During a checkpoint, SQL Server synchronizes the contents of the transaction log and the disk by performing these steps:

1. Flush all dirty pages to the disk. A dirty page is defined as a buffer cache page that has had modifications made to it since the last checkpoint. These modifications need to be written to the disk to ensure data integrity.

2. Truncate the transaction log, if the 'truncate log on checkpoint' option has been set. We discuss transaction log truncation in more detail elsewhere in this chapter.

3. Note the time of the checkpoint in the transaction log. This timestamp is very important for future automatic recoveries, since it tells SQL Server exactly when the transaction log were synchronized.

Checkpoints can be requested by the user or run automatically by SQL Server. Users can request checkpoints by running the CHECKPOINT command. Automatic checkpoints occur:

- When the time specified in the 'recovery interval' parameter has arrived; we discuss recovery interval below

- When shutting down the database engine

- When you change a system configuration option with the 'sp_dboption' procedure

Recovery interval

At the start of this section, we discussed how SQL Server uses automatic recovery to ensure database integrity upon system restart. One important setting that affects automatic recovery, along with transaction log and checkpoint performance, is the recovery interval. This setting tells SQL Server the maximum allowable amount of time (in minutes) per database that the engine can take when recovering after a system failure. If SQL Server determines that the transaction log has become so full that the amount of recovery time would exceed the recovery interval setting, SQL Server performs a checkpoint. You can set the recovery interval by running the 'sp_configure' stored procedure. You can also set it via the SQL Enterprise Manager's Server Configuration screen. The default value is five minutes; you can set it anywhere between 1 and 32767 minutes. Once you make this change, it takes effect immediately; there is no need to restart SQL Server.

If you find that your transaction log is filling up or if you determine that checkpoints are taking too long, consider lowering the recovery interval parameter. This forces SQL Server to make more frequent checkpoints, which should reduce the overall amount of time it takes to complete this important operation.

Note that there may be situations where SQL Server still takes a long time to complete its recovery, despite your recovery interval setting. Generally, this happens when a large, lengthy transaction was running prior to a sudden system shutdown. The engine may require substantially more time than specified by the recovery interval parameter to come up during this kind of situation.

Managing log usage

As we've seen elsewhere in the chapter and book, it's a good idea to proactively manage your usage of the transaction log. In this section, we briefly itemize these suggestions. How can you actively manage your log usage?

- **Size the log correctly for your environment.**   We've discussed this topic in detail elsewhere, but it bears repeating: One of the easiest ways to control log usage is to have sized the log correctly in the first place.

- **Disable transaction logging for unnecessary operations.**   You can "turn off" logging for certain types of operations, such as the bcp utility and the SELECT INTO command. You can control this behavior on the SQL Enterprise Manager's edit database option screen. Be careful when choosing this option; you won't be able to use the transaction log to restore your system's state in the event of a problem.

- **Avoid long transactions.**   SQL Server can only free the transaction log up to the beginning of the oldest uncompleted transaction. This can lead to a "frozen" system, until you finally close out the offending transaction. One of the most common causes of this problem is application code that lets the user leave a transaction open indefinitely. You can prevent this by always making sure that the begin and end of your transactions are not separated by user input: It's better to let the user enter data, then start and finish the transaction.

- **Regularly back up or truncate the transaction log.**   Regardless of how you handle your completed transaction logs, you must take action. You can simply truncate the transaction log on checkpoints, but remember that this means that the contents of the log won't be available if you have to restore from a database backup at some point in the future. If you want to keep your transaction logs, you'll need to back them up regularly.

- **Avoid completely full transaction logs.**   You should always try to prevent the log from completely filling up. However, if this happens, you can reclaim log space by simply dumping the transaction log with the 'truncate_only' or 'no_log' options. This discards the transaction log without making a backup copy and should only be used when you've completely run out of space and need to free up log space immediately. If you're in a production environment and have just run the dump transaction command, consider backing up your database right away, since you won't be able to use the transaction log to recover data in the event of a major system failure.

Transaction logs and mirroring

We discussed this important topic earlier, but it bears repeating here: If you only have enough disk drives to mirror one object, that object should be the transaction log. This simple procedure greatly increases your data's chances of surviving a serious disk failure, since there will be a second workable copy of the transaction log.

SQL Server – Log object

You can use the SQL Server Log object in the SQL Performance Monitor to oversee the current state of your transaction logs. In this section, we examine the statistics tracked by this object. You can add these statistics to your performance chart:

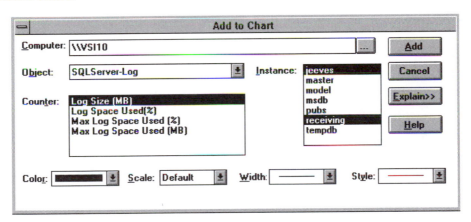

Figure 12.34

Statistics

Log size: The log size statistic shows the current transaction log size for a particular database. Unless you're changing the transaction log size on-the-fly, you won't see any changes to this statistic.

Log space used: The log space statistic used shows the current state of the transaction log's free space. You can monitor this statistic to see how close the transaction log is to capacity. In the following sample, the transaction log is getting close to being filled:

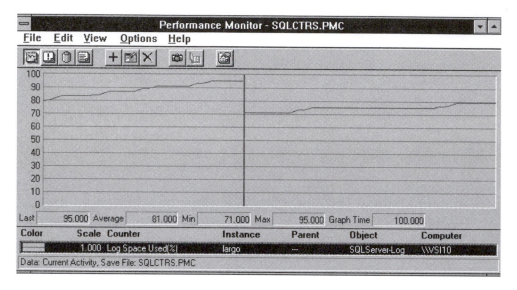

Figure 12.35

Remember that once the log fills up, all database modification activity halts until the log is truncated. Applications receive this error message:

```
Msg 1105, Level 17, State 2
Can't allocate space for object 'Syslogs' in database
'largo' because the 'logsegment' segment is full. If you
ran out of space in Syslogs, dump the transaction log.
Otherwise, use ALTER DATABASE or sp_extendsegment to
increase the size of the segment.
```

Once you receive this message, you must either dump or truncate the transaction log. After taking this step, you'll be able to continue with your normal operations.

Max log space used percentage: SQL Server 6.5 introduces this new statistic, which shows the maximum percentage of used transaction log space for a particular database. How can you interpret this information? It's best to think of this new indicator as a transaction log "high-water mark" that can help you decide if your logs are sized correctly.

For example, suppose that shortly after starting SQL Server, a database's transaction log reaches 25 percent of capacity before you back up the log and free its space. If you were monitoring this statistic, it would reach 25 percent and stay there, despite your freeing the transaction log. Later, if you reached 65 percent of transaction log capacity, this indicator would climb to, and hold at, 65 percent until:

1. You restarted the engine.

   —or—

2. The amount of used transaction log space percentage exceeded this number.

This metric can be very useful in trying to determine if your transaction logs are sized correctly. If a database's transaction log was too small, you would observe this statistic hovering above 85 percent or more. This would mean that your activities caused the transaction log to fill up to 85 percent of capacity and that you might benefit from increasing transaction log space. Conversely, if this number never passed the 50 percent level, you've probably allocated too much space to the transaction log, since you never reach 50 percent of capacity.

Max log size: This indicator, new in SQL Server 6.5, shows us the maximum amount of transaction log space that was used for a particular database since SQL Server was most recently started. This statistic is similar to the 'maximum log space used percentage' indicator; the difference is that this value is measured in megabytes, rather than in percentages. You can also use this metric to ascertain whether you've defined the right amount of transaction log space. If you quickly reach the limit of the transaction log's storage capacity, you probably need to add space. On the other hand, if you use only a small fraction of available transaction log volume, you defined an overly large transaction log.

Examples

Let's look at a few examples of how you can use the SQL Server logs object in the performance monitor. In the first example, we're monitoring log space usage for the 'quasar' database:

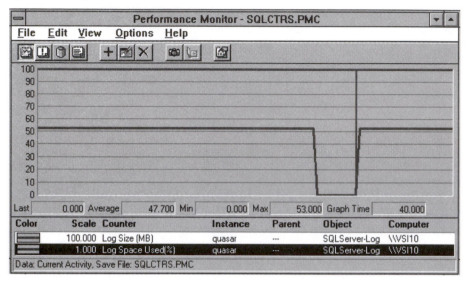

Figure 12.36

Notice how we've changed the scale of the log space element: By raising the scale, we're able to have this indicator stay at the top of the graph. This makes it easier to see the effects of log space usage. We've just cleared the transaction log: Observe how the log space used element has decreased from approximately 52 percent down to near 0.

In the next example, we've set an alert to notify us if the transaction log used percentage reaches 60 percent or more:

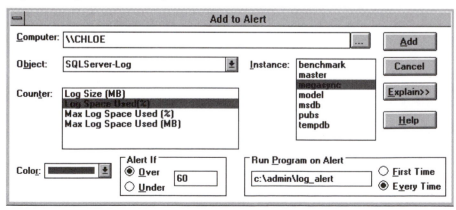

Figure 12.37

Taking this method one step further, we programmed this alert to run a program that dumps the transaction log when SQL Server detects this threshold.

Finally, we've added the new indicators found in SQL Server 6.5 that track the maximum log usage percentages:

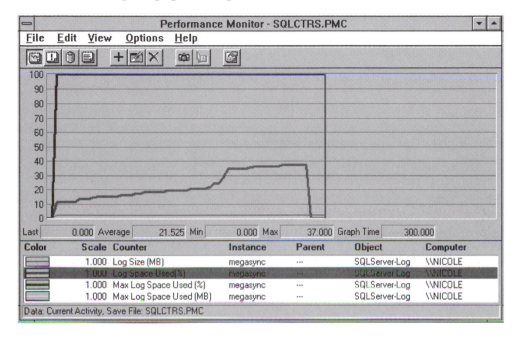

Figure 12.38

Notice the two uppermost lines: the top line represents the maximum log usage percentage, which reached 100 percent earlier in our session. The next line down is the current log usage percentage. We've just dumped the transaction log, so this line drops. However, the top line stays at 100 percent, since that represents the maximum log usage percentage and can't be reset by dumping the log.

Configuration parameters

Logwrite sleep: It's most efficient if the SQL Server transaction log buffer is full or nearly full when a write to the log occurs. You can help control this behavior by setting the logwrite sleep parameter. This configuration option tells the engine to delay writing to the transaction log if the buffer is not yet full. The valid range of values is between 0 and 500 milliseconds. For example, if you set 'logwrite sleep' to 100, SQL Server waits 100 milliseconds before writing to the transaction log if the transaction log buffer is not yet full. If you set the value to -1, SQL Server never delays writing to the transaction log, regardless of the current state of the buffer.

Take care when configuring logwrite sleep. Any performance gains that you are able to realize by delaying the log writing event can be offset by a potential loss of data. This data loss can happen should SQL Server experience a failure before the committed transaction log records have been written to disk. We also discuss logwrite sleep and its relation to the 'transactions per log record' statistic in our section on I/O topics.

The DBCC utility and engine information

In Chapter 9, we saw how to use DBCC to learn more about our system's disk state. However, DBCC can help us in other areas as well. In this section, we explore some of these additional alternatives.

MEMUSAGE

You can get a detailed overview of your system's memory status by running DBCC MEMUSAGE:

```
DBCC MEMUSAGE

Memory Usage:
```

	Meg.	2K Blks	Bytes
Configured Memory:	8.0000	4096	8388608
Code Size:	1.7166	879	1800000
Static Structures:	0.2385	123	250048
Locks:	0.2480	127	260000
Open Objects:	0.1068	55	112000
Open Databases:	0.0031	2	3220
User Context Areas:	0.8248	423	864824
Page Cache:	3.3020	1691	3462416
Proc Headers:	0.0795	41	83326
Proc Cache Bufs:	1.3359	684	1400832

```
Buffer Cache, Top 20:
```

DB Id	Object Id	Index Id	2K Buffers
1	1	0	14
1	640005311	0	11

1	36	0	7
1	2	0	5
1	5	0	4
1	99	0	4
1	1	2	3
1	3	0	2
1	5	1	2
1	45	255	2
2	2	0	2
3	2	0	2
4	2	0	2
5	2	0	2
6	2	0	2
6	8	0	2
8	2	0	2
1	1	1	1
1	2	1	1
1	3	1	1

```
Procedure Cache, Top 5:


Procedure Name: sp_server_info
Database Id: 1
Object Id: 361052322
Version: 1
Uid: 1
Type: stored procedure
Number of trees: 0
Size of trees: 0.000000 Mb, 0.000000 bytes, 0 pages
Number of plans: 1
Size of plans: 0.003166 Mb, 3320.000000 bytes, 2 pages

Procedure Name: xp_msver
Database Id: 1
Object Id: 1036530726
Version: 1
Uid: 1
Type: stored procedure
Number of trees: 0
Size of trees: 0.000000 Mb, 0.000000 bytes, 0 pages
Number of plans: 1
Size of plans: 0.000578 Mb, 606.000000 bytes, 1 pages

Procedure Name: xp_snmp_getstate
```

```
Database Id: 1
Object Id: 937054374
Version: 1
Uid: 1
Type: stored procedure
Number of trees: 0
Size of trees: 0.000000 Mb, 0.000000 bytes, 0 pages
Number of plans: 1
Size of plans: 0.000578 Mb, 606.000000 bytes, 1 pages

Procedure Name: xp_sqlregister
Database Id: 1
Object Id: 969054488
Version: 1
Uid: 1
Type: stored procedure
Number of trees: 0
Size of trees: 0.000000 Mb, 0.000000 bytes, 0 pages
Number of plans: 1
Size of plans: 0.000578 Mb, 606.000000 bytes, 1 pages

Procedure Name: sp_sqlregister
Database Id: 1
Object Id: 1001054602
Version: 1
Uid: 1
Type: stored procedure
Number of trees: 0
Size of trees: 0.000000 Mb, 0.000000 bytes, 0 pages
Number of plans: 1
Size of plans: 0.000822 Mb, 862.000000 bytes, 1 pages
```

What does all this information mean? DBCC MEMUSAGE begins by reporting on the current state of overall system memory. This covers a number of important indicators, including:

- How much memory is assigned to SQL Server
- Current lock memory requirements
- Current open object memory requirements
- Procedure cache information

The report describes several other internal SQL Server memory structures as well.

SQL Server uses three units of measure for all reported numbers:

- Megabytes
- 2-K blocks
- Bytes

Next, DBCC MEMUSAGE provides a detailed memory profile of the 20 biggest objects found in the buffer cache. You can use this information to get a better understanding of SQL Server's current caching profile. For example, since the report shows the database and object IDs, it is not hard to pinpoint the database and object name by using simple SQL queries:

```
select * from sysdatabases where dbid = 1
```

Once we know the database name, we can then switch to this database to run a query against the sysobjects table:

```
select * from sysobjects where id = 640005311
```

This profiling knowledge can help you go a long way when trying to decipher a difficult performance puzzle.

Finally, DBCC MEMUSAGE gives us a itemized report describing the current procedure cache condition for each of the top 12 objects. These objects can include:

- Defaults
- Rules
- Stored procedures
- Triggers
- Views

In the example above, there are only five objects in the procedure cache. For each object, SQL Server describes several characteristics. The most important information relates to the number of trees and plans for the object. DBCC depicts the size of all trees and plans in megabytes, bytes, and pages.

OPENTRAN

One common dilemma facing SQL Server administrators is learning the current state of transactions. Remember that long or never-ending transactions are the cause of many obstacles to a well-running system. These barriers can include spurious long transaction messages, poor response, and overflowing transaction logs. Luckily, you can use the DBCC OPENTRAN command to get more information about the oldest active transaction, which, in many cases, is the culprit. For example, suppose that you receive a message that the transaction log for the 'largo' database is full. As part of your research, you run:

```
dbcc opentran (largo)

Transaction Information for database: largo

Oldest active transaction:
        SPID            : 14
        UID             : 3
        SUID            : 3
        Name            : user_transaction
        RID             : (3335 , 33)
        Time Stamp      : 0001 00010464
        Start Time      : Feb 25 1996 12:26:34:430PM
```

How can you understand this report? The 'start time' item refers to when the transaction began. If today's date is February 28, we know that this transaction has been open a long time. The 'time stamp' element is meaningful to SQL Server only as an internal timestamp indicator. Next, we can look at the 'spid' number. This number is SQL Server's internal system process ID. You can run 'sp_who' to get more detailed data:

```
sp_who

spid status    loginame hostname blk  dbname cmd
---- --------  -------- -------- ---- ------ ----------------
 .      .         .        .       .     .      .
14   sleeping ken      VSI10    0    largo  AWAITING COMMAND
 .      .         .        .       .     .      .
```

It appears that Ken, running on host VSI10, is the user who corresponds to system process ID 14. Another way to get the user name would be to link the UID output from DBCC OPENTRAN to the 'sysusers' table:

```
select * from sysusers where uid = 3

suid   uid    gid    name                       environ
------ ------ ------ ------------------------   -------
3      3      0      ken                        (null)
```

Moving on in DBCC OPENTRAN's output, we next examine the 'name' element. In this case, name is set to 'user_transaction,' which means that this particular transaction was started by a user, rather than by SQL Server itself. RID refers to the current row ID and operation ID accessed by the transaction.

What happens if there are no active transactions when you run this report? SQL Server returns a message to this effect:

```
Transaction Information for database: largo
     No active open transactions.
```

PERFMON

The PERFMON option lets you combine several individual SQLPERF options into one report. These options include:

- IOSTATS
- LRUSTATS
- NETSTATS

We'll cover each of these topics in more detail in the SQLPERF section.

PINTABLE

In normal operation, SQL Server allocates shared memory pages on an as-needed basis: The engine continually scans the buffer pool, looking for pages that no longer need to be kept in shared memory. For most environments and applications, this is fine. As an administrator, however, there may be instances where you want SQL Server to keep all or part of a table in memory, regardless of whether the engine wants to use those pages for something else. You can use the DBCC PINTABLE command to make this happen. Let's look at an example that illustrates how to use this option.

Suppose that you are administering a system that makes use of a relatively small lookup table. For fastest results, you want this table always resident in shared memory. If you use DBCC PINTABLE, SQL Server keeps the table's pages alive in shared memory. Note that this doesn't happen all at once: As you read the pages from the table into shared memory, SQL Server then prevents other pages from taking your special table's space. To run this command, you need to know the database ID and table ID:

```
DBCC PINTABLE (6,80003316)

WARNING: Pinning tables should be carefully considered.
If a pinned table is larger or grows larger than the
available data cache, the server may need to be
restarted and the table unpinned.
```

There are very few SQL Server operations that result in a warning message. This is one that does. The reason that SQL Server warns you about pinning tables in memory is that it's possible that you might fill up so many pages that the engine may not be able to continue. You would then need to shut down the engine, restart it, and then unpin the table. For this reason, make sure that you pin only those tables that are substantially smaller than available shared memory. Also, remember that SQL Server has very sophisticated algorithms that help it determine when to free up buffer pool pages: Chances are that your performance will be as good or better if you simply let these algorithms do their work.

UNPINTABLE

The opposite of the DBCC PINTABLE operation is DBCC UNPINTABLE. When you choose this command, SQL Server gradually replaces the table's pinned pages with other pages. This doesn't happen all at once: If no other activity happens on your system, the pinned table's pages stay resident. As we saw earlier, you may have to unpin a previously pinned table if it has caused complications for SQL Server.

PROCCACHE

This option, new with SQL Server 6.5, lets you receive the same information about stored procedure caching through DBCC as you would learn from the SQL Performance Monitor:

```
DBCC PROCCACHE
```

num proc buffs	num proc buffs used	num proc buffs active
688	13	3

proc cache size	proc cache used	proc cache active
684	149	49

ROWLOCK

As we saw in our analysis of SQL Server's locking options, version 6.5 lets administrators and developers implement row-level locking for insert operations on certain tables. You can use the DBCC command to enable or disable this capability, known as Insert Row Locking (IRL):

```
DBCC ROWLOCK (6,16003088,1)
```

This command turns on IRL for the table that corresponds to object ID 16003088 in database 6. The object ID column maps to the 'id' column in the current database's 'sysobjects' table, while the database number can be found in the 'dbid' column in 'master' database's 'sysdatabases' table. The final parameter is a flag that can be either 1 (enable) or 0 (disable).

If this method is too cumbersome for you, consider writing a stored procedure to handle the system table lookups.

SQLPERF

As we've discussed, SQL Server often provides administrators with a diversity of alternatives when searching for performance information. The performance monitor and SQL Enterprise Manager utilities both furnish crucial statistics. However, don't forget that DBCC also affords the same figures. You can use the SQLPERF option, along with any or all of the following subparameters:

- **IOSTATS.** This covers I/O information since the last time that you started the server. We cover these indicators in more detail later in this chapter.

Statistic	Value
Log Flush Requests	33.0
Log Logical Page IO	18.0
Log Physical IO	24.0
Log Flush Average	1.375
Log Logical IO Average	0.75
Batch Writes	24.0
Batch Average Size	1.84615
Batch Max Size	4.0
Page Reads	202.0
Single Page Writes	90.0
Reads Outstanding	0.0
Writes Outstanding	0.0
Transactions	87.0
Transactions/Log Write	3.625

```
(14 row(s) affected)
```

- **LRUSTATS.** LRU stands for the Least Recently Used queue, which is the internal shared memory structure. SQL Server presents a number of important shared memory parameters, all of which we cover later in this chapter.

```
Statistic                       Value
------------------------------- --------------------
Cache Hit Ratio                 91.8033
Cache Flushes                   0.0
Free Page Scan (Avg)            0.0
Free Page Scan (Max)            0.0
Min Free Buffers                204.0
Cache Size                      1627.0
Free Buffers                    1432.0

(7 row(s) affected)
```

- **NETSTATS.** This criterion displays network utilization numbers, which we describe in this chapter's section on memory.

```
Statistic                       Value
------------------------------- --------------------
Network Reads                   0.0
Network Writes                  923.0
Command Queue Length            0.0
Max Command Queue Length        0.0
Worker Threads                  5.0
Max Worker Threads              5.0
Network Threads                 0.0
Max Network Threads             0.0

(8 row(s) affected)
```

- **RASTATS.** SQL Server uses refined techniques for read data in advance; this parameter cites the current statistics for read-ahead operations. We explain these parameters in the efficient memory management section of this chapter.

```
Statistic                       Value
------------------------------- --------------------
RA Pages Found in Cache         32.0
RA Pages Placed in Cache        11.0
RA Physical IO                  4.0
Used Slots                      0.0
```

- **THREADS.** We have discussed threading and how Windows NT and SQL Server use this powerful technique. Let's examine how you can use the THREADS parameter in conjunction with DBCC SQLP-ERF:

```
DBCC SQLPERF (THREADS)
```

Spid	Thread ID	Status	LoginName	IO	CPU	MemUsage
1		sleeping	(null)	0	0	1
2		sleeping	(null)	0	0	0
3		sleeping	(null)	15	0	0
4		sleeping	(null)	3	0	0
5		sleeping	(null)	0	0	0
6		sleeping	(null)	0	0	0
7		sleeping	(null)	0	0	0
8		sleeping	(null)	0	0	0
9		sleeping	(null)	0	0	0
10	37(0x25)	runnable	sa	5	581	1
11	69(0x45)	runnable	laoshi	12	6640	5
12	162(0xa2)	runnable	buddy	0	1422	5
13	61(0x3d)	runnable	ken	0	351	5

(13 row(s) affected)

This report lists:

1. **SQL Server's system process ID.** This is a number that the database engine assigns to the process.

2. **The thread ID.** This is the Windows NT operating system thread identifier.

3. **The thread's state.** A thread can have a number of discrete states.

4. **The thread's owner.** This is the login name of the thread's owner. If the system owns the thread, this indicator shows null.

5. **I/O usage.** This is a count of the number of I/Os performed by the thread.

6. **CPU usage.** This indicates how much CPU the thread has consumed.

7. **Memory usage.** This itemizes the amount of memory employed by the thread.

- **LOGSPACE.** You can use DBCC SQLPERF's LOGSPACE option to get a quick overview of your entire system's current transaction log status:

```
DBCC SQLPERF (LOGSPACE)
```

Database Name	Log Size (MB)	Log Space Used (%)	Status
packages	55.0	76.044932	1

```
largo              200.0          14.995432          0
msdb               2.0            0.292969           0
pubs               0.0            0.0                1
tempdb             0.0            0.0                1
model              0.0            0.0                1
master             0.0            0.0                1
```

(7 row(s) affected)

USEROPTIONS

SQL Server 6.5 introduces a new DBCC parameter: USEROPTIONS. This parameter lets you see what SET options have been enabled for your current connection. For example, look at this script and output:

```
DBCC USEROPTIONS
SET NOCOUNT ON
DBCC USEROPTIONS

output:

Set Option                       Value
------------------------------   -------------------------
textsize                         64512
language                         us_english
dateformat                       mdy
datefirst                        7

(4 row(s) affected)

DBCC execution completed. If DBCC printed error
messages, see your System Administrator.

Set Option                       Value
------------------------------   -------------------------
textsize                         64512
language                         us_english
dateformat                       mdy
datefirst                        7
nocount                          SET

(5 row(s) affected)
```

Chapter 13

Database Parameters and User Configuration

SQL Server provides administrators with a variety of configurable parameters to make database access more efficient. In this chapter, we examine each of these options in more detail. Some of these options don't have a significant effect on performance, whereas others can drastically alter system response. You set these options in a variety of ways, including the SQL Enterprise Manager configuration screen, the 'sp_configure' and 'sp_dboption' stored procedures, and the SQL Enterprise Manager 'Edit Database' screen:

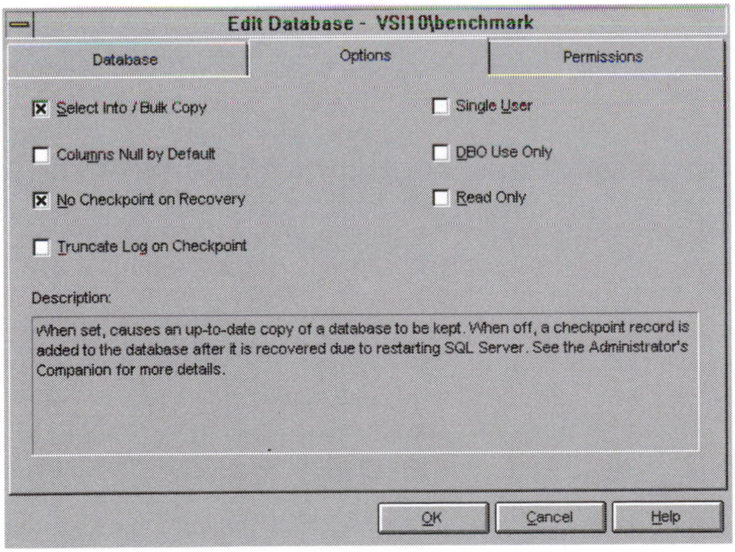

Figure 13.1

Another way to create databases and set database options is to use the 'CREATE DATABASE' SQL statement.

sp_helpdb

Before we describe the various database options you can set, let's examine the 'sp_helpdb' system procedure. You can use this stored procedure to learn about all of your system's databases, or you can get information on a single database only:

```
sp_helpdb
```

```
name      db_size    owner      dbid  created    status
-----     -------    ------     ----  ------     ----------------
largo     7.00  MB   navrochet  6     Jan 28 1996 no options set
master    17.00 MB   sa         1     Jun  7 1995 trunc. log on chkpt.
model     1.00  MB   sa         3     Jun  7 1995 no options set
msdb      4.00  MB   sa         5     Jan 25 1996 trunc. log on chkpt.
pubs      3.00  MB   sa         4     Jun  7 1995 trunc. log on chkpt.
quasar    53.00 MB   natalie    7     Feb 13 1996 no options set
tempdb    2.00 MB    sa         2     Feb 22 1996 select into/bulk-
copy
```

```
sp_helpdb largo
```

```
device_fragments            size           usage
--------------------------   -------------  ----------
datadevice1                 5.00 MB        data only
logdevice1                  2.00 MB        log only
```

Single large database versus multiple small databases

One mistake that SQL Server developers and database administrators frequently make is to divide up their information into several small databases, rather than storing the data within one, larger database. Why is this a problem? Remember from our earlier discussions that one way that SQL Server speeds processing is to take advantage of its memory buffers to reduce disk I/O. These memory buffers hold data, indexes, and stored procedures. When a process needs access to one of these resources, it first looks in the appropriate memory cache area. On a busy system, it's not uncommon to see a very high percentage of these requests satisfied from memory, rather than from disk. This speeds up access by diminishing the number of times that the engine must make a costly disk inquiry.

When you've divided up your data into numerous small databases, chances are that users won't be able to share much of this information, leading to degraded performance. Let's look at an example to help clarify what we mean. Suppose that you're maintaining a manufacturing system that supports your organization's worldwide operations. Further, suppose that this system all resides on one large server. You've chosen to divide your data into separate databases, based on geography. Therefore, you have a great deal of data, subdivided into databases such as 'WestEurope,' 'EastEurope,' 'WestNorthAmerica,' etc. Your reason for doing this was to segregate information so that users would see data only for their particular region. As part of this strategy, you've duplicated a great number of your lookup tables among the small databases. This does indeed keep users from being distracted by nonpertinent information, but it comes at a high price: a greatly reduced potential for memory caching. Even though users may be examining similar information (e.g., identical copies of lookup tables in each database), the engine can't take advantage of memory caching across databases.

For example, what happens if Ted is currently looking for part number 20993 in the 'parts' table in the 'WestNorthAmerica' database and Alex, using the 'EastEurope' database, needs to find the same part? Ted has already pulled the appropriate page into memory, yet Alex won't see that page, because although Alex is reading a row on the same page, he's retrieving it from a different database. If you had used one, large database to hold this data, instead of several small databases, Alex' process wouldn't need to issue a disk read request, since the page would already be in memory. If you multiply the number of unnecessary read requests by the number of users, it's easy to see how performance could be adversely impacted.

Lost caching opportunities don't only affect data; stored procedures can also be shared among users (although the engine needs to generate query plans if the procedure is already in use). This means that in addition to requesting superfluous data reads, users are also missing opportunities to share stored procedure code.

While there certainly are situations that require such an approach, it's a good idea to try and avoid the temptation to create many small databases where one large repository would suffice. If your goal is to limit data access to appropriate users, you have a number of alternative choices, including key design and views.

Direct system table updates

You can configure SQL Server to let users make direct changes to the engine's internal system tables. The 'allow updates' flag controls this behavior. Normally, users make changes to these tables via SQL Server's internal stored procedures. Any direct attempts meet with an error. However, setting this flag to true lets users circumvent these procedures and perform direct modifications to these tables' contents.

Be very careful when setting this flag. Users can cause severe damage to your database by making incorrect changes to these tables. For example, someone could rename all tables by updating the 'sysobjects' table, thereby preventing further access to these database objects.

Number of open databases

This parameter controls the number of open databases that SQL Server can support at one time. The parameter can range between 5 and 32,767. If you don't set this value high enough, it's possible that users may receive error messages from the engine, informing them that there can be no more open databases.

Number of open objects

This configuration value tells SQL Server the maximum number of database objects that can be open at one time. Database objects include:

- Tables
- Views
- Stored procedures
- Rules
- Defaults
- User-defined data types

This parameter can range between 100 and over 2 billion, with a default value of 500. How can you establish a realistic value? Generally, you should raise this number if you expect to have:

- A large number of objects
- A large number of users accessing these objects at any given time

If you make this number too small, your users may receive error messages from the engine stating that there can be no more open objects. This can be very inconvenient, since it's possible that the user may not be able to proceed until someone else disconnects. Setting this number too high consumes extra memory, since SQL Server must define internal memory structures to support these additional objects. The amount of extra memory is not very significant, however, which is an argument in favor of keeping this number high.

Stored procedure cache

Once SQL Server has defined all necessary internal memory, any leftover memory can be assigned to the stored procedure cache and the data cache. This parameter tells the engine what percentage of leftover memory should be assigned to the procedure cache. Caching procedures can help lead to better performance, since recent, already-executed procedures may already be in memory when other users need them. This can be significant, because any activity that reduces physical disk I/O always helps.

This parameter can range between 0 and 99 percent; the default value is 30. This default means that any leftover memory is divided between the procedure and data cache, with 30 percent going to procedure and 70 percent going to data. If your application makes almost no use of stored procedures, consider lowering this parameter. On the other hand, if you anticipate heavy use of stored procedures during normal system operation, try raising the value higher. As with any other parameter, try to test this value in isolation: Don't change five parameters at once.

SQL Server 6.5 introduces some additional stored procedure cache statistics that you can observe through the performance monitor. We discuss these new indicators elsewhere in this chapter.

Create for load

If you're creating a database that you intend as the destination for an earlier database backup, check the 'create for load' option. Taking this step helps speed up the data restore process, since SQL Server doesn't initialize all pages in the database before proceeding. Considering the number of pages found in a medium-to-large sized database, the cost savings can be substantial. Once the load is finished, other users can then access the database.

Database read-ahead cache

You can control essential SQL Server read-ahead behavior through a variety of configuration settings, including:

- Read-ahead cache hit limit
- Read-ahead cache miss limit
- Read-ahead delay
- Read-ahead prefetches
- Read-ahead slots per thread
- Read-ahead worker threads

We explore these settings in much greater detail in Chapter 16.

Database size

You can configure the default size of all new databases by setting this parameter, which can range between 1 and 10000 megabytes. The default value is 2 megabytes, which you can override by setting this parameter or by supplying a different value when you run the CREATE DATABASE command.

Regardless of the value you choose for this option, it must be no smaller than the current size of the 'model' database. When you create a new database, SQL Server uses the 'model' database as a guide for the new database.

Recovery interval

The recovery interval parameter can have a major impact on the amount of time necessary to restart the SQL Server engine after a system failure. We covered this parameter in Chapter 12, during our review of checkpoints and transaction logging.

Controlling user connections

SQL Server administrators can configure the maximum number of active user connections by setting the 'user connections' option. This selection varies by server type. If the number of active connections meets this value, the next attempted connection receives an error message:

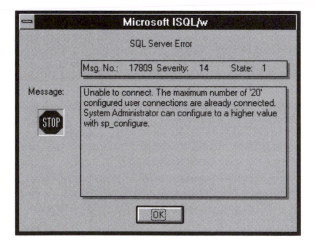

Figure 13.2

SELECT INTO/bulk copy

Recall from our discussions earlier in the book that it's a good idea to avoid filling up the transaction log. However, certain operations are prone to just that negative effect. Fortunately, you can instruct SQL Server not to log two of the most common culprits for transaction log consumption: the bcp utility and the SELECT INTO command. When you set the 'select into/bulk copy' flag, SQL Server doesn't place records of these two operations into the transaction log, thereby conserving valuable space. In fact, you can't even use the 'SELECT INTO' SQL syntax without setting this option. If you try, you'll get an error message back from the engine:

```
1> select *
2> into jugadores
3> from equipos
4> go
Msg 268, Level 16, State 2:
You can't run SELECT INTO in this database. Please check
with the Database Owner.
```

Bulk copies also run much faster when they're not logged by the engine. This is another reason to set this flag if you expect to use SELECT INTO or the bcp utility. One caution about bulk copy operations: If your table has indexes, SQL Server still logs these operations even if you set this flag to true. If you expect to load large amounts of data into a table, consider dropping and then rebuilding the indexes after the load is finished.

As we discussed earlier, be careful when disabling transaction logging. If a problem should arise during a nonlogged operation, you won't be able to use the transaction log to restore your database to its state prior to the operation.

DBO use only

SQL Server supports the concept of three types of users:

- **sa.** This is the system administrator, who has access to all databases.
- **dbo.** This is the actual database owner.
- **Standard user.** This is a normal system user.

You can set this flag to tell SQL Server to restrict access to the database to the 'dbo' user.

No checkpoint on recovery

When SQL Server performs an automatic recovery, it normally runs a checkpoint at the end of the recovery process. The recovery process records this checkpoint, unless you've set this flag to true. When set to true, SQL Server doesn't perform the checkpoint upon completing recovery.

Read-only

Setting this flag tells SQL Server to allow users to look at data, but not to make any changes. If a user attempts to update data or perform any write operations, they'll receive an error message:

```
1> create table mambo (chacha char(10))
2> go
Msg 3906, Level 16, State 1:
Attempt to BEGIN TRANsaction in database 'largo' failed
because database is READ ONLY.
```

You can tell if a database is read-only by looking at the icon from SQL Enterprise Manager:

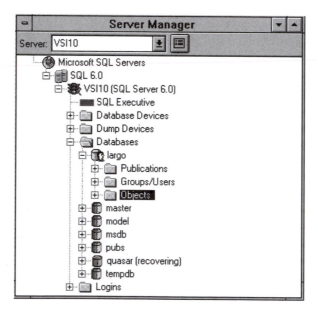

Figure 13.3

In this case, the 'largo' database is read-only.

Single user

You can tell SQL Server to allow no more than one user at a time to access a database by setting this flag to true. If any additional users attempt to connect to the database, they'll receive an error message:

```
1> use largo
2> go
Msg 924, Level 14, State 1:
Database 'largo' is already open and can only have one
user at a time.
```

Certain operations, such as shrinking a database, require that you restrict database access to single-user mode.

Columns null by default

You can direct SQL Server to treat all new columns as being either nullable or non-nullable. If you set this flag to true, all new columns will accept null data entry, with the exception of primary keys.

Truncate log on checkpoint

As we've discussed earlier, it's not good for the transaction log to fill up. You can set this flag to request that SQL Server delete all committed transactions from the transaction log after each checkpoint. The effect of this operation is that your transaction log never stores old, committed transaction records and is, accordingly, likely not to fill.

There is a potentially serious drawback to this strategy: It won't be possible for you to perform periodic dumps of the transaction log. Therefore, if your system fails before you've dumped the database, you stand to lose committed transactions that would have been found on the transaction log dumps. If you feel that you can deal with this possibility and you're concerned about running out of transaction log space, you can use this option to greatly diminish the risk of overflowing the transaction log.

User configuration and administration

SQL Server, through the SQL Enterprise Manager utility, the 'sp_monitor' stored procedure, and the performance monitor, bestows a large number of useful statistics on database and system administrators. In this section, we examine these statistics in detail, along with some examples that demonstrate how you can use their information to discover and minimize potential bottlenecks.

SQL Server Users object

You can get a variety of information from the SQL Server Users object by se-lecting it from the performance monitor:

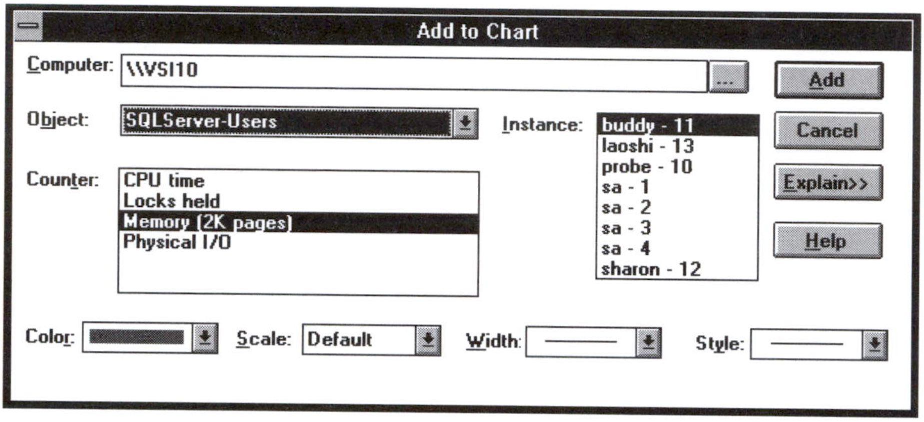

Figure 13.4

Statistics

CPU time

When users connect to an SQL Server engine, they begin consuming resources. Administrators can use this statistic to track the cumulative amount of logical I/O time that each user connection has occupied. This data can be useful when comparing the relative differences among users for this vital resource.

Locks held

When users view or alter data, they require various types of locks. This indica-tor stores a count of the number of locks that a user connection is currently holding. This number can be deceptive; all locks are not equal.

By way of example, suppose that you're observing this statistic for two us-ers: Jeff and Scott. Jeff is holding 25 locks, while Scott is holding 145 locks. Who is locking more resources? As it turns out, Jeff is locking more information than Scott. Recall from our earlier discussions about lock escalation that there are times where SQL Server may "promote" a number of page and extent locks into a single table lock. In this case, Jeff has requested so many page locks for a particular table that the engine has locked the entire table for him. This greatly reduces concurrency for all other users. Scott, conversely, has only locked several dozen pages in a few tables. He has a higher overall count than Jeff, but he is affecting fewer users.

Memory

Database memory is a crucial commodity. This number displays the overall amount of memory consumed by the user's connection. Keep in mind that this number actually represents the number of 2 K pages that the user has requested. Administrators can incorporate this information into analysis designed to find those users that place extra burdens on the system.

Physical I/O

Each time that a user asks for information from the database, SQL Server attempts to satisfy the request by looking into the buffer pool. Hopefully, the data is already present in the pool. If not, the engine is forced to make a physical I/O request. In addition, when a user stores or updates information in the database, SQL Server eventually makes a physical I/O call to update the disk drive.

This statistic helps administrators observe the total amount of physical disk I/O (reads and writes) requisitions for a particular user's current database activity. This is especially helpful for long-running queries, since when the user starts a new activity, the number is reset.

You can use this knowledge to help you understand what degree of data caching is present on your system. Low physical I/O numbers generally indicate that the engine is satisfying user inquiries within shared memory. High numbers mean that the disk drives are getting exercised, looking for this elusive information.

Maximum users connected

Version 6.5 adds a new SQL Server object statistic that tracks the maximum number of connected users while you are observing the engine. Technically, while this statistic is part of the general SQL Server object, it relates more closely to the SQL Server Users object.

Examples

Let's look at a few examples of how to use the users object from the performance monitor. Bear in mind that you can also use the SQL Enterprise Manager utility to learn even more detail about user sessions; we'll combine these two utilities later.

In the first example, we're looking at all statistics for one of our user's sessions:

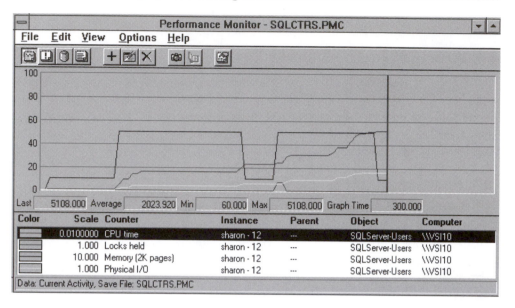

Figure 13.5

Sharon is periodically starting and stopping a database insert process. Notice how we've changed the scale on the CPU time counter; lowering the scale helps make this number more readable. Observe how the CPU counter continues to trend upward, regardless of the state of the user's connection. It does so because this counter is cumulative; it always rises over time, since the cumulative total can only move upward. If Sharon were to log off, this number would drop to zero, since she was no longer on the system. Other indicators, such as locks and memory, fluctuate according to user activity.

In our next example, we're comparing memory usage between two users:

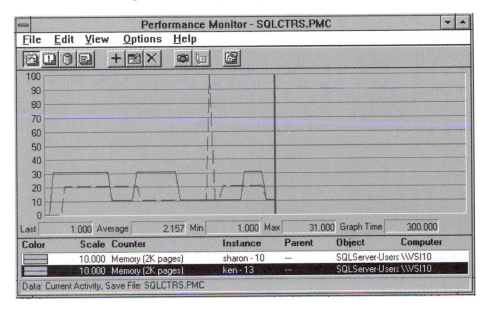

Figure 13.6

We've increased the significance of the numbers to make the graph easier to understand. This type of comparison among users can be very helpful when trying to spot trends.

In the next example, we're watching one user's lock condition:

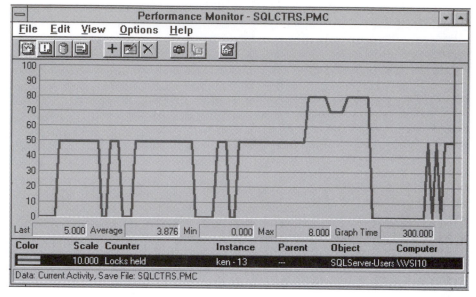

Figure 13.7

Notice how we've increased the width of the measurement line: try experimenting with a variety of line styles, colors, and thickness. Your goal should be to make your graphs as readable as possible. In this example, we've asked SQL Server to alert us should Ken's total number of locks exceed four. In real life, you'd probably set this number much higher. In any case, SQL Server continually monitors Ken's lock status. Once his total number of locks exceeds four, SQL Server registers the event on the alert screen:

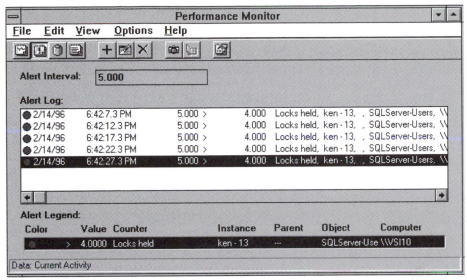

Figure 13.8

Finally, we have created a report to watch all SQL Server User object information for two users:

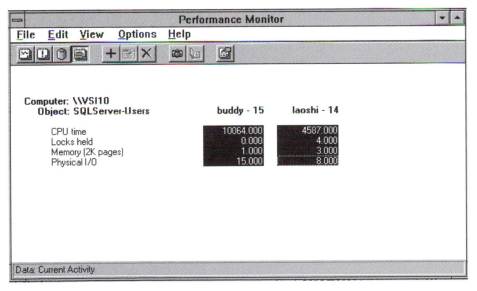

Figure 13.9

There are dozens of ways that you can use the users object to monitor user status and performance conditions. As in many administrative tasks, the best course of action is to experiment. You may be pleasantly surprised with the variety of knowledge you can gain from effective monitoring.

Chapter 14

Network Parameters

One of Windows NT and SQL Server's greatest strengths is the high degree of integration between the operating system, database engine, and networking software components. In this chapter, we delve into how you can evaluate networking status reports, as well as the impact of several configuration parameters on network performance.

Statistics

Administrators can use the SQL Server object within the performance monitor to obtain networking information. Let's spend some time examining these networking indicators.

NET—command queue length

SQL Server uses worker threads to process incoming processing requests from remote users and systems. It's possible that during periods of peak activity, some of these incoming solicitations may have to wait for a worker thread to become available. As an administrator, you can use this counter to monitor how many database requests are currently waiting for available resources.

If you observe this number either climbing or remaining high, it usually means that your system is not efficiently manipulating these incoming units of work. What can you do to improve performance (and reduce this statistic)? Basically, you have two choices:

1. **Increase the number of worker threads.** Adding worker threads can diminish the overall wait times for incoming requests. We covered this topic in Chapter 12.

2. **Reevaluate your distributed processing architecture.**   It's
    possible that your current distributed processing architecture is in-
    sufficient for your data management needs. For example, you may be
    relying too heavily on one central server; no matter how many worker
    threads you allocate, you'll never be able to lighten the backlog.

NET—network reads per second

When communicating with other database instances, SQL Server uses the Tab-
ular Data Stream (TDS) protocol. TDS is an extremely efficient protocol for database communication. This statistic follows how many TDS packet reads SQL
Server makes each second. The higher the number, the heavier the network
traffic.

NET—network writes per second

Just as the 'network reads per second' statistic tracks the number of TDS reads
each second, this statistic follows how many TDS writes SQL Server makes
each second. A high number for this indicator means that your system is performing numerous distributed writes.

Configuration

Packet size tuning

You set SQL Server's network packet size by setting the 'network packet size'
parameter. This parameter, which can range between 512 and 32767, defaults
to 4096 bytes. How can you know if you should change this value? If your network supports a variety of protocols, such as TCP/IP, IPX/SPX, or DECNet™,
it's a good idea to configure this value to match the most efficient setting for the
most heavily used protocol. In addition, it's wise to use larger packet sizes if you
plan on moving large blocks of data between servers. On the other hand, if most
of your work is transactional (e.g., frequent, small bursts of information), use a
smaller packet size.

   With SQL Server 6.5, administrators have the added capability of using the
SQL Enterprise Manager utility to make this setting:

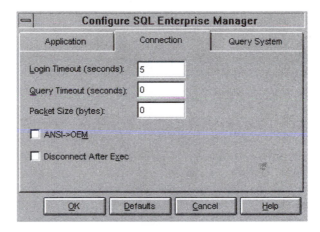

Figure 14.1

Remote access

If you don't want remote users to have access to your system or if you don't want users on your system to connect to remote systems, you can set the remote access configuration parameter. The default value is 1, which means that users on other systems have the ability to log into your database server. In addition, users on your machine can connect to other SQL Server systems.

To disable either or both of these behaviors, set this parameter to 0. Be careful if you decide to eliminate this capability; many developers have built applications that make use of information stored on remote servers. If you suddenly isolate your database server, well-running applications may cease working.

Remote login timeout

Users generally don't like it if attempts to log in to remote databases take an infinite amount of time. It's better for the database server to return an error after a certain amount of time passes. You can use the 'remote login timeout' configuration parameter to control SQL Server's reaction when a remote server is not able to satisfy the login request.

This parameter can range between 0 and over 2 billion seconds, with a default value of 5. This means that the engine waits, by default, five seconds before returning an error message when it is unable to connect to a remote server:

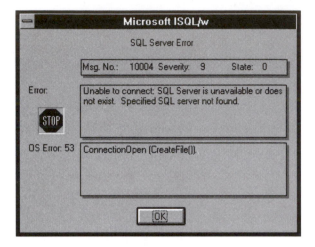

Figure 14.2

If you set this value to 0, SQL Server waits an infinite amount of time before returning an error. The flaw of this approach is that users rarely have an infinite amount of time to wait. If you are concerned about the quality or speed of your network, however, raising this setting from five to ten seconds may not be a bad idea. This increase might make the difference between a no-connect scenario and a slow-connect scenario.

Remote query timeout

Just as you control the amount of time it takes for SQL Server to return an error when attempting a remote login, you can control remote query conduct via the remote query timeout parameter. This value, which can range between 0 and over 2 billion seconds, tells SQL Server how long to wait during a remote query before returning an error to your application.

Setting this option to 0 means that SQL Server waits indefinitely before returning an error during a remote query. Ordinarily, you should avoid this setting, since it's not helpful for your applications to halt while waiting for remote queries to operate. On the other hand, raising this value in cases of slow or poor networks can be beneficial; a few more seconds may be all that it takes for a previously failed query to return successfully.

SQL Server user-defined counters object

SQL Server 6.5 introduces a new way for administrators and programmers to use the performance monitor to track site-specific information. This new feature consists of 10 predefined, empty stored procedures that you can customize to produce information on a wide variety of topics.

Let's look at how you can take advantage of these user-defined counters. Suppose that you want to use the performance monitor to help track the relative size of two tables. You would need to take these steps to make this happen:

1. Grant the 'probe' user permission to connect to the database.

2. Grant 'probe' SELECT permission on all appropriate tables.

3. Drop the 'sp_user_counter1' procedure:

   ```
   drop procedure sp_user_counter1
   go
   ```

4. Create a new 'sp_user_counter1' procedure:

   ```
   create procedure sp_user_counter1
   as select count(*) from jeeves.dbo.tab1
   go
   ```

5. Add this counter to your performance monitor.

6. Perform steps 3 through 5 for each counter you want to add. A total of 10 stored procedures are available for user-defined counter activity.

The following graphic shows a monitoring session where we're observing the number of row counts in two different tables:

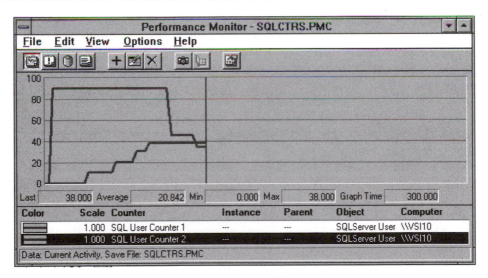

Figure 14.3

You can get very imaginative with user-defined counters. For example, suppose you're running a distributed database environment and want to know how large a particular table is on a number of different systems. You could write your own stored procedures to interrogate these databases, but how would you display the results? User-defined counters let you combine the power of stored procedures with the graphing capabilities of the performance monitor.

In another example, you can use user-defined counters to track database data itself. Imagine that you are managing an OLTP system. One of your goals is to continually monitor the average length of time that it takes to satisfy a customer request. You can use one of the preallocated stored procedures for this purpose:

```
drop procedure sp_user_counter4
go
create procedure sp_user_counter4 as
select avg(response_time) from response
go
```

You can then track the output from this stored procedure via the performance monitor.

Be aware of these restrictions when using user-defined counters:

1. Your stored procedure or SQL statement can return only one integer value. If you attempt to graph a user-defined counter stored procedure that brings back other information, you won't see meaningful results for the counter.

2. The 'probe' account must have permission to execute the procedure.

Chapter 15

SQL Enterprise Manager

In this chapter, we examine, in detail, all of the information that the SQL Enterprise Manager reports regarding user activity. We'll display all of these statistics later in this chapter, when we review some examples.

Detail activity

Status: Status shows the current condition for the process.

Process ID: This is the numeric identifier that SQL Server assigns to each separate process.

Login ID: This is the identifier or alias that the user or process used when connecting to the database.

Database: This is the current database that the user or process is accessing.

User name: This is the actual user name that identifies the process.

Command: This is the command running for the connection when you brought up the screen. You can update the command to be more current by pressing the refresh button.

Host: This is the machine where the user or process resides. For system processes, such as lazywriter and checkpoint sleep, this value is left blank, since they reside, by definition, on the current machine.

Application: This is the name of the application that the user or process is running. For system processes, this is left blank.

Blocked by: If the user or process is blocked, this field shows the process ID of who is responsible for the block.

Blocking: If this user or process is blocking others, this field shows a non-zero value. A zero value means that the user or process is not blocking anyone else.

Lock type: If the user or process is holding a lock, SQL Server displays an icon showing the type of lock. If there is no lock, then SQL Server displays "(No Locks)" instead.

Locked object: If the user or process has locked an object, SQL Server displays the object name in this field.

Group name: This field provides the user's database group name.

CPU usage: This shows the cumulative amount of logical I/O that the user or process has consumed since connecting to SQL Server.

Physical I/O: This shows the current amount of physical I/O operations that the user's or process' database operation has performed.

Host process: This is the hexadecimal process ID assigned by the NT operating system.

Examples

Let's look at some examples of how to use the SQL Enterprise Manager to get detailed information about database operations.

In the first case, we're examining the user activity dialog box:

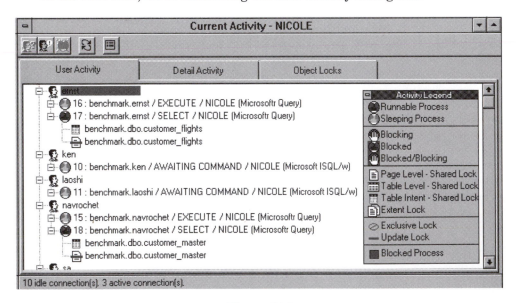

Figure 15.1

To make these examples more clear, we included the dialog box that shows the meaning of all graphic symbols. SQL Server 6.5's graphics now include icons for insert and link page locks:

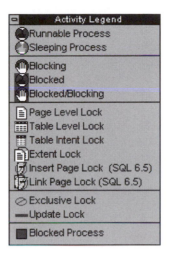

Figure 15.2

What can we learn from this screen? For each user, there are several important clues regarding current activity. Let's begin by focusing on user 'ernst.' Simply by examining this first screen, we know that:

1. Ernst has two connections.

2. His process IDs are 16 and 17.

3. He is connected to the 'benchmark' database for both sessions.

4. Both connections were made through Microsoft Query.

5. Process 16 is sleeping, while process 17 is runnable.

6. Process 17 has a table intent shared lock on the 'customer_flights' table.

7. Process 17 also has a page-level update lock on the 'customer_flights' table.

Focusing on the detail activity dialog box, we can learn more about these two processes:

Current Activity - NICOLE

Status	Process ID	Login ID	Database	User Name	Command	Host
●	11	laoshi	benchmark	laoshi	AWAITING COMMAND	NICOLE
●	12	sa	master	dbo	INSERT	NICOLE
●	12	sa	master	dbo	INSERT	NICOLE
●	12	sa	master	dbo	INSERT	NICOLE
●	13	sa	benchmark	dbo	EXECUTE	NICOLE
●	14	sa	benchmark	dbo	AWAITING COMMAND	NICOLE
●	15	navrochet	benchmark	navrochet	EXECUTE	NICOLE
●	16	ernst	benchmark	ernst	EXECUTE	NICOLE
●	17	ernst	benchmark	ernst	SELECT	NICOLE
●	17	ernst	benchmark	ernst	SELECT	NICOLE
●	18	navrochet	benchmark	navrochet	SELECT	NICOLE
●	18	navrochet	benchmark	navrochet	SELECT	NICOLE

10 idle connection(s). 3 active connection(s).

Figure 15.3

Current Activity - NICOLE

Host	Application	Blocked By	Blocking	Lock Type	Locked Object	Group Name
NICOLE	Microsoft ISQL/\	0	0	(No Locks)		public
NICOLE	MS SQLEW	0	0	🗄	tempdb.dbo.#inf	public
NICOLE	MS SQLEW	0	0	(No Locks)	SQL Server Inter	public
NICOLE	MS SQLEW	0	0	(No Locks)	SQL Server Inter	public
NICOLE	Microsoftr Query	0	0	(No Locks)		public
NICOLE	Microsoftr Query	0	0	(No Locks)		public
NICOLE	Microsoftr Query	0	0	(No Locks)		public
NICOLE	Microsoftr Query	0	0	(No Locks)		public
NICOLE	Microsoftr Query	0	0	🖨	benchmark.dbo.	public
NICOLE	Microsoftr Query	0	0	📇	benchmark.dbo.	public
NICOLE	Microsoftr Query	0	0	🖨	benchmark.dbo.	public
NICOLE	Microsoftr Query	0	0	📇	benchmark.dbo.	public

10 idle connection(s). 3 active connection(s).

Figure 15.4

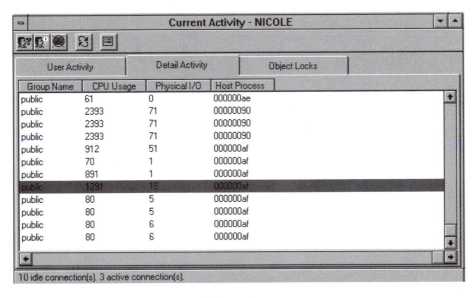

Figure 15.5

The detail activity dialog box helps us understand these additional facts about processes 16 and 17:

1. Ernst logged in with a user ID of 'ernst.'

2. Neither of these processes is blocking anyone else, nor is either blocked by anyone.

3. Their current, cumulative CPU usage.

4. Their current, cumulative I/O usage.

5. Their Windows NT operating system process IDs.

We can learn even more about any of these rows by double-clicking on the row:

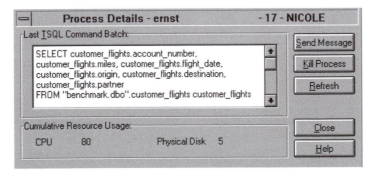

Figure 15.6

We could have gotten this same information by double-clicking on the original row in the user activity dialog box. This is a very helpful tool to determine the exact SQL or database operation that a user or process is running. If we determine that this is a "runaway query," we can use this dialog box to kill the process. Be very careful when taking this step; users are somewhat unhappy if a legitimate query suddenly disappears. Fortunately, we can also take less drastic action by sending a message to the user:

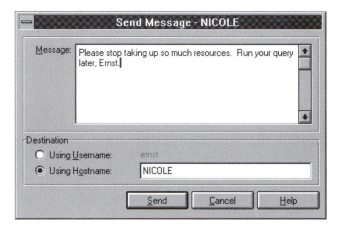

Figure 15.7

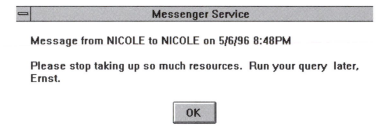

Figure 15.8

Switching to the object locks dialog box gives us a condensed screen, showing us only those processes that are holding object locks:

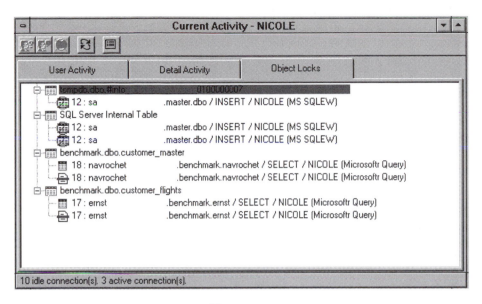

Figure 15.9

As with most tools, the best way to learn how to use the SQL Enterprise Manager is to run it regularly. It's most effective if you run the tool during periods of varied system activity, which will broaden your exposure to the large number of potentially different system states.

Chapter 16

Efficient Replication

Replication is a key component of SQL Server's architecture. In this chapter we turn our attention to how you can use replication in the most efficient manner possible. We begin by briefly covering some key replication terms and theories. These serve as a foundation for our more detailed discussions on improving replication performance.

What is replication?

In a nutshell, replication is an operation that takes information from one source and copies it to a destination. Replication is built in to SQL Server 6.0 and is simple to enable and maintain.

Why replicate?

By replicating data, administrators can safeguard their information, as well as make it available for others to see. Let's look at some scenarios where you could use replication to enhance your information strategy.

Reporting

Suppose that you maintain a production database server in a manufacturing environment. Your primary database server continually polls factory floor equipment and places these manufacturing statistics into an SQL Server database. Besides this primary operation, managers and executives use query tools to construct various data searches and reports. Lately, however, performance problems have arisen. Users complain that it takes a long time for their queries to finish running. You've also noticed that the polling operations are taking longer and longer to complete. Most disturbingly, you've gotten reports that some of these polling processes may have timed out during peak production periods. What is happening? Chances are that the sheer load of user queries and reports is bogging down overall system response. This would have the effect of delaying user reports, as well as lengthening polling time, and possibly even causing the poll processes to time out.

How can you use replication to get around this quandary? By discussing the situation with your users, you learn that they need "fresh" data. Taking your conversations further, you discover that what they mean is that they want information that is no older than two hours. Fortunately, you can easily configure replication to provide this data within a two-hour window. Armed with this requirement, you create a secondary server. You set up replication so that the primary server sends data to the secondary server every 30 minutes. This means that your users can query from the secondary server, without having any impact on the primary server. After installing and configuring the secondary server, you notice an immediate betterment in user reporting response time. You're also pleased to find that your polling processes are now completing in half the time they used to need. Finally, you haven't detected any timeouts either.

Distributed information

Distributed database and processing environments are becoming more common each day. However, the act of distributing this data among a network of computers is one of the most frustrating challenges facing database administrators in these leading-edge environments. Previously, administrators needed to write SQL scripts and programs to extract and move data. These programs usually required manual control and frequently failed. In addition, remote site information was often out-of-date, given the built-in delays found in any manual process. However, with SQL Server replication, you can set up an automatic, efficient, and easy-to-administer distribution infrastructure.

Suppose that you are managing a distributed financial application. One of your more important data components is a tax table. This table contains tax rates for each of your company's locations, is quite large, and is maintained at your headquarters office. Furthermore, data values for this table change frequently, since localities constantly change their tax laws. Your task is to maintain local copies of this table at each remote site. Each site needs only its own tax rate information; other sites' values don't matter. One of the most difficult parts of your job deals with keeping these sites up-to-date. It seems that no matter how much you try, some location always seems to be working with old data.

You can use SQL Server's replication feature to create local copies of the tax table at each site. Instead of replicating the entire tax table to all locations, you can set up horizontal partitioning so that SQL Server replicates based on a key value. This means that you can send specific tax table information to the appropriate destinations, which helps reduce network costs, since you are sending less data to each site. An even greater benefit is the automatic updates that replication provides; as soon as a change is made on your central database, SQL Server broadcasts the alteration to all affected outposts.

Read-only data

One of the benefits of replication is that replicated tables are treated as read-only on the subscribing server. This can help protect database integrity. For example, using the sample financial application that we just described, suppose that you want to prevent field personnel from making changes to the local copies of the tax table. You could enforce these rules by revoking insert, update, and delete privileges from all users. This is not a very elegant solution, since it complicates legitimate data changes. A better solution is to use the built-in, read-only aspect of SQL Server's table replication. Following this approach means that the central server will be able to replicate onto remote servers, yet users at the remote sites won't be able to make any changes.

Replication terms

Before we acquire our skills in optimal replication strategy, let's consider some important replication terms and concepts.

Tight consistency

You can think of a tight consistency replication architecture as one in which changes to the source database are immediately made in the destination database. For example, if a user adds a record to the 'environment' table on machine A, the database source, the same record is added to the 'environment' table on machine B. What makes this architecture notable is that machine B's database gets updated immediately: There is no time delay between the machines. This means that a user on machine B will see the new 'environment' record as soon as the user on machine A commits her transaction.

There are benefits to this approach, chiefly in the area of consistency and user confidence: If you know that replication is happening immediately, you can be confident that you will see "real" data in the destination database. However, there are also several drawbacks to this approach, such as:

- **Network quality.** If you're running a slow or inconsistent network, you'll have problems trying to implement a tight consistency model, since the source database will constantly be waiting on network response to complete its work.

- **Response.** Even on a fast network, tight consistency is hard to achieve, since the database engine is under constant pressure to keep the replicated location up-to-date.

- **Growth.** While you may be able to implement tight consistency across two or three machines, you'll have a hard time making it work when your organization grows to 5, 10, or 20 machines. The above obstacles become nearly insurmountable as your environment grows.

For these and other reasons, SQL Server uses the loose consistency model.

Loose consistency

With loose consistency, which is the method chosen by the designers of SQL Server 6.0, the database engine still needs to ensure that data is transmitted between replication sites in a timely and accurate manner. However, the pressure to keep data flowing in real time between sites is no longer present. What does this mean for your users? Basically, they can count on the data that they see in a replicated database being accurate, but not up to the exact moment. If the machines containing the databases are continually connected, there still is a small time lag between the act of changing data on one database and its appearance on the replicated database. In many cases, however, this time lag is not significant and has no effect on usability. If the databases reside on machines that are only intermittently connected, then changes on the source database won't be reflected on the destination database until the machines have a chance to communicate.

SQL Server uses the loose consistency replication model for a number of reasons, including:

- **Network quality.** If your network is low quality or if you can't expect to maintain constant connections between machines, then the tight consistency model won't work for you. SQL Server uses loose consistency because this model can still work, even if you have some network limitations.

- **Network speed.** With loose consistency, network speed is not the crucial component that it is with tight consistency.

- **Growth.** A loose consistency approach lets you add more SQL Server databases to your replication configuration without bogging down performance.

The transaction log is at the heart of SQL Server's loose consistency replication architecture. Changes made in the transaction log on the source database are applied to the target database. How does SQL Server keep track of all of this information? There are several important processes that taken together make up a scheduling engine. The scheduling engine handles the actual details of knowing when and where to replicate any information. These modules are the log reader, synchronization, and distribution processes. We'll look at each of these processes in more detail later in this chapter.

Data Publication

Publication is an important replication concept. When data is said to be published, it is available to be replicated elsewhere. You can think of publication as in the literary sense: When information has been published, you can read it.

Article

Articles are collections of information to be replicated, taken from a table. For example, if you want to replicate all new rows from the 'purchases' table, SQL Server treats this data as an article. If, at the same time, you want to replicate all new rows in the 'billing' table, this is another article.

Publication

A publication is, simply put, a grouping of articles. Using our earlier literary metaphor, think of a publication as a magazine, containing a number of articles on various subjects. Each subject can be thought of as an article.

Subscriber

A subscriber is a database that asks for and obtains publications, just as in the case of a magazine. The subscriber then has a copy of the information contained in the articles found in the publication. Note that since the data contained in the articles is coming from elsewhere, the subscriber may make changes to the information, but these changes won't be reflected in the publisher's database.

Beginning with SQL Server 6.5, you can now replicate to any database that has an ODBC driver, rather than only to SQL Server databases. This greatly increases the power and flexibility of replication.

Distribution database

SQL Server uses a dedicated database as a repository of replication information. This dedicated database is known as the distribution database. This database holds replicated information until it is passed on to the appropriate
subscribers. Note that users don't have any access to this database: it is for system use only.

To get a better understanding of this database, let's look at some of the tables that it uses to maintain replication information:

- MSjob_commands

  Each transaction can have one or more commands. This table holds a
  record of these commands and has this layout:

Table 16.1   MSjob_commands

column name	type	purpose
publisher_id	smallint	The server ID number of the publishing server
publisher_db	varchar	The actual name of the published database
job_id	integer	A number that identifies the job
command_id	integer	The identifier of this command
art_id	integer	The article's identifier number
incomplete	bit	A flag that states whether the command is all contained in this record or whether it spans multiple entries
command	varchar	The actual command or portion of the command

- MSjob_subscriptions

  The distribution database uses this table to track what articles are of
  interest to certain subscribers:

Table 16.2   MSjob_subscriptions

column name	type	purpose
publisher	varchar	The name that you've assigned to the publishing server
publisher_id	smallint	The server ID number of the publishing server
publisher_db	varchar	The actual name of the published database
subscriber	varchar	The subscriber's name
subscriber_id	smallint	The identifier for the subscriber
art_id	integer	The article's identifier

Table 16.2 MSjob_subscriptions (Continued)

subscriber_db	varchar	The name of the subscriber database
status	tinyint	The status of the subscriber 0 : inactive 1 : subscribed 2 : active
ts	binary	The published subscription's timestamp
status	tinyint	Reserved for future use

- MSjobs

  This table is very important: It holds the actual transactions that are to be replicated and has the following schema:

Table 16.3 MSjobs

column name	type	purpose
publisher_id	smallint	The server ID number of the publishing server
publisher_db	varchar	The actual name of the published database
job_id	integer	A number that identifies the job
type	tinyint	The type of the job: 0 : An SQL command 1 : No operation command 2 : An SQL script 3 : A native bcp command 4 : A character bcp command 5 : A manual synchronization
xactid_page	integer	The transaction's page
xactid_row	smallint	The row number for the transaction
xactid_ts	binary	The transaction's original timestamp
entry_time	datetime	The time that this row was added to this table

- MSsubscriber_info

  This table holds detailed information about the replication jobs that SQL Server must run:

Table 16.4 MSsubscriber_info

column name	type	purpose
publisher	varchar	The name assigned to the publisher
subscriber	varchar	The name assigned to the subscriber

Table 16.4   MSsubscriber_info (Continued)

type	tinyint	An indicator that shows the subscriber type: 0 : SQL Server 6.0 1 : ODBC
login	varchar	Login ID
password	varchar	Password
commit_batch_size	integer	How many transactions should be run on the subscriber before a COMMIT TRANSACTION is issued
status_batch_size	integer	How many transactions should be run on the subscriber before it updates the status indicator
flush_frequency	integer	How many hours (at a minimum) before transactions that have already been replicated to other subscribers can be removed from this database
frequency_type	integer	An indicator that shows the time scale for this operation
frequency_interval	integer	How long between 'frequency_type' operations
frequency_relative_interval	integer	When the 'frequency_type' is monthly, this field shows the relative interval for the day
frequency_subday	integer	This shows how often to rerun the operation for intervals below one day (e.g., per second, per minute, per hour)
frequency_subday_interval	integer	How much time should elapse between operations that take place with subday frequency
active_start_time_of_day	integer	The time when this task is active
active_end_time_of_day	integer	The time when this task ceases to be active
active_start_date	integer	The date when this task is active
active_end_date	integer	The date when this task ceases to be active
retryattempts	integer	A count of how many times SQL Server should retry this operation if it fails
retrydelay	integer	A count of how many minutes SQL Server should wait between retries

- MSsubscriber_jobs

  This table provides the relationship between the subscriber and all
  appropriate jobs destined to be run against that subscriber:

Table 16.5 MSsubscriber_jobs

column name	type	purpose
job_id	integer	The job's identifier number
publisher_id	smallint	The server ID number of the publishing server
publisher_db	varchar	The actual name of the published database
subscriber	varchar	The subscriber's name
subscriber_id	smallint	The identifier for the subscriber
command_id	integer	The command's identifier

- MSsubscriber_status

  This table tracks the status of all jobs run for all subscribers:

Table 16.6 MSsubscriber_status

column name	type	purpose
publisher_id	smallint	The server ID number of the publishing server
publisher_db	varchar	The actual name of the published database
job_id	integer	The job's identifier number
subscriber_db	varchar	The subscriber's database name
subscriber_id	smallint	The identifier for the subscriber
completion_time	datetime	The time when this row was put into this table
status	integer	The status for this job
delivery_latency	integer	How many seconds it took between the time this row was inserted here and it was sent to the subscriber database
delivered_jobs	integer	How many jobs are still present in the distribution database that have already been sent to the appropriate subscriber
delivery_rate	integer	How many jobs per second were executed in the last batch dispatched to the subscriber

Log reader process

As we saw earlier, SQL Server uses the transaction log on the publication server as the source of all replication information. The log reader process is responsible for monitoring the publication server's transaction log. When the log reader locates a transaction affecting a table that has been marked for replication, it duplicates this change into the distribution database. This process is automatically started by the SQL Server engine; you don't need to be concerned with its administration.

Synchronization process

When you add a new subscriber to your replication environment, SQL Server uses a specialized process to synchronize the new subscriber with the existing replication configuration. This synchronization process makes sure that the system tables and replication schema are correct. Like the log reader process, SQL Server automatically starts and stops the synchronization process.

Distribution process

To complete the replication operation, SQL Server needs to take the information found in the distribution database and duplicate it on the subscription servers. The engine uses the distribution process to make this happen. This process, which is started automatically by the engine, locates the appropriate transactions in the distribution database and implements them at the correct destination.

SQL Server Replication-Published DB object

You can use the SQL performance monitor to track several important replication publishing statistics.

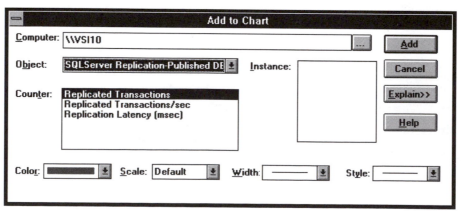

Figure 16.1

Statistics

Replicated transactions: This indicator shows how many transactions are present in the replication log. These are transactions that are due to be replicated but have yet to be placed into the distribution database.

Replicated transactions per second: SQL Server lets you use this statistic to track how many replicated transactions are happening each second.

Replication latency: This number shows the latency, or delay, between the time a transaction is marked for replication and the time that it actually replicates. Milliseconds are the unit of measurement for this statistic.

SQL Server Replication-Subscriber object

You can use the SQL performance monitor to track several important replication subscription statistics.

Statistics

Delivered transactions: This statistic keeps a running count of how many transactions have placed into the distribution database.

Delivered transactions per second: This measures how many replication transactions per second the subscription server is able to perform.

Delivered latency: There is normally a small delay, or latency, between the time a transaction is placed into the distribution database and the time that it is executed against the subscription server. This counter keeps track of these delays, which are measured in milliseconds.

Undelivered transactions: This indicator monitors how many transactions are present in the replication database that have not been sent to the correct destination. There are several reasons why a transaction may not have been delivered:

- The destination database may not be running.
- The network may be down.
- The transaction has not yet been sent.

Replication stored procedures

There are numerous stored procedures that SQL Server uses to create, maintain, and monitor replication. In this section, we itemize these stored procedures. Note that some of these stored procedures are used by other types of operations in addition to replication. Finally, keep in mind that the tasks performed by many of these stored procedures can also be accomplished by using the SQL Enterprise Manager utility.

Table 16.7   Replication stored procedures

procedure name	purpose
sp_addtask	Add a scheduled replication task
sp_droptask	Drop a scheduled replication task
sp_helptask	Display details about a particular task
sp_addpublisher	Create a new publication server
sp_addsubscriber	Create a new subscription server
sp_changesubscriber	Change the status of an existing subscriber
sp_dboption	Set a database's capability for publishing or subscribing
sp_droppublisher	Drop an existing publication server
sp_dropsubscriber	Drop an existing subscription server
sp_helpdistributor	Provide details about a distribution server
sp_helpserver	Provide a list of replication servers
sp_helpsubscriberinfo	Provide details about a subscription server
sp_replsync	Acknowledge that a subscriber has finished synchronizing
sp_addarticle	Define an article and associate it with a publication
sp_addpublication	Create a new publication
sp_articlecolumn	Assign a column to an existing article
sp_changearticle	Alter an article's details
sp_changepublication	Modify a publication's profile
sp_droparticle	Drop an existing article
sp_droppublication	Drop an existing publication, along with all associated articles
sp_enumfullsubscribers	Provide an itemization of subscribers that have selected all of a publication's articles
sp_helparticle	Furnish details regarding an article
sp_helparticlecolumns	List all of the columns in an article
sp_helppublication	Return details about a particular publication
sp_helppublicationsync	Show facts about a synchronization assignment

Table 16.7 Replication stored procedures (Continued)

sp_helpreplicationdb	List all replicated databases for a server
sp_addsubscription	Subscribe to a particular article
sp_changesubscription	Alter the details about an existing article or group of articles
sp_changesubstatus	Modify the status of a particular subscriber
sp_dropsubscription	Delete an existing subscription
sp_helpsubscription	Provide details about an existing subscription
sp_subscribe	Subscribe to a specific article inside a publication
sp_unsubscribe	Stop subscribing to a specific article inside a publication
sp_helpreplicationdb	Note if a database is a destination for replication
sp_distcounters	Provide all details about each subscriber
sp_MSkill_job	Delete a specific job from within the distribution database; all other jobs remained unaffected
sp_replcleanup	Delete already-executed jobs from the distribution database queue
sp_replica	Instruct SQL Server to treat a table as a replica, rather than the original
sp_replcmds	Show the commands that make up transactions that are set to be replicated
sp_replcounters	Provide all details about each replicated database
sp_repldone	Refresh the record that shows when the server last processed a distributed transaction
sp_replflush	Empty the current article cache
sp_replstatus	Refresh SQL Server's internal replication tables
sp_repltrans	Display all transactions that are set to be replicated but haven't yet been officially noted as distributed

Efficient replication

Now that we've reviewed how SQL Server supports replication, let's look at some specific suggestions regarding how you can make your replication as efficient as possible.

Replication topology planning

If you're planning to implement SQL Server's replicating technology, consider devoting some time in advance to creating a well-designed replication topology. Your research should cover a number of important topics, including:

- **Levels of replication.** One advantage of advance planning is that it lets administrators come up with creative alternatives to traditional architecture. One area where this is especially true is when you are trying to determine the number of levels of replication. Recall that a subscription server is capable of publishing its subscribed information. You can use these "publishing subscribers" to help you construct a multilevel replication architecture. These multilevel environments have the potential to be faster than single-level configurations; it's more likely that a multilevel topology can eliminate costly long-distance connections by using intermediate machines.

- **Frequency of replication and load balancing.** Regardless of the frequency of your replication tasks, it's always a good idea to avoid situations where you encounter overly high processing and network loads. This can happen in cases where you are replicating to a large number of subscription servers. If you ask that all subscription servers receive replicated information at the same time, it's possible that your system or network may bog down, given the potentially heavy data load. It's more efficient to launch these update tasks on an alternate basis, with each subscription server receiving its information at a slightly different time.

- **Reducing replication overhead.** After you define a replication relationship, SQL Server must synchronize databases between publishers and subscribers. This procedure can consume large amounts of system resources. Accordingly, anything you can do to reduce the amount of work necessary for this synchronization should help improve overall performance. One simple step to follow is to use automatic synchronization after you've subscribed to a publication. This approach batches synchronization tasks, rather than running them in real time after a new subscription.

At the end of this process, you'll be rewarded with an efficient, effective replication strategy that should suit your needs for a long time to come.

Transaction log

As we have seen, SQL Server's replication algorithms rely on the publication database's transaction log to provide details on those transactions that need to be replicated. The log reader process searches the transaction log for operations that have been marked for replication, then copies this information into the distribution database. Once a transaction has been copied between the publication and distribution databases, the original transaction log record can be freed as part of the standard transaction log backup/dump routines.

Good transaction log throughput is critical to your efforts to keep your database server running efficiently. Factoring replication into the picture merely increases the importance of the transaction log. Therefore, what steps can you take to ensure that your transaction log can handle the extra burdens of replication?

- **Allow for enough space.** It's never much fun to run out of transaction log space. Your system can come to a complete halt, since no data modifications can take place when the transaction log is full. Replication has the potential to increase log space requirements, since the log reader process can only free up transactions once they have been replicated. We've already seen that some time may elapse between the initial transaction and the subsequent replication event. This means that it's possible that your previously well-sized transaction log may suddenly seem too small once you begin replicating information.

- **Place the log on a speedy device.** Regardless of whether you employ replication or not, the transaction log should always be on a fast disk drive. An excessively slow transaction log disk drive can cast a wide shadow over the rest of your system's performance. Replication itself adds extra transaction log reads by the log reader process. These additional read requests can then further increase overload if the transaction log's disk drive is already overworked.

- **Avoid long transactions.** Long transactions can contribute to a full transaction log, which in turn can have a devastating effect on response. Since there may be significant gaps in time between the time a transaction is marked for replication and the time that replication happens, anything you can do to help reduce transaction length can be helpful.

- **Mirror the transaction log.** One common use for replication is to help preserve data integrity. It's worthwhile to remind you again that by mirroring the transaction log, you increase the odds that you'll be able to weather any disk predicaments that you may chance upon. Mirroring also helps keep replication up and running when the primary disk fails.

Memory

For your system to function as a publication and distribution server, or as a remote distribution server, you must have at least 32 megabytes of RAM, with a minimum of 16 megabytes allocated for SQL Server. Other than these prerequisites, there are no other additional memory requirements for replication.

Control amount of published data

Just because you can replicate a specific table doesn't mean that you should. Sometimes, administrators replicate unnecessary tables. This increases the work for all machines in your environment, places added burdens on your network, and enlarges the amount of disk space necessary on subscription machines.

Before you add a table to a publication, try to be certain that you should, in fact, replicate the table. If you figure that replication is the right step to take, your next judgment should be whether you can replicate on a horizontal or vertical basis. Either of these types of operations reduce the sheer amount of information being passed among systems. For example, suppose that you want to replicate an account table that has several million rows. Your first question should relate to whether or not this table is a good candidate for replication. Assuming that it is, your next question should ask if all subscription servers will want all information in this table. Chances are that you can subdivide this data, based on either a horizontal or vertical basis.

Taking these extra steps can yield surprisingly good performance amplification, since you may have sharply reduced the amount of information flowing among your systems.

Primary keys

SQL Server won't be able to implement replication for a table if the table doesn't have any primary keys defined. However, primary keys are important for many other reasons aside from replication. As we discussed in Chapter 3, primary keys help improve database integrity, reliability, and performance.

SQL Server 6.5 introduces a slight exception to this rule. If you haven't defined a primary key for a table, you can still replicate the table, but only through an operation known as a "snapshot." Snapshot replication means that SQL Server makes a one-time copy of information between the publisher and subscriber. Realistically, most administrators want replication to be an ongoing event, which highlights the importance of primary keys

Foreign keys

Beginning with SQL Server 6.5, you can disable foreign key constraint checks during replication operations. This can help hasten performance, since the act of constraint checking can take some time, especially on those tables with many foreign keys. You can request this new behavior by adding NOT FOR REPLICATION to your CREATE TABLE and ALTER TABLE foreign key and constraint statements.

Control number of publications

If you want to replicate a table among one or more subscribers, try to avoid duplicate replication work. This duplicate work often happens when administrators add the same table to more than one publication. This extra overhead can reduce performance on all machines participating in the replication topology, as well as increase network loads. To bypass this problem, examine your current publications before creating a new one. You might be surprised to learn that a particular table is already part of an existing publication.

Appendix A

Case Studies

Real-world performance problems rarely happen in isolation. Typically, administrators and developers face a multitude of intertwined problems and obstacles. In this appendix, we present a number of case studies, each featuring multifaceted performance impediments. After we describe the problems, we propose a variety of solutions, with references to the sections in this book that provide additional information.

Although this appendix does not cover every potential bottleneck that you might encounter, we've tried to realistically combine a number of problems in each case. See if all or part of these cases resemble the challenges that you face in your daily responsibilities. If they do, try testing some of the solutions described here to see if they help alleviate your performance problems.

Case study 1

You're the database administrator on a new project. You work with a team of four programmers creating a new system for order entry. As development has proceeded, you've begun to receive reports of strange database anomalies from your developers. After analyzing the situation in more detail, you determine that these anomalies can be broken down into a number of distinct problems, including:

- **Slow search performance.** Certain lookup programs have terrible response time when searching for particular pieces of information. This is especially alarming given that your database contains a bare minimum of data and will only grow over the coming months.

- **Data truncation.**   Developers report that there are certain situations where they've noticed character field truncation when moving data between tables.

- **Sluggish INSERT/UPDATE/DELETE response.**   During testing, you become aware that it's taking a long time to make modifications to data in one particular table. SQL Server finds the data very quickly; the problem appears to happen only when actually changing data.

- **Conversion errors.**   Periodically, developers encounter this error message when testing queries:

```
Msg 260, Level 16, State 1
Disallowed implicit conversion from datatype 'char'
to datatype 'int'
   Table: 'development.dbo.table2',
   Column: 'id_number'
   Use the CONVERT function to run this query.
```

Let's address each of these obstacles individually. Since performance is of the highest concern, you turn your attention to this topic first. You learn that most of the complaints from developers and testers occur when querying this table:

Table A.1   beneficiary_plans

beneficiary_number	plan_type	start_date	end_date	...
1767-CE-3992	SeniorGold	Mar 12 1996	Nov 15 2005	...
6995-AX-9931	Budget	Aug 01 1987	Dec 01 2000	...
9002-BN-1212	JuniorTin	Feb 14 1990	Dec 03 2002	...
.	.	.	.	.

You ask to see an example of a problem query, along with its query plan:

```
select * from beneficiary_plans
where beneficiary_number like '%CE%'

STEP 1
The type of query is SELECT
FROM TABLE
beneficiary_plans
Nested iteration
Table Scan
```

The problem isn't a lack of an index on the 'beneficary_number' column, since querying for an exact match on that column yields:

```
select * from beneficiary_plans
where beneficiary_number = '1767-CE-3992'

STEP 1
The type of query is SELECT
FROM TABLE
beneficiary_plans
Nested iteratio
Using Clustered Index
```

You realize that the reason for slow performance lies in SQL Server's use of a table scan to satisfy the request. Why is the engine choosing the table scan approach rather than using the clustered index? The explanation for this behavior is that SQL Server has no choice but to perform a table scan, since your query syntax doesn't allow the engine to use the index. Keep in mind that the engine can't use an index if you are searching on a substring: The search syntax must start from the left of the field and work toward the right. In this case, you're attempting to locate all records that have 'CE' in the middle. How can you change your query so that you can find this information and use an index? Realistically, if this is your goal, then this table needs to be altered. You could add another column that contains only the middle two bytes of the 'beneficiary_number' column. Remember from our discussion on good relational database design that your fields should be as atomic as possible. In this case, chances are that the 'beneficiary_number' field could be broken down into a number of meaningful subcomponents. Each of these components could then be indexed, either individually or collectively. If you need more advice on relational database construction, see Part 1 on creating a well-designed database.

With regard to data truncation, your research shows you that the problem data typically relates to customer names and addresses. You discover that the programmers have been creating their own work tables, as well as defining variables in stored procedures and programs using diverse field sizes. For example, some programmers define the customer's last name as 20 bytes, whereas others use up to 40 bytes. You realize that there is no standard size for these fields. You have two choices to resolve this problem: you can define and publish a data dictionary, showing the size and type of all elements in the system; another method would be to create a library of user-defined data types and then produce a listing of all of the new types. Regarding the customer's last name, you could create a new type called 'name_type' or 'last_name_type' (or any other meaningful name), then assign it to be as large as you need. Developers could then use the user-defined type instead of estimating the correct size:

```
create table #mytemp (...last_name name, ...)
```

For more detail on user-defined data types, see Chapter 2.

Your next investigation deals with the lethargic response that you're receiving when making a change to a particular table. You invoke the SQL Enterprise Manager to get a better idea about the table:

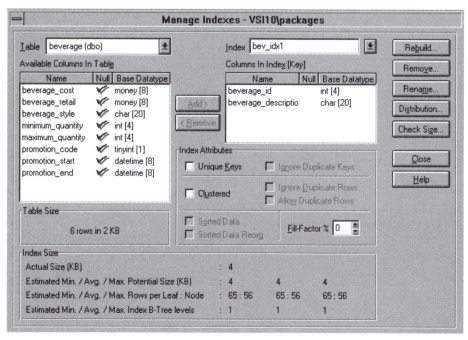

Key	Identity	Column Name	Datatype	Size	Nulls	Default
🔑	✓	**beverage_id**	int	4		
		beverage_description	char	20		
		beverage_cost	money	8	✓	
		beverage_retail	money	8	✓	
		beverage_style	char	20	✓	
		minimum_quantity	int	4	✓	
		maximum_quantity	int	4	✓	
		promotion_code	tinyint	1	✓	
		promotion_start	datetime	8	✓	
		promotion_end	datetime	8	✓	

Figure A.1

You next look at the index screen:

Figure A.2

The drop-down dialog box for indexes shows:

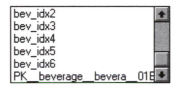

Figure A.3

You can also use the 'sp_helpindex' stored procedure to get more detail about a table's indexes:

```
index_name   index_description                   index_keys
-----------  --------------------                ----------
PK__beverage clustered, unique, primary key..beverage_id
bev_idx1     nonclustered located on default beverage_id,
                                                beverage_description
bev_idx2     nonclustered located on default beverage_cost
bev_idx3     nonclustered located on default beverage_retail
bev_idx4     nonclustered located on default promotion_code
bev_idx5     nonclustered located on default promotion_start
bev_idx6     nonclustered located on default beverage_style
```

You notice that there appears to be a relatively large number of indexes in place on this table, especially when compared against the number of columns. Recollect that one likely cause of slow performance when modifying data is an excess amount of indexes. Each time you make a change to data within a table, SQL Server needs to update the appropriate indexes as well. In addition, these index updates can trigger additional internal index balancing work by the database engine. All of this can add up to delayed replies for interactive applications.

For tables that don't receive many interactive updates, chances are that these extra indexes would not be a problem, since the columns that make up the indexes would not be updated. However, in cases like this, where the data in an underlying table is constantly being modified, try to decrease the overall number of indexes. If you need to run queries or reports on the table that necessitate these indexes, you can:

1. **Replicate the table to another location.** As we've seen in Chapter 16, SQL Server comes with robust data replication. One widespread use for data replication is to create query-only tables that can be accessed by users without fear of negatively impacting production database response.

2. **Create temporary indexes.**   If you need to run month-end reports on these types of tables, you can always create your extra indexes, run the reports, and then drop the indexes after finishing. Your reports still run quickly, and you also can help reduce drag on normal, day-to-day operations.

3. **Replace the clustered index on 'beverage_id' with a non-clustered index.**   Keep in mind that each time you add a row into a table that has a clustered index, SQL Server needs to ensure that the table's pages remain clustered correctly. This can lead to extra work for the engine, as it strives to insert the new rows into the clustered index. If the pages are relatively full, SQL Server may need to split the pages and adjust appropriate pointers. Page splitting may also require that pointers for the other indexes on the table be updated as well.

For more detail on this topic, see Chapter 3, "Indexing Strategies."

Next, you start scrutinizing the sporadic conversion problem. What does the error message mean? Should you learn more about the CONVERT function? Chances are that when you come upon this error, your tables or variables are not defined as being the same data type. The error occurs when you try to join between these disparate data types. To get around the problem, you could make use of the CONVERT function, but this treats the symptom, rather than the underlying problem. As we saw in Part 1 on good database design practices, it's always a wise idea to have all join columns match, in both data type and size. Consequently, the best approach to eliminating the problem is to thoroughly examine all of your tables to make sure that all of the potential join columns agree on these important characteristics. This may take some work, but it will be worth it all through the development and production cycles. For more information on join columns, see Chapter 3 in Part 1, as well as chapters in Part 2.

Case study 2

You've just accepted a job administering a 12-month-old application that tracks attendance, test scores, and other important statistics for a school district. After you've started working, your new manager approaches you with a long list of problems that must be resolved within two weeks. Somehow, no one told you about this during the interviewing process. Nevertheless, you resolve to do your best to eliminate as many of the trouble spots as quickly as you can.

Once you've analyzed the list of problems, you assign the highest priority to these particular issues:

• **Test scores table modification.**   The users need you to modify the 'test_scores' table to prepare for upcoming exams.

- **Resolving insertion error message.** User applications periodically receive error messages when attempting to insert data into a number of important tables.

- **Design enhancement.** It seems that certain students have been using friends as stand-ins for standardized tests, such as the SATs. To counter this behavior, school administrators have decided to take pictures of all students and then have these pictures displayed on a monitor when the students arrive to take their tests.

Beginning with the need to alter the 'test_scores' table, you learn that the table has this layout:

Table A.2   test_scores

student_id	test1	test2	test3	test4
3334	87	90	76	81
3335	65	68	57	72
3336	90	98	92	89
.	.	.	.	.

The user explains to you that the school district has recently changed its policy: Students now have five major tests each semester. Therefore, the table needs to have a new column added to hold the fifth score. While listening to the user explain her ideas for the table, you realize that there is a fundamental problem with this design. What happens if the school district later decides to test even more frequently? Will you continually need to add additional columns each time this happens? You also recognize that many of the existing applications are going to fail with the new design, since they were hardcoded to deal with this table as it stands today.

From a relational database standpoint, this table violates the first normal form, which states that a table must not have repeating fields of the same data within a row. This table has column after column of test scores. For completely static, unchanging environments, this is not necessarily a problem. However, as you've learned, users have a way of rapidly altering the database landscape. With all of this in mind, you suggest a different way of storing this information. This new technique will protect you, along with future administrators, from needing to change the database schema each time the number of tests changes:

Table A.3   test_scores

student_id	test_number	grade
3334	1	87
3334	2	90

Table A.3   test_scores (Continued)

3334	3	76
3334	4	81
3335	1	65
.	.	.

This approach also frees you from the unpleasant task of changing application programs with every schema change. Unfortunately, you realize that for
this particular instance, you can't escape making the alterations to the programs.

While on the subject of programmatic difficulties, the users report receiving this error from time to time:

```
Msg 2627, Level 14, State 1
Violation of PRIMARY KEY constraint
'PK__attendanc__atten__7A122857': Attempt to insert
duplicate key in object 'attendance'.
Command has been aborted.
```

To learn more about the 'attendance' table schema, you generate an SQL
script, using the **SQL Enterprise Manager's** utility:

```
/****** Object:  Table dbo.attendance    Script Date:
8/17/96 10:01:47 PM ******/
if exists (select * from sysobjects where id =
object_id('dbo.attendance') and sysstat & 0xf = 3)
     drop table dbo.attendance
GO

CREATE TABLE dbo.attendance (
     attendance_id int NOT NULL ,
     student_id int NOT NULL ,
     attendance_date datetime NOT NULL ,
     attendance_code smallint NOT NULL
)
GO

/****** Object:  Table dbo.attendance    Script Date:
8/17/96 10:01:48 PM ******/
ALTER TABLE dbo.attendance WITH NOCHECK ADD
     CONSTRAINT PK__attendanc__atten__7A122857 PRIMARY
     KEY   CLUSTERED
     (
```

```
            attendance_id
      )
GO


/****** Object:   Table dbo.attendance     Script Date:
8/17/96 10:01:55 PM ******/
setuser 'dbo'
GO


setuser
GO
```

You now understand that the error message relates to a violation of the primary key constraint. This means that someone is attempting to insert a duplicate value on the 'attendance_id' field. This is puzzling: No users have direct access to the table. Instead, data is entered into the table via a Visual Basic program. Clearly, the program works for the vast majority of cases. Why would it fail on rare occasions? As you examine the code, you make a crucial discovery: The author of the program had written a routine to generate the 'attendance_id' sequence number. It's possible that during peak periods of activity there was a conflict between different instances of the program. Fortunately, there is a relatively simple way to resolve this problem. You can assign the 'identity' property to the 'attendance_id' sequence number column. This change informs SQL Server that you want the engine itself to generate the auto-sequencing number for this column. In fact, you can even have the engine start from the current maximum number:

```
select max(attendance_id) from attendance


----------
90093
```

With this knowledge, you now know what the seed value for the table should be (90094). Unfortunately, you'll need to unload the table, drop it, and then re-create it with the 'attendance_id' column defined with the identity attribute, because SQL Server doesn't let you add this property to an existing column. You also need to change your INSERT statements from:

```
insert into attendance values (...)
```

to:

```
insert into attendance
(student_id, attendance_date, attendance_code)
values (...)
```

You need to make this change because SQL Server now generates the 'attendance_id' column: There's no need to provide a value. One final note on this topic: When unloading and then reloading tables using an identity column, make sure that you don't lose referential integrity between tables, since it's possible that the newly generated key values for a particular table may not match existing relationships among other tables.

Focusing on the design challenge of capturing and displaying student images, your management originally wanted to store these images on the file system and store a pointer to the image in the database:

Table A.4   student_profile

student_id	last_name	first_name	...	image_file
3334	Patrick	Geoffrey	...	d:\pictures\3334.gif
3335	Carroll	Clyde	...	d:\pictures\3335.gif
3336	Lombardo	Peter	...	d:\pictures\3336.gif
.	.	.	.	.

You are concerned about the extra work necessary to "join" the 'image_file' column with the correct image from the disk. In addition, you are worried about the extra backup and restore work that this approach might cause. After pondering these factors, you realize that this extra work is unnecessary: You can use the image data type to store the pictures inside the database itself:

Table A.5   student_profile

student_id	last_name	first_name	...	image_content
3334	Patrick	Geoffrey	...	0x6173...
3335	Carroll	Clyde	...	0x5595...
3336	Lombardo	Peter	...	0x9932...
.	.	.	.	.

When you write your student record retrieval program, all pertinent information is now stored with the parent row, eliminating the need for extra work to find the image on the file system.

Unfortunately, after implementation of the above image solution, certain problems arise. Users tend to add or update student pictures in large batches. Sometimes, during these insert or update operations, the application receives this message from SQL Server:

```
Msg 1105, Level 17, State 2
Can't allocate space for object 'Syslogs' in database
'students' because the 'logsegment' segment is full. If
```

```
you ran out of space in Syslogs, dump the transaction
log. Otherwise, use ALTER DATABASE or sp_extendsegment
or increase the size of the segment.
```

All work comes to a halt until you back up or dump the transaction log. You are very perplexed—until you added the 'image_content' column you had never seen this error before. Why is this happening now? The answer lies in the effect that text and image columns can have on the transaction log. Recall that text and image columns can hold up to two gigabytes of information. If you log this information, you'll quickly overflow the transaction log, and SQL Server is unable to continue work when the log is full. The reason that the log overflow happens sporadically is related to the number of active users, along with the particular tasks they're performing. It's possible that given a slightly lower workload, you would never encounter this error. However, in any case, you must correct the situation so that the problem is eliminated. What's the best way to proceed? You have at least two choices:

- **Change the way you work with image columns.** Many application tools let you insert, update, and delete text and image information without the overhead of transaction logging. This will eliminate the strain on your transaction log, as well as enhance performance, but at the cost of reduced database integrity. Bypassing the log means that it's possible that an image could be lost if your system crashed between the time of the insert and the corresponding checkpoint operation. If you are concerned that your system may indeed crash periodically (due to power outages or other problems) and you won't easily be able to reconstruct the text or image data, consider using the next alternative.

- **Increase the size of the transaction log.** Another alternative you can employ when faced with overflowing transaction logs is to allocate more space. This is the path of least resistance, since disk space is becoming less expensive each year. However, keep in mind that increasing transaction log space is not a permanent solution, especially if you expect your overall system usage to increase over time. Even if you arrive at the right figure, you still may fill the log during a period of heavy system activity.

Case study 3

You're the database administrator for an executive information system (EIS). Senior management uses this system to track sales at each of your company's 350 restaurants. Each restaurant is open 24 hours a day and generates dozens of transactions per hour. Lately, you've been hearing some complaints from your users that the system isn't running as fast as they'd like. Specifically, they cite the amount of time it takes to get results from their reports.

As usual, when you ask the users to identify individual queries or reports, they respond by saying that all of the queries and reports are too slow. Still, you decide to move forward and focus on one heavily used report, figuring that if you can overcome its bottlenecks, you'll be able to do the same for the rest of the application.

The report that you choose to work on tracks daily sales at all of your company's restaurants. Once an hour, your central computer polls each restaurant and uploads the transaction file. This file contains detailed information about each check, including what was ordered, when it was ordered, and how much it cost. Once the transaction file is uploaded, you post all the details into the 'item_history,' 'ticket_history,' and 'item_ticket' tables:

Table A.6   item_history

restaurant_id	item_id	item_cost	order_time
.	.	.	.
209	45	12.99	Jan 30 1998 12:09PM
209	2	1.99	Jan 30 1998 12:10PM
152	101	7.99	Jan 30 1998 12:10PM
.	.	.	.

Table A.7   ticket_history

restaurant_id	ticket_id	ticket_total	ticket_time
.	.	.	.
175	130995	34.18	Jan 30 1998 1:18PM
175	130996	106.92	Jan 30 1998 1:19PM
298	207889	56.71	Jan 30 1998 1:20PM
.	.	.	.

Table A.8   item_ticket

restaurant_id	ticket_id	item_id
.	.	.
95	103392	18
95	103392	6

Table A.8   item_ticket (Continued)

304	909553	41
304	909553	33
304	909553	11
.	.	.

The hourly sales report sums up, by restaurant, all of the sales for the current day. As you review the program, you realize that it spends the majority of its processing time retrieving and summing up the individual sales detail records. What would happen if you simply kept a summary table and acquired your daily sales information from it, rather than continually rereading the 'ticket_history' table and recalculating the sales figures? You could update this new table as records came in from the field, thereby spreading the processing load more evenly over the day.

Your new summary table could have this format:

Table A.9   daily_sales_total

restaurant_id	sales_date	sales_total
.	.	.
25	Jan 29 1998	12099.21
25	Jan 30 1998	6733.09
.	.	.
26	Jan 29 1998	9508.94
26	Jan 30 1998	8801.53
.	.	.

If you placed a unique composite index on the 'restaurant_id' and 'sales_date' columns, you could quickly locate the appropriate row to update as the latest hour's sales data came in. Once you found the right row, you would only need to update the 'sales_total' column to reflect the most recent hour's added sales. When you ran summary reports, you could then read this (smaller) table, instead of churning through mountains of data. For more information about the benefits of storing historic data versus continually recalculating summaries, see Chapter 2 in Part 1 on efficient relational database design.

As an alternative approach, you could simplify the amount of custom programming necessary to gather all of this information by taking advantage of SQL Server's built-in replication features. By replicating specific details from each restaurant, you can automate the polling process, as well as increase your confidence that you are locating and transporting correct information. In addition, replication lets you increase the frequency of communication from restaurants to the central system, thereby providing management with more timely information. Given the low cost of hardware and simplicity of replication, you can even create a network of destination machines, which serves to diminish the load on the monolithic central computer.

Improving one report doesn't mean that your work is done, however. You decide to focus on your system's I/O performance, since you know that a slow-running I/O subsystem can have a far-reaching impact on overall system response. When you first installed SQL Server on the central system, you didn't explicitly create any devices other than master. This means that your transaction log and all of your data are stored on this device, which maps to drive C. After the system had been up and running for a few months, you purchased two additional disk drives, which leaves you with the following configuration:

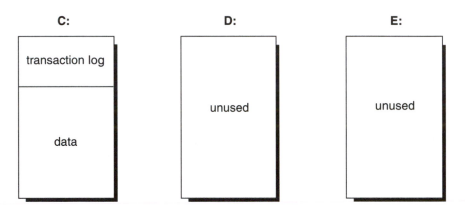

Figure A.4

You realize that if you did a better job of spreading the load among your disk drives, you should get better I/O performance. In this case, that means spreading your data among all available disk drives. You also observe that you could lose important data if the drive containing the transaction log failed. With this in mind, you come up with a new disk layout:

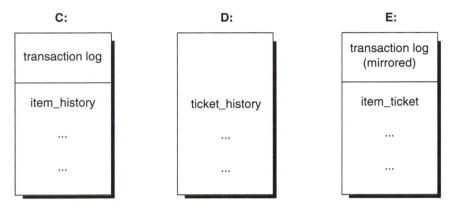

Figure A.5

This should help balance the amount of I/O work required of each drive, as well as increase the likelihood of surviving a disk failure. Remember that regardless of mirroring, nothing can take the place of a well-designed backup strategy. For more information about the relationship between disk layout and SQL Server engine performance, as well as disk mirroring, see Chapter 12 on maintaining an efficient SQL Server engine.

After you've solved all of the above problems, your users are very grateful. However, an administrator's work is never done, and only a few days go by before the users are asking for additional queries and reports. In particular, one user wants you to construct a query that summarizes information in the 'ticket_history' table. She'd like to classify tickets based on their price, using these criteria:

1. If the ticket is less than $10.00, it fits into the 'budget' category.
2. If the ticket is between $10.01 and $29.99, it fits into the 'inexpensive' category.
3. If the ticket is between $30.00 and $45.00, it fits into the 'moderate' category.
4. Anything higher is considered 'expensive.'

At first, you considered using a Transact-SQL stored procedure to group and summarize this information. Then you remember that you can use the 'case' expression to simplify your work:

```
select restaurant_id,
       ticket_id,
       ticket_total,
       . . .
       . . .
       "Ticket category" =
       case
           when ticket_total < 10
         then "Budget"
          when ticket_total >= 10 and
               ticket_total <= 29.99
             then "Inexpensive"
          when ticket_total >= 30 and
               ticket_total < 45
             then "Moderate"
          when ticket_total >= 45
             then "Expensive"
       end
from ticket_history
```

We discuss the CASE function in more detail in Chapter 5, "SQL Tips."

Case study 4

In this case study, you are a consultant called in to a small manufacturing company that has been experiencing a high degree of turnover in their systems department. Management wants your help in resolving a number of serious problems. Most of these difficulties relate to application and engine performance, but some relate to the operating system itself. Complaints include:

- No accountability regarding system administration
- Excessive amount of time to start the engine
- Concurrency problems
- Sluggish server operating system performance

You start your work by examining the system administration situation. It turns out that there have been four SQL Server administrators over the last 15 months. Each has left the position, either voluntarily or with some assistance from management. These types of conditions don't bode well for a well-running database environment. Your first task is to educate management about the importance of SQL Server administration. Security is a big part of administration, so you are dismayed to learn that all analysts and programmers, as well as some users, have the "sa" password. This means that no one can be held accountable for system administration. In addition, well-publicized "sa" passwords often lead to serious security breaches. Consequently, you work with the new SQL Server administrator to bring the security situation up-to-date. This means altering the "sa" password, as well as removing any expired logins from the system.

Examining the complaint about the amount of time that it takes to start SQL Server, your first action should be to learn if there are any stored procedures that are automatically started when the engine starts. To do this, you would first run the 'sp_helpstartup' stored procedure:

```
sp_helpstartup

Startup stored procedures:
------------------------------
re_index_detail
audit_trail_report
check_security
kyles_awesome_procedure
security_monitor
   .    .    .    .
   .    .    .    .
load_sample_data
build_indexes
```

You wonder what all of these procedures actually do. This is compounded by the lack of accountability: Any number of analysts, programmers, or end users may have created these procedures. Reviewing these names leads you to believe that there is a high degree of duplication among the procedures. You also suspect that many of these procedures have no useful purpose. Making matters worse is that these procedures were then set to run whenever SQL Server started, which can have disastrous effects on system performance and may even damage data integrity.

With this in mind, you begin the painstaking task of examining each stored procedure in detail. What's the best technique to use? You can disable all of these startup procedures by setting trace flag 4022. This trace flag tells SQL Server not to run any of the auto startup routines. You decide that this is the best route to follow, since you suspect that none of these procedures have any values. However, you begin to get numerous complaints from users, all of whom are experiencing this type of message:

```
Msg 208, Level 16, State 1
Invalid object name 'storage_location'.
```

As it turns out, perhaps taking the all-or-nothing approach wasn't the best idea. It appears that at least one of the stored procedures had some value. Disabling the startup stored procedure meant that one or more tables were no longer present, thereby causing application failures. Unfortunately, you must now review the instructions contained in each startup procedure. You can use the SQL Enterprise Manager's Manage Stored Procedures dialog box to display the code that makes up a stored procedure:

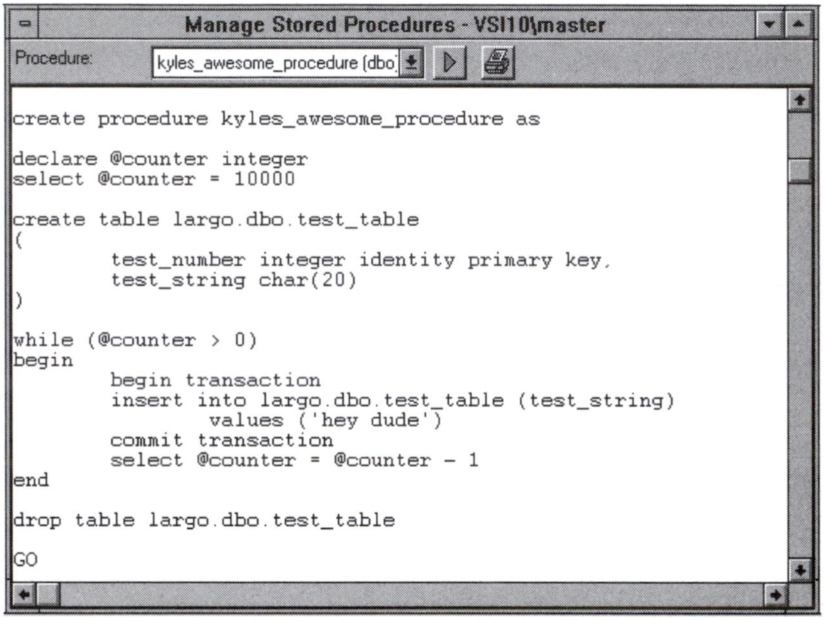

```
Manage Stored Procedures - VSI10\master

Procedure:  kyles_awesome_procedure (dbo) ▼  ▷  🖨

create procedure kyles_awesome_procedure as

declare @counter integer
select @counter = 10000

create table largo.dbo.test_table
(
        test_number integer identity primary key,
        test_string char(20)
)

while (@counter > 0)
begin
        begin transaction
        insert into largo.dbo.test_table (test_string)
                values ('hey dude')
        commit transaction
        select @counter = @counter - 1
end

drop table largo.dbo.test_table

GO
```

Figure A.6

This is very distressing. It appears that someone named Kyle wrote a stored procedure that creates a table and then issues 10,000 insert statements into the table. Making matters worse, he then drops the table, which made it very difficult for you to find. It seems that you will need to review each startup stored procedure in detail to decide which should be kept versus which should be discarded. Fortunately, after a few days, you have removed all unnecessary startup procedures.

You next turn your attention to the concurrency problems. It seems that large reports often contain stale or out-of-date information. In particular, one report runs against a large transaction table. The report is run during the middle of the day and usually consists of a number of old values by the time it finishes. What's the best way to advance in these types of circumstances? You begin by looking at the SQL code that makes up the report's main query:

```
declare C_materials insensitive cursor for
    select * from materials where
    latest_modification_date = @todays_date
```

The report then opens the 'C_materials' cursor and fetches data until there is no data left to read. You know that the 'materials' table contains thousands of rows, and users are making changes to it throughout the day. How can you increase the likelihood that the report will locate timely information? There are several approaches that you can apply:

- **Determine an acceptable timeliness threshold.**   If the underlying rows are changing all through the day, you need to work with your management and the user community to resolve what constitutes "timely data." Theoretically, your report might never end if you continually had to restart the process each time a row changed. Perhaps you could run the report at night or during another low-volume time.

- **Improve report speed.**   This is an often-overlooked technique to improving concurrency. If the problem is that too many users are trying to modify the same information, one way that you can reduce the number of contentious users is to speed up their work. One way would be to make them type faster, but this might anger some workers. Instead, why not see if you can improve on query performance, either by reworking the query, modifying indexes, giving hints to the optimizer, or any number of other tactics. You might find some previously missed solution to the problem without having to resort to more strenuous schemes.

- **Change the cursor type.**   In the cursor example listed above, the original developers decided to use an insensitive cursor. Remember from Chapter 7, "General Tips," that an insensitive cursor makes a copy of the original table. SQL Server then performs all cursor operations against the copy, not the base table. This means that the owner of the cursor won't see any changes made to the original data, even if it happens much later during the cursor's existence. In addition, in numerous circumstances SQL Server builds a temporary work table to hold the cursor's contents. It's possible that you could run out of temporary storage space in conditions where the base table is very large and hence requires a large temporary table.

  In this case, contemplate a slight change to the cursor declaration. Once you remove the 'insensitive' request from the DECLARE CURSOR statement, SQL Server keeps you advised about any changes to the data:

```
declare C_materials cursor for
select * from materials where
latest_modification_date = @todays_date
```

Your report now receives fresher information. There's also no need for any temporary tables. However, this tactic still doesn't solve all concurrency problems; there still can be obstacles brought about by the transaction isolation level, which brings us to our final point.

- **Review the transaction isolation level.**   Recall from our earlier concurrency review that you can use transaction isolation to increase or decrease the timeliness of your information. Developers have a choice of three different transaction isolation options:

  - **Read uncommitted.**   This is the least restrictive transaction isolation level. Your programs can see more data, but the likelihood of "phantom" or erroneous data increases. Given that your users want an error-free report, this is probably not the best choice for this situation.

  - **Read committed.**   This transaction isolation level only shows you committed data. However, it's possible that another user may change underlying data after your cursor has read it. This level also doesn't seem restrictive enough for the current circumstances.

  - **Repeatable read.**   This transaction isolation level prevents other users from changing underlying data until your query finishes with the entire table. This is the most restrictive transaction isolation level, but it comes at a price: Other users may find themselves "locked out" while your query runs. However, given that this report must be correct, it's probably a good idea to raise the transaction isolation level to this setting.

Finally, you look into why users are experiencing sluggish operating system response on the server. You begin by looking at memory, since memory is often the most significant factor in performance. The server has a total of 64 megabytes of RAM. To learn SQL Server's memory setting, you could use the SQL Enterprise Manager or simply run the 'sp_configure' stored procedure. You choose the latter:

```
sp_configure 'memory'

name    minimum       maximum       config_value run_value
------  -----------   -----------   ------------ -----------
memory  1000          1048576       57344        57344
```

It appears that a previous administrator, in an effort to speed up the engine, assigned too much memory to SQL Server. You validate this hypothesis by running the performance monitor to examine page file usage and data caching:

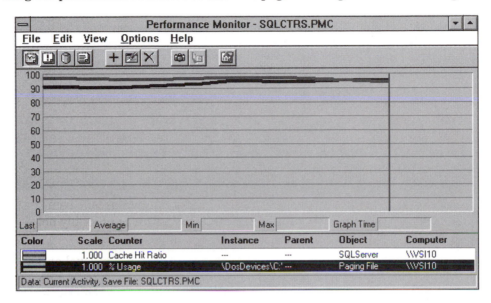

Figure A.7

Notice how high both the cache hit ratio and page file usage numbers are. The high cache hit ratio means that from SQL Server's perspective, there is plenty of memory. However, a high page file usage percentage usually means that either your paging file is too small, or that your system is swapping too much. One cause of too much paging is a shortage of memory. By assigning excessive memory to SQL Server, you run the risk of forcing the Windows NT operating system to swap to obtain necessary memory. Unfortunately, SQL Server statistics alone won't show this problem. In fact, if you monitor the cache hit ratio, you may think everything is fine. For this reason, don't forget that SQL Server doesn't exist in isolation; it's wise to track operating system indicators as well as database statistics.

In this case, you recommend lowering the SQL Server memory parameter. It's best to lower the number gradually, while keeping track of the same statistics. Chances are that you can run with a much lower memory setting while preserving good SQL Server performance.

Case study 5

You are maintaining a merchandising system for a large clothing retailer. Your database holds over one gigabyte of information and is accessed by about 25 users at one time. One of the most critical parts of your application is an inventory receiving system, which these users employ to log the large number of incoming shipments received each day. Lately, certain users have complained of degraded response, especially during the middle of the merchandise check-in process. In addition, you've observed that periodically the system comes to a complete halt for a few moments. Adding to the mystery is the strange fact that it seems to break out of the halt situation on its own, with no administrator intervention.

Before beginning, you run the 'sp_helpdb' stored procedure to learn more about the current size of the database:

```
sp_helpdb receiving

name          db_size       owner dbid created     status
-----------   ----------    ----- ---- ----------  ----------
receiving     1014.00 MB    sa    6    Apr 5 1996  subscribed

device_fragments                 size          usage
------------------------         ------------  --------
datadevice1                      1000.00 MB    data only
logdevice1                         14.00 MB    log only
```

Your first concern is the performance problem. After analyzing the puzzle, you locate the problem in the check-in program's query routine. This program uses the following algorithm when checking in merchandise:

```
create a temporary table
load rows from the master merchandise table into the
     temporary table
for each piece of new merchandise
     search the temporary table for a match
     if a match is located
       display details on the screen
     else
       add a new record to the master merchandise table
     end if
     update the detail merchandise table
end for each
```

So far, everything seems fine. The master and detail merchandise tables are well indexed; you run some test queries and the query plans look good. Where can the problem lie? Recall from our earlier study of temporary tables that you shouldn't forget to place indexes, where appropriate, on these temporary objects. You examine the temporary table creation logic:

```
create table #checkin_lookup
(
```

```
        merchandise_id integer,
        merchandise_description varchar(40),
        . . .
        . . .
    )
    go
```

It seems that there are no indexes on this table. This means that each time your program performs a lookup, the optimizer is forced to use a table scan to locate information:

```
select merchandise_description
from #checkin_lookup
where merchandise_id = 20032

STEP 1
The type of query is SELECT
FROM TABLE
#checkin_lookup
Nested iteration
Table Scan
```

This can be extremely expensive, especially when you realize that the '#checkin_lookup' table can have up to 30,000 rows. Adding an index to the temporary table makes a big difference:

```
create index cl_merchandise_id on
       #checkin_lookup(merchandise_id)

select merchandise_description
from #checkin_lookup
where merchandise_id = 20032

STEP 1
The type of query is SELECT
FROM TABLE
#checkin_lookup
Nested iteration
Index : cl_merchandise_id
```

Adding indexes to temporary tables aren't the only area for potential improvement. Other possibilities include the following:

- **Use multiple disk drives to support temporary tables.** We explored this topic in Chapter 11, "Disk Management." Since the temporary table SQL creation logic lets you specify a segment, you can spread the temporary table I/O load to several disk drives.

- **Consider storing the tempdb database in RAM.**   We discussed this topic in Chapter 11. You can instruct the engine that you want to keep this database within SQL Server's RAM space. This has the potential to help performance by reducing the amount of I/O necessary to move data from these temporary tables into memory. You're able to realize this benefit since the data will already be present in RAM. However, before you take this step, make sure that your environment has enough memory and that you explicitly create most of your temporary tables.

- **Update statistics.**   Don't forget to run this vital command on temporary tables if the tables are of significant size (e.g., greater than 250 rows). This is particularly important when you place more than one index on a specific temporary table.

Next, you turn your attention to the system "freezes." What can cause a system to freeze? Generally, these kinds of events are prefaced by a full transaction log. Recall from our earlier review that SQL Server relies on the transaction log to store detailed information about each database modification. If the log fills up, the engine has no choice but to suspend all data modification until you remove the blockage. You can confirm that the transaction log is the cause of this problem by monitoring the SQL Server log object:

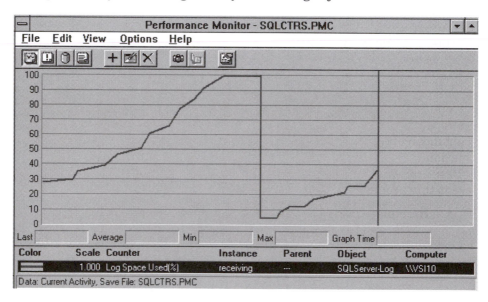

Figure A.8

From this chart, we can see that the transaction log does indeed fill up. What's interesting about this chart is that the log doesn't stay full; something seems to free it after a little while.

Another way to monitor the log would be to set an alert:

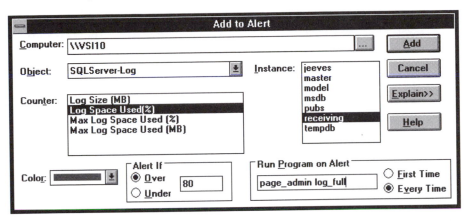

Figure A.9

You set this alert so that it runs a paging program whenever the transaction log hits 80 percent of capacity. This will help you take appropriate steps prior to the system halting.

Now that you know why the system is halting, your next job is to determine what frees the log. With a little more investigation, you learn that there is a stored procedure that gets called by one of the programs. This stored procedure performs a 'dump tran' operation, which frees the transaction log. However, this is not good from a data backup and restoration perspective. If you dump transaction logs without backing them up, you can potentially lose data if your system should crash and you are forced to restore an earlier backup. The restore operation will reestablish data up to the point of the backup; any subsequent operations will be lost without a good transaction log backup. Dumping the log means that you've asked SQL Server to "throw away" this important information.

Based on what you've learned, you decide to follow two courses of action to prevent this problem from happening again:

- **Increase transaction log size.**   After researching the problem, you determine that the transaction log was too small for the overall amount of data. In most cases, the transaction log size should equal at least 10 percent of overall data storage. Given that your database holds 1 gigabyte of information, you choose a transaction log size of

100 megabytes, which is far more the current 14 megabytes. We discuss transaction log sizing in much greater detail in Chapter 12 on efficient engine administration.

- **Perform regular transaction log backups.**   You can often learn much more than performance information whenever you analyze your system's operations. In this case, you detected a potentially serious operational problem relating to dumping the transaction log. You can greatly minimize the likelihood of lost data simply by backing up the transaction log on a regular basis. When you combine this approach with your earlier decision to increase the log size, chances are that you won't encounter a full transaction log anytime soon. We discuss transaction log sizing and backups in Chapter 12 on efficient engine administration.

Appendix B

SQL ReplayVersion 1.10

Shareware product of AZ Databases, Inc.
Authors: Andrew and Katrin Zanevsky

CONTENTS:

1. PRODUCT DESCRIPTION

SQL Replay collects data about SQL Server activity by making periodic snapshots of system information. Recommended snapshot interval is 1 minute, which may be adjusted to your particular environment needs. Information is derived from system tables, sysprocesses, syslocks, and some of the SQL Server global variables.

Collected data allow you to review past SQL Server activity, and find performance problems or bottlenecks, research locks contention, or heavy usage time intervals. Essentially the system allows you to execute stored procedures sp_who, sp_lock (simplified), and sp_whoactive (proprietary format of AZ Databases) "of the past".

Note: sp_whoactive is a stored procedure developed by AZ Databases, Inc. It will not be present on your system unless you have previously obtained it from AZ Databases or other sources and installed it on your SQL Server.

Part of SQL Replay is fully automated and will collect statistics on the background. You don't have to watch or administer it once you have set it up.

Another part of the system is reporting stored procedures that will allow you to review collected data and produce various reports of past SQL Server activity. These procedures have several different output formats and numerous report options. Reports will be available only after SQL Replay has been installed and continuous data collection has been initiated.

You may also write ad hoc queries on SQL Replay tables to research specific problems or produce customized reports of SQL Server activity statistics.

2. SYSTEM REQUIREMENTS

This product has been developed for Microsoft SQL Server for Windows NT versions 4.2x and 6.x. It may work with Sybase SQL Server but certain modifications may be required depending on the SQL Server version.

A special database called "replay" will be set up on your SQL Server upon installation. The monitoring process will accumulate significant amounts of data in the database. Space requirements should be carefully considered, because it is possible that you will overflow your database as a result of using SQL Replay. Space requirements may range from under 1 MB to several MB. Default size of the database is 30 MB.

Table size depends on the following:

- the average level of activity on your SQL Server (P), defined as the average number of system processes (as reported by sp_who),
- the average locking activity, defined as the average number of users holding table locks (U), and the average number of different tables locked by a user at a time (T),
- the number of days for which logs are kept: processes and locks log (Da), and global variables log (Dv),
- frequency of activity snapshots, defined as the number of snapshots made per hour: activity (Fa) and global variables (Fv).

Approximate minimum space estimate formula:

$$\text{Space (MB)} = (\,P/625 + U{*}T/1940\,) * Da{*}Fa + Dv{*}Fv/1000$$

E.g. A hypothetical system has an average of 20 system processes, 5 of which are locking 2 different tables each. 60 activity and global variables snapshots are made per hour (one per minute). Activity log is kept for 3 days and global variables log is kept for 7 days. Space requirements for such system are:

$$\text{Space (MB)} = (\ 20/625 + 5*2/1940\ ) * 3*60 + 7*60/1000 = 7.1\ \text{MB}$$

It is recommended to reserve more space for unexpected surges in system process and locks activity.

3. INSTALLATION

3.1. Upgrade from version 1.0x:

If you have previously installed SQL Replay version 1.0x, then you should only execute command file UPGRADE.CMD with two parameters - SQL Server name and sa password:

> UPGRADE Server Password

Please review the file WHATSNEW.TXT for version 1.10 changes description. Database space requirements have not changed.

3.2. New installation:

Installation may need to be customized for your specific environment. Please read each instruction carefully before implementing. SQL Server DBA experience is required to perform SQL Replay installation.

- Calculate space required for "replay" database using formula above.

- Set up device "replay" with the chosen size (default - 30 MB). We recommend using SQL Server administration tools for this task - SQL Enterprise Manager (SEM) or SQL Administrator. Optionally you may execute the provided T-SQL script REPLDEV.SQL to create the new device, but you must manually modify the file to specify drive and path for the new device, and device size (as the number of 2K pages) if it should be other than 30 MB.

- Create database "replay" of the chosen size (default 30 MB) on SQL Server device "replay". We recommend to keep both data and transaction log on the same device. Use SQL Server database administration tools for this task. Optionally you may execute script REPLDB.SQL to create the database but you must manually modify the file to set the chosen database size (in megabytes).

- Set database options "trunc. log on checkpoint" and "select into/bulk-copy" (optional) to "true" for the replay database. You may use administration tools or execute T-SQL script OPTIONS.SQL to complete this step. It is assumed that transaction log of replay database will not be preserved, because replay database data is not critical to user applications stability. You may, however, decide to change these options and set up periodic backups of transaction log and the database.

- Execute T-SQL script files SNAPSHOT.SQL and REPORTS.SQL from any SQL Server query interface to install necessary objects. Note: All objects are installed in the replay database.

- We recommend to grant full permissions on SQL Replay objects to public. Execute T-SQL script ALLGRANT.SQL from any query tool to complete this task. Do NOT execute this script if you want to restrict access to SQL Replay objects. You may set up permissions yourself using SQL Server administration tools. Keep in mind that periodic snapshots and purges should be made under an account that has full permissions on SQL Replay objects (especially important on SQL Server 4.21).

4. SCHEDULING MONITORING PROCESS

4.1. Choose configuration parameters:

- activity snapshot interval (default = 1 minute);
- log information expiration period for processes and locks activity data (default = 7 days);
- log information expiration period for global variables data (default = 7 days).

4.2. Scheduling on SQL Server 4.21:

On SQL Server 4.2x you need to modify and use script file REPLAY.SQL and command file REPLAY.CMD to schedule periodic activity snapshots.
   Modify file REPLAY.SQL as follows:

- If you wish snapshot interval other than 1 minute, then find the line that reads "waitfor delay '00:01:00'" and change the delay '00:01:00' in quotes to the desired snapshot interval (format - HH:MM:SS).

- If you wish to set old data purge delay to non-default values, then find the line that reads "exec past_purge" and change procedure's first parameter to the desired processes and locks expiration period in days and set second parameter to the desired global variables expiration period in days.

- Save modified file REPLAY.SQL on your SQL Server hard drive. (e.g. in directory C:\REPLAY.)

Modify command file REPLAY.CMD as follows:

- Substitute user login name (or use "sa") and password, and specify the path to REPLAY.SQL file on your hard drive where indicated.
- Save modified file REPLAY.CMD on your SQL Server hard drive.

REPLAY.CMD begins an endless loop that takes snapshots of SQL Server activity and records them in log tables. Before starting the loop it checks whether SQL Replay has already been started. If another instance of SQL Replay is detected, the second execution will not spawn another process and will harmlessly terminate.

Beware that if you kill the monitoring process or if it is terminated (e.g. because SQL Server service is stopped), it will not reincarnate, until REPLAY.CMD is executed again. Therefore, it is recommended to schedule REPLAY.CMD for execution every hour or several hours. If one instance is stopped for any reason, another one will soon be spawned. We strongly recommend to upgrade to SQL Server 6.X, since it has a much more flexible native scheduler.

For example, if you have stored REPLAY.CMD in directory called C:\replay and you want to schedule the task to start daily at 2AM, execute the following from a command prompt:

```
at 2:00AM /INTERACTIVE /EVERY:M,T,W,Th,F,S,Su "c:\replay\RELAY.CMD"
```

Important: You don't have to execute REPLAY.CMD every minute! Once started it will continue making snapshots every so often until terminated.

4.3. Scheduling on SQL Server 6.x:

On SQL Server 6.x we recommended to use SQL Executive Scheduler to schedule tasks. Files REPLAY.SQL and REPLAY.CMD are not needed.

Execute T-SQL script SCHEDULE.SQL from any query interface to set up SQL Replay tasks with default parameters (you may then manually reset tasks in the SQL Executive Task Management). Two tasks will be scheduled:

- Activity Snapshot task will be executed every minute.
- Activity Purge task will be executed every day at 3:10AM and will purge all audit data older than 7 days.

To change frequency of either task do the following:

- In SEM open Task Manager (Server/Scheduled Tasks).
- Open Task Edit window (double-click on the task).
- Open Task Schedule window ("Change" button on the bottom).
- Reset task frequency as desired.
- Save changes (click on "OK" button to close Task Schedule, then click on the "Modify" button on the Task Edit window).

To reset audit data expiration delays in task Activity Purge:

- In SEM open Task Manager (Server/Scheduled Tasks).
- Open Task Edit window (double-click on the task).
- In the "Command" box change parameters of stored procedure past_purge: set the first parameter to the desired expiration period for processes and locks information and the second parameter to the desired expiration period for global variables data. Both parameters represent the number of days.

We strongly recommend to turn on "trunc. log on checkpoint" database option in your msdb database or set up periodic transaction log dumps. Otherwise, msdb transaction log will overflow because SQL Executive starts making updates in msdb once you schedule any tasks, and updates the history in msdb. If you do not turn this option on then you need to set up transaction log dumps by other means (e.g. through the alert engine).

5. SOFTWARE LICENSE AGREEMENT

AZ Databases, Inc. grants you the right to use the software product SQL Replay as follows.

- This software product is distributed free as a shareware.
- Under no circumstance shall AZ Databases, Inc. be held liable for any direct or indirect damages that may arise from use of this product. You understand and accept risks of using shareware software on your database system. Potential problems include but are not limited to the following:
  - Performance overhead imposed by SQL Replay may slow down or even lock some of your transactions.
  - Disk space needs to be reserved for SQL Replay database.
  - Replay database may overflow and require manual intervention to clean.
  - msdb database (SQL Server 6.x only) transaction log may overflow if you do not turn on the option "trunc. log on checkpoint" and do not dump transaction log periodically.
  - The number of user connections may exceed the limit set on your server due to additional processes logging system activity.
- You may install this product on any number of SQL Servers in your company.
- You cannot resell the whole product or any part of it without prior written permission of AZ Databases, Inc.

- You have the right to redistribute this product free of charge if the recipient accepts this license agreement unaltered and you do not change the contents of this package.

- If you redistribute this product you agree not to make any alterations and must preserve all comments in the source code and documentation indicating rights and authorship of AZ Databases, Inc.

- You have the right to alter the product software for your company's exclusive use only. By making alterations you will waive your rights to limited technical support of this product from AZ Databases, Inc.

- AZ Databases, Inc. reserves the right to discontinue further development and support of this product at any time in its sole discretion.

6. SUPPORT

AZ Databases, Inc. does not make any guarantee or commitment of support. We value your input and will make reasonable (in our discretion) efforts to answer user questions, resolve problems, and possibly release new enhanced versions of the product. You are encouraged to contact us with suggestions on further improvements of the software.

For limited technical support contact AZ Databases, Inc. at:

fax and voice-mail: 847/419-0190

e-mail: 71232.3446@compuserve.com

AZ Databases, Inc. provides consulting, development, and database administration services for clients using Microsoft SQL Server and Sybase systems. We distribute this product SQL Replay as a shareware in order to help your business to manage database systems and to demonstrate our expertise in SQL Server area. We will appreciate any business and client referrals that you may have for us.

7. DATABASE OBJECTS

71. Tables:

`past_globvar_last_snapshot`	Last snapshot of global variables
`past_locks_last_snapshot`	Last snapshot of locks
`past_processes_last_snapshot`	Last snapshot of system processes
`past_globvar`	Global variables log
`past_locks`	Locks log
`past_processes`	System processes log

Tables past_globvar, past_locks, and past_processes are synchronized by snapshot_time. You can use that fact when writing your own ad hoc queries on these tables.

7.2. Table past_globvar columns:

```
snapshot_time        datetime,
interval_sec         smallint,
connections          smallint,
cpu_busy             smallint,
idle                 smallint,
io_busy              smallint,
total_errors         smallint,
total_read           smallint,
total_write          smallint,
process_count        smallint
```

7.3. Table past_locks columns:

```
snapshot_time        datetime,
id                   int,
dbid                 smallint,
spid                 smallint,
lock_count           int
```

7.4. Table past_processes columns:

```
snapshot_time        datetime,
active_ind           char(1),
spid                 smallint,
suid                 int,
hostname             char(10),
locks                int,
delta_locks          int,
logical_io           int,
delta_logical_io     int,
physical_io          int,
delta_physical_io    int,
blocked_by_spid      smallint,
blocks_count         smallint,
cmd                  varchar(16),
status               char(10),
dbid                 smallint
```

7.5. Stored Procedures:

`past_snapshot`	Makes a single snapshot of system processes, locks, and global variables.
`past_purge`	Purges old data in system processes, locks log and global variables log.
`past_activity`	Produces reports of past activity on system processes and locks.
`past_globvar_report`	Produces reports of past activity on global variables.

8. SQL REPLAY REPORTS

8.1. Stored procedure past_activity

`past_activity` produces several different reports of past SQL Server activity.

Usage: `past_activity` `Option,Tfrom,Tto[,Filter]`

Option = { `"who"`/`"whoactive"`/`"lock"`/`"help"` } - output format specification,
allowed option synonyms: `who=w, whoactive=active=a, lock=l, help=h=?;`
`Tfrom, Tto` - report time interval in any SQL Server datetime format,
Filter specifies output filter criteria:
- user login name (as found in syslogins), it may contain `"%"` to request a 'like' search for login name in syslogins (limitation: there must be exactly one matching name),
- `spid` (system process id number as reported by sp_who),
- `"all"` - no filter,
- `"active"` - report processes that showed activity,
- `"growing"` - report processes with growing logical or physical i/o,
- `"blocking"` - report not blocked processes that were causing blocks,
- `"host=XXXXXXXXXXXX"` - report processes with hostname XXXXXXXXXXXX,
- `"cmd=XXXXXXXXXXXXXXXX"` - processes executing command XXXXXXXXXXXXXXXX,
- `"logical>NNNNN"` - report processes with logical i/o increment > NNNNN,
- `"physical>NNNNN"` - report processes with physical i/o increment > NNNNN,

Filter keywords: `all,active,growing,blocking,host,cmd,logi-cal`, and `physical` may be prefixed with "/" to avoid confusion with `login` names. Default: Filter=all.

8.2. Stored procedure past_globvar_report

`past_globvar_report` produces numeric or pseudo-graphical report of past global variables changes.

Usage: `past_globvar_report Tfrom ,Tto [,Format [,Zoom]]`

`Tfrom, Tto` - report time interval in any SQL Server datetime format,
`Format =  0` specifies numeric output (default),
`Format = [1,255]` specifies bar width for pseudo-graphic output,
choose
the value based on your screen width, so that the whole activity bar is visible without scrolling the screen to the right.
`Zoom` `= 0` - one report line per snapshot (default),
`Zoom` `> 0` - one report line per <Zoom> minutes (average values).

AZ Databases, Inc. is currently developing additional stored procedures to analyze activity log data and produce more reports. Register your product to promptly receive future updates (see REGISTRATION above).

9. REGISTRATION

AZ Databases, Inc. is continually improving and enhancing SQL Replay. In order to promptly receive new product releases please register by sending us the following information:

Personal contact information:
a. Name _____
b. Position _____
c. Companyname _____
d. Street address _____
e. City, state, zip _____
f. Telephone (optional)_____
g. Fax (optional)_____
h. E-mail (optional, preferred) _____

Business facts about your company:

i. Type of business _____
j. Ownership: __private   __public
k. Number of employees _____

l. Does your company outsource or consider outsourcing SQL Server devel-opment, DBA, and support?   __Yes   __No

Technical information about your SQL Server software and hardware:

m.How many SQL Servers do you have? _____

n. What is the size of your largest database? _____

o. How many users concurrently access them? _____

AZ Databases, Inc. reserves the right to include your company name in its list of clients, that may be used for promotional and advertisement purposes.

All other information that you supply will be kept strictly confidential and will never be sold or otherwise redistributed without your explicit written per-mission.

```
*  *  *  *  *  *  *  *  *  *  *  *  *  *  *  *  *  *  *  *  *  *  *  *  *  *  *  *
*  Send your registration to:                                  *
*       e-mail (preferred): 71232.3446@compuserve.com          *
*        fax and voice-mail: 847/419-0190                      *
*       mail: 89 Manchester Dr., Buffalo Grove, IL 60089       *
*  *  *  *  *  *  *  *  *  *  *  *  *  *  *  *  *  *  *  *  *  *  *  *  *  *  *  *
```

SQL Server, Microsoft SQL Server, Sybase, Sybase SQL Server, and Windows NT are trademarks or registered trademarks of Sybase Inc. and Microsoft Corp. AZ Databases, Inc. is not associated with these companies.

Index

LICENSE AGREEMENT AND LIMITED WARRANTY

READ THE FOLLOWING TERMS AND CONDITIONS CAREFULLY BEFORE OPENING THIS SOFTWARE PACKAGE. THIS LEGAL DOCUMENT IS AN AGREEMENT BETWEEN YOU AND PRENTICE-HALL, INC. (THE "COMPANY"). BY OPENING THIS SEALED SOFTWARE PACKAGE, YOU ARE AGREEING TO BE BOUND BY THESE TERMS AND CONDITIONS. IF YOU DO NOT AGREE WITH THESE TERMS AND CONDITIONS, DO NOT OPEN THE SOFTWARE PACKAGE. PROMPTLY RETURN THE UNOPENED SOFTWARE PACKAGE AND ALL ACCOMPANYING ITEMS TO THE PLACE YOU OBTAINED THEM FOR A FULL REFUND OF ANY SUMS YOU HAVE PAID.

1.	**GRANT OF LICENSE:** In consideration of your purchase of this book, and your agreement to abide by the terms and conditions of this Agreement, the Company grants to you a nonexclusive right to use and display the copy of the enclosed software program (hereinafter the "SOFTWARE") on a single computer (i.e., with a single CPU) at a single location so long as you comply with the terms of this Agreement. The Company reserves all rights not expressly granted to you under this Agreement.

2.	**OWNERSHIP OF SOFTWARE:** You own only the magnetic or physical media (the enclosed media) on which the SOFTWARE is recorded or fixed, but the Company and the software developers retain all the rights, title, and ownership to the SOFTWARE recorded on the original media copy(ies) and all subsequent copies of the SOFTWARE, regardless of the form or media on which the original or other copies may exist. This license is not a sale of the original SOFTWARE or any copy to you.

3.	**COPY RESTRICTIONS:** This SOFTWARE and the accompanying printed materials and user manual (the "Documentation") are the subject of copyright. The individual programs on the media are copyrighted by the authors of each program. Some of the programs on the media include separate licensing agreements. If you intend to use one of these programs, you must read and follow its accompanying license agreement. You may not copy the Documentation or the SOFTWARE, except that you may make a single copy of the SOFTWARE for backup or archival purposes only. You may be held legally responsible for any copying or copyright infringement which is caused or encouraged by your failure to abide by the terms of this restriction.

4.	**USE RESTRICTIONS:** You may not network the SOFTWARE or otherwise use it on more than one computer or computer terminal at the same time. You may physically transfer the SOFTWARE from one computer to another provided that the SOFTWARE is used on only one computer at a time. You may not distribute copies of the SOFTWARE or Documentation to others. You may not reverse engineer, disassemble, decompile, modify, adapt, translate, or create derivative works based on the SOFTWARE or the Documentation without the prior written consent of the Company.

5.	**TRANSFER RESTRICTIONS:** The enclosed SOFTWARE is licensed only to you and may not be transferred to any one else without the prior written consent of the Company. Any unauthorized transfer of the SOFTWARE shall result in the immediate termination of this Agreement.

6.	**TERMINATION:** This license is effective until terminated. This license will terminate automatically without notice from the Company and become null and void if you fail to comply with any provisions or limitations of this license. Upon termination, you shall destroy the Documentation and all copies of the SOFTWARE. All provisions of this Agreement as to warranties, limitation of liability, remedies or damages, and our ownership rights shall survive termination.

7.	**MISCELLANEOUS:** This Agreement shall be construed in accordance with the laws of the United States of America and the State of New York and shall benefit the Company, its affiliates, and assignees.

8.   **LIMITED WARRANTY AND DISCLAIMER OF WARRANTY:** The Company warrants that the SOFTWARE, when properly used in accordance with the Documentation, will operate in substantial conformity with the description of the SOFTWARE set forth in the Documentation. The Company does not warrant that the SOFTWARE will meet your requirements or that the operation of the SOFTWARE will be uninterrupted or error-free. The Company warrants that the media on which the SOFTWARE is delivered shall be free from defects in materials and workmanship under normal use for a period of thirty (30) days from the date of your purchase. Your only remedy and the Company's only obligation under these limited warranties is, at the Company's option, return of the warranted item for a refund of any amounts paid by you or replacement of the item. Any replacement of SOFTWARE or media under the warranties shall not extend the original warranty period. The limited warranty set forth above shall not apply to any SOFTWARE which the Company determines in good faith has been subject to misuse, neglect, improper installation, repair, alteration, or damage by you. EXCEPT FOR THE EXPRESSED WARRANTIES SET FORTH ABOVE, THE COMPANY DISCLAIMS ALL WARRANTIES, EXPRESS OR IMPLIED, INCLUDING WITHOUT LIMITATION, THE IMPLIED WARRANTIES OF MERCHANTABILITY AND FITNESS FOR A PARTICULAR PURPOSE. EXCEPT FOR THE EXPRESS WARRANTY SET FORTH ABOVE, THE COMPANY DOES NOT WARRANT, GUARANTEE, OR MAKE ANY REPRESENTATION REGARDING THE USE OR THE RESULTS OF THE USE OF THE SOFTWARE IN TERMS OF ITS CORRECTNESS, ACCURACY, RELIABILITY, CURRENTNESS, OR OTHERWISE.

IN NO EVENT, SHALL THE COMPANY OR ITS EMPLOYEES, AGENTS, SUPPLIERS, OR CONTRACTORS BE LIABLE FOR ANY INCIDENTAL, INDIRECT, SPECIAL, OR CONSEQUENTIAL DAMAGES ARISING OUT OF OR IN CONNECTION WITH THE LICENSE GRANTED UNDER THIS AGREEMENT, OR FOR LOSS OF USE, LOSS OF DATA, LOSS OF INCOME OR PROFIT, OR OTHER LOSSES, SUSTAINED AS A RESULT OF INJURY TO ANY PERSON, OR LOSS OF OR DAMAGE TO PROPERTY, OR CLAIMS OF THIRD PARTIES, EVEN IF THE COMPANY OR AN AUTHORIZED REPRESENTATIVE OF THE COMPANY HAS BEEN ADVISED OF THE POSSIBILITY OF SUCH DAMAGES. IN NO EVENT SHALL LIABILITY OF THE COMPANY FOR DAMAGES WITH RESPECT TO THE SOFTWARE EXCEED THE AMOUNTS ACTUALLY PAID BY YOU, IF ANY, FOR THE SOFTWARE.

SOME JURISDICTIONS DO NOT ALLOW THE LIMITATION OF IMPLIED WARRANTIES OR LIABILITY FOR INCIDENTAL, INDIRECT, SPECIAL, OR CONSEQUENTIAL DAMAGES, SO THE ABOVE LIMITATIONS MAY NOT ALWAYS APPLY. THE WARRANTIES IN THIS AGREEMENT GIVE YOU SPECIFIC LEGAL RIGHTS AND YOU MAY ALSO HAVE OTHER RIGHTS WHICH VARY IN ACCORDANCE WITH LOCAL LAW.

ACKNOWLEDGMENT

YOU ACKNOWLEDGE THAT YOU HAVE READ THIS AGREEMENT, UNDERSTAND IT, AND AGREE TO BE BOUND BY ITS TERMS AND CONDITIONS. YOU ALSO AGREE THAT THIS AGREEMENT IS THE COMPLETE AND EXCLUSIVE STATEMENT OF THE AGREEMENT BETWEEN YOU AND THE COMPANY AND SUPERSEDES ALL PROPOSALS OR PRIOR AGREEMENTS, ORAL, OR WRITTEN, AND ANY OTHER COMMUNICATIONS BETWEEN YOU AND THE COMPANY OR ANY REPRESENTATIVE OF THE COMPANY RELATING TO THE SUBJECT MATTER OF THIS AGREEMENT.

Should you have any questions concerning this Agreement or if you wish to contact the Company for any reason, please contact in writing at the address below.

Robin Short
Prentice Hall PTR
One Lake Street
Upper Saddle River, New Jersey 07458